JUNGLE LABORATORIES

JUNGLE LABORATORIES

*Mexican Peasants, National Projects,
and the Making of the Pill*

Gabriela Soto Laveaga

Duke University Press
Durham and London
2009

© 2009 Duke University Press

All rights reserved

Printed in the United States of America on
acid-free paper ∞

Designed by Heather Hensley

Typeset in Warnock by Tseng Information
Systems, Inc.

Library of Congress Cataloging-in-Publication
Data appear on the last printed page of this
book.

Duke University Press gratefully acknowledges
the support of the Department of History of the
University of California, Santa Barbara, for
providing funds toward the production of this book.

To the memory of my father,
Professor Hector Soto-Pérez,

and to the Mexican men
and women who for decades
gathered barbasco

CONTENTS

In the summer of 1997 I participated as a graduate-student researcher on a binational research team which was documenting the medicinal plants of the Mixteca of Oaxaca. I never, however, made it to the Mixteca. Instead I stumbled onto a project that would lead me in the opposite geographic direction, in search of giant yams in southern Mexico.

The team was funded in part by the National Institutes of Health, the Instituto de Química at UNAM (Universidad Nacional Autónoma de México), and the Museum of Man in San Diego. As the sole historian on the team, my role in documenting medicinal plants was not entirely clear to the American researchers and their Mexican counterparts. This confusion proved fortuitous, since I was assigned to spend a month in Mexico City's National Herbarium while the team's chemists and biologists pondered why I had been hired. Housed in the basement of the Siglo XXI hospital, Mexico's high-tech public health institution and symbol of medical progress, the National Herbarium became for nearly a month a calming alternate world hidden away beneath Mexico City's chaotic traffic. It is there that I learned to press and catalogue medicinal plants, marvel at their uses, and tolerate the oppressive mothball stench which stays in your clothing and skin but acts as an undisputed bug repellent. And there was where I first heard of barbasco.

As part of my herbarium training, I was expected to participate in a two-week seminar for medical doctors hailing from various backgrounds and regions of Mexico. The goal of the program was to educate physicians trained in Western institutions about alternative approaches to health and medications. Specifically, participants were to consider the role of plants in a state-sanctioned project to offer alternative healing methods to Mexican people. The objective was to revive and legitimate this knowledge and slowly begin a medical revolution of sorts by training those who prescribe medications to accept alternative forms of conceiving illness and healing. During one of these presentations, the director of the former Mexican Institute for the Study of Medicinal Plants offhandedly mentioned that few people knew that the oral contraceptives were derived from a wild Mexican yam. I was intrigued. Could this be true? If so, why was this not common knowledge? Why did some historical narratives persist while others languished forgotten? This book is a result of those initial questions.

ACKNOWLEDGMENTS

As this project expanded in scope, the debts I accrued also increased. Although I cannot acknowledge here everyone who helped, inspired, or questioned this book, I wish to express my gratitude to those who most influenced my thought process.

In particular, for their intellectual guidance and mentorship, I thank Warwick Anderson, Eric Van Young, Dain Borges, Charles Briggs, and Carlos Vélez-Ibáñez.

I can never sufficiently thank the dozens of rural Mexicans who set their work aside to respond to my questions about barbasco, but I can state here that the stories they shared, which were crucial for this book, are what allowed me to obtain fellowships, grants, and my current job. While I cannot name them all, the most important interviews are listed at the beginning of the bibliography. I am particularly thankful to Isidro Apolinar of Chiltepec, Oaxaca, and his family who welcomed me, often for several hours at a time over the span of five years. Indeed, this book would be a very different one if it weren't for the time that dozens of individuals, such as Don Isidro, gave to me at different stages of this book's production.

I am extremely grateful to the Mexican scientists who patiently explained chemistry, botany, and biology in terms that a historian could grasp. While I cannot list them all here, I am indebted to Dr. Ricardo Reyes Chilpa and his graduate students at the Institute of Chemistry at UNAM, Maestra Abigail Aguilar and her incredible research team at the Herbario IMSS (Instituto Mexicano del Seguro Social) in Mexico City, Dr. Alfredo Pérez Jiménez of the Institute of Biology at UNAM, Ing. Carlos Huerta at Universidad Autónoma de Chapingo,

Ing. Luis Ernesto Miramontes in Mexico City, Dr. George Rosencranz in Palo Alto, California, and Dr. Arturo Gómez-Pompa of UC Riverside. Any errors in explaining their fields of expertise are entirely my own.

This book followed me through many academic institutions as I pursued a doctoral degree and took up a tenure-track appointment and a postdoctoral fellowship. At each stage I have been fortunate to engage in conversations—private and in seminars—which have furthered my initial musings. At UC, San Diego, I thank my graduate cohort and Professors Eric Van Young, Christine Hunefeldt, and Cristena Turner. At UC, San Francisco I thank the faculty at the Department of Anthropology, History and Social Medicine, and the Bay Area Med Heads for raising questions about molecules and race, in particular Adele Clarke, Vincanne Adams, Phillipe Bourgois, Dorothy Porter, Nick King, and Brian Dolan. At the Center for U.S.-Mexican Studies, where I was a researcher in residence from 1999 to 2001, I thank a lively and engaging cohort of scholars of Mexico.

This project would have taken much longer to complete without the generous financial assistance of a Fulbright–García Robles Fellowship; a Ford Foundation Dissertation and Postdoctoral Fellowship; a UC President's Postdoctoral Fellowship; a UC-MEXUS grant; a Center for U.S.-Mexican Studies fellowship; a UCSB (University of California, Santa Barbara), Career Development Grant; and various UC Academic Senate travel grants.

Although writing is a solitary endeavor, a great group of friends never allowed me to feel lonely. I especially thank Eunice Stephens, Natalie Ring, Marcela Guadiana, Emily Edmonds, Delia Cosentino, Courtney Gilbert, Adriana Zavala, Jon Yohannan, J. Fernando Corredor, Adam Warren, Karla Ibarra, Josh Dunsby, Elena Songster, and Angela Vergara.

Douglas Sharon, Bonnie Bade, and Teresa May were supportive of this project from its embryonic stages.

I acknowledge the support of my colleagues at UCSB, who read and commented on sections of the final manuscript, in particular Sarah Cline, Cecilia Méndez, Mike Osborne, Anita Guerinni, Adrienne Edgar, and Erika Rappaport.

Nicole Pacino's excellent research skills were invaluable in locating images and documents at the later stages of this manuscript. In Mexico, Nora Crespo aided me in photocopying in the AGN as well as locating some crucial, uncatalogued files. I also thank Don Raymundo in Galería 3 and Erika Mosqueda in the reference section of the AGN. In addition, I thank Carlos and Vicky Ortega and their children, Adriana and Carlos, for warmly and constantly opening the doors of their house in Mexico City and always making me feel at home. In Oaxaca City, Monica Guadiana and Angel Domínguez always had a place for me to sleep, even on the shortest of notices.

I also appreciate the dedication of three anonymous Duke University Press reviewers. Their lengthy and frank assessment of an earlier draft made this, I am certain, a much more complete and, hopefully, better book. I am grateful to Duke University Press editor, Valerie Milholland, for believing that one day this book would get done, to Miriam Angress for her help at each step of this process, and to Leigh Barnwell for her tireless assistance with images. I also thank Mark Mastromarino for understanding and generously giving me more time and Sonya Manes for copyediting. I also thank Patricia Rosas for her ten-hour plus days with the manuscript. They all worked to make this a better book.

Though my intellectual debts are many, it is the emotional support I have received from my parents, Consuelo and Hector Soto, and my sisters— Ana and Carmina—which I can most definitely never repay. Finally, I can never fully express my gratitude to my partner on the dance floor and in life, Stephan Krämer. Without Stephan's daily support and understanding, this project would have taken much longer to complete. *Du bist mein Alles.*

My father, Professor Hector Soto-Perez, arrived in the United States in 1965 and set about to learn his first words of English. Eight years later he received his Ph.D. at USC and for nearly twenty-five years taught at Cal State, Los Angeles. Though he longed to return to Mexico, he instead made it his life's work to teach about the land he had left behind and to demand rights for Mexicans in this country. He unexpectedly passed away as this manuscript's first complete draft was being written. From my father's intense nostalgia, I learned, as a young girl, to love Mexico, initially mimicking, and later making my own, the sentiments that only an immigrant can have. This book is dedicated to him.

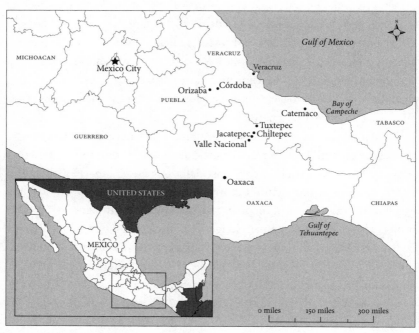

MAP 1 Map of Mexico with the main barbasco towns of Oaxaca.

It was early August, and the campesinos shifted uncomfortably on the rows of wooden benches. [1] *The sounds and smells of the humid jungles of the Chinantla region in eastern Oaxaca surrounded the tiny meeting hall and blended with those produced by sweaty, restless bodies. Attending official meetings was something new for most of these struggling peasants. Some nervously picked at the dirt beneath chipped nails while others tightly clasped hands callused and swollen from coaxing coffee from tired lands. They were there to learn about the uses of a root, a wild yam called barbasco, which the majority harvested and sold for cash to buy food for their families. These campesinos wrested the root from the ground, hauled it over rough terrain, and sold it miles from their homes on the same day they picked it. As the speaker began, they listened in what seemed uncomfortable disbelief. Certainly he could not be serious. They laughed nervously, jostled one another, and waited impatiently for the meeting to end. But the speaker, Melquíades Santiago, also a campesino and the president of their local union, persisted. He earnestly explained that the tiny blue pills that he was passing out to attendees had once been barbasco. Through what he called a "chemical process," a substance in the gnarled tuber had been transformed into potent medications. Moreover, he insisted that the little round pill could cure aches, pains, and the "worms in their stomach" that caused cramps and gave them diarrhea.*

The year was 1983, but in a 1999 interview, Santiago would recall that when he left the meeting hall the ground outside was strewn with tiny colored pills. Most of the campesinos at the meeting had not believed him.

It is not, however, the pill-throwing actions of these peasants which make this particular meeting remarkable. Instead it is the carefree use of chemical terms such as diosgenin *and* progesterone *which Santiago, a campesino with no formal education, used when recalling the event. That this educational meeting even took place is noteworthy since a mere decade earlier, men similar to those at the meeting had used slivers of chemical knowledge to contest local social hierarchies and produce their own interpretation of science in the Mexican countryside.*

This book is about a forgotten chapter in Mexican history: the search for wild yams called barbasco. Products derived from barbasco altered modern medicine, aided advances in science, and, arguably, granted millions of women some control over reproduction. When we open our medicine cabinets today, it is likely that we find medications that in earlier versions were derived from compounds found in barbasco. From 1940 to the mid-1970s, these yams were the ideal source material for the global production of synthetic steroid hormones. Mass production of progesterone, cortisone, and, eventually, oral contraceptives was possible because of the availability of Mexican yams.

Beyond the history of a tuber, this book is an exploration of the local and social consequences of the global search for medicinal plants. Specifically: What happens in rural Mexico when global trends lead international laboratories to confer value to a local weed?[2] This story is significant for several reasons. It forces us to reconsider how local and national histories affect globalized science and markets. It urges us to rethink the means by which Mexican peasants attained social and political legitimacy in the late twentieth century. And it also invites us to discuss the power and the malleable meaning of science in the most unusual of spaces, the Mexican countryside, during a crucial time, the 1970–76 populist regime. Additionally, this story contests the idea that science could only be copied but not produced in Latin America, a region that for many was, at best, on the periphery of knowledge production.[3]

In the late 1940s barbasco became a valuable resource when it replaced *cabeza de negro*, another dioscorea, as the ideal raw material for making synthetic steroids. By the 1950s while Mexican and foreign scientists researched, experimented on, and catalogued varieties of barbasco, United States Senate hearings were trying to determine the fate of the root in Mexico. By 1960 more than 2 million women in the United States were using the Pill, and more than 100,000 Mexican peasants were gathering the raw material used in its production. In 1975 the Mexican president, Luis Echeverría, attempted to nationalize the steroid hormone industry. The parastatal he created to manufacture steroids from barbasco would close in 1989.

Barbasco's importance to Mexican science, politics, and rural development is eclipsed only by its significance to the world. In the 1950s, for example, the search for the mass production of cortisone was seen as "an unrestrained, dramatic race involving a dozen of the largest American drug houses, several leading foreign pharmaceutical manufacturers, three governments, and more research personnel than have worked on any medical problem since penicillin."[4] In May 1951 an article in *Fortune* magazine under the intriguing headline "Mexican Hormones" reported that "the biggest technological boom ever heard south of the border" was that synthetic cortisone could be derived from Mexican wild yams.[5] But the surprises did not stop there. When referring to the laboratory where research on wild yams was conducted, Carl Djerassi, the co-discoverer of the Pill, wrote in his memoirs, "Syntex [the laboratory] as a company, and Mexico, as a country, deserve full credit as the institutional site for the chemical synthesis of an oral contraceptive steroid."[6]

In the 1950s the potential medicinal use of Mexican yams seemed inexhaustible, versatile, and almost miraculous. Barbasco contains a substance, diosgenin, that chemists can transform into synthetic progesterone, from which all other hormones, such as cortisone, can be easily manufactured. Chemical work on barbasco transformed Mexico from a "presumably backward" country, as it was described in press releases, into the world's premier supplier of synthetic hormones.[7] Mexico monopolized this production until the late 1960s, when domestic politics and alternative sources of raw materials deposed Mexico from its steroid-producing throne.

Barbasco, in the form of synthetic cortisone, brought relief to millions suffering from rheumatoid arthritis. Research with diosgenin by the Mexican chemist Luis Ernesto Miramontes yielded what he initially believed to be a substance that would prevent women from experiencing miscarriages—but, ironically, it turned out to be the basis for oral contraceptives. A few months after this discovery, Gregory Pincus, with the relentless advocacy of the family-planning crusader and benefactor Margaret Sanger, used barbasco to continue his own research on viable oral contraception in the United States. Despite this history, few today associate Mexico with steroid hormone production.

This is surprising because at the height of the barbasco trade, more than ten tons of wild yams were removed from the tropical humid areas of Oaxaca, Veracruz, Tabasco, and Chiapas on a weekly basis. Comparatively, in the 1960s approximately 3,000 kilograms (3 tons) of corn were collected per hectare during an *entire* harvest.[8] In 1975 the price per kilo of barbasco was virtually the same as it had been when it was first collected in 1942, 10 to 60 Mexican centavos, less than one American nickel. By contrast, Synalar, an anti-inflammatory medication derived from diosgenin, sold for the equivalent of several dollars in Mexican pharmacies of the time. Although other authors have explored the intricate, often contentious relationship that developed between foreign steroid hormone laboratories and the Mexican state over control of the yam trade and the medications derived from it, they did not focus on a basic question: How did so many yams make it out of the jungles and into the hands of laboratory scientists?[9]

This book, then, answers that explicit question and explores the implication that thousands of Mexicans were needed to remove barbasco from southeastern Mexico. Despite the sheer numbers of individuals and yams involved in the barbasco trade, few within Mexico remember barbasco today. One can speculate that the end product, patented medications, was so far removed from the raw material that it was impossible to make the connection. Or, conversely, barbasco had no monetary value before the 1940s, and hence it attracted little, if any, national attention outside of rural Mexico.

Within Mexico the barbasco root and the people who harvest it might well have continued to be ignored or overlooked had it not been for the populist administration that came to power in 1970. As part of his vision of what he called a "new Mexico," President Luis Echeverría (who held office from 1970 through 1976) insisted that a better Mexico was one that regulated its population growth. Echeverría, fully aware of the United Nations' and the World Health Organization's population control programs of the 1970s, intended to seize control of the highly lucrative steroid hormone industry and create a domestic pharmaceutical industry, a move that would give Mexico much-needed control of patented medications and, of course, oral contraceptives.[10]

In addition, controlling the barbasco trade would allow the Mexican government to organize thousands of unemployed and potentially rebellious yam pickers at a time of increased social unrest in rural Mexico. Consequently, Echeverría's solution, a state-owned company called Proquivemex, opened its doors in 1975 with the ambitious mission of producing enough domestic pharmaceuticals from Mexican medicinal plants to compete with and eventually replace transnational laboratories. But in addition, and in a novel fashion, Proquivemex promised to represent and organize Mexican peasants and educate them about the wild yam—and, by extension, about the rudiments of chemistry. If peasants could learn the true value of the wild yam, the populist argument went, then they could reap the financial profits of harvesting barbasco, a privilege until then enjoyed only by some caciques or local strongmen. Eventually, as the founding charter of Proquivemex promised, campesinos would also control the state laboratory entrusted with producing steroid hormones. Indeed, campesinos would occupy the space reserved for scientists.

At first glance these promises resemble other far-fetched ones made during Echeverría's populist regime, but placed within the larger context of Latin American history they appear less absurd, though no less questionable. Since the late nineteenth century Latin American governments had embraced scientific theories that promised to hold the key to explaining and transforming their racially and economically diverse societies.[11] Science and pseudoscientific ideas were heartily and intimately intertwined with the politics of state formation. Social Darwinism; eugenics, in its multiple manifestations; positivism and degeneracy—to name a few—were the tools used by politicians to explain why governments could regulate the actions of their "diseased" citizens, who most often suffered from poverty, illiteracy, unemployment, and racial stereotypes. Governments imported, produced, and molded scientific language and programs to reform their plebian constituencies and create healthy citizens.[12] For many governments, rural and indigenous peasants posed a particularly difficult roadblock to progress. How to integrate these sectors of society into the national fabric while distinguishing them from the *gente decente* (literally, the "decent citizens")?

Mexican leaders before Echeverría had attempted to answer this question by various means. Some, such as President Porfirio Díaz (1876–1911) and his cabinet, aptly named the "Científicos," were more overt in their designs than others. Given these trends, it should not be too remarkable that

Echeverría would believe that science, in this case chemistry, could, if not fix, then aid the decaying countryside. What is surprising, however, is that some barbasco pickers took science, this language of elite social control, and made it their own.

Barbasco in Mexico

The history of barbasco is partly that of a project of modernization imposed by a government that in the 1970s attempted to redefine the Mexican nation while grappling to retain political power in the countryside. Those the government chose to include as part of this modern project is what makes this story compelling. Arguably root pickers—indigenous, poor, and uneducated—were in many respects the antithesis of modernity, but in their capacity as gatherers of the root they became the essential link to finally bring a modern project to Mexico: domestic patented medications. The inherent ideological contradictions in this plan reveal much about Mexico at the end of the twentieth century. As the government promoted the continuance of a "campesino way of life," its imposed projects illustrated how little the government understood the social and economic interactions which allowed Mexicans in the countryside to exist in the mid-twentieth century.

By incorporating Mexican peasants into the history of medical discoveries, this book challenges previous histories which place the scientist and the laboratory at the center of the tale. But by focusing on rural Mexico and Mexicans, my intent is certainly not to imply that campesinos became research scientists; rather, I seek to point out that a political moment invited yam pickers to believe that they could produce steroids. In the past few decades, historians of Latin America and, more recently, historians of science have written histories that add to or question traditional narratives by incorporating the historical perspective of workers, patients, prostitutes, and the colonized among others.[13] With regard to the history of oral contraception, several scholars have challenged the U.S.-centric version by incorporating within a single narrative the participation of Mexico, Puerto Rico, and the Netherlands.[14]

This book pushes that particular narrative further by postulating that some Mexican campesinos actively engaged in the knowledge production of steroids for personal and communal gain. By 1976 a handful of men in the area surrounding Tuxtepec, Oaxaca, were making their fortunes—both social and economic—as intermediaries between transnational pharmaceutical companies and peasant pickers. Employees for foreign laboratories learned to rely on the diosgenin-yield predictions of these campesinos to forecast manufacturing needs for the coming year. In addition, these local men could speak the language and understand the local social networks that were alien to laboratory employees but crucial for obtaining barbasco. Some men, such as Melquíades Santiago from the introductory vignette, managed to rise through the ranks of the barbasco trade by controlling the information that was disseminated. With that, social divisions were created based on chemical knowledge.

Beyond the Laboratory

Exploring the changes that occurred in rural Mexico as a result of the barbasco trade reveals the transformative and malleable social power of science once it leaves the confines of the laboratory and is linked to a populist agenda. The resourcefulness of financially and politically marginalized Mexicans who used their knowledge of barbasco to their advantage clearly emerges from the narrative. Indeed, barbasco in the 1970s became another tool for people accustomed to exploiting every available opportunity to attain social legitimacy. For example, when campesinos traveled to Mexico City to meet with the president of Mexico or with directors of transnational pharmaceutical companies to debate the price of barbasco, it altered regional social hierarchies that had been in place for centuries. By including rural Mexicans in the narrative of discovery, I press readers to accept that scientists, both domestic and foreign, were not working in a cultural vacuum: they relied heavily on rural Mexicans' knowledge of soil conditions, growth cycles, and the minute particularities between different species of yams.

Despite the distinction between elite knowledge production and routine labor—as these campesinos' actions would certainly be labeled—steroid research could not have occurred without the participation of Mexican campesinos. The American chemist Russell Marker acknowledged this when he returned in 1969 to rural Veracruz and handed a plaque to the descendants of the Mexican peasant who tracked down the first wild yams for him in 1942. In so doing, Marker recognized the presence of Mexican peasants in the act of discovery. By blurring the lines between those who produce knowledge, in or outside the laboratory, who performs a routine job—the scientist measuring compounds or the campesino digging up specific yams—becomes more ambiguous.

When historians of science asked, "Who is capable of engaging in science?" they encouraged us to include, for example, gender in our analysis of European science production.[15] Bringing campesinos and the action of the Mexican government into the narrative of steroid hormone synthesis lets us analyze how local and national events influenced global science production and how world events influenced Mexican campesinos and how they interpreted and internalized those events. Other studies have shown that when scientific centers arose as historical actors, "both science and the locality were changed by the event."[16] However, the case of barbasco in Mexico goes one step further by demonstrating how locals appropriated science to redefine themselves.

One of the key differences in the manipulation of the barbasco root's meanings was that scientists and politicians thought of it as the precursor to steroid hormones. Their understanding and knowledge of the tuber were linked to the steroid industry, pharmaceutical laboratories, and global markets. Those who searched for and dug up barbasco, on the other hand, were working from a completely different knowledge base: rural Oaxaqueños thought it was a weed, a tool for fishing, a plant with powerful medicinal properties, and a crucial source of sorely needed cash. It would be decades before the chemical properties of barbasco would be widely understood by rural Mexicans. Nonetheless, they developed a knowledge of the plant equal in sophistication to that of the scientists. They used their knowledge of rain patterns, differing root colors, and variations in vine width to determine when and where they could dig up the best roots. That thousands of campesinos did not use microscopes to make their determinations did not invalidate their methods. In fact, to develop a systematic understanding of the root, Mexican ecologists in the 1950s imitated the barbasco-tracking techniques used by thousands of Mexican campesinos.

Twenty years later, peasants, in turn, mimicked the language of chemistry, freely using *progesterone* in letters to the Mexican president as a way to gain social legitimacy within Mexico. In his book *Peasant Intellectuals*, the historian Steven Feierman explored how peasants, rarely considered intellectuals, at crucial moments, "organized political movements of the greatest long-term significance, and in doing so elaborated new forms of discourse."[17]

This was the case in the mid-1970s, when campesinos began sending hand-written letters to the president to demand roads, schoolhouses, and electricity. The letter writers stressed their knowledge of *esteroides*. The global need for barbasco, which is found nearly exclusively in southern Mexico, and the actions of rural yam pickers forced the Mexican government to reconsider the role of campesinos. In the context of barbasco, Mexican peasants had to be recognized as producers of knowledge—quite simply, only campesinos knew where and how to obtain the raw material needed for continued steroid research.

Commodities

The history of barbasco may echo the familiar tale of Latin American commodities exploitation, but it is significantly different. While the parallels with, say, rubber are many, commercial cultivation of barbasco was never successful. Despite attempts to export seedlings and grow them in the United States and other countries, Mexican barbasco resisted transplantation. When it was grown successfully in Guatemala or Puerto Rico, the diosgenin content plummeted compared to that found in plants indigenous to Mexico. The yam, like the petroleum of southern Mexico, had to be tracked, extracted, and transported for processing elsewhere before being exported. Similar to coffee and tobacco, it had to be dried at the source, but unlike silver, another major Mexican commodity, surprisingly few myths surrounded the extraction of barbasco. Of the Latin American commodities, one may be tempted to find similarities with Andean coca, which must also undergo a chemical process before acquiring its street value as cocaine and whose demand drove the development of strong local and transnational social networks.[18] Cocaine, like diosgenin, is a historically recent commodity. But unlike cocaine's illicit associations, diosgenin continued to garner praise from scientists and politicians alike. Recent histories of commodity markets have taken care to examine the social and political consequences of particular trades, and this history pushes us to think how local practices (political and social) impact the world economy.[19]

Bioprospecting

When I initially set out to do my research—immersed in literature on medicinal plants, bioprospecting, and the rights of a nation over its own natural resources—I believed that this would be a historical case of locals and pharmaceutical companies battling over the patent rights to the medicinal properties of plants. I knew that there had been a movement to nationalize barbasco in the 1970s, so I assumed that it would be traditional healers and local root pickers who began the movement claiming ownership of the knowledge about barbasco. It was not a farfetched assumption, since the story had many of the key elements of today's current battles against pharmaceutical companies. But then I looked deeper. The story of barbasco in Mexico is more complex than that.

Bioprospecting is understood as the exploration of "potentially profitable biodiversity and biodiversity-related knowledge," for commercial purposes.[20] Several scholars have observed that the word itself is inappropriate and the concept legally flawed because its foundation is the patenting of traditional knowledge. In other words one cannot patent knowledge that has existed for generations as an invention. The expected outcome is that local communities will profit as much as well as those interested in the pharmaceutical potential of their natural resources. Biopiracy, for its part, is the blatant exploitation of traditional knowledge and chemical compounds through legal means, usually via patents. Using this terminology, the initial stages of the barbasco trade in the 1940s, 1950s, and 1960s could be labeled biopiracy. By the 1970s, under President Luis Echeverría, there were some attempts at reform. The study of barbasco contributes to the debate on bioprospecting by illustrating how the drive to obtain medicinal plants integrated science (via pharmaceutical laboratories) and indigenous knowledge.

By using the case of barbasco and, in particular, of those who picked the yam, I push the argument beyond biopiracy, benefit sharing, and the controversy over traditional knowledge, which has often dominated the discussion. Recent scholarship has elucidated the links between medicinal plants and pharmaceutical-industry or university researchers, as well as the often-lopsided relationship between the industry and local participants.[21] Historicizing the case of barbasco lets me add to these discussions by showing that local allegiances and power structures do not remain static over time—an exploited campesino may, ten years later, be the exploiter of future yam pickers. In other words barbasco pickers were not always unified, universally exploited, or equally savvy about their relationship and agreements with industry and the State, as the Melquíades Santiagos of this history illustrate. Moreover, engaging the discipline of history in discussions about bioprospecting allows for a closer examination of the long-term sociocultural effects of the ongoing search for medicinal plants. The quest for medicinal plants may be driven by the aim of transnational interests, but a successful outcome is directly intertwined with the history, politics, and social conditions of the people and the environment in which the medicinal plant is found.

The case of barbasco illuminates that argument by showing how the history of the locality influenced the relationship that the Mexican rural community would have with the steroid hormone industry. Although this conclusion seems obvious, few case studies have traced the history of a place from before the arrival of transnational laboratories, during the point of contact, and after the pharmaceutical industry's involvement has waned.[22] It is at that juncture—the coming together of traditional modes of existence in the countryside and of modernity in the guise of cutting-edge steroid-hormone research—where we learn how a sector of Mexican society functioned at a time of economic crises and how the malleable meanings of science aided this endeavor. In understanding the subtle nuances of apparent contradictions—such as campesinos and steroid hormones—we can better explain the history of a country in which such contradictions can take place.

Bioprospecting in the 1940s

Although I am applying it here, the word bioprospecting was not widely used until the 1990s. Instead, for example, the Mexican campaigns against pharmaceutical laboratories during the populist regime of the 1970s used a discourse of nationalization and empire, which, given the populist regime of the time, seemed appropriate. In this case the imperial reach manifested itself in the guise of pharmaceutical laboratories that held the promise of health while taking natural resources in exchange. But this rhetoric also opens up for analysis the image that the laboratory played in Mexican national projects.

Other scholars have richly examined the contradictory image of the laboratory as a pristine space that excluded "dirty and uncivilized" locals.[23] But the history of barbasco in Mexico shows us that some of the lowliest of rural locals—yam pickers—came to believe that even the restricted spaces of the laboratory would open to them if they mastered the chemical lingo. As others have shown before, laboratories are places where society and politics are renewed and transformed, so by placing a laboratory in the jungle the Mexican government unwittingly created the venue that would further the illusion that the Revolution's promises could be kept.[24]

Bringing the campesinos' experiences into the story enables other connections to emerge. As with field botanists who "use spatial and locational ways of knowing" and who know that they will be held to laboratory standards, barbasqueros soon learned that the yams they selected would be analyzed, weighed, and possibly rejected based on norms stipulated by outsiders.[25] These rules, intended to standardize yams, intertwined with each locality's specific history and social relations and so determined the impact that barbasco would have in the region. This study focuses mainly on the area surrounding Tuxtepec, Oaxaca, and it reflects that region's labor networks and ethnic history.

Barbasco and Mexican Peasants

Although scholarly works have studied the participation of U.S. and European scientists in the discovery of synthetic hormones and the collapse of the Mexican steroid industry, those works entirely omit the modern history of the barbasco-producing region.[26] Most recently, Myrna Santiago in her treatment of oil discovery in northern Veracruz, Christopher Boyer in his analysis of the timber industry in Michoacán, and Stuart McCook in his exploration of Caribbean crops, among others, have challenged scholars to link social transformations and land-tenure questions to the study of the environment.[27] Within that same vein, a study of barbasco extraction from Mexico's jungles lets us analyze pivotal changes in rural relationships, peasant organizations, and the links between the countryside and the capital at a time of diminished government subsidies for rural areas. Therefore, this analysis to some extent also questions the traditional depiction of Mexican campesinos in the second half of the twentieth century (1960–80), when, arguably, being a campesino was already anachronistic.

In exploring the actions of the Oaxacan barbasqueros in this region, I carry the process of peasantization beyond the postrevolutionary period (1917–40), beyond the post–Second World War era, and into the heart of the "Mexican Miracle" (sustained economic growth from 1940 to 1968) and beyond it (1968–89). Whereas scholars such as Florencia Mallon, Christopher Boyer, Gil Joseph, Daniel Nugent, and Alan Knight have analyzed the politicization of what they call the "rightful heirs of the Revolution," they also demonstrated that this group identity was neither timeless, preconstituted, nor, in fact, a group.[28] Instead, they have shown that the idea of a Mexican peasantry arose after the Revolution, when government subsidies geared toward the countryside enticed former *vecinos, agraristas*, and peons to consider and cautiously embrace this new label of campesino. I argue that this active construction of a campesino identity did not stop or slow down for peasants or a mythmaking State as the century progressed; rather, as the term became too loaded, people in the countryside actively sought other, more appealing identities (for example, barbasqueros). Christopher Boyer contends that an "imagined collective heritage of this sort can be a powerful political platform on which to build a new social identity."[29] Thus, the wild yam became a convenient metaphor that politicians, activists, and even painters used to illustrate what Mexico could become. But for many, barbasco was more than a metaphor; it was the means used by campesinos in southern Mexico to creatively attain legitimacy in a changing Mexican society.[30] This study spans 1941–89, nearly fifty years of Mexican history, and reflects how global affairs—the Second World War, industrialization, populism, and neoliberalism—through the influence of barbasco, left a particular imprint on the countryside.

Mexicans and Science

The use of barbasco did more than call into question campesino identity. For poor campesinos to be able to extract barbasco from the jungle and deliver it to waiting laboratories required a complex web of local buyers, processors, and liaisons with the pharmaceutical companies that, in some locations, relied on centuries-old networks of trade and preexisting notions of race and class. In addition, skilled Mexican technicians in urban areas were required to carry out experiments to determine the purity of the diosgenin, the chemical compound found in the yams. The grade or value of a given root was measured by its diosgenin content, which varied from 3.5 percent to almost 6.5 percent. The more diosgenin a particular yam held, the more valuable it was. Roots found in and around Tuxtepec consistently yielded an average of nearly 5 percent pure diosgenin. Further up the production chain, Mexican chemists continued experimenting in their search for new, usable products. I am aware of the presence of these hundreds of Mexican men and women in laboratories throughout Mexico, but their story is for another book.

I do allude to the participation of Mexican scientists in exploring how barbasco became the source of study and funding for modern ecology studies in Mexico. In 1959, the Mexican government pressured the pharmaceutical companies to either share private research on barbasco and pay increased taxes for its exploitation or contribute funding to a domestic research commission to study the yam; most opted for the latter. The result, the Commission for the Study of the Ecology of Dioscoreas, became one of Mexico's premier research units and served as a training ground for many of Mexico's current leaders in biology, botany, and chemistry. Although the commission's aim was the scientific documentation of all the yam's properties, the social component of the barbasco trade—the pickers—would eventually garner the interest of the nation.

Barbasco also redefined the landscape because the yams' growth patterns did not respect state borders. During Echeverría's populist administration and at the height of the nationalization campaigns of the steroid hormone industry (1975–77), Mexico's barbasco regions, which encompass several southeastern and southwestern states (Tabasco, Chiapas, Veracruz, Oaxaca, part of Puebla, and smaller regions in México and Michoacán), were divided into six zones, each of which represented a cluster of communities where locals harvested barbasco. The zones mimicked pharmaceutical companies' parcellation of the barbasco-rich lands of southern Mexico in the decades leading up to the nationalization campaign. For example, most of the barbasco harvested in Veracruz before the campaigns was fermented, dried, bundled, and shipped to Syntex in Mexico City. Locals in Oaxaca, however, sold barbasco to buyers for subsidiaries of the German corporation Schering-Plough, while root pickers in Chiapas, Tabasco, and Puebla sent their yams to other laboratories, of Dutch or American origins. In 1975, when the Mexican government intervened, it modeled its own zones on these barbasco clusters. Many of the interviews for this study were done in the compact Región Tuxtepec (roughly Tuxtepec to Valle Nacional). So, although political boundaries are one way to approach the study of the impact of barbasco on rural Mexico, I found that analysis centered on the created spaces of production zones and laboratory supply networks offered a stronger focus for seeing the impact of the yam.

By the mid-1970s Mexican politicians linked the arrival of much-anticipated progress (in the form of roads, money, and employment) in the area of Tuxtepec, Oaxaca, to the control of the barbasco trade. By 1975 barbasco, more than any other tropical commodity, appeared to hold the promise of economic and social transformation. What could be more astonishing than a gnarled root containing chemical compounds that, once tweaked, could halt conception or, altered in another way, could alleviate swollen joints? Officials reasoned that if the Mexican government could control the industry, then maybe the countryside could also, like barbasco, be transformed into something more useful.

Many campesinos thought likewise. At a time when Mexico's impoverished and increasingly landless rural inhabitants were seen as proof of the government's inability to fulfill the promises of the Revolution of 1910, many campesinos began to join independent organizations that pledged to restore lands into peasant hands, through violence if needed. Because the Revolution had failed them, some reasoned, they would make their own changes. Hence, barbasco gave the government the opportunity to use the ruling party's tactic of institutional co-optation, linking yam pickers into peasant organizations in areas where the government sought control. These actions confirm that the nation's process of invention did not end with the Revolution, but continued, often in contradictory forms, well beyond the twentieth century.

For a time, barbasco equally gripped the imaginations of both those who embraced the rhetoric of imperialism and those who saw in the wild yam a chance for Mexico to compete on equal footing with nations that produced, not just consumed, science. Barbasco so engrossed the Mexican national imagination that artists and activists produced cartoons, slogans, and even ballads to the wild yam. Even the muralist David Alfaro Siqueiros would immortalize barbasco in a painting, *El tesoro de la selva* (Treasure of the Jungle) commissioned by Syntex Corporation. This painting is now housed in its former headquarters, currently Roche Pharmaceuticals in Palo Alto, California.

A Note on Sources

When framing this project about barbasco and rural Mexico, my initial intention was to use oral histories and interviews only as supporting material to information I would find in the archives, principally Mexico's National Archives (AGN). However, I encountered what many researchers working on Mexico's recent history have found: uncatalogued, misplaced, or missing archives. After several months in Galería 3 of the AGN, I was given permission to climb to the second floor and personally sift through the documents from President Luis Echeverría's administration, which were mislabeled in the archive guide.[31] After fruitless months of sorting through several hundred of the almost 5,000 unmarked boxes, I had only a few dozen sheets that mentioned barbasco. During this time, I also interviewed botanists, chemists, and former employees of Proquivemex—following any lead and collecting any personal documents from that time that might help me understand the impact of barbasco in Mexico. I spent time looking in the archives of the Secretariat of Agrarian Reform (Secretaría de Reforma Agraria, SRA) and the National Agrarian Registry (Registro Agrario Nacional, RAN). After a few months, I decided to stop and go instead to Tuxtepec, Oaxaca.

In the information I had found up to that point, various documents mentioned that the Región Tuxtepec contained the richest barbasco in Mexico. Tuxtepec was also the location where, with much fanfare, a government processing plant for yams had been inaugurated with the promise that eventually campesinos would be running it.

A veritable laboratory in the jungle, the Proquivemex plant in Tuxtepec was one of the areas where the impact of barbasco was strong enough to shift the seemingly immobile power structures that had persisted for centuries.

Returning from Oaxaca in 1999, I was fortunate to meet the first director of Proquivemex, Alejandro Villar Borja. He had saved nearly five boxes of company documents. Among these were newspaper articles that had been meticulously cut and labeled, though many were missing page numbers or dates. Not surprisingly, most of the information pertained to the 1975–77 period, the time when Villar Borja had been active in the barbasco trade. He allowed me to photocopy most of his personal papers in exchange for my cataloguing them and creating a database of the records. Years later, in 2004, I would find copies of many of these papers in the AGN.

In addition, I interviewed more than fifty former barbasco pickers and several local *beneficio* (processing plant) owners using a basic questionnaire (see the appendix). I conducted three oral histories, one each in Chiltepec and Valle Nacional, Oaxaca, and in Catemaco, Veracruz. In 1999, 2001, and 2004 I returned to re-ask questions or clarify details with the people I had interviewed. I spent the most time with Isidro Apolinar of Chiltepec, Oaxaca. Apolinar, a former barbasquero, slowly rose up the ranks of local-level barbasco associations to become the treasurer of the national-level association in the early 1980s. I also interviewed former and current bureau-crats of the state-owned company Proquivemex; officials of the National Peasant Confederation (CNC) in Tuxtepec, Valle Nacional, and Mexico City; environmental research groups (Red Mocaf and Conabio); employees from former and existing federal agencies (Hacienda, FIFONAFE, SAGAR, SARH, SEMARNAP); and several Mexican scientists, including Luis Ernesto Mira-montes, co-discoverer of the Pill, members of SEMARNAP (Secretariat of the Environment, Natural Resources and Fishing; formerly Instituto Nacional de Investigaciones Forestales [INIF]); and former members of the Com-mission for the Study of Dioscoreas. In California, I interviewed George Rosenkranz in Palo Alto, and Arturo Gómez-Pompa in Riverside, and I at-tempted unsuccessfully to interview Carl Djerassi. Rosenkranz, together with Miramontes and Djerassi, held the patent for the first oral contracep-tives; Gómez-Pompa was the first director of the Commission for the Study of the Ecology of Dioscoreas.

The issue of objectivity is a constant for any researcher. When one shares a meal or helps complete a chore so an informant can talk about barbasco, it makes objectivity more difficult. To overcome this, whenever possible, I verified informants' stories. Although my research deepened my admiration for the campesinos of Oaxaca and Veracruz, in this book, I have tried to remain true to my profession and maintain an analytical view. Whenever I discuss someone who was accused of graft or corruption in an interview or archival material, I substitute a pseudonym for that person's name. All my other interviewees gave their permission for me to use their real names.

Most of the interviewees, in both laboratories and the countryside, were male. Given that the most lucrative products derived from barbasco were oral contraceptives, the story would seem incomplete without at least a few female voices. I purposefully sought interviews with campesino women, but these efforts were often thwarted when the husband came to the door and answered my questions. The archival material I reviewed yielded only a few references to women. Clearly, women participated in the barbasco trade, but the dearth of female presence in the historical record reveals the blunt reality of the hierarchy of barbasco production and trade. Neverthe-less, barbasco gathering affected the lives of rural women. The historians Francie Chassen-López and Steve Stern, among others, have shown how minor changes, such as a corn mill, altered social relations in the Mexi-can countryside. So, it is likely that the exploitation of a root that could be picked equally by men, women, and children had a strong impact on the lives of women in the region. When harvesting barbasco, women would work in groups to dig up the yam, and, in areas where jobs were scarce, to obtain cash on their own. While one can speculate about the levels of independence that barbasco brought to women of the region, these changes were not immediately noticeable during my initial queries into the barbasco trade in 1999.

I did not have a predetermined method for selecting my interviewees for two reasons: First, as a visitor, I did not live in the communities that would potentially give me access to family networks. Second, the sheer quantity of barbasco removed from this region almost guaranteed that everyone of a certain age had at some point gathered, bought, or sold barbasco. Daily, I rode the bus that connects Tuxtepec to Valle Nacional and debarked at various stops, taking footpaths that led to milpas, ranches, or settlements. I would approach everyone I saw, male and female, to ask about barbasco. When I reached communities of a few dozen homes, such as Cerro Concha, I went door to door. Also, in Jacatepec, where I spent much of my time, an owner of a *tiendita* (shop) gave me permission to sit outside his store, and a local resident let me sit on her porch. From those vantage points, I could ask anyone who walked past if they had had some involvement with the barbasco trade. I asked a standard set of questions that sometimes led to lengthier conversations.

Since I had very little documentation, I always ended my conversations by asking if anyone had any papers that mentioned barbasco. It was interesting to see what had been saved: barbasco IOUs from 1975 and the early 1990s,[32] as well as a 1976 peasant organization manual and 1967 PRI identity card,[33] handwritten notes on the tons of processed barbasco,[34] a roster of barbasco transports (by foot, *chalupa* [raft], or "beast,"),[35] and the most intriguing item—photocopies of Proquivemex stocks.[36]

On two occasions—once in Catemaco, Veracruz, and another time near Jacatepec, Oaxaca—people showed me how to track down and gather barbasco. In Valle Nacional, at the area's lone surviving facility for processing barbasco, I was allowed to watch men prepare to ferment the root and later rake it on concrete slabs. I filmed nearly fourteen hours of interviews with some of these men and women and reduced it to a thirteen-minute documentary that is available at Geisel Library at the University of California, San Diego.

In addition to the AGN and Villar Borja's personal papers, I used Oaxaca's municipal and state archives and archival material in Mexico City and the Estado de México. In the United States, I relied mainly on archives at the Chemical Heritage Foundation in Philadelphia and in chemist Russell Marker's personal papers in the Paterno Library at Pennsylvania State University.

Given my intent to write this history from the perspective of what happened in Mexico, some readers may find it curious that I spend nearly three-quarters of chapter 2 discussing a chemist from the United States, Russell Marker. I knowingly chose to do so for several reasons. First, Marker was the leading scientist to initiate contact with and rely on campesinos for harvesting the root. Second, his participation in the history of steroid hormone discovery has often been overshadowed by his eccentric nature without acknowledging the impact of his actions in the Mexican countryside. Third, I wished to examine the myth that Russell Marker saw campesinos fling barbasco into a river and was able to grasp its chemical powers from the suds it produced. This falsehood is treated as fact in various books. I argue that Marker, more than many of his contemporaries, understood that a scientist needed to leave the laboratory to develop the field of steroid hormones. Hence Marker, like Mexicans, has not been accurately represented in the history of barbasco.

I must add a note on sources and serendipity. In late 2004 Nora Amanda Crespo, a student I had hired to photocopy items in the AGN, mentioned that she had seen the Proquivemex archives. Having spent months searching for them, I was doubtful. In February 2007, while beginning research on a new project, I asked someone in the AGN Reference Section. He assured me that the AGN did not house that archive. A few days before departing, a young Reference Section employee, Srita. Erika Mosqueda, asked about my previous research project. When I mentioned barbasco she gave me a blank stare, but when I mentioned Proquivemex, she told me that I could find the company archives in Galería 2. She explained that the Proquivemex catalogue (*guía*) did not circulate, but as an AGN employee, she could bring it to me. So, in February 2007, after years of searching, I discovered that several hundred boxes containing the financial and administrative minutiae of the parastatal company had been in the AGN all along. After my initial disheartened shock, I realized that had this information been found earlier, I might never have gone to Oaxaca. I would certainly have written a vastly different book, one centered on a company and not on campesinos who casually mentioned steroids. Although I looked at several dozen boxes, the entire collection awaits fresh eyes.

The Book's Organization

I have divided this book into nine chapters. In the first I chart the history of the Región Tuxtepec, in particular the area of the Chinantla in Oaxaca's Papaloapan region. Here harvesting barbasco would eventually become so common that even small children would dig up enough to buy their sweets.[37] Discussion focuses on the type of labor and crops that were common to the area before barbasco was transformed from a pesky weed into a valuable commodity.

Chapter 2 begins by examining the various pharmaceutical discoveries in Europe and the United States that drove the American scientist Russell Marker to search in southern Mexico for a more reliable source of the raw material for synthetic steroid hormones. In 1944 he helped found Syntex, one of Mexico's leading pharmaceutical companies. The extraction and payment methods Marker established in rural Mexico at that time would persist almost unchanged for more than three decades.

Chapter 3 details how the inhabitants of the Chinantla learned from outsiders that laboratories were buying wild yams by the sackfuls, and how these campesinos began to track down and process barbasco. Everyone— women, men, and children—could harvest barbasco, though it was mainly men who ventured into the jungle thickets in search of the root.

Chapter 4 addresses the role of science in Mexican politics and follows the building of the Mexico-based steroid industry with the participation of an ever-growing number of foreign companies. After the synthesis in 1951 of cortisone based on barbasco, the most prominent pharmaceutical houses in the world anchored subsidiaries in Mexico. As these companies became more powerful, the Mexican government attempted to regulate the barbasco trade. One result of these regulatory efforts was the government's creation, in 1959, of the Commission for the Study of the Ecology of Dioscoreas, which was wholly funded by multinational foreign companies but run by Mexican scientists. Mexico's scientific community was initially unaware of the importance of barbasco and its ecology. That resulted in a race between Mexicans and foreign researchers, in which Mexican scientists were spurred on and eventually surpassed foreign efforts.

Chapter 5 explains that as late as 1974 the wild yam's value was still relatively unknown outside of barbasco-harvesting regions. This situation changed when a group of students, fleeing to Chiapas after the 1968 student protests that the Mexican government violently suppressed, discovered that locals had been selling a regional root to pharmaceutical companies for several decades. The students first took their findings to President Echeverría, who was touring the state of Chiapas, and eventually to the national press.

Chapter 6 focuses on President Echeverría's nationalization of the barbasco industry and the creation of the government-subsidized processing company, Proquivemex. In particular, this chapter analyzes a confluence of events in the early 1970s that made barbasco, and its role in Mexico, the subject of national debate.

Chapter 7 explores the struggle between Proquivemex and transnational corporations over the price of barbasco and the back-payment of profits to peasants. Although profit was a goal of the company, the social agenda regarding peasants illustrates that Proquivemex was a product of the populist era.

Returning to the Región Tuxtepec chapter 8 explores how the Proquivemex teach-ins engendered subtle changes in the local population. Proquivemex's tight link to the outgoing president, Echeverría, along with the expected lack of cooperation from transnational pharmaceutical companies, contributed to the company's failure as a business venture. Although a handful of indigenous men and women acquired an unprecedented level of wealth as a result of the barbasco trade, the majority of yam pickers, laboratory employees, and technicians did not reap the financial rewards associated with the steroid industry. In addition, although all pickers were labeled campesinos, there were distinct differences among them: Some owned land, some were squatters, and some were day laborers. And although they were, in their majority, indigenous, nearly twenty distinct ethnic groups participated in the barbasco harvest. That they all came to be lumped together under the identity of barbasqueros speaks to the loss of subtle identity markers when a group is associated with a commodity.

Despite Proquivemex's failure as a business venture, some of its social goals prevailed—the topic explored in chapter 9. For example several campesino leaders went to Schering's laboratories in Germany, where they learned how barbasco was chemically transformed into steroids. In addition campesinos founded their own independent organizations linked to barbasco production, and several former barbasqueros rose through the ranks of the National Barbasco Producers and Collectors Union (Unión Nacional de Productores y Recolectores de Barbasco, UNPRB), the national organization, and began to acquire power, as well as land, in their native states. But Proquivemex, like so many federally funded projects of the time, was burdened by graft, corruption, and a misunderstanding of the situation in the Mexican countryside—and, disastrously, a failure to stay apprised of the changing steroid hormone industry. As federal funds declined, a desperate group of campesinos marched to the capital to demand that the now moribund barbasco trade be revived so that their livelihood would continue. Proquivemex hobbled along for nearly a decade until President Carlos Salinas de Gortari's neoliberal reforms led to the company's dissolution in 1989. Ultimately, through the history of the wild yam, we are able to track politicians' loss of interest in the Mexican campesino.

A Brief Note on Use of Terms

I have opted to use the word *jungle* over the more academically appropriate *tropical forest* because most local people today do not call the area "bosque tropical." Moreover in the 1940s and 1950s the foreign press invariably described the barbasco trade as the "jungle-root" industry.[38]

Campesino, which I will use interchangeably with *peasant*, has a multi-faceted meaning in rural Mexico. Though it describes, in its broadest terms, someone who comes from the *campo*, or countryside, there are few campesinos who can live exclusively off the land. Consequently, this term encompasses individuals who come from the countryside but who might make extra income as construction workers, domestics, or part of the informal economy. The word also connotes a certain ethnic background, since most campesinos are indigenous. Finally, although barbasco collection entailed digging, I do not refer to these campesinos as barbasco diggers. I opted to retain the local use of *collectors*, *gatherers*, and, mostly, the arguably incorrect *pickers*. Local strongmen and transnational pharmaceutical companies insisted that collecting barbasco was not hard work because it could be *picked up* off the ground. This linguistic choice ensured that pickers were not appropriately remunerated for their work. In the 1970s barbasco pickers themselves used a similar designation, *recolector* (harvester, picker), to describe their labor.

THE PAPALOAPAN, POVERTY, AND A WILD YAM · 1

In July 1964, Isidro Apolinar woke up at dawn, strapped on his huaraches, and walked into the jungle that surrounded his small hut.[1] He carried a tree branch whittled to a sharp point, three tortillas with salt, and an empty sack. The spearlike branch would help him dig in the moisture-heavy dirt, the tortillas and salt would ward off his hunger, and, if he were lucky, the sack would bulge with wild yams before he returned home that evening. When money ran out, which was often, or work was not available, which was becoming more frequent, these tubers were the only means he had to feed his family. But his family did not eat them. Instead, Apolinar sold them to waiting local buyers who swiftly shuttled them out of the region. He would not learn until a decade later that pharmaceutical laboratories were using barbasco, the wild yam, to meet the growing global demand for oral contraceptives.

The daily life of Isidro Apolinar offers a glimpse into how the barbasco trade changed the lives of southern Mexican peasants. In this chapter, we explore the historical context of the barbasco-rich Papaloapan region with its centuries-old harvesting of regional cash crops that transformed local labor and social relations into a stereotype of monoculture. This chapter also looks at how local rulers and federal politicians dreamed of harnessing the region's potential and bringing progress to the area in the nineteenth century and twentieth. But in embracing projects such as tobacco and, later, dams and indiscriminate logging, local and national policy further exacerbated centuries-long ethnic divisions which allowed a small and mestizo minority to thrive off the labor of the indigenous majority.

The Region—Oaxaca's Papaloapan

Isidro Apolinar grew up in San José Chiltepec, a speck of a village in eastern Oaxaca.[2] The area of the Chinantla, the third largest tropical forest in Mexico, spans an estimated 80,000 hectares of jungle.[3] The region boasts seven climatic zones and incredible botanical diversity in a mere 9,623 square kilometers.[4] But the rugged, undulating topography, with its seemingly endless hills and crevasses, also served to isolate pockets of indigenous settlements from the arrival of politically driven "modernity and progress" that sought to transform the area in the nineteenth century and early twentieth. The remoteness of certain indigenous settlements posed a particular problem that was publicly addressed as early as 1848, when the governor of the state of Oaxaca, Benito Juárez, noted "the absolute necessity to open ports and roads for the progress of commerce, industry and agriculture."[5] An anonymous letter, written more than twenty years later, again encouraged another Oaxaca native, President Porfirio Díaz, that building roads "was one of the first steps in the progress of a nation."[6] Even so, it would not be until 1952, more than a century after Juárez's initial request, that the first road connecting Chiltepec to the rest of the region was finished. However, although roads would eventually be built and railroad track laid, this would not benefit everyone in the region. Instead, the arrival of infrastructure would speed up the removal of the region's wealth. Additionally, paved roads also made it easier to differentiate between mainly indigenous and hard-to-access places and the more urban and mestizo towns.

The Papaloapan Basin's 46,517 square kilometers stretch into three states: Oaxaca, Veracruz, and Puebla. Fifty-one percent of the region is in Oaxaca, 37 percent in Veracruz, and 12 percent in the state of Puebla.[7] Within this territorial expanse the landscape shifts from the eroded lands of the Mixteca Alta, where "there is no way that man or beast can live off the land" to the lush vegetation of the Valle Nacional.[8] It was not uncommon for normally dreary government reports to turn to hyperbole when attempting to describe the endless green of the lower Papaloapan in Oaxaca. As one official wrote in 1952, "As we continue to climb the vegetation becomes more exuberant, dense, and tangled until it becomes sheer vitality. . . . The Cuenca's wealth in forestry products is immense, it is here where one can find precious woods like cedar, *caoba* [mahogany], *nogal* [walnut], *fresno* [ash]."[9]

Sentence after sentence of government reports list the commercial goods found in the area.

The Oaxacan portion of the Papaloapan is home to at least five major ethnic groups, among them Chinantecos, Popolucas, Mixe, Mixtecos, and Zapotecos. Yet a 1949 federal report identified eleven major indigenous languages spoken in the region.[10] Describing the region as a "mosaic," it provided a racially tinged description, when the writer claimed that some of these indigenous groups "by their miserable circumstances live almost forgotten by the world," and were "still living in a stone age."[11] The writer went on to add that in contrast to these indigenous Mexicans there were other communities in which "modern life exists in a similar way to that of large cities."[12] With "progress" localized in the larger towns, the author of the report was certain that in 1949 the Papaloapan was in a constant struggle between the "primitive and the modern."[13]

One palpable manifestation of this struggle was the lack of healthcare in the midst of endemic diseases linked to poverty, with river blindness (onchocerciasis), malaria, and hookworm among the most common.[14] As a young boy Isidro Apolinar recalled traveling two and half hours by foot to Tuxtepec to receive a foul-tasting dosage of medicine "for worms." The Apolinar children then shared a Coke to wash away the bitter taste. It remained a vivid memory for Isidoro because it was the only medical attention that he recalled receiving as a child. It may well be that Apolinar was given a dose of chenopodium combined with carbon tetrachloride, as part of the hookworm campaigns organized under the auspices of the Rockefeller Foundation, which in 1931 sponsored a health unit in Tuxtepec.[15]

Another marker of marginalization was the absence of basic infrastructure that by the 1940s was spreading throughout Mexico. Growing up in Chiltepec in the 1930s, Isidro Apolinar was not familiar with paved roads, light bulbs, or running water. He traveled on footpaths and obtained water for drinking, cooking, and washing by hauling small buckets from the lazy Río Nacional, a river that inched its way through the jungle that was constantly reclaiming the borders of Apolinar's village. Nearly all of his neighbors spoke only Chinanteco, and although some also spoke Spanish, the local language, or regional *dialecto*, was, as he explained, the preferred way of communicating. But not everyone in Chiltepec was Chinanteco: These fertile lands attracted men and women from as far away as central Mexico.[16]

Despite their varied origins, nearly all of Apolinar's neighbors were farmers. A 1952 report from the federal Commission of the Papaloapan River Basin, where Chiltepec is located, reported that just over 84 percent of the basin's population relied on "agriculture and related activities" for subsistence.[17] However, around that time, Mexico entered a period of food crisis, and even farming became a precarious profession. Unable to subsist, campesinos found it necessary to seek out day-labor jobs on nearby ranches and plantations or odd jobs in construction to feed their families.

As a child, Apolinar rarely ate meat. Instead, he feasted on the tropical fruits—pineapples, mangos, grapefruit, bananas—that grew plentifully in the jungle, as well as the vegetables cultivated on his father's plot of land. Any maize that the family did not use for subsistence they sold to one of two men who paddled down the river from Tuxtepec every eight days. Negotiating a fair price was impossible because the lack of roads impeded competing buyers from reaching Chiletepec. Those who came by boat paid a meager ten centavos per kilo of corn, whereas a small bag of animal crackers, a rare but treasured treat, cost twenty centavos. Consequently, Apolinar's family had limited access to cash. They were not alone. A 1949 study revealed that 76.8 percent of the Oaxacan part of the Papaloapan (926,672 people) lived in shacks (*jacalitos*), an indicator of poverty.[18]

Defying 1940 census data, which placed Oaxaca's illiteracy rate at nearly 80 percent,[19] Apolinar went to school for three years—enough to know "when middlemen were cheating him," as he put it—though buying a notebook or a even a pencil was a financial strain on his family. Nearly seventy years later, he clearly recalled the anxiety of shaving off the remaining lead from a pencil stub or carefully erasing the pages of a used notebook to do his homework. His family was by all measurable standards poor, but he said they managed to get by, primarily by taking on extra jobs. For example, Apolinar's mother washed neighbors' clothes and made fresh tortillas to sell, and his father worked on a farm tending a lemon grove. In addition, outsiders would occasionally buy *palmita* (a type of decorative frond), rubber, or local plants through the middlemen, who on their weekly trips to the region told locals of any goods that the outside demanded. Apolinar's first job, like that of most children of Chiltepec, was to thread leaves of tobacco on the remaining *plantaciones* for twenty centavos a day.[20]

He also helped his father clear the family's minuscule plot of land by throwing away pesky tubers called barbasco, whose vines twined their heart-shaped leaves around the family's precious stalks of corn.

Historical Context

Since the 1400s outsiders have coveted the wealth in what was once the Gran Chinantla—where Chiltepec, Tuxtepec, and Valle Nacional are now located. In 1455, the Mexicas, having already established their Aztec empire in central Mexico, came into the region. They transformed nearby Tuxtepec into a garrison of the empire and exacted tribute in the form of cotton, natural dyes, cacao, bird feathers, and gold—items that were already staples of trade in the area—from the surrounding ethnic groups, mainly the Chinantecos, Mazatecos, Cuicatecos, and Popolucas.[21] Although the Aztecs allowed some religious and cultural autonomy, the people of the Gran Chinantla engaged in regular uprisings. By the early 1500s, the Chinantecos were one of several subjugated groups that continuously contested Aztec rule.[22]

The first Spaniards arrived in the area in 1520 in search of gold. Allegedly Aztec emperor Moctezuma, knowing the Europeans' lust for gold and wanting to teach the rebel region a lesson, pointed the foreigners in the direction of the Chinantla.[23] Within a few years, forced labor and epidemics reportedly reduced a thriving population of nearly 100,000 Chinantecos to less than 2,000.[24] The riches of the Chinantla were so obvious that Hernán Cortés claimed the region for himself and tried unsuccessfully to make it part of his daughter's dowry. By 1534 the Gran Chinantla was directly under the jurisdiction of the Spanish crown, but the region would never come completely under Spanish domination. The rugged terrain did not aid imperial ambitions and neither did the complex local languages. Missionaries pled unsuccessfully with the Spanish crown to enforce the region's use of the indigenous lingua franca, Nahuatl.[25] Nevertheless, shortly after the conquest, the Chinantla became one of New Spain's most important agricultural regions, producing native cotton as well as European staples, mainly wheat, rice, sugarcane, apples, and grapes.[26]

In 1821, after a protracted eleven-year war, Mexico achieved independence from Spain. The fledgling nation, however, spent much of the remaining century defending its borders from Spain, France, and, unsuccessfully in 1846–48, from the United States. Militarily defeated, an exhausted Mexico continued an internal political, and often armed, struggle to try to determine which political future—empire, monarchy, republic, or federal statehood—should be the correct path. Benito Juárez, a Zapotec Indian from Oaxaca, would rise to the presidency, and bearing the calling card of liberals, he would demand separation of church and state. Liberal reforms targeted both corporately owned church property and communally held indigenous land. These were expropriated and sold to wealthy private owners. This shift in land ownership gave rise to the powerful haciendas, fincas, and plantations that concentrated thousands of acres of fertile land in the hands of a single, usually mestizo, family and transformed thousands of indigenous groups into peons on the lands they formerly held. By the late nineteenth century, much of Tuxtepec's lands were mid- or large-sized haciendas devoted to coffee, tobacco, or cacao monoculture. Smaller plantations dedicated to rubber, cotton, pineapple, sugarcane, and wheat production also thrived. In 1910, Tuxtepec had the highest concentration of commercial agricultural properties in Oaxaca, with 202 haciendas totaling 769,830 hectares (an average of 3,800 hectares per hacienda), which represented more than 27 percent of the state's total.[27] Porfirio Díaz's iron-fisted rule (1876–1911) brought simmering calm to Mexico. During the Porfirian era, national interest focused on the region and investment in plantaciones of tobacco, banana, sugarcane, and cotton increased. Recent scholarship has contested the belief that Oaxaca remained isolated from Porfirian modernization and the effects of the regime's implosion, the 1910 Revolution. The noted Oaxacan historian Francie Chassen-López argues that Oaxaca was a central recipient of Porfirian funding, but the focus was on ports and urban spaces, while much of the remaining region languished.[28]

As early as the 1880s the Tuxtepec region in the Papaloapan Cuenca had already prompted visionary politicians and businessmen to write about it. A Mexican ambassador to Washington and yet another Oaxaca native, Matías Romero, extolled the virtues of its cotton and coffee. But he also added that the area lacked "human labor (*brazos*) and a salubrious climate." As Romero explained in his study of the region, "The scarcity of labor made it necessary to turn to the people of the sierra and the valleys of Oaxaca, who come attracted by a daily wage of fifty cents. . . . Despite this there is still scarcity of labor in Tuxtepec and often the cotton harvest, or part of it, is lost because of insufficient labor."[29] Nearly a century later, a 1958 report echoed Matías Romero's study when it described how "drawn by the illusion of fertile land, the settlers instead carry the weight of tropical diseases." Furthermore, "the climate of the Cuenca is in its majority tropical and unsanitary, and hence . . . is a vector of illnesses that have for centuries sapped the strength of men," making it a challenge to reap profits from this fertile land.[30] The climate is so extreme that summer temperatures often reach an oppressive 100 degrees in the shade. Thus, finding laborers to work in the fertile valleys has been a constant struggle for landowners since the nineteenth century. Labor shortages were also a bane in one of the basin's microregions, Valle Nacional.

Valle Nacional

Historically, Apolinar's village, Chiltepec, has been overshadowed by the notoriety of its neighbor to the south, Valle Nacional. Mere miles from each other, both towns fall within the district of Tuxtepec in the Papaloapan River Basin. The torturous climate and rugged topography did not deter big landowners in Valle Nacional. Mexico's public image of peace and prosperity was unceremoniously ripped away in a 1910 denunciation that accused Valle Nacional of being "undoubtedly the worst slave hole in Mexico." With those words, John Kenneth Turner forever—and internationally—linked the region to the cruelty brought on by monoculture.[31] Posing as an American investor, Turner, a muckraker and socialist sympathizer, became a supporter of the Mexican Liberal Party and spent much of 1908–10 traveling incognito through the henequen plantations of the Yucatán and the central valleys of Oaxaca gathering evidence for a book exposing the Porfirian regime.[32] Written certainly to shock a foreign audience, his account, however, is filled with details gained by the unprecedented access that he had posing as a potential financial backer. In that guise he witnessed how the rebellious Yaqui of northwestern Mexico were herded like cattle onto trains, separated from their families, and forced to labor in the fields cutting henequen leaves, the source of twine. But, Turner confessed in his exposé, the horrors of the Yucatán did not prepare him for what he witnessed in Valle Nacional.[33]

Turner recorded how 15,000 men, women, and children arrived yearly to labor in the tobacco fields of Valle Nacional. None were expected to live more than eight months, a fact that prompted Turner to rename it the Valley of Death (Valle de la Muerte) for the certain fate that awaited each new laborer.[34] Turner was caught by the arresting beauty of this fertile plain but noted that the rough terrain made it difficult for laborers to walk from the train station or the port to the valley's plantations.

The answer to Valle Nacional's labor shortage was partly solved by over-flowing jails from as far away as central Mexico, from which unsuspecting petty thieves, drunks, or those who had incurred the wrath of local *jefes políticos* (political bosses) were loaded on trains bound for the haciendas of Valle Nacional. Turner documented the charges against one set of prisoners who arrived at El Hule railroad depot, what he called "the Gateway to the Mexican Hell":

> Of our ten friends from Pachuca, all had been arrested and put in jail, but not one had been taken before a judge. Two had been charged with owing money that they could not pay, one had been arrested when drunk, another had been drunk and had discharged a firearm into the air, the fifth had shouted too loudly on Independence Day, September 16th, another had attempted rape, the seventh had had a mild-mannered quarrel with another boy over the sale of a five-cent ring, two had been musicians in the army and the tenth had been a clerk of *rurales* and had been sold for paying a friendly visit to the previous two while they were in jail serving out their sentence for desertion.[35]

Other laborers arriving in Valle Nacional had been deceived. They un-wittingly signed up for what they believed was a good-paying job in a dif-ferent state, only to find themselves sold to one of the plantations in Valle Nacional. This practice of *enganchar* (hooking labor), inspired a turn-of-the-twentieth-century *corrido* (ballad) that bemoaned the fate of those un-fortunate men sent to work in Valle Nacional and the women they left be-hind.[36]

Plantation owners could purchase male laborers for between forty-five and sixty American dollars, depending on the seasonal scarcity of labor, with women and children selling for half those prices. These reluctant workers traveled to El Hule, Oaxaca, by train and then continued on foot, crossing rough terrain and rivers. If malaria and other tropical diseases did not kill them, then certainly the lack of food and intense work schedule would. Men, women, and children all labored from as early as 4:00 A.M. until nightfall and were forced to sleep together in longhouses with only straw mats on the floor. In a scene reminiscent of Voltaire's *Candide* and his travels through the sugar plantations of South America a century earlier, Turner describes:

Everywhere we saw the same things—gangs of emaciated men and boys at work clearing the ground with machetes or ploughing the broad fields with oxen. And everywhere we saw guards, armed with long, lithe canes, with swords and pistols. Just before we crossed the river the last time into the town of Valle Nacional we spoke to an old man with a stump of a wrist who was working alone near the fence. "How did you lose your hand?" I asked. "A *cabo* [foreman] cut it with a sword," was the reply.[37]

Ambassador Matías Romero makes mention of the *contrata*, or debt peonage, and criticizes those who attempted to escape because they inconvenienced the planter, who "not only loses the advance payment but also has a shortage of arms when he most needs them."

Memories of the labor practices of Valle Nacional still linger. In 2004 Apolinar, then a robust seventy-four year old, crouched to illustrate how owners of plantations made a noose around a worker's neck and tied the other end to the worker's foot, wrapping it around either the toe or ankle. Although Apolinar had not been alive to witness the infamy of the plantations of Valle Nacional—and the certainty of this account was lost in his memory—Apolinar's father had told his children vivid stories about the notorious contraption that forced the laborer to maintain a bent position, ideal for picking crops and for discouraging any plans of escape. The cautionary tale also served to remind his children that a person should try to secure his own piece of land, so as to not be subject to the whims of local masters.

After tobacco came cycles of coffee, cotton, sugar, and rubber production, and eventually Valle Nacional and much of the Papaloapan region became one of the world's leading banana-producing zones. Under the banner of "progress and development," large tracts of lush jungle were cleared for cultivation. In 1909, the American-owned Standard Fruit Company set up its headquarters in Tuxtepec, where the company bought 11,000 hectares in the area, "a four-hour ride on the Tuxtepec River," and imported 1 million Roatan banana plants from Jamaica.[38] Along with the United Fruit Company, Standard reproduced the labor conditions of the tobacco and coffee haciendas. By 1932, Standard was the main exporter of bananas from Mexico.[39] Bananas would redefine the region as tobacco had before. At the end of the twentieth century, the decaying remains of the Casa Verde, as the multinational's local headquarters was called, were still standing in Tuxtepec's central plaza, next to the cathedral and the municipal offices.[40] The ruins were a reminder that in 1940 a banana spore, *chamusco*, which three years earlier had decimated the United Fruit Company's holdings in Central America, had infested Mexico's banana-growing region.[41]

The cycles of monoculture went beyong the Papaloapan. Mexico's unbalanced use of farmland led to corn shortages in several states, and by 1940 Mexico was spending "about 1 million pesos to import" the basic ingredient in tortillas, one of its key food staples.[42] President Manuel Avila Camacho (1940–46) was well aware of the difficult situation in the countryside. In addressing a group of Mexican agronomists on July 8, 1941, he noted, "Whenever I visit the countryside I realize that it needs credit," for even when an individual has excellent lands, he "is still in dire poverty."[43] But in a disquieting contradiction, Avila Camacho authorized, for example, the annual export to the United States of 25,000 tons of sugar during the Second World War, although domestic demand exceeded production.[44] Furthermore, despite increased peasant demands for arable land during the Avila Camacho administration, nearly 900 acres in Acapulco, in the neighboring state of Guerrero, were sold to Getty-Presidente interests, co-owned by J. Paul Getty, for a risible four pesos per square mile.[45]

The Papaloapan Commission

For decades the possibility of harnessing the power of the Papaloapan River—Mexico's second largest—fueled dreams of national prosperity. Enormous federal government subsidies flowed into the area in an attempt to stimulate the region's development in the 1940s. Most of the funding went to building roads, schools, bridges, and irrigation infrastructure.[46] Rather than diminishing class differences, this influx of federal funds exacerbated social exclusion: The region remained polarized, with its indigenous population exhibiting high rates of illiteracy, disease, and poverty.

Although about 55 percent of Papaloapan has thin topsoil and erosion-prone mountainous terrain that make grazing difficult and agricultural production labor intensive, the other 45 percent, mostly northeastern Oaxaca and southern Veracruz, is lush and fertile. Despite the region's economic potential, however, periodic flooding delayed plans for roads and railroads into the Papaloapan Basin until the mid-twentieth century. The flooding finally prompted the creation of a commission to study the problem.

Commission of the Papaloapan River Basin

The founding of a regional development program, the Papaloapan Commission, in 1947 can be traced directly to one particularly devastating tropical downpour that occurred in September 1944.[47] Preconquest settlers called this area Tlalocan, after Tlaloc, the Aztec god of rain and lightning and evidence of pre-Hispanic flooding has been found in the area, but it was apparently not as frequent or intense as the twentieth-century floods.[48] In 1921, 1927, 1929, 1931, 1935, and 1941, "the settlements [along the rivers] were inundated for two or three months, with enormous losses to agriculture, which brought about the danger that in time this fertile region would be converted into an unproductive wasteland."[49] When the tributaries of the Papaloapan flooded, they dislodged giant roots—barbasco—which, when tossed about in the river currents, produced a sudsy substance. Locals, familiar with this sight, explained that the river was *embarbascado*, or "full of barbasco," and, they added that without fail, dead fish would follow the appearance of suds in the water.[50]

The floods of September 1944 were the most catastrophic, destroying 75 percent of Tuxtepec: the commercial center and district capital of the region. The historian Tomás García Hernández recorded that on September 23, 1944, after three days of continuous flooding, with houses floating in the river and stores and offices inundated with mud, the municipality set all its prisoners free so they could get to higher ground to save their lives.[51] The federal government declared Tuxtepec a disaster area and released emergency funds.

Created by presidential accord in 1947, the Papaloapan Commission was the first "tropical development scheme" in Mexico, with the modest mission of "conquering the tropics."[52] Initial projects focused on providing health and sanitation to make it a more salubrious place for the thousands of workers and colonists who would descend on and eventually populate the region. In addition to spraying with DDT, sewers and proper drainage systems were built alongside kilometers of roads and sidewalks. Often compared to the Tennessee Valley River Project in the United States, this development plan's teams of engineers, anthropologists, and botanists made the Papaloapan one of the most studied regions at a time when the tropics beckoned with promises of development and prosperity. The Papaloapan did not disappoint.

In less than twenty years industrial production had soared by nearly 10 percent, reaching 2,265 million pesos.[53] By 1964, for example, one-third of the nation's sugar came from sixteen mills located in the fertile basin, which also housed several beer-bottling facilities, a paper mill, and a textile plant—all of which added to the impression that, as President Echeverría would later say of any developing region, "the Revolution made it here."[54] However, as development made its way across the region, ethnically indigenous Mexicans were edged onto less desirable, marginal lands. But outsider influence was not a new trend either in the area of the Chinantla or in the Papaloapan as a whole.

Local Consequences of National Progress

In 1951, when Apolinar was twenty-one and recently married, an influx of newcomers arrived in the surrounding areas. They were mostly Mazatecos relocated by the government after the construction of the Miguel Alemán Dam on the Tonto River, one of the tributaries of the Papaloapan, flooded their lands. This dam was billed as the largest in Latin America, and it created a giant artificial lake, with a surface that spanned 4,700 square kilometers, making it Mexico's second largest, after Lake Chapala.[55] More than 30,000 disproportionately indigenous and non-Spanish-speaking Mexicans were displaced, even though the dam's construction was trumpeted as bringing Mexico closer to the modern era by providing electricity and water to faraway cities (mainly Mexico City) and by stopping the periodic flooding along the riverbeds.

Twenty years later another dam, Cerro de Oro, would displace thousands of Chinantec families, when more than 25,000 fertile hectares were flooded in the name of development; it uprooted and severed traditional networks by scattering the relocated residents throughout Veracruz and Oaxaca.[56] As recently as 2000, campesinos had yet to see the public benefits the government promised from the dam.[57] Those who did benefit, however, were cattle ranchers whose lands no longer flooded.[58] The displaced were scattered in one of the poorest regions in the state of Oaxaca. For locals such as Apolinar the influx of displaced farmers meant more competition for jobs. At the time, the early 1950s, he earned one peso daily by caring for others' livestock, but even with additional odd jobs, it was difficult for him to care for a growing family that would eventually total ten children.

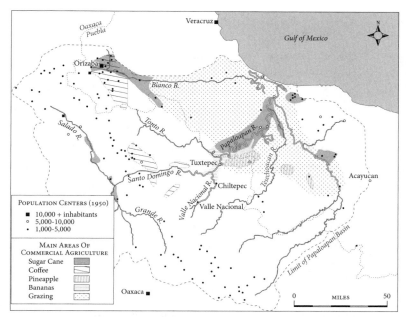

MAP 2 A Papaloapan Basin map showing the main cash crops, roads, and cities in the region in the late 1940s and 1950s.

Within Map 2:

POPULATION CENTERS (1950)
■ 10,000 + inhabitants
○ 5,000-10,000
• 1,000-5,000

MAIN AREAS OF COMMERCIAL AGRICULTURE
Sugar Cane
Coffee
Pineapple
Bananas
Grazing

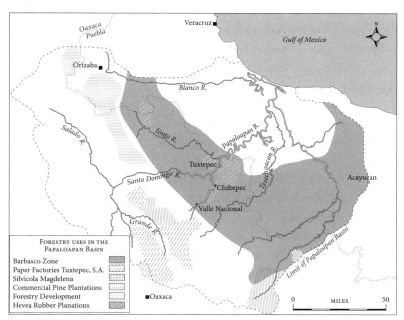

MAP 3 By the 1970s, as this map illustrates, barbasco was considered one of the leading "nontimber" sources of income in the region, competing in some areas with traditional cash crops.

Within Map 3:

FORESTRY USES IN THE PAPALOAPAN BASIN
Barbasco Zone
Paper Factories Tuxtepec, S.A.
Silvicola Magdelena
Commercial Pine Plantations
Forestry Development
Hevea Rubber Planations

Both maps from Enrique Beltrán and Jorge L. Tamayo, eds., *Recursos naturales de la cuenca del Papaloapan* (Mexico City: Comisión del Papaloapan, 1977).

Stagnant wages and growing unemployment were not particular to the Chinantla. The shift in the early 1940s from a national focus on an agrarian society to industrialized urban spaces had a strong impact on the countryside: between 1940 and 1960, the number of landless peasants throughout the Mexican countryside grew dramatically. Although the amount of accessible farmland increased a modest 11 percent in these years, the peasant population increased 59 percent during the same time period.[59] As the number of available field hands grew, the number of workdays per peasant decreased from 190 per year in 1950 to 100 days in 1960. Locally, Apolinar attributed much of the ensuing community violence—mainly murders—to the area's general unemployment and increasing poverty that spread a *desesperación* (hopelessness) that also led many of his friends and Apolinar himself to begin to drink.[60]

The area of the Chinantla, in particular, experienced an extraordinary demographic explosion.[61] Between 1921 and 1990 the population increased from 27,942 to 110,223 inhabitants.[62] Recent studies have revealed that this growth was not uniform but was concentrated in pivotal towns, reflecting certain zones' integration into the national economy.[63] In 1921 only 4 communities in the Chinantla had more than 1,000 inhabitants;[64] by 1990 that number had increased to 22, indicating a great shift in internal migration. In fact until the 1990s, Chinantecos tended to migrate within the general geographic area of the Chinantla despite its lack of employment opportunities, a trend suggesting that inhabitants must have been depending on local secondary sources of income to remain in the area.[65] If so, what sources were they relying on?

A report from the Papaloapan Commission in 1970 yields some clues about what local peasants were doing to remain in their communities. The authors list barbasco—the annoying root that plagued the Apolinar family's cornfields—as one of two main products of the region, the other being timber.[66] This study concluded that from 1954 to 1964, barbasco revenue was a whopping five million of the total fourteen million pesos reported as revenue from forest production from all the municipalities of Tuxtepec, Yaveo, and Choapan. The five million figure becomes more significant because it was generated in only five years, from 1954 to 1959. A two-volume report on the findings completed by the Papaloapan Commission in 1977 devotes entire maps to the main sources of income in the area: the paper factory, pine lumber, rubber plantations, and "zones of barbasco." The map shows that barbasco production had eclipsed traditional crops; the largest area for potential sources of income in the Papaloapan was devoted to the exploitation of barbasco.[67] For a region historically linked to the profitable use—and abuse—of land, this fact is indeed curiously significant.

It was in the 1960s when Apolinar first heard that local buyers were purchasing as much barbasco as one could dig up. In searching for barbasco he joined a veritable army, an estimated 25,000 families, or approximately 125,000 Mexicans, who by 1974 had or were actively gathering barbasco. Collecting the root to sell would be the first step in Apolinar's long affiliation with the yam. Yet he, like most of the pickers, did not know why he was being paid to gather barbasco. To begin to answer that question, the next chapter turns to the international laboratories in Europe and the United States, where the pressing need to find barbasco arose.

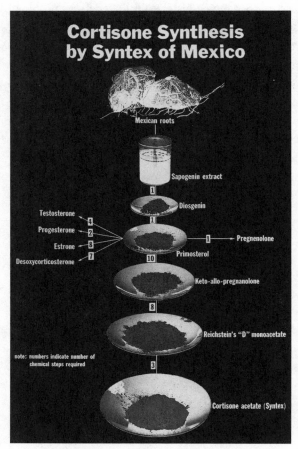

FIGURE 1 Poster showing the multiple steps needed for cortisone synthesis from barbasco, circa 1951, when Syntex was still a Mexican company. Photograph by Ezra Stoller © Esto.

MEXICAN PEASANTS, A FOREIGN CHEMIST, AND THE MEXICAN FATHER OF THE PILL

Surely Alberto Moreno, a Veracruz store owner, must have been surprised. The balding gringo who stepped into his rural general store and asked Moreno where one could find giant roots looked more like a librarian than an adventurer.[1] The year was 1942, and with the rumble of war, few foreigners were venturing far from home, fewer still into Mexico's countryside. There certainly were not many foreigners near Córdoba, Veracruz. But the man, Russell Marker, was not lost; rather he had purposefully traveled from wintry Pennsylvania to this spot in his search for dioscoreas. Marker, unable to speak Spanish, somehow communicated his desire for *cabeza de negro*, so named by the locals because, as he would later describe, some roots "that are not deformed by trees growing close to it look like the perfect head of a negro sticking out of the ground."[2] The following day Moreno helped Marker load two giant samples of the tuber onto the roof of a public bus bound for the neighboring town where Marker was staying.

In neighboring Oaxaca, Isidro Apolinar, then twelve years old, was dutifully ridding his father's *milpa* of dioscoreas, while Marker was desperately seeking the aid of local Mexicans to help him find the wild yams. His quest in the 1940s would lay the foundation for the global steroid hormone industry that transformed reproductive medicine and pain management in the twentieth century. But none of this would have been possible if Marker had not found local Mexicans to help him track and harvest the root.

Often described as "the most remarkable chemist" one could encounter, Russell Marker is credited with making possible the "ready and low-cost supply of steroid hormones" to which we are accustomed today.[3] In the 1960s the author of *Steroid Drugs*, Norman Applezweig, explained that Marker "single-handedly created an industry which has brought vast wealth and prestige to Mexico and immeasurable benefits to the health of many millions throughout the world."[4] While Marker's accomplishments are indeed extraordinary, Applezweig's comment erroneously leads one to assume that, first, Marker had no help in Mexico, and, second, that the Mexican nation profited from his discoveries. In this chapter we begin to explore the first mistaken assertion, by analyzing the often recounted tale of Marker in Mexico, his interaction with campesinos, the creation of the Syntex laboratories, and the eventual research on barbasco that would lead to the successful synthesis of an active oral contraceptive. We will examine the second assumption, that Mexico gained monetarily from this discovery, in later chapters. Although Russell Marker arrived in Mexico City in late fall 1941, the quest that led him to the jungles of Veracruz a few months later had begun decades earlier and thousands of miles away.

Russell Marker

Marker was born in 1902 in the sleepy town of Hagerstown, Maryland, in a one-room log cabin that still stood in the mid-1980s virtually unchanged but for an added brick exterior.[5] The eldest son of white sharecroppers, Marker's graduating junior high school class had only three students, two of whom went on to high school. Marker's drive to attend high school posed real challenges since it required a daily two-mile walk to a station, a four-mile train ride, and another mile walk to classes. Furthermore, Marker was continuing his studies against his father's wishes. Perhaps it was at this time that Marker honed the personality traits—a dogged determination and a way of ignoring physical obstacles and authority figures—that would later astound and befuddle colleagues. Despite his father's protests Marker graduated in three years, intent on going to the University of Maryland. When he arrived on the College Park campus the year after the end of the First World War, the registrar, anxious to enroll any student, accepted Marker in the sciences even though he had never taken a single science class.[6]

In summer 1918, intent on not falling behind, Marker picked up a chemistry text and began analyzing how to solve the problems. Before the end of the summer he had gone through the entire textbook. For the next three decades chemistry would dominate his life. His self-driven nature and independent approach to solving chemical problems would also prove to be invaluable traits decades later when he traveled to Mexico.

After graduating, Marker began working on improving chemical products that would in one way or another affect the lives of nearly everyone in the United States.[7] For example, anyone who has filled a car's tank with gasoline has unknowingly encountered Marker's remarkable ability to confront chemical riddles head-on. In 1926, while working at Ethyl Gasoline Corporation, a couple of Marker's colleagues were frustrated by the constant evaporation that changed gasoline's properties. In response Marker offered to find a hydrocarbon with a constant boiling point. What we now casually refer to as the number of octanes we put into our cars is based on Marker's research, which revealed that the standard for testing gasoline was 90 or 92 octanes. His reputation for solving problems caught the eye of Frank Whitmore, future dean at the Pennsylvania State College (which would become Penn State University), and also that of the chemists at the Rockefeller Institute, where he was hired to make compounds for more established researchers.

Recently isolated steroids had fascinated Russell Marker since his college days, but it was at the Rockefeller Institute where he first began to study them in earnest. After reading several articles about German researchers' successes with steroids, he realized that there would be a "big demand for them eventually."[8]

In a move that would characterize his life as a professional chemist, Marker quarreled with his superiors over his research on steroids, and he abruptly left the Rockefeller Institute in 1934 and went to teach organic chemistry at Pennsylvania State College. There, under the aegis of a Parke, Davis & Company research grant, he relentlessly pursued his research into the manufacture of synthetic steroid hormones.

Hormones, the Body's Messengers

Although hormones are now "the most widely used drugs in the history of medicine," the concept of hormones was not understood until 1905—and it would take another two decades before pharmaceutical companies could mass-produce them.[9]

Hormones, manufactured in glands, are organic chemicals that move through the bloodstream to exert particular effects on the activities of organs or tissues in other parts of the body. Scientists often describe hormones as messengers in the body; the best way to explain their function is by studying examples of when hormones do *not* function.

One of scholars' favorite examples is Addison's disease. In the early 1850s Dr. Thomas Addison, a physician at London's Guy Hospital encountered a patient who mysteriously died. The man's symptoms included an unstoppable wasting away, a weakened heart, anemia, gastric problems, and a leathery coloration on certain parts of the body. Addison was unable to perform an autopsy, and five years passed before another patient appeared at the hospital with the same bizarre symptoms. This time Addison performed an autopsy.[10] He found that all of the organs appeared to be in perfect working order—all, that is, except for the withered remains of what had been the adrenal glands. In the following decade other patients would present the strange set of symptoms and, once autopsied, they all revealed the same shriveled adrenals. Inductive reasoning led Addison to conclude that an insufficiency of the adrenals caused the symptoms. Physicians working on Addison's disease later discovered that the cause was not the adrenals themselves but the lack of the hormones that they normally would produce. A famous sufferer of Addison's disease, President John F. Kennedy, was dependent on synthetic steroids. His condition was a carefully guarded secret even well after his death.[11] The same inductive reasoning that led researchers to the discovery of Addison's disease also led to the 1923 discovery of insulin for managing the "dreaded disease," diabetes.[12]

A hormone, then, is a substance that propels metabolic effects that would otherwise lie dormant. Hence, the word *hormone*, derived from the Greek *hormao*, means to excite or arouse.[13] Each chemical "message" is tailored differently. For example as children approach their teenage years, the pituitary gland sends out hormone signals to the rest of the body that trigger the process of sexual maturation. Other signals are sent at the onset of menarche, at the various stages of the menstrual cycle, when a woman becomes pregnant, or at menopause. In all of these examples hormones are responsible for informing other organs about a body's altered state so that the body can accommodate and change for the duration of, say, a pregnancy.

Glands and hormones together form the endocrine system; the study of this system and its disorders is endocrinology. But not every hormone is a *steroid*, a word meaning "like a sterol."[14] Sterols are solid alcohols found in animals and plants, the most common in humans being cholesterol. All sterols have the same molecular structure, consisting of four interconnected rings joined by carbon atoms. All substances that share the same four-ringed starting structure are steroids.

Two major types of steroid hormones are essential for human life. The first, sex hormones, control the reproductive system.[15] These hormones are divided into androgens (male hormones), estrogens (female hormones), and progestogens (hormones that regulate pregnancy and the menstrual cycle). The other steroid hormones regulate metabolism and ensure the survival of the individual. Because these hormones originate in the cortex (outer wall) of the adrenal glands, they are called adrenocortical hormones, corticosteroids, or corticoids.[16] Once physicians understood the role of hormones in the body, they also grasped how to fix dysfunctions by giving the body the hormones it lacked. Replenish these substances, the hypothesis went, and patients would be cured. The stage was set for what is now termed *hormone replacement therapy*—literally, giving large, sustained doses of a hormone— the remedy for these hormone-deficiency ailments. The concept was simple, but one significant problem remained: researchers seemed incapable of reproducing hormones synthetically, that is, outside of the human body.

To shed light on the difficulties inherent in synthesizing these molecules, I have reproduced the diagram on page 44. Each number represents a carbon atom. Cortisone and other hormones have an oxygen atom in position 11, but chemists could not replicate this structure in a laboratory. Therefore, to find substitutes for human hormones, scientists first needed to uncover the composition of these hormones and find the chemical reaction that would attach the correct atom to the correct place.[17]

Controlling Sex Hormones

Scientists entering the exciting new field of sex endocrinology were confronted with the stark fact that they were dealing with research materials— testes and ovaries—that were not readily available in any research laboratory. Whereas gynecologists had easy access to ovaries in the nineteenth century and early twentieth because of the common practice of removing them to treat hysteria, irregular bleeding, and even menstrual cramps, research scientists had no regular access to gonads.

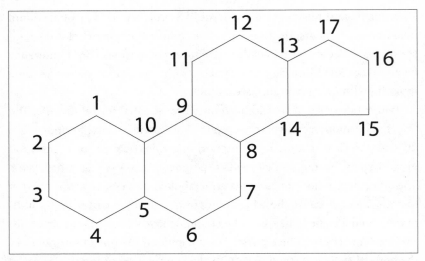

FIGURE 2 Steroid hormones are crucial substances for the proper functioning of the body. All steroids have the above ringed structure.

Complaints about the lack of access to more research material grew in the 1920s, when the focus of research shifted from biological function to chemical isolation and identification of sex hormones.[18] Initially, without direct access to organic starting material, the pharmaceutical industry contracted exclusively with slaughterhouses. This practice would lead to the dependence of future researchers (gynecologists, physiologists, and chemists) on pharmaceutical companies for a guaranteed supply of animal glands. Furthering pharmaceutical companies' control of steroid hormone production, Europeans built a powerful cartel based on patents and cross-licensing agreements in the 1930s.[19] Most of these pharmaceutical patents were based on methods for synthesizing sex hormones from cholesterol found in the spinal cords of cattle. Quite rapidly the study, control, and production of steroid hormones passed from individual chemists to large drug houses who had enough capital to finance the required research.[20]

In 1926 two German scientists discovered that pregnant women's urine happened to be far more active than the best ovarian extracts. Moreover, "the supply of urine was both abundant and inexpensive."[21] Female sex hormones were first isolated in 1929 from the urine of pregnant women, and two years later, scientists extracted male sex hormones from male urine. In 1938 female sex hormones were also isolated from male urine, confirming earlier speculation that men and women possessed both female and male hormones.[22] The delay in chemically isolating these substances was due entirely to the limited availability of raw material, because active substances occurred in only small quantities. A researcher recalled his travails in extracting estrogen from male urine, where it occurred in such small amounts that from "17,000 liters of male urine . . . we succeeded in obtaining 6 milligrams of a single crystalline."[23] In sum the minuscule extracts were incredibly valuable.

Doctors, clinicians, and gynecologists interested in furthering their study of sex hormones struggled to collect urine. For example, in the 1920s, the biochemist Edward Doisy, with the help of a nurse in the outpatient clinic of St. Louis University School of Medicine, gave each obstetric patient a one-gallon bottle and instructed her to fill it with urine and return it on the woman's next trip to the clinic. Later, "when more urine was needed, Doisy had to himself deliver and collect two-gallon bottles from the homes of obstetric patients—a time-consuming task."[24]

In 1930 the same German scientists who discovered the properties of human urine also found metaphorical hormonal "gold in the urine of pregnant mares,"[25] when they determined that it "was superior to human urine as a source of female sex hormones."[26] This discovery greatly aided pharmaceutical companies' commercial production of female sex hormones because horses' urine was cheaper to obtain than that of humans.[27]

Although European and American researchers raced to discover as many hormones as possible, their clinical utility remained undetermined. As one author has explained, "Sex hormones may best be portrayed as drugs looking for diseases."[28] Why, then, were researchers competing against each other to try to unlock the workings of hormones?

Linked to researchers' inherent drive for scientific exploration were expectations that these substances would be profitable once scientists determined their medicinal uses. Early tests revealed that continued application of hormones relieved illnesses ranging from minor or severe skin conditions to diabetes. In the early 1920s the use of female hormones was restricted to treating menstrual disorders—mainly amenorrhea (lack of menstruation)—but by the late 1920s female sex hormone therapy was touted as the remedy for "menopause, infertility, and problems of the genital organs."[29] The market for hormones increased when clinical trials for female sex hormone therapy spread from the gynecological clinic to the psychiatric and derma-tology clinics.[30] By extending the range of disorders that female sex hor-mones could treat, pharmaceutical companies made most women, for most of their life, potential consumers—an incredible stroke of marketing genius. With hormones being marketed as "cure-alls," the demand increased, as did the need for larger quantities of raw material.

Marker and the Pursuit of Hormone Research

Given the popularity of steroid research at the time it is not surprising that Russell Marker was also intrigued by these substances. But he had to leave the Rockefeller Institute when his proposal to derive them from "vegetable material" was deemed unacceptable research.[31] In 1934 during the depths of the Great Depression, Marker left his US$4,400 per year at the Rocke-feller Institute and opted for a severe pay cut—an annual salary of a mere US$1,800, without explicit patent royalties—at Pennsylvania State Univer-sity. This financially risky decision would later prove to be the first step in Marker's solution to the hormone supply problem, but, more important for this history, it would ultimately lead Marker to Mexico.

For a time, however, it appeared that Marker was not going to go very far beyond the confines of the Penn State labs. In contrast to the wealth of equipment and chemicals at the Rockefeller Institute, he had only "a kilo of very dirty cholesterol" to work on at Penn State. Tenacious researcher that he was, Marker spent a full year repeating the experiments that he had read about in journals, giving him a foundation for his own original research. Be-tween 1935 and 1943, Marker published 147 scientific papers on sterols and took out seventy-five patents for Parke, Davis & Company.[32] At this time, he also worked on deriving hormones from bull urine.[33]

By the late 1930s estrone (female hormone), as well as androsterone and testosterone (male hormones), had already been isolated. Marker, however, was intrigued by progesterone, the sex hormone thought to be necessary for pregnancy. In the early 1930s doctors had recognized that insufficient estrogen in women was responsible for painful and irregular periods and that insufficient progesterone led to "habitual aborters."[34] As Marker con-centrated his efforts on sex hormones, he joined the worldwide race to at-tempt to synthetically (and commercially) re-create outside the body what, up until the twentieth century, only glands could produce. In the search for steroid hormone substitutes, the plant kingdom became the next frontier.

The Quest for Diosgenin

Marker reasoned that vegetable sterols were the solution to steroid hormone production shortages, even though chemists had been unsuccessful in replicating animal hormones from plant material. He knew that sterols are found in the botanical order Liliales—which includes the onion, asparagus, and lily families—and the genus *Dioscorea*, which covers yams, desert yuccas, and agaves.[35] In particular Marker was looking for saponin compounds and their derivatives, sapogenins. The structure of sapogenin includes "a long pendulous 'side-chain,' rather like a tail, attached to the four rings of the molecule"[36]—a structure similar to that of cholesterol, the fatty substance the body uses for making steroids. To make steroids such as progesterone out of cholesterol, the side chain must be removed by chemical reaction, a process that "the body can accomplish without difficulty."[37]

Marker sought to do something novel: undo the side chain from sapogenin so it would simulate progesterone. Within months of beginning this research, Marker succeeded, using the root of the sarsaparilla plant.[38] As the *New York Times* reported on December 18, 1939, other hormones could also be derived from the root, mainly testosterone—which, the article informed, "gives bass voices to effeminate men, restores ambition to work in aging men," and "gives the will to succeed to younger men who have lacked that quality."[39] But even more important, Marker's discovery would ensure that "hormones would become generally available at low prices."[40] The chemical procedure for removing the side chain from sapogenins is now called the Marker degradation, and it is still used, virtually unchanged, in large-scale production of synthetic hormones today. Decades later, his research would lead to the first commercially viable oral contraceptive.

Although Marker's experiment was successful, the initial yield of progesterone from sarsapogenin was too small to be commercially viable. Undaunted, Marker continued his research. He suspected that greater amounts of sapogenin could occur in other plants of the sarsaparilla family. According to various sources, Marker not only enlisted the help of botanists from throughout the southern United States and northern Mexico but also spent the summer of 1940 traveling in search of a plant with a larger yield of sapogenin.[41] In particular Marker was seeking a sapogenin known as diosgenin, which he correctly surmised would act as a direct link to the production of progesterone.

By 1938 Marker had decided that "no plant in northern North America contained sufficient material to be an inexhaustible source of steroids for medicinal purposes."[42] Consequently, he traveled to Texas, where he stayed in the home of a botanist friend. While there, he grabbed a book on the vegetation of arid lands for bedtime reading. As Marker explained in his memoirs, "Halfway through I was galvanized by a photo of an enormous root (tuber) whose caption only mentioned that 'this specimen was collected just where the highway from Mexico to Veracruz, between Orizaba and Córdoba, crosses over the Barranca [gorge] de Métlac.' So I went there."[43] Marker left the United States for Mexico in late 1941. But getting to that location in eastern Mexico would prove to be a greater challenge than he had anticipated—one that might have dissuaded any other researcher.

In Search of the Wild Yams

In spite of several dozen versions describing Marker's initial adventurous foray into Mexico—which had him either cleverly observing natives as they fished with the root or "tirelessly hunting that 'ideal' plant" in jungles where "parrots screamed, alligators bellowed, and monkeys chattered . . . where the roar of a jaguar or puma often broke the night's silence as he huddled before his lonely campfire"—in reality, Marker began his search in the U.S. embassy in Mexico City and not by "crossing *barrancas* choked with vines so thick it was difficult to distinguish them from the occasional boa constrictor."[44]

Because of the Second World War, the U.S. embassy had issued a travel warning urging Americans to stay out of Mexico. This may be the reason that Marker was the only foreigner traveling on the train into Mexico in the fall of 1941.[45] Although Mexico had strengthened its relations with the United States, Marker's impression was that "No one knew for sure to which side Mexico would give its nod of support."[46] Few at Penn State agreed with Marker's plans to do research in Mexico, and many expressed concern for his safety.

Marker already had permission from the U.S. Department of Agriculture to "import without restriction," as long as all legal plants were "free of soil and plant litter."[47] However, when he arrived at the U.S. embassy, staff told him to return later because it would be very hard for him to obtain a government-issued permit to collect plants in Mexico. Marker interpreted this rebuff as another indication that "Mexico tended to be pro-German."[48]

Years later in a letter to the president of a pharmaceutical company, Marker included two photographs taken during this time in the countryside, and he repeated that "at this time the U.S. was at war with Germany and Mexico tended to be pro-German" and so, as an American, he felt unwelcomed.[49]

Perhaps Marker's poor reception was a reaction to his letter of introduction, which described his project as "working on some hormone projects intimately related to the National Defense."[50] It seems implausible, though, that Mexicans in the countryside would have seen this letter. Mexico declared war on Germany and the Axis countries on May 22, 1942, shortly after Germany sank two Mexican tankers in the Gulf of Mexico. Even though Mexico had aligned with the United States, during Marker's second trip into Mexico, he nonetheless felt threatened for being a citizen of the United States.

Corroborating Marker's perception that Americans were unwanted, the historian John Hart found that in the 1940s in the states of Chiapas, Oaxaca, and Tamaulipas, most Americans chose to settle in cities because rural Mexicans tended to reject them.[51] There are two possible explanations. First, resentments were not linked to current events (that is, the ongoing war) but rather to the 1938 oil expropriation. Second, some campesinos may have resented President Manuel Avila Camacho's proposed war scarcity (*carestía*) policy, since it resulted in exports to the United States of foodstuffs much needed by the rural population.

This was the first but not the last time that Marker's national identity would hamper the search for dioscoreas. In January 1942, to the surprise of embassy employees, Marker returned to Mexico. He had arranged to have a Mexican botanist with a plant-collecting permit accompany him to Veracruz in search of cabeza de negro, *Dioscorea mexicana*.[52] Hoping to collect many plant specimens Marker rented a truck and a driver and waited for the botanist to arrive. The mission was quickly derailed when it became apparent that the botanist had his own plant-collecting agenda, to say nothing of the fact that his girlfriend and her mother were in tow.[53]

In describing this first attempt at collecting plants Marker explained in a letter:

We experienced much difficulty with the natives and the botanist decided to return to Mexico when we reached Tehuacán where this photo was taken. On the return trip to Mexico City the hostility was so great toward me as an American that the Botanist got two soldiers to accompany us back. One of these has a gun and the other had an overcoat, the army was so poorly equipped in those times.[54]

Marker returned empty-handed to Mexico City, and the U.S. embassy told him to go home. Instead, he asked where he could catch a bus to take him to the area where the giant root grew.[55] Several hours later Marker was on his way to Orizaba, Veracruz.

Wild Yams in Veracruz

Throughout the small towns that dot Mexico's countryside mom-and-pop stores are sprinkled by the dozen. These days, soft drinks, potato chips, peanuts, and candy bars share crowded shelf space with feminine products, screwdrivers, toilet brushes, twine, and stationery paper. Toys dangle tantalizingly from the ceiling; prepackaged pastries lie alongside freshly baked bread; and sugar, flour, cooking oil, and corn tortillas are at hand. Most often the owner of a *tiendita* has some source of either temporary or fixed income in addition to profits from the shop. Some shop owners, such as Alberto Moreno in Fortín de las Flores, owned a coffee-drying slab, which implied that he either grew coffee plants or ran a side business as a collection site.[56]

Tienditas, where people trade gossip as easily as maize and pineapples, are prime sources for local information—so it is not surprising that upon arriving in Veracruz Marker headed for a such a place.[57] Alberto Moreno's store—appropriately called Aquí Me Quedo (Here I'll Stay)—was located on the main road.[58] According to Marker, although he spoke very little Spanish and Moreno spoke no English, Marker communicated that he wanted samples of the giant root. Moreno told Marker to come back the following day.[59] When he returned he found two large dioscoreas, exactly the tubers he had been searching for.

Moreno packed the tubers into bags and loaded them atop a bus that would take Marker back to Orizaba. But when he arrived both bags were missing. As he desperately tried to communicate his loss to the driver, a policeman approached and, Marker recalled, "I understood that he wanted some money to give them back. I had a ten-dollar note in my pocket and I handed that to him. He took that and gave me one of the roots."[60] Having no other bills Marker was unable to purchase back the other root, so he set off with only one giant yam.

This short anecdote from Marker's memoirs shows how the rules had changed for him: at the time, no market existed for dioscoreas (either cabeza de negro or barbasco), so the tubers were of no value to anyone but him—but the policeman had taken advantage of that. While in Mexico, Marker would be constantly reminded that in contrast to working in the pristine conditions of his university laboratory, he was functioning in a remarkably different setting with a different set of laws that required him to become familiar with doing science beyond the walls of a laboratory. He had to learn a completely new, more sophisticated level of human interaction that ranged from pacifying a botanist with a permit, to engaging the shopkeeper Alberto Moreno, to bribing a policeman. One could argue that Marker, more than many of his fellow scientists, would understand how fully local people and local customs could shape science production and discovery. This crucial human component would alter and redefine how Mexico and the rest of the world would research and develop steroid hormone production.

A relationship, however, does not always constitute a dialogue or even acknowledgment of the other party. Despite Marker's initial contact and later friendship with Moreno, he would never meet the people who ended up expanding the hormone-production industry that his search precipitated: the more than 100,000 pickers who came to rely on the barbasco trade and on whom Marker and other scientists would be fully dependent. Without the yam diggers' labor, researchers could not have proceeded with their chemical experiments or, ultimately, with the creation of commercial hormone-based medications. The initial labor relationship Marker established with Moreno would also determine how local Mexicans would, in the future, perceive their role in the pharmaceutical companies' search for medicinal plants: from uninformed root gatherers to, eventually and surprisingly, vocal agitators for change in the countryside.

Thus, in 1942 the root itself was not as important as what could be obtained *in exchange for* the root. A few local people were immediately able to make a profit as suppliers of dioscoreas, and that would lead to thirty years of inequality between those who understood its value—chemical, monetary, or political—and those who never fully grasped its financial and political importance.

Back at Penn State

When Marker returned to Penn State, he set about experimenting on his lone cabeza de negro. He chopped up some of the root, dried it, and isolated diosgenin—the crucial first step to synthetically producing steroid hormones. In early February 1942 Marker sent part of the root to Parke-Davis laboratories in Detroit, where company chemists learned the relatively simple task of extracting large quantities of diosgenin from the tuber.[61] Despite this remarkable achievement, the discovery was met with odd indifference not only at Parke-Davis but also by the rest of the pharmaceutical industry. This reaction went against all logic. First, Mexico had an abundant supply of cabeza de negro; second, Marker had discovered that local people were able and willing to go into the jungles to dig it up; and, most important, work in the laboratories had proven cabeza de negro to be a remarkable source of raw material for the production of hormones. The main problem, however, was that the yam was known to be found only in Mexico, which, in 1942, was seen as an insurmountable obstacle. The unenthusiastic reaction of then president of Parke-Davis, Dr. Alexander W. Lescohier, reveals much about Mexico's image among scientists at that time.

Years earlier off the coast of Acapulco Lescohier suffered a severe case of appendicitis.[62] He was rushed from the ship to a hospital where he received such "rough treatment" at the hands of Mexican doctors that he was convinced he would die. Based on that harrowing experience Lescohier was certain that "nothing could be done in Mexico."[63] So when Marker and Oliver Kamm, then director of research for Parke-Davis, excitedly insisted that hormone production from wild yams was viable and easy, Lescohier brushed aside the idea. Lescohier was so certain that Mexico was inappropriate for a process as sophisticated as hormone production that he refused to divert any Parke-Davis funds to the effort, in spite of the results from the Detroit laboratory.[64] Instead, Lescohier countered that progesterone could be derived from pregnanediol extracted from bull urine, as Marker had earlier demonstrated. Parke-Davis would "have a stable of bulls in here just like we have a stable of horses. We'll get a thousand bulls if necessary and just collect the urine. But there's no use of thinking of going to Mexico City because it can't be done in the first place."[65]

Lescohier was not alone in thinking that science production in Mexico was simply a fool's dream. Regarding the "precarious adventure" of working in Mexico, researchers cited among the many obstacles: "The Mexican pharmaceutical industry was virtually non-existent: there were no facilities for processing the black root, and what was more the cabeza de negro was hardly the most accessible of source material, for it grew in steamy hilly jungle[s] where nobody in his senses ever went. And was Mexico politically stable? How could any large company setting up an establishment there be sure of the future."[66]

The comment about Mexico's political stability most likely also referred to the oil expropriation by then president Lázaro Cárdenas's government in 1938, which hit American interests the hardest.[67] Moreover, the erroneous image of Mexico as a technologically backward nation whose citizens were ill prepared to grasp the complexity of chemistry would be a constant theme to justify future actions by transnational pharmaceutical laboratories. A chemist's account of the time reinforces the myth: instead of "Ph.D. colleagues and well-educated technicians" foreign chemists had to manage a laboratory with "one college graduate and several charming, but giggly, señorita-assistants who had not finished high school."[68] These images of Mexicans as brimming with charm but allegedly lacking in serious professionalism would also play a part in how the drug companies evaluated and remunerated labor at every step of the hormone-production process.

Added to business and scientific concerns were worries about infrastructure and labor. The drug companies pointed out that

Mexico was a rough country with inadequate transportation and poor industrial facilities. Digging isolated wild plants and hauling tons of unwieldy tubers out of jungles and across mountains was surely doing things the hard way, not to mention the labor problem. No, it was just too farfetched for serious consideration by American businessmen.[69]

Writing in 1965, another author concurred that in the 1940s "Mexican politics were unstable." A key worry was that

Mexico had neither scientists nor technicians capable of running a hormone processing plant. Hundreds of thousands of dollars of capital would have to be risked just getting set for production. And who knew whether, by then, European or American chemists would not have found equally effective ways of improving the old methods of hormone extraction?[70]

Undaunted by the brush-off he got from Parke-Davis, Marker made the rounds of pharmaceutical companies that might be interested in investing in Mexican wild yams.[71] He trudged to Merck, Ciba, and Schering-Plough, but despite the certainty of significant profits, no company was interested in taking the risk of sinking money into the hormone-producing tubers of Mexico's jungles. Marker's university supervisors at home were also unconvinced. In a letter congratulating him for the "difficult isolation of kryptogenin" the dean of Penn State, F. C. Whitmore, reluctantly added "as regards the collecting trips [in Mexico] I would say they represent a necessary evil" in which could be seen "no possibility of the valuable results from your botano-chemical studies coming to an end in the near future."[72]

Given the world's staunch refusal to foresee any potential chemical industry in Mexico, the history of hormone production might have developed much later than it did. But Marker was not intimidated about having to pursue nontraditional scientific methods in Mexico. Accounts of what happened next vary depending on the source, but in general they all agree that Marker, on his own, financed his return to Mexico. So with no pharmaceutical backing and begrudging permission from the university administration, Marker went to Mexico, rented an erstwhile pottery shop in Veracruz, and converted it into a makeshift laboratory.[73]

In 1979 the chemist Carl Djerassi interviewed Russell Marker in Palo Alto, California. Marker revealed not only his tenacity but also the serendipitous spirit of his discovery:

> Then I decided that I was going to go into it myself and I withdrew from the bank about half of my meager savings and went to Mexico, where I collected 9 or 10 tons of the root from the natives that found the original two plants for me. . . . The man that had collected the original had . . . a little store and a small coffee-drying place right across the street. We collected material and he chopped it like potato chips and dried it in the sun, and I took it up to Mexico City and had it ground up. I found a man that had some crude extractors there; he extracted it with alcohol and evaporated it down to a syrup. And that I took back to the United States to a friend of mine who had a laboratory. I made arrangements with him

that if he would do the rest of the financing and let me use his laboratory, I would give him one-third of the progesterone that we got. I told him that I expected a little over 2 kilos. But we ended up having a little over 3 kilos and he took a kilo of it. At that time he was getting [US]$80 a gram for it [from animal sources].[74]

The Emergence of Syntex Laboratories

After synthesizing more progesterone than had ever been synthesized before, Marker and his colleague had more than 3,000 grams—at the time, worth approximately US$240,000.[75] Having obtained the elusive female hormone in vast quantities, Marker now needed a buyer. According to later accounts in scientific journals (*Steroids, Chemical Education,* and *Journal of American Chemical Society*), popular magazines (*Life, Newsweek, Time,* and *Fortune*), and books on various medical topics, Marker unexpectedly showed up at Mexico City's Laboratorios Hormona S.A., which marketed natural hormones derived from animal sources, among other pharmaceuticals. Marker would later reveal that, knowing little Spanish, he had flipped open a phone directory and searched under the word *hormonas.* The owners of Laboratorios Hormona were a Hungarian lawyer, Emeric Somlo, who sometimes added *doctor* to his name, and a German chemist, Federico Lehmann, who initially met with Marker. The German immediately associated Marker's name with articles in chemistry journals. Most importantly he grasped the meaning of Marker's discovery.[76] Subsequent meetings with Somlo cemented the idea of establishing a Mexican company devoted to the industrialization and production of progesterone. Given that Marker had no capital, he offered to provide the scientific know-how while Somlo and Lehman brought in the funds—but Marker was guaranteed 40 percent of the profits from the new company. Syntex, whose name was derived from the words *synthesis* and *Mexico,* opened its doors in January 1944,[77] and in less than a decade it became the major supplier of synthetic hormones to European and American pharmaceutical companies.[78]

Fortune magazine proclaimed in an article published in 1951 that Syntex's "jungle-root chemical industry" was probably "the biggest technological boom ever heard south of the border."[79] Marker's lone findings had upset the European monopoly of steroid hormone production. Moreover, with his synthesis in full swing, the price of progesterone dropped from US$80 to less than $1 per gram. At that point, the scientific world's hormone-seeking gaze shifted from European slaughterhouses to the jungles of southeastern Mexico.[80]

Business and Science

Marker abruptly left Syntex less than one year after forming a partnership with Somlo and Lehmann. According to later interviews Marker claimed that his partners refused to pay him his share of the profits. In retaliation— and in an interesting example of how scientific knowledge is combined with the politics of knowledge—Marker sabotaged his former company by switching and mislabeling reagents.[81] George Rosenkranz, Marker's successor, made the following observations shortly after his arrival at Syntex:

> It soon became obvious that my predecessor, the brilliant, but secretive and suspicious Marker, did not want anybody to know the secrets of his processes . . . Reagents and intermediates all carried strange code names. For example, the hydrogenation catalyst was labeled, "silver." Solvents were identified by the workers by weight and smell.[82]

In the power struggle over the chemical synthesis of diosgenin, the one thing Marker retained was the actual knowledge of the process. By controlling the disparate chemicals used in processing, he ultimately controlled the end product and could easily stop the manufacture of sex hormones. In other words, in the late 1940s, the steroid production process in Mexico was constrained almost in its entirety by this single, somewhat eccentric entrepreneur and scientist. Years later, in the 1970s, that situation would change: Mexican peasants, some wholly unaware of chemical processes, were able to stop steroid hormone production by regulating the amount and type of wild yams that they extracted from the jungle.

In 1945 Marker, penniless, left Syntex. With the help of a friend and several Mexican technicians who left Syntex with Marker, he set up a rudimentary laboratory in nearby Texcoco. Within a year, he was able to process nearly thirty kilos of progesterone.[83] Marker had continued to collect new varieties of dioscoreas, and one of these was called barbasco by locals. As Marker explained, "It had almost pure diosgenin . . . I couldn't use that earlier because I found it at a place called Tierra Blanca. The only way you could get it out of there during the war was to put it on a boat and take it over to Veracruz."[84]

FIGURE 3 Several technicians from Syntex followed Marker in 1945 to his new start-up laboratory, Botanica-Mex S.A., but the company was beset with problems from the beginning. Here Russell Marker and his employees sit on a pile of diosgenin. Pennsylvania State University Archives, Paterno Library.

The new company, Botanica-Mex S.A., was plagued by troubles that would become familiar to all independent companies that attempted to compete with Syntex: threats, rough treatment, and monopolies.[85] Within a year Botanica-Mex S.A. was taken over by Gedeon Richter S.A.; in May 1946 the company was moved to Mexico City, and its name changed to Hormosynth S.A.[86] Less than six years later, in 1951, the name was again changed, to Diosynth S.A., and the company was sold to Dutch Organon. In the early 1980s it was one of the six leading companies producing hormones in Mexico, again under a new name: Esteroidal S.A. de C.V.[87]

Disappointed with the business aspect of discovery and science production Marker chose to abandon chemistry in 1949. He explained: "I had put hormones into production in Mexico. That's what I went to Mexico for." Furthermore, he refused to take out patents making his hormone-production process available to all. After the failure of Botanica-Mex he effectively disappeared from public view until 1969, when he resurfaced at the Mexican Chemical Society's commemoration in his honor.[88] The details of Marker's life, when they appear in print, are remarkably similar because researchers have relied on the same scant sources. As Marker explained in a 1983 letter to Frank Koch, the head of Syntex Corporation, "Unfortunately when I retired from Chemistry in 1949 I destroyed all the reprints of my scientific publications and correspondence in order that I would never be tempted again to return to scientific work."[89] In 1983, approached about contributing to an exhibit on the history of steroid hormones in Mexico, Marker confessed in a letter that "now I regret that I destroyed all my notes" because it forced him to rely instead on the public record of the various universities and laboratories where he had worked.[90] Although Marker would never practice chemistry again he traveled often to Mexico where, for the next five decades, he trained silversmiths to reproduce silver pieces originally made by Thomas Germain in the early eighteenth century and which later, under orders from Madame de Pompadour, had been melted down to help finance France's wars.[91]

Of the chemists linked to steroid production in Mexico Marker was the one who had the most direct contact with Mexican peasants. He may well have found a substitute raw material for hormone production elsewhere had it not been for the participation of Alberto Moreno and the men Moreno hired to find the root. Years later, in 1990, Marker publicly acknowledged his debt to Moreno by handing Adolfina, Moreno's daughter, a framed picture of himself and a plaque that stated, in English and Spanish, "Russell Marker collected plants here with Alberto Moreno in January 1942 for Chemical Research at the Pennsylvania State University. This resulted in the formation of Syntex S.A., in March 1944 for the production of steroidal hormones."[92]

After sharing a crucial and prominent role in some of the twentieth century's discoveries Marker had laid the groundwork for other scientists to further his research. Marker's life certainly seemed worthy of a movie and, indeed, in 1974 he was back in Veracruz to supervise a German television production about his time in Mexico.[93] Marker again resurfaced in Mexico on December 4, 1976, when the directors of the state-owned company for the production of steroid hormones, Proquivemex, asked that he speak out in defense of Mexican indigenous barbasco pickers.[94] Marker's dramatic departure from chemistry would not, however, alter the need for more wild yams.

Barbasco—*Dioscorea composita*

As mentioned, by 1949 a raw material for hormone production that was superior to cabeza de negro was found in a *Dioscorea* "called 'barbasco' by the natives"—unlike cabeza de negro, this root "had almost pure dios-

FIGURE 4 *The Treasure of the Jungle*, painted in the 1960s by the famed artist David Alfaro Siqueiros, was commissioned by Syntex Laboratories. The painting currently hangs in former Syntex headquarters, now Roche Pharmaceuticals, in Palo Alto, California. This reproduction of the painting was used as a cover for a steroid conference in Mexico. Pennsylvania State University Archives, Paterno Library.

FIGURE 5 In 1990 Marker was again honored by the Mexican Chemical Society. During his visit he traveled to Veracruz to, in turn, hand a plaque to the daughter of Alberto Moreno in recognition of Moreno's role in finding *cabeza de negro* (*Dioscorea mexicana*). This 1969 picture from Marker's personal photo album has his typed description at the side. Pennsylvania State University Archives, Paterno Library.

genin."[95] This find led to an explosion in the Mexican hormone industry. Whereas cabeza de negro took anywhere from six to nine years to mature enough to have significant commercial levels of diosgenin, barbasco contained nearly 6 percent diosgenin yields in plants half that age. Moreover, those in the industry had reason to believe that the supply of barbasco was inexhaustible. Also, earlier concerns over the feasibility of a labor-intensive collection process vanished when Mexico's worsening economic instability in the countryside provided large numbers of willing pickers and a new business-friendly regime replaced President Lázaro Cárdenas's populism. Future discoveries at Syntex would be credited to George Rosenkranz, Luis Ernesto Miramontes, and Carl Djerassi, who were responsible for continuing the research on wild yams.

George Rosenkranz and the Study of Chemistry in Mexico

George Rosenkranz, a Hungarian-born chemist, was taking advantage of Fulgencio Batista's presidential decree allowing all emigrants to settle in Cuba when the owners of Syntex contacted him.[96] Somlo and Lehmann were desperately seeking someone who could continue the work that Marker had so abruptly left behind. For some time Rosenkranz had been extracting saponins from imported Mexican yams because most Cuban yams yielded only sitosterol. Rosenkranz took on the position of director of technical and scientific operations at Syntex in Mexico, where he was able to synthesize progestogens, androgens, estrogens, and corticoids—all from cabeza de negro.

Despite this remarkable feat and the obvious advantages of diosgenin as a cheaper starting material for hormone production, pharmaceutical companies still did not consider the Mexican steroid industry a serious alternative to the "oceans of pregnant mares' urine."[97] In addition potential investors did not want to get embroiled in a pending patent case. As sociologist Gary Gereffi, who studied Syntex laboratories, explained,

> The patent pressures came from both sides. Syntex's sale of hormones was inhibited by the Europeans' product-and-use patents, which put Syntex customers at legal risk. At the same time, Syntex was being sued by Parke-Davis, which had tried to protect itself with worldwide rights on Marker's processes but slipped up by not filing Marker's patents in Mexico.[98]

As a result of these difficulties, the European steroid cartel continued to enjoy a virtual monopoly from 1947 to 1949, and Syntex sold only small quantities of progesterone, which at the time was a hormone still looking for a stable market.[99]

Rosenkranz's work in the Mexican chemical industry highlighted the perceived lack of trained Mexican chemists. "Applying the same solution as in Cuba, [Rosenkranz] started a Ph.D. program" at the National Autonomous University (UNAM).[100] He also actively lobbied for financial support for Mexico's famous Instituto de Química, established in 1941 on the UNAM campus. Rosenkranz's intentions were to train Mexican chemists to work with steroids specifically derived from barbasco. Today the Instituto continues to be a flagship in Mexico's ethnobotanical research.[101] As Rosenkranz continued to work on sex hormones extracted from barbasco, world demand once again would determine the focus of the study of hormones.

The "Cortisone Famine"

In autumn 1941 a rumor circulated that the Germans were purchasing immense quantities of adrenal glands in Argentina. The rumor exploded into an alarming version that "Nazi pilots were able to fly to forty thousand feet and higher because they were being hopped up with injections of an adrenal cortex hormone."[102] Lending support to this story, an American researcher had in fact discovered that laboratory rats appeared to be more resistant to oxygen deprivation when they were administered continual doses of cortical extracts. But to produce an altitude-tolerance booster for the thousands of American pilots being trained at that time, all the cattle and pigs in the entire United States would have had to be slaughtered.[103] Consequently, a synthetic alternative would have to be found. The government gave Merck & Co. the task of finding a way to synthesize hormones from other primary material. Although the company produced several hundred grams of a synthetic—called Compound A—it had no useful effect in humans.

Later intelligence reports confirmed that the Nazi-pilot rumor was unfounded, so the remaining Compound A was converted to Compound E, cortisone. Later in the decade cortisone was injected into a terminally ill patient who had been bedridden and paralyzed by rheumatoid arthritis pain for five years. Within days the patient was walking without so much as a limp.[104] After six months of testing with synthetics researchers found that daily injections alleviated the symptoms of rheumatoid arthritis. Although the treatment was not a cure, daily injections produced a near-complete remission in even the most severe cases of crippling arthritis.[105] Nevertheless, in reporting the findings at a physicians' meeting in April 1949 Merck chemists disclosed that it would be months before they could produce any more cortisone for experimental purposes. Moreover, no one knew when cortisone could be mass produced, much less the cost of the product. According to an article published in *Life* magazine in 1951: "The drug has been so scarce that it is probably a black market item in some quarters. Though the number of arthritics in the U.S. is estimated at well over a million, there is only enough cortisone to treat a small fraction of them."[106]

As the news spread from medical circles to the general public "every pharmaceutical concern in the country was anxious to play a role in ending the tragic shortage of cortisone," and, certainly, to cash in on the profits as well.[107] Within a few weeks nearly a kilogram of cortisone had been produced, enough to treat thirteen patients for six months. But every dose cost more than a thousand dollars to produce,[108] making the treatment available to the likes of, say, the Kennedys—who, it was rumored, stashed cortisone in bank vaults for the future president—but not to the general public.[109]

Cortisone was scarce because the starting materials, cattle bile and other organic substances, were extremely difficult to extract. In one example of an effort to synthesize enough cortisone to meet the incredible demand, the Worchester Foundation for Experimental Biology "devised a scheme for producing 50,000 grams of cortical hormone a month by setting up each day 1,000 fresh beef adrenals in an ingenious glassware apparatus that kept the glands alive by pumping blood, oxygen, and penicillin into them."[110] Even though it was easy to oxygenate that famous number-eleven spot— recall the steroid diagram on page 44—when the gland was part of a living being, it was still too costly a process. Upjohn Pharmaceuticals had also experimented with the adrenal glands of 2,200,000 hogs, but the cost per gram of cortisone produced was nearly US$800.[111] The cost was still too high and the quantities still too low to treat effectively the significant numbers of people with rheumatoid arthritis in the United States.

Carl Djerassi: Syntex, Cortisone, and an Amazing Mexican Yam

The invention of fermentation chemistry demonstrated that bacteria and molds were a cheaper, more efficient means for obtaining steroids. Despite this discovery, dioscoreas, especially barbasco, would remain the most versatile source for obtaining the purest forms of synthetic hormones. Carl Djerassi, the Austrian-born American chemist who joined Syntex in 1949, described the search for cortisone as a chase in which "the new ways of producing cortisone come as the climax to an unrestrained, dramatic race involving a dozen of the largest American drug houses, several leading foreign pharmaceutical manufacturers, three governments, and more research personnel than have worked on any medical problem since penicillin."[112]

Schering Corporation even attempted to coax Russell Maker out of retirement: A letter dated September 26, 1949, implied that "our purposes in handing you this check [for US$1,000] is simply to defray your expenses in a matter of mutual interest . . . working together towards our common objective of finding a product which will solve the problem of rheumatoid arthritis."[113] Schering correctly guessed that "plant sources offer the greatest opportunity for real advancement towards the ultimate objective of obtaining Cortisone for all who need it."[114] But Marker, despite overtures by Schering and many others, would not be involved in this chapter of steroid discovery.

As the search for a plentiful and ready supply of cortisone continued, scientific journals reported with astonishment that tiny Syntex in Mexico had beaten out the larger and better-financed research teams. *Harper's Bazaar* said it best when it reported, "The cortisone production problem was solved . . . it should be noted that the leader in the race was a chemical manufacturer in presumably backward Mexico."[115] American magazines such as *Fortune* and *Life* detailed how, once again, Syntex and a Mexican tuber had helped solve a global shortage of hormones.[116] But barbasco's real value was reinforced when researchers in Upjohn's laboratories in Kalamazoo, Michigan, developed a method that used an enzyme to place an oxygen atom at location 11 of the four-ringed hormone molecule. This discovery was important for Mexico "because it allowed steroids made from diosgenin to be used as *intermediate* materials in the manufacture of cortisone and its derivatives."[117] Progesterone produced by Mexican barbasco would become the preferred source to meet the growing demand for cortisone.

Barbasco's value had crossed national borders and become popular outside of Mexico—but within Mexico, few knew that the country's jungles were helping to solve a global race for medications.

In the early 1950s as more researchers began to experiment with various synthetic alternatives to progesterone, the product derived from Mexican

FIGURE 6 Mexican scientists gaze at cabeza de negro (*Dioscorea mexicana*), which barbasco (*Dioscorea composita*) replaced as the primary source of synthetic steroids in the late 1940s. This image first appeared in a 1951 *Life* magazine article after it was announced that life-saving cortisone could be derived from Mexican yams. Photograph by Juan Guzmán.

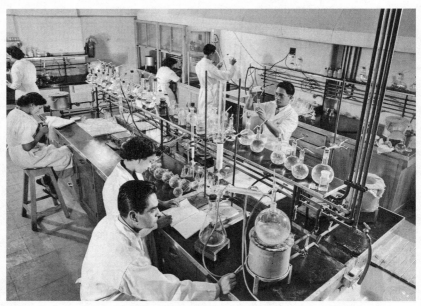

FIGURE 7 Mexican scientists at work in Syntex Laboratories. In 1951 *Fortune* magazine proclaimed that Syntex had made "the biggest technological boom ever heard south of the border." Photograph by Ezra Stoller © Esto.

FIGURE 8 Initial images of steroid research in Mexico stressed the exotic elements of conducting research in a developing country. The original 1949 caption for this image explained that "the main Syntex plant above, is a former gunpowder mill built upon the remains of a seventeenth century castle. Girl operators synthesize male hormones on the lower level, female hormones on the upper." Photograph by Ezra Stoller © Esto.

FIGURE 9 Called "barbasco flour," diosgenin was the foundation for the production of synthetic steroid hormones. Here a Mexican technician at Syntex in Mexico City measures the "flour." Photograph by Ezra Stoller © Esto.

yams continued to be the purest form available. American chemists found that the Syntex product was between four and eight times more effective than natural progesterone when taken orally.[118] In July 1951, Upjohn asked Syntex for the unheard amount of ten tons of progesterone at forty-eight cents per gram (the going rate was US$2 per gram), and Syntex agreed to manufacture it. It later became known that Upjohn had found a way to convert progesterone into hydrocortisone, which in turn could be used to produce the much-sought-after cortisone. The increased output of steroid hormone that Syntex produced effectively challenged the former European hormone cartel, with the result that more consumers were able to purchase medications that formerly had been prohibitively expensive.

The continued scarcity of an effective treatment for arthritis, "man's most crippling disease," prompted other foreign-led pharmaceutical companies to establish themselves in Mexico.[119] In the following decade, as these companies moved into Mexico ready to exploit barbasco, it became clear that although Syntex had no monopoly on the root, the company did have a crucial element: the "most highly organized collection system."[120] Even though the Mexican government created Laboratorios Farquinal in the 1950s as part of Industria Nacional Químico Farmacéutica S.A. de C.V. to control the chemical and pharmaceutical subsidiaries that Mexico had taken over from the Axis countries during the Second World War, it became too difficult to compete with the powerhouses of established laboratories like Syntex.[121]

Luis Ernesto Miramontes and Mexico: The Birthplace of the Pill

Few Mexicans and even fewer non-Mexicans, know that Luis Ernesto Miramontes—according to patent number 2,744,122—is the co-discoverer of the chemical compounds that led to the global production of oral contraceptives. In the most common narratives Americans Margaret Sanger and Katharine McCormick seek out Dr. Gregory Pincus in Worcester, Massachusetts, to develop the Pill. Pincus agreed to work with them because he was aware of studies that progesterone could work as an anti-ovulent. What is usually left out from this popular history is that research on progesterone was conducted in Mexico City at Syntex. As Miramontes explained during an interview, "If I hadn't been working at Syntex there would not have been a Pill until much later when someone else would have thought of discovering noretisterona."[122] Miramontes's story is a counternarrative to the well-known history of the discovery of the Pill and the individuals who played a role in its development—not in the United States but, surprisingly, in Mexico, the pivotal beginning for contraception development. The initial research for the Pill was conducted in the Syntex laboratories in Mexico City using barbasco as the starting raw material.[123]

Born in 1925 in the Mexican state of Nayarit, Miramontes knew from an early age that he wanted to become a chemist. He was at the prestigious Institute of Chemistry at the National Autonomous University (UNAM) in Mexico City working on his chemistry degree when he learned about the work taking place at Syntex with wild yams. Syntex had an agreement with the Institute in which the company provided solvents and money in exchange for offering student internships and potential future positions at Syntex Laboratories. Miramontes was a "very good experimenter" who was able to complete complex syntheses in record time. In 1950 Carl Djerassi took note of the young student and invited him to join Syntex as his own assistant. Since Miramontes still had not completed his degree at that time, he worked at Syntex in the mornings and then dashed back to the University to continue working on his thesis.

In the early 1950s Syntex, as were most other research laboratories, was involved in corticoid research to attain cortisone, but Miramontes was assigned to work on synthesizing other compounds. He was trying to find an orally efficient synthetic progesterone that could replace the painful injections used by women with a history of miscarriages.[124] On October 15, 1951, after months of working seven days a week he concluded the synthesis of norethindrone. He carefully detailed the reaction in his daily notebook, and was heartily congratulated by Djarssi and Rosencranz.

Ironically, as Miramontes explained about the substance he had synthesized, "I knew that it would have oral activity but I didn't know about the Pill. I did not even imagine it. Nor at the beginning did Djerassi, nor Rosenkranz imagine that everything related to the Pill would come about [because of these experiments]."[125]

Miramontes's chemical reaction ended up transforming how governments defined population growth, but not in the way that he anticipated. Despite being listed as second author in the article that reported the synthesis of norethindrone, Miramontes claimed in 2004 that he remained unaware of what he had done for nearly a year, until he read in chemical journals what his work had achieved for Syntex. After five years as a chemist for Syntex, Miramontes would go on to work briefly for Searle,

FIGURE 10 On October 15, 1951, the Mexican chemist Ernesto Miramontes performed an experiment that would later lead to the manufacture of oral contraceptives. Here a young Miramontes, in white lab coat, stands with President Miguel Alemán. Courtesy of the Miramontes Family.

another transnational pharmaceutical company, and teach at UNAM before spending the rest of his career working for PEMEX, Mexico's state-owned petroleum company. With nearly forty national and international patents Miramontes was honored in 1986 with Mexico's Andrés Manuel del Río award for chemistry, and in 1992 the General Hospital in Tepic, Nayarit, was renamed "Luis Ernesto Miramontes Cardenas" Hospital.

In 2001, the fiftieth anniversary of the Pill, Miramontes and George Rosenkranz (Carl Djerassi was unable to attend) were honored in Mexico City's General Hospital auditorium because their discovery laid "the foundation for contraception based on hormones."[126] According to Miramontes these would be the few times that he was honored in Mexico for his contribution to contraception. While he was seldom publicly acknowledged for his work, in 1964 Miramontes's name appeared, together with those of Djerassi and Rosencranz, next to the discovery of oral contraception as the U.S. Department of Patents' "forty most important patents" of the previous two centuries together with, among others, Edison, Pasteur, and the Wright brothers.[127]

In 1955 the fertility specialist Dr. John Rock selected Enovid, Searle Pharmaceuticals' oral contraception formula, over Syntex's version, norethindrone. This simple choice guaranteed that the United States and not Mexico would be celebrated for the rest of the twentieth century as the birthplace of the Pill.

As a Mexican chemist's crucial role in the history of contraception slowly slipped into historical amnesia, an increased demand for barbasco drew rural Mexicans—who, like Isidro Apolinar, were struggling to find employment and make a living—into the nation's southern jungles.

The photographer Ezra Stoller captured visual proof of the barbasco trade boom. While on assignment in Mexico in the early 1950s, he shot several hundred images of peasants, laboratories, and yams. *Newsweek* and *Fortune* magazines ran stories with Stoller's photos that introduced Americans to the story of barbasco. His documentary images are remarkable for many reasons. First, the sheer quantity of barbasco being delivered—by boat, horse, or the backs of men—is significant because it had been a mere eight years since Russell Marker had first asked Moreno for wild yams. Even if they were taken on a delivery day, the images support estimates that by the early 1950s barbasqueros were removing several dozen tons of barbasco from the jungles per week. These images are also worth examining more closely because they record the method of trade, delivery, and weighing of the yams, which would remain virtually unchanged for more than two decades (as would the price paid for barbasco). It is likely that when Marker first traveled to Mexico he could not have envisioned the labor networks that would emerge from his request for a wild yam. Moreover, he could not have grasped that political transformations and medical discoveries in the 1950s would ultimately drive a global quest for steroid hormones.

Conclusion

The late nineteenth century and early twentieth saw a revolution in scientists' grasp of the functioning of hormones. As understanding increased, pharmaceutical companies struggled to produce medications based on synthetic hormones that could be administered to compensate for hormonal shortages that cause illnesses. The challenges of using animal organs or human and animal urine as starting materials in chemical steroid–producing processes were almost insurmountable. But then a young chemist, Russell Marker, proposed experimentation on plant materials as a substitute for animal and human raw materials. Although his research proposal was not well received the notoriously stubborn scientist persisted.

In 1941 he traveled to Veracruz from Pennsylvania on a scientific hunch that yams found in the jungles of southeastern Mexico could yield more sapogenin than the yucca plants found in the American Southwest. The collection of yams, which Marker's quest set in motion, would endure unaltered in southeastern Mexico for nearly four decades. Marker's scientific zeal had initiated a revaluing of a plant that the residents of southeastern Mexico had considered a mere weed. The world's growing demand for steroid hormones derived from diosgenin, the substance contained in cabeza de negro and later in barbasco, led to the need for a workforce of thousands of able-bodied Mexicans to harvest the tubers. With the number of unemployed peasants growing in Mexico's barbasco-rich regions, these jobs proved to be an important escape valve for the country's labor pressures.

Before hormones could be neatly packaged, scientists had to leave the confines of the laboratory and enter social spheres not normally associated with their discipline—such as women's clinics, barracks, and peasant communities. The result was a complex intertwining of scientific know-how and everyday experiences surrounding the search for sex hormones. By putting a price on cabeza de negro, then on barbasco, the hormone-production industry brought together two different value systems that normally had been insulated from each other: the scientific model of research and development and the southeastern Mexican peasant's mode of production. In this merging of science with peasant life people's social roles and obligations would be reshuffled.

In the early 1960s Isidro Apolinar inherited some land from an aunt and thus began to grow more crops. But subsistence farming in the humid tropics was not an easy task on a small plot of land. In addition to nutrient-poor soil, he waged a near-constant battle with the excessive vegetation and the insects, reptiles, birds, and small rodents living in the lush vegetation. Furthermore, dozens of vinelike plants seemed to pop up in the fields overnight between the rows of carefully planted corn and beans. Among the most persistent of these was barbasco (*Dioscorea composita*), the same root Apolinar helped his father rip from the family's cornfield when he was a child. The root was so implacably invasive, he recalled, that one could even find it growing under the hammock in the front yard or under the clotheslines behind the house. But medical discoveries taking place far outside the Chinantla would change the way Apolinar viewed the plant and determine his and the region's future.

For example, by 1952 Dr. John Rock had set up trials on the Pill in Haiti, Puerto Rico, and Mexico City; by May 1960 the FDA approved Searle's Enovid to be sold as an oral contraceptive. Within two years more than 2.5 million women were on the Pill. In 1962 the FDA approved the oral contraceptive developed at Syntex under the name Ortho-Novum. This approval translated into the need for more raw material for synthesizing hormones.

This chapter describes how locals such as Apolinar became aware of the barbasco trade and how they learned to track and harvest it. Interviews with more than fifty former barbasco gatherers revealed that many found barbasco collecting unremarkable, simply another in a long list of informal tasks which allowed them to subsist at a time of increasing economic hardship in rural Mexico. Their nonchalance reminds us that what constitutes a weed is not only localized but also socially constructed. In southeastern Mexico locals often call plants that outsiders might consider a weed *buen* or *mal monte* or *acahual* (secondary vegetation like shrubs). These plants are often viewed as vital to ecosystems.[1] Those familiar with barbasco's medicinal properties often described it as a "noble plant," but those who harvested the yam, unaware of its value, often described it as "something from the monte." Barbasco was seen as part of the acahual which was often selectively cleared to plant crops. But outsiders in the Chinantla would redefine barbasco's value in the mid-twentieth century when they sought, no longer cash crops, but the molecules that made up some of the region's native plants. As the quest for medicinal plants became more specific, so did the role of Mexican peasants.

Barbasco in the Oaxacan Countryside

Apolinar and his neighbors for the most part ignored barbasco or removed it from their cornfields. Occasionally they would use it for fishing. They would dig up the tuber and carefully dam a stretch of a nearby stream. After slicing the root with their machetes, they would fling the barbasco into the dammed pool. The moment the root made contact with the water, a sudsy foam emerged on the surface. Within minutes, fish appeared, gasping for air. Farmers had to be careful not to throw in too much or to toss it into running water—especially rivers. Locals had observed that if barbasco floated downstream and a pregnant cow happened to drink from the water, she would miscarry.[2]

Local *curanderos* (healers), however, knew that barbasco had other properties: when fermented in alcohol and placed directly on aching joints, it relieved the pain. A traditional healer from Jacatepec, Heladia Portugal, called barbasco a "noble but also powerful plant." She had learned from her mother, a midwife, that "you boil the *camote*, [and] all it takes is one glass" of this warm brew for barbasco to be an effective abortifacient.[3] When questioned, local curanderos seldom used barbasco for abortions because it was so potent that it could kill both the fetus and mother. As healer Portugal insisted, "No one has come [to me] to abort. I would not give it for an abortion because then I would be a killer (*asesino*)."[4] Another, unconfirmed, local use of barbasco was to substantiate or disprove adultery.[5] A Mexico City chemist interested in reviving the barbasco trade in 1999 insisted—although no scholarly literature supports his claim—that as late as the 1950s, women in the Chinantla who were suspected of adultery were given a beverage made from barbasco. Inevitably, they became bloated and developed blotching and bruising. This was taken as a visible sign of their guilt.[6] Interestingly, however, an early story of why Marker opted to switch from cabeza de negro to barbasco has him brewing a tea "as instructed" by a local healer and drinking it to relieve arthritis pain.[7] By the next morning, "he was covered with bruises: his blood had hemolyzed because of the saponin."[8] After testing the root he found it to have "three to four times" more diosgenin than previous roots. In the Chinantla, healers had an almost exclusive knowledge of the root's medicinal uses, and the campesinos generally regarded barbasco as having little utility. Certainly the tuber had no monetary value for them.

In 1952, a decade before Apolinar went in search of barbasco, the first road connecting Chiltepec to the rest of the region was built with much fanfare. Running from Chiltepec to Tuxtepec, it earned Chiltepec a brief description on a map that accompanied a Papaloapan Commission report of that year, which proclaimed that it was "the most important route that crosses the Sierra toward Oaxaca [City]."[9] Nevertheless, Apolinar rarely traveled beyond Tuxtepec, less than twenty miles to the northeast. He had, as he remarked, "no reason to do so." Unbeknownst to him the arrival of the road coincided with the global need for cortisone and the rush to find more barbasco in Mexico's tropical forests. Just as trains had been used in an earlier era to haul away mountains of bananas and tobacco, the roads would become crucial in the barbasco trade.

News of the world beyond Apolinar's village arrived by way of a radio, a crucial technology in an area where in the 1950s 67 percent of the basin's total population still "did not know the alphabet."[10] The government in its broadcasts encouraged campesinos to obey the dictates of the patria and not the priest.[11] Male campesinos were "encouraged to read agrarian law and technical manuals" to become better and more productive citizens.[12] As a good disciple of Mexico's postrevolutionary propaganda, Apolinar was most interested in the presidential elections, when representatives from the Institutional Revolutionary Party (PRI)—or the Liberal Party, as Apolinar chose to call it—came and urged everyone to vote.[13] These events were the rare occasions when Apolinar and his neighbors truly felt that Chiltepec mattered to the rest of the country. Apolinar's relatives became active in politics, and his father won the municipal presidency of Chiltepec twice. At the time of his father's death, Apolinar—who to this day saves his 1967 PRI membership credential in a plastic grocery bag—promised his father that he would never change political parties. His allegiance would forever be with the party that somehow always managed to come to his little village, and he would support any PRI-driven projects for developing the region—even one as remarkable as the *Dioscoreas* project, which in 1975 would promise to turn wild yams into pharmaceutical wonders.

Dioscoreas

From the standpoint of human ecology, yams are fascinating plants to study. Within the genus *Dioscorea* we encounter species that provide food in the diet of the hungry populations of the pantropical world. . . . On the other hand, there are other species of this same genus with properties that can be used for the prevention of birth or at least used to curb the increasing world population.[14]

Dioscorea is the scientific name under which yams, "the potato of the tropical and subtropical countries" are classified.[15] The botanical name *Dioscoreas* is derived from the name of the Greek herbalist Dioscorides, one of the earliest ethnobotanists to record the healing powers of plants. As detailed in chapter 2 one local species, a cousin of barbasco and one of the first types of yams to be found by foreign chemists, is *cabeza de negro*, so called because the tuber's rough, fuzzy, pineapple-like surface was thought to have resembled a black man's head. Like many wild yams cabeza de negro and barbasco can be lethal if ingested without heating. Edible yams have been cultivated for thousands of years; the wild-growing, poisonous variety was used in traditional Mesoamerican pharmacopeia as a remedy for rheumatism, snakebites, muscular pain, and skin diseases, and as we saw, a poison to kill fish.

In times of famine the campesinos would cook the wild sapogenin-containing yams before eating them in order to avoid potentially fatal hemolysis, the breakdown of red blood cells with the subsequent release of hemoglobin.

Six to eight hundred *Dioscorea* species grow throughout the world.[16] Of these about a hundred are found in Mexico, and of that number, fewer than five contain diosgenin, the chemical compound needed to produce synthetic steroid hormones in commercial quantities.[17]

The Florentine and the Cruz Badiano codices catalogue dozens of tubers known to the natives of Mesoamerica before the arrival of the Spaniards.[18] In the nineteenth century tonics using *Dioscorea villosa* were widely popular in the United States. People considered an infusion of the wild yam, also known as China root or yam root, to be "a valuable remedy in bilious colic."[19] Suggested treatment was for "an ounce of the powdered root [to] be boiled in a pint of water and half of it given as a dose."[20] In 1836 a certain Dr. Miller of Neville, Ohio, valued "the tincture highly as an expectorant, as a diaphoric [perspiration stimulant], and in large doses as an emetic [to produce vomiting]."[21]

The name *barbasco* is widely used throughout Latin America to describe a plant, root, or vine containing a paralysis-inducing substance. When crushed it can be used for fishing. This generic name is so common that barbasco appears often in literature. Stories by Gabriel García Márquez (for example, "Blacaman the Good, Vendor of Miracles"), Mario Vargas Llosa's novel *The Storyteller*, and even Ramón González Montalvo's 1960 novel about a Salvadoran peasant uprising (appropriately titled *Barbasco*) have featured characters using barbasco. Even the Popol Vuh, the sacred book of the Maya, describes fishermen using the root.[22]

There are plants with similar chemical properties throughout Latin America. In a nonfiction work, *Medicine Quest*, Mark Plotkin writes that while in Paramaribo, Suriname, local Maroons told him that tapirs eat the stems of a plant they call nekoe, which contains rotenone. Locals allegedly observed the tapirs eating nekoe and defecating into streams, followed by stunned fish rising to the surface.[23] This led the Surinamese to use nekoe for fishing.

The Shuar of Ecuador and the Nukak of Colombia also use barbasco to fish, but it is a species different from the Mexican barbasco discussed here. The Ecuadoran barbascos comprise a rotenone-containing tree bark or plants of a subtropical species belonging to the genus *Lonchocarpus*.[24] The active compound found in Mexican barbasco is glycoside of diosgenin.

Some *Dioscoreas*, including Mexican barbasco, contain chemical substances called sapogenins, which create suds when the root is sliced and dunked in water. But, more important, when subjected to an extraction process, sapogenins yield diosgenin, a precursor for making the synthetic hormones progesterone, estrogen, and testosterone.

Gathering Barbasco

Apolinar could not recall who told him that local people were buying barbasco, but he vividly recalled the nearly fifteen years he spent gathering it in the nearby jungle. Looking back on that grueling work, he and many other barbasqueros repeated that "only the desperate pick barbasco every day." Unfortunately, by the early 1960s unemployment in the area was growing and many people were becoming "desperate" enough to depend on barbasco as their primary means of subsistence.

Most former root pickers explained that they learned their skill by observing others in their community dig for the root. Some older barbasco pickers, however, recalled that representatives of a company or even local middlemen brought samples of barbasco to their communities. Carrying leaf samples or the actual tubers, these outsiders showed locals the commodity middlemen were now eager to purchase. A leader in the national barbasquero movement, Pedro Ramírez, remembered how an outsider had come to his hometown of Minatitlán in Veracruz bearing barbasco roots, leaves, and a vine.[25] Though he couldn't remember how much he was initially paid, nearly everyone he knew while growing up was familiar with barbasco and had at one point gathered and sold the root. For some, barbasco was ancillary income, and if they spotted it on their way to or from their corn or bean fields, for example, they would dig it up to earn a few extra cents.[26]

With its fibrous, branchlike root structure, barbasco competed with the roots of local agricultural products, mainly corn and beans. Because the root spread underground, even farmers' slash-and-burn techniques could not eliminate it. In fact, slashing and burning produced more barbasco because the high temperatures caused by fire served to stimulate the yams' growth.[27] In addition all pieces of the yam broken off by plows or other cultivation tools sprouted new plants. The root could grow at altitudes up to 4,200 feet and required at least 50 inches of rainfall per year, conditions typical of the Chinantla.

According to some older pickers, as late as the early 1960s barbasco was so abundant in the area between Tuxtepec and Valle Nacional that they had

FIGURE 11 Tracking barbasco was made more difficult by similar-looking vines, the presence of poisonous snakes, and muddy terrain that often "swallowed" huaraches. Image circa 1950, possibly in Veracruz. Photograph by Ezra Stoller © Esto.

only to walk a few feet from their homes to uncover several kilos of the yam. As demand increased, however, campesinos had to search deeper in the jungle, making it more difficult and potentially more dangerous to find the increasingly elusive root. Some interviewees reported that as early as 1976 or 1977 barbasco had become extinct in some areas.[28]

Despite barbasco's tenacity and abundance, most root pickers had trouble spotting the vine with its heart-shaped leaves because the foliage of *Dioscorea composita* resembles the leaves of other *Dioscorea* species.[29]

Furthermore, untrained pickers could not tell the depth, girth, or age of a root from the aboveground foliage, putting them at a serious disadvantage since it was the older roots that contained higher levels of diosgenin.

In the jungle, the dense vegetation invaded and swallowed footpaths. *Barbasqueros* (yam pickers) had to hack at vines and underbrush at every step they took. Vines similar to barbasco tenaciously hugged tree trunks;

others snaked their way across the jungle floor. On finding a true barbasco vine, an experienced barbasquero carefully noted its width because thicker vines denoted older and consequently larger roots. Locals prized these giant yams: a single root could weigh upwards of 60 kilograms (nearly 120 pounds), a find that became rarer as more individuals began to remove the tubers.

Once the root pickers found a vine they began to dig. Most *Dioscoreas* send down roots vertically for about one meter that then branch out horizontally, making removal of the root much more difficult. Experienced, better-prepared pickers would bring a *coa*, a tree branch fashioned into a digging stick by whittling a sharp end on one side. If neither a coa nor a shovel were available, then pickers dug with their hands—although, as some later complained, "the root sometimes made the skin beneath our nails burn."[30] Fallen trees, steep ravines, and thick mud made for slow progress. The picker constantly stopped to catch his breath, remove huaraches from the clutches of the mud, or carefully sidestep bushes that might hide poisonous snakes.

Former root pickers consistently mentioned the ever-present fear of snakes—mainly the venomous *nauyacas*.[31] Of 47 barbasqueros interviewed, 40 claimed to have known someone who had been bitten by a snake while looking for barbasco.[32] Although this number at first seems exaggerated, given that Mexico is home to approximately 580 species and subspecies of snakes, of which more than 20 percent are poisonous, coupled with the tendency of most campesinos to wear open-toed huaraches, the high percentage of snakebites becomes more believable. Another possibility is that stories of snakebites represented more of a cautionary tale often repeated for younger pickers.[33] Child root pickers were at particular risk from snakebites since their small bodies were more vulnerable to the poison. Interviewed when he was 32 years old, Paulino Hernández recalled that as a 5-year-old boy, he had accompanied his father into the jungle. His job was to shake off the dirt that clung to fresh roots while his father searched for more barbasco. Because Hernández owned no shoes, his father carried him on his back so the boy could avoid the thorns and snakes in the underbrush.

Finding barbasco was a dirty job. Once gatherers located the vine they often dug with bare hands to try to trace the growth of the yams. Moreover, the first generation of root collectors was made up of some of the poorest men and women in the region, so they rarely owned shovels. After they dug up the tubers, they chopped them into smaller pieces, which they placed in a burlap or plastic sack. The barbasqueros knew that by leaving behind a small portion of the yam, it would, like a potato, regenerate. As the demand increased, fewer and fewer pickers left even the smallest pieces in the ground.

For pickers who owned a machete entering the jungle was easier, but no less strenuous, because they had to hack away at overhanging foliage and bushes. Even so, twigs, rocks, and spiny plants still managed to bruise and cut huarache-clad or bare feet. The machete itself posed a danger when pickers used it as a digging tool because if it struck a rock, it could rebound and leave deep gashes on legs or arms. In addition the unevenness of the ground was responsible for frequent and dangerous falls. The humidity was relentless and enervating; even standing still one sweated. As a final aggravation swarms of tiny insects feasted incessantly on root pickers' uncovered arms and legs.

The hazards of a day of root picking did not end with barbasqueros' efforts in the jungle—the dangers continued during the journey to sell the tuber at a collection site. Despite obvious exhaustion most pickers had to walk a long distance to the collection center. Since harvested barbasco begins to rot within hours after picking, losing density and weight through shriveling, pickers had to get there as quickly as possible since the roots were bought by the kilo. Those who were not near a river or a road had to maneuver down narrow, steep dirt paths that often turned into slippery mudslides with the frequent rain, a treacherous situation for tired people carrying a heavy load of roots. Barbasqueros could expect to walk anywhere from thirty minutes to two hours to sell what they had found.

Pickers who lived near a river could float barbasco downstream and into Tuxtepec using small rafts made of pieces of wood strung together with rope. When the trade became more sophisticated, men with small boats would scour the banks for campesinos waiting to sell their barbasco. When pickers were close to roads, they usually transported barbasco on wooden carts pulled by either man or mule.

Many barbasqueros left their homes at dawn to avoid the heat and did not return until five or six in the afternoon, often having eaten, as Isidro Apolinar often did, only dry tortillas with salt. Once they returned home, if they had not passed a river or stream, pickers needed to find water to wash the thick, dried mud off their bodies. As one erstwhile buyer remarked,

FIGURE 12 Dioscoreas had to be swiftly transported to local buyers because they began to rot soon after being dug up. This *merma*, or loss of moisture, led to weight loss, causing yams to fetch less money. Photograph by Ezra Stoller © Esto.

one could easily tell those who had picked barbasco because of how they emerged from the jungle.[34] In the evening those who had collected barbasco tended to any cuts; men did chores, women cooked meals, and all prepared for the following day. The work was so intense that bones ached for days after gathering barbasco.

Collection Sites and Local Middlemen

As word spread throughout the Chinantla that locals were buying barbasco, rustic handwritten signs informed pickers where they could sell the yams. At these *centros de acopio* (collection sites) the campesinos could sell their roots to *acopiadores* (middlemen). The acopios were in their homes, backyards, stables, or sheds. By the late 1960s nearly a thousand informal collection sites were scattered throughout southeastern Mexico.

According to one former buyer, Alejandro Weber (El Turco), the acopiadores were *hombres de confianza*, trustworthy men who had been hand-
picked for certain characteristics, such as their ability to speak Spanish and
an indigenous language, their familial relations or links to the local strongmen, and an acopio that was near a road or river.[35] Many acopiadores had
established relationships with the local indigenous community because
they had already been buying crops from those people, including corn, bananas, coffee, and rubber. In turn local, usually mestizo, representatives of
the pharmaceutical companies gave each acopiador a floor scale, several
dozen burlap bags, and sometimes extra coas or machetes. Pickers could
purchase the latter items in exchange for barbasco. In most instances the
middlemen paid barbasqueros with cash from the truckers who hauled the
barbasco away or from the owners of the *beneficios* (processing plants where
the barbasco was dried and fermented).[36]

Because middlemen usually paid in cash, they had significant power in
their communities. As one barbasquero recalled when asked why he and
others would not walk the extra hour to Valle Nacional, where the price
for barbasco was sometimes twenty centavos higher per kilo, he responded
that the local buyer, Turco, "would not let us sell in Valle"—an attempt to
keep pickers from bypassing his collection site.[37] The likely reason for this
restriction was that the acopiadores received a commission for every kilo of
barbasco they purchased, making it advantageous to have barbasqueros sell
only to them. In explaining the financial incentive Turco, the former buyer,
gleefully remarked, "I earned almost more than the ones who dug it out."[38]
Consequently, some acopiadores encouraged, or even forced, certain communities to sell to them by threatening to not purchase other crops grown
by a picker if he or she sold their barbasco elsewhere.

Some entrepreneurial individuals with extra cash also started independently purchasing barbasco. For example once Turco decided to purchase
barbasco in the late 1960s, he simply posted a sign outside his house in
Jacatepec and confidently waited for people to come because "other than
barbasco there was no other source of work." He soon became known as a
barbasco buyer and truckers hired by beneficio owners would drop off cash
to him every week. As he recalled, "barbasco poured in. In one day I would
buy a ton [of barbasco]."[39]

As money began to flow into the region, coupled with the thin regulation
of the barbasco trade, abuses linked to buying barbasco increased. For ex-

ample some barbasqueros in Valle Nacional were paid with *vales* (coupons) that they could redeem only at the local store, which often was owned by the same acopiador.[40] Not surprisingly the local barbasco buyer came to replicate on a smaller scale the traditional strongmen in the region. The practice of *enganchar* (hooking) created a form of debt in which the individual barbasquero, or an entire community, was obligated to sell barbasco exclusively to the lender. In addition the large sums of money handled by one member of the community—the buyer—began to create class divisions, especially when acopiadores acquired horses, built cement houses (traditional homes are made of wood), and even bought cars with their barbasco commissions.[41] Despite the newfound power and wealth of many acopiadores they were still quite low in the barbasco hierarchy, since they had to rely on the owners of the beneficios, who distributed money to them.

Instead of paying the pickers, some middlemen gave them a machete or coa and told them that they could pay for the tool with installments of barbasco. The acopiador also loaned money to barbasqueros who, on some days, were unable to gather enough barbasco to support their families. A buyer, Lorenzo León Felipe, explained this practice: "That old man, Don Angel Rodríguez, left me enough money for the purchase [and] they [barbasqueros] would sometimes ask for a loan. I'd give them an advance on their pay; I'd hook them in, so to speak."[42] Entire communities would also be "hooked" by credits into continuing to sell to specific buyers. But there were other subtle ways to gain loyalty from widely dispersed communities. León Felipe explained that in searching for barbasco-selling communities to exploit, he would "go to Tehuacán and buy 100 pencils, 100 notebooks, and two boxes of gum" to hand out to the children of potential sellers.[43] León Felipe also relied on the local authorities:

> I would say to the *comisariado* [delegate] of Arroyo de Banco, "Listen, wouldn't you like to gather barbasco? All right, then. I will leave 500 pesos, and sign this voucher that I gave you 500 pesos and you can pay me with barbasco." When [the comisariado] started picking barbasco, he would come and tell me, "I have 2,000 kilos of barbasco so why don't you send me the car?" I would send a buyer [and instruct him], "Go and get barbasco from that guy. If there's any left over, if it's more barbasco you pay him, then give him the coupons. Rip them up in front of him and if he wants more money, then make him another coupon."[44]

FIGURE 13 Dioscoreas were taken to collection sites, usually the yards of local men, where sacks were inspected for excess mud, twigs, and nonvaluable yams. Circa 1950. Photograph by Ezra Stoller © Esto.

Barbasco buyers had specific tasks that later, in the 1970s and 1980s, were recorded in writing.[45] Buyers had to inspect each of the sacks and visually check the roots. With this quick visual scan, they were specifically looking for an excess of nonbarbasco material—sticks, stones, mud, or garbage that the picker might have accidentally or purposefully put into the sacks. The buyer would then weigh them on large metal scales and pay the root picker in cash. When the government took charge of the barbasco trade in 1975 this once simple step became bureaucratized, and the buyer would have to fill out a form in triplicate.

In 1998–99, as documentary evidence of the quantities of barbasco collected in the area, a former buyer produced a short stack of saved receipts that spanned 1975 to 1991.[46] The quantities are staggering. For example, on July 14, 1975, at his site he collected 51 sacks, or 2,059 kilos; 4 days later, he

FIGURE 14 Here a buyer, or *acopiador*, weighs the dioscoreas. Photograph by Ezra Stoller © Esto.

sent 32 sacks by small boat; on July 21, *peones* carried off another 40 sacks on their backs. All told, in a single week he collected nearly 125 sacks of barbasco. Interestingly, this particular buyer was part of a tiny community, Cinco de Oro, on the outskirts of Jacatepec. Even in 1999 it consisted of little more than a handful of scattered homes a 40-minute walk from the main highway. This implies that the buyer was receiving barbasco from people living in even more remote communities. By the mid-1980s the receipts were photocopied forms containing many details: the name of the driver, if the roots were transported by truck; where the barbasco was sent; total kilos of cut barbasco versus total kilos of fresh barbasco; where it was bought, at what price, and total numbers of sacks. In addition, in a clear effort to control increasing graft, the later receipts also included the amount of the commission given to the buyer.

The fluctuation in numbers of sacks may reflect the financial situation in the countryside, but it also suggests that in later years barbasco was becoming scarce, although evidence of this is mainly anecdotal in more remote areas. Equally noteworthy is the amount of cash—several tens of thousand pesos on average in a single week—that was entering and circulating in the Chinantla. Hence, the receipts also reveal that middlemen were beginning to acquire a clear and growing financial and social influence.

The price paid for barbasco exploited the root pickers, but they were not passive sellers of yams. Tales abound among former buyers of cunning pickers who fashioned mud to resemble roots, soaked roots and sacks in water before selling them, or threw in rocks and twigs to make the sacks weigh more. For example, taking advantage of the almost-daily afternoon rains, pickers would walk with a sack on their back, letting the rainwater soak the burlap before walking into an acopio. These small, everyday forms of resistance allowed pickers to earn a few more cents for their labors.

Beneficios

For most root pickers, the acopio was their last stop before heading home after a long day. But for the barbascos, the trip had barely begun. Barbasco was transported to the beneficios by road; on overflowing trucks or in lumbering mule carts; or via water, on rafts or small barges. In 1975, when Echeverría's government became interested in barbasco, it was even proposed that barbasco be airlifted out of the dense jungle.[47]

The simple beneficios employed many campesinos to mix, ferment, and dry barbasco. The workers learned to experiment until they could achieve the purest yields of diosgenin. By the 1960s nearly 300 beneficios were located throughout southeastern Mexico.[48] From 1951 to 1975 in the area of Tuxtepec most beneficios were privately owned, primarily by local men. The six transnational pharmaceutical companies involved with the barbasco trade in Mexico owned the others.

Emilio Fortín, an owner of a beneficio in Catemaco, Veracruz, one of the few still functioning in 1999, explained that he came from Spain in 1954 to join his father, a political refugee in Mexico. The father's thriving beneficio sold all of its barbasco to Syntex. Fortín explained that 1999 had been a slack (*flojo*) year, but "at the height of the trade, about thirty years ago, the companies bought 15,000 tons of dried barbasco [per year]."[49] He clarified that this meant the beneficio had purchased 75,000 tons of fresh barbasco. In 1999 he had bought only 125 tons from "my indigenous buyers in the sierra,"

FIGURE 15 The
lack of roads in
the area made it
necessary to float
barbasco down
streams and rivers
in small barges,
such as the one
pictured. Decades
later, during Eche-
verría's presidency,
there was talk of
airlifting barbasco
out of the jungle.
Photograph by
Ezra Stoller © Esto.

FIGURE 16 The
alleged inexhaust-
ible supply of bar-
basco transformed
social relations in
rural areas as tons
of yams were picked
on a weekly basis.
Official government
numbers suggest that
upwards of 125,000
families depended on
barbasco picking for
survival by the late
1960s. Photograph
by Ezra Stoller © Esto.

FIGURE 17 After fermenting for several days, the yams needed to be dried on concrete slabs, where granules were constantly turned with "rakes." Workers were not permitted to wear shoes, despite the intense heat. Photograph by Ezra Stoller © Esto.

and he calculated that it had taken 300 to 400 campesinos to gather that much.

The beneficio consisted of a large slab of concrete surrounded on all four sides by an open-air building with a tin roof similar to the drying blocks for coffee—in fact, many of these were former coffee-drying facilities that had been abandoned when the price of coffee dropped.

It was rather astonishing to step out of the thick cover provided by the jungle and encounter a dirt road leading to a paved open space as large as a city block on which sat large vats and blending machines. When the drivers dropped off the root cargo at the beneficio, workers inspected the delivery to ensure that it was indeed *Dioscorea composita* or *Dioscorea floribunda*, the diosgenin-containing yams. Before washing the root to remove any excess dirt a beneficio worker carefully wrote the provenance of each load. If it had not yet been finely chopped or sliced, workers cut it manually using a machete. After chopping, the barbasco was placed into a processor with regulated amounts of water that produced a thick, brown pastelike substance. This paste was then placed in large tin basins where it fermented for three to four days—emitting a sweet rotten-apple smell. Next, workers laid the fermented pulp out to dry on the cement slabs, raking it periodically. As it dried, the paste crumbled into fine, earth-toned granules: the coveted diosgenin "flour." Those who raked the barbasco flour were not allowed to wear shoes, because each grain that might adhere to their huaraches was of value. Hence they walked barefoot on cement heated by the sun, and often complained of swollen, painful feet. Once the flour dried it was bagged, labeled, and shipped to waiting laboratories. When the flour arrived at the laboratory it was tested, and the purity of diosgenin, ranging from approximately 3 percent to 6.4 percent, determined the price paid for barbasco.

When pickers sold their barbasco at a beneficio and happened to inquire where so much of it was going and what it was used for, they were usually told that it was used to make laundry soap. Not just any soap but the highly popular Fab.[50]

Former owners of beneficios today remain the political and financial elite in the area. Elderly Gabriel Cué, whose son was running for political office in 2000, recalled the "time of barbasco" as the boom time for Tuxtepec. Already an influential landowner in the 1950s he was approached by Syntex and agreed to sell only to that laboratory; other beneficio owners in the region contracted directly with Beisa.

Beneficio owners hired men from nearby communities to work on transforming barbasco. Some of these *chalanes* (assistants) eventually became highly skilled, developing a way to purify the root so that it could yield higher percentages of diosgenin. Because outsiders paid not only for quantity but also for quality, these men became valuable, practical "chemists." The next chapters explore what it meant to have Mexican campesinos associated, even if somewhat informally, with transnational pharmaceutical companies.

Conclusion

Barbasco picking was a curiously egalitarian job: men, women, and children, widowed and married, landed and landless, could all harvest the root. The only apparent common denominator was that pickers were poor and mainly indigenous. Only in 1975, when the government began processing barbasco, would some of the pickers, such as Isidro Apolinar, learn that the plant did not grow only in the Papaloapan of Oaxaca—it could also be found in the neighboring states of Veracruz, Tabasco, Chiapas, Puebla, and, on a much smaller scale, in parts of Guerrero and Michoacán. In those places, too, the word had spread that as much barbasco as pickers could carry had to be brought to the collection sites.

Before barbasco could leave the Chinantla, it had to be transformed—the root could not leave the jungle in its raw state. Although peasant pickers were key to the extraction of barbasco, various levels of middlemen made the entire process function. After picking, the root had to be slivered, fermented, dried, measured into labeled sacks, and then sent to a laboratory (in either Orizaba, Veracruz, or Mexico City). This multitiered, specialized process reinforced preexisting fortunes by concentrating the power of barbasco collection in the same hands as those who previously controlled coffee, tobacco, and other commercialized crops. In addition, it created a never-before-seen flow of cash in some areas as some campesinos replicated, on a much smaller scale, the power of the middlemen in their communities.

As more Mexicans began to search for barbasco, interest in the dioscorea was also growing in the United States and in Europe. The next chapter examines how international demand altered the intensity of the trade and how chemical knowledge slowly began to filter into remote pockets of the Chinantla.

The Second World War had ushered in an era of expectations for a stronger relationship between Mexico and United States. Mexican politicians believed that by joining America militarily a new partnership based on mutual cooperation and devoid of fears of American expansionism would emerge. Mexico provided foodstuffs and manual labor in exchange for financial support for its growing infrastructure. The official press furthered this air of cooperation by amply reporting in the early 1940s on the "friendly" resolution of the 1938 expropriated petroleum as well as commercial treaties, among other good-will projects.

In the aftermath of the Second World War German property and patents in the United States and Mexico were seized. Confiscated German laboratories, in this case Schering, catapulted the United States into an industry until then controlled almost exclusively by Europeans. But the creation of a steroid hormone industry in the Western Hemisphere would focus on Mexico and not the United States, for barbasco was believed to grow only in Mexico. American attempts to control the Mexican steroid industry would illustrate to some that expansionism in the twentieth century was no longer a question of territory but of legal (patents) control of capital and natural resources.

Changes were also taking place in the countryside. Calculating yam yields, speculating about future harvests, and mixing solvents to produce higher concentrations of diosgenin were becoming routine tasks for some campesinos of southeastern Oaxaca. Less than one decade after Russell Marker's impulsive trip to Veracruz, the record number of yams being harvested in Mexico had transformed barbasco into a booming commodity. Hence the barbasco trade in the 1950s is worthy of study because harvesting tons of barbasco had become unremarkable.

This chapter discusses the creation of a commission and protectionist measures and legislation crafted to attempt to retain Mexican control of barbasco. In addition it examines how Mexican ecologists made barbasco politically important by redefining the role the nation should play in the steroid hormone industry. But, unaware of the flurry of political and scientific activity, campesinos in the Papaloapan continued to dig up ever-larger quantities of barbasco.

Barbasco in Washington, D.C.

At 11:05 A.M. on Thursday July 5, 1956, in Room 457 of the Senate Office Building in Washington, Senator Joseph C. O'Mahoney, chairman of the Subcommittee on Patents, Trademarks, and Copyrights, called the meeting to order. For that day and the next two, Senator O'Mahoney would hear testimony against a Mexico City–based company, Syntex S.A., and its attempts to monopolize control of a wondrous wild yam.[1]

A few months before the hearings, in spring 1956, Mexican Syntex had been sold to the American-based Ogden Corporation, but Syntex did not need to be an American company for the United States to claim jurisdiction over the case. Under investigation were allegations that Syntex had secured and then violated agreements giving it "valuable rights to use patents owned by the United States Government." Syntex had allegedly restricted the export from Mexico of products "made from the barbasco root" and potentially entered into a "cartel agreement" by edging out other companies.[2] For two days the subcommittee heard testimony from chemists, businessmen, and physicians who explained the importance of barbasco to the United States and, ultimately, to the world. Discussions centered on the charges that Syntex had established a barbasco monopoly in Mexico. But at the heart of the investigation, I argue, was the fact that botanists had failed to successfully cultivate the yam in commercial quantities outside of southern Mexico. The availability of raw barbasco in Mexico had made it possible for foreign and Mexican chemists and technicians to produce original and extremely significant scientific research.

The struggle to control the industry in the midst of growing international demand for barbasco prompted Mexican officials to force pharmaceutical companies to fund scientific research on barbasco in Mexico. The achievements of the resulting scientific commission would be stunning.

A Growing Barbasco Market

By the late 1950s Mexico was producing nearly 90 percent of the world's steroid hormones.[3] A Mexican monopoly replaced a European-controlled trade, and the focus of the steroid hormone industry definitively changed "from technology to raw materials."[4] Despite attempts to look for substitutes, diosgenin's versatility as a steroid starting material made it far superior to other alternatives.[5] The other leading starting material, cholesterol, had only two intermediate compounds that could be made into commercial steroid products, but diosgenin yielded 16-dehydropregnenolone (16-D), which is the basis for virtually all "pharmaceutically interesting" steroids.[6]

Moreover, the supply of barbasco seemed to be inexhaustible. Don Cox, a field botanist hired by Syntex in 1952 to determine the quantity of barbasco, assured the company that no matter how much barbasco was dug up, the plant was not in danger of extinction because slash-and-burn techniques common in the area actually aided its spread.[7] It seemed that Mexico possessed everything needed to transform it into a leader in the lucrative pharmaceutical game—the raw material, a willing workforce, and a captive market. Within Mexico, however, the situation was more complex.

During the late 1950s seven companies were processing barbasco in Mexico and only one of those, Beisa, was a subsidiary of a transnational corporation.[8] But by the 1960s the small, independent companies had disappeared, and all of the companies processing barbasco became subsidiaries of larger corporations. More disturbingly, none was Mexican.

Scholars have used Mexico's loss of control of the steroid hormone industry to illustrate dependency theory. This worldview theory posited that developing countries were doomed to be exploited by wealthier nations because of, among other criteria, lack of technology and thwarted attempts at financial independence.[9] Although previous research sustains this analysis of the steroid industry, I contend that Mexico did profit—scientifically, at least—from the presence of transnational corporations. The source of Mexico's scientific gains can be found, ironically, in Syntex's determination to edge out foreign and domestic competition and find a plentiful supply of barbasco for its own buyers.

Syntex Grows

In 1954, a mere ten years after its founding, Syntex—with 3,000 workers, including 150 chemists and technicians, and reported annual sales of 5 million dollars—was the largest steroid-producing company in the world.[10] But since the early 1950s smaller companies within Mexico had begun to sell diosgenin to European cartels, thus undercutting Syntex's profits. In 1951, at the behest of Syntex, the Mexican government raised taxes on the export of barbasco-derived products from these smaller companies and later limited the number of permits to buy specific quantities of barbasco from campesinos.[11] In response several foreign company owners, among them the famed African American chemist Percy Julian, demanded an explanation of the Mexican government's apparent collusion with Syntex, which had not been deprived of permits. The president of Syntex denied any wrongdoing, but at the Senate hearings Julian insisted that earlier attempts to build a company in Mexico had failed because "the permit was denied at every turn," mainly due to "the objection of the Syntex Company."[12] Similarly, in his memoirs, Russell Marker recalled how after leaving Syntex, its management coerced and threatened him at every turn when he attempted to establish Botanica-Mex.[13] Although similar testimony was heard from other frustrated entrepreneurs who argued that Syntex was receiving unfair privileges, the actions of the Mexican government, placed within a historical context, were not that uncommon. Although shortages created by the Second World War strengthened the relationship between Mexico and the United States, American entrepreneurs who competed with Mexican interests "suffered."[14] On June 29, 1944, the Mexican government passed a regulation requiring at least 51 percent Mexican ownership in any foreign-owned company. This measure was part of a larger project to "ensure the freedom of private initiative."[15] But often Mexico's lack of "capital, expertise, and patents," meant that Mexican stakeholders could not insist on the majority percentage in new undertakings with their foreign counteparts.[16] At the time the steroid industry was an exception.

Historical Context

The post–Second World War era was a prosperous one for Mexico. The middle class continued to grow, as small factories throughout Mexico "took advantage of the cheap and abundant source of electric power and began to transform the economy and the face of the nation."[17] Accelerating this transformation was the 1953 peso devaluation, which not only stabilized the economy but also enticed foreign investment. President Miguel Alemán (1946–52), unlike his predecessor Avila Camacho (who had been "cordial but cautious" toward foreign investment), publicly announced that he wanted the United States to participate in Mexico's economic development.[18] Investors did not wait long. As increasing numbers of tourists from the United States took advantage of the improved exchange rate, they saw "familiar signs advertising General Motors, Dow Chemical, Pepsi-Cola, Coca-Cola, Colgate, Goodyear, John Deere, Ford, Proctor & Gamble, Sears Roebuck, and other corporate giants," most of whom would not have invested in Mexico a mere ten years earlier.[19]

The administration of Miguel Alemán and Adolfo Ruiz Cortines (1952–58) both implemented protectionist measures and legislation designed to encourage domestic producers to participate in import-competing ventures.[20] For example the dollar–peso exchange rate was fixed at 12.50 in April 1954, and would remain at that level through August 1976, and general tariffs were changed to protect newly emerging Mexican industries. Both administrations insisted on a high degree of industrialization, seeing the production of automobiles and other manufactured goods as the means to attain financial prosperity for Mexico.

Initial attempts to control the steroid hormone trade took place in this political climate. Mexico's *Diario Oficial*, the daily publication of government proceedings, declared on May 7, 1951, that the export tax on "tubers, roots, stems, and other plant parts or extracts in any shape," particularly those that contained "sapogenins," would increase.[21] Notably, the export tax was 100 pesos for those extracts used in their pure form as medicinal plants, but any further chemical synthesis of the plant was taxed at 500 pesos. This tax was a direct response to the barbasco trade. Since dioscoreas could not be exported in their plant form, at least one chemical synthesis had to be performed in Mexico. This ensured that barbasco extracts were taxed at the higher bracket and that some labor, beyond simple yam gathering, was performed in Mexico.

A key aspect of rapid industrialization in Mexico was, however, low wages in urban areas. In the countryside these financial changes coincided with an increase in population and fewer lands to distribute, which in turn led to surging unemployment. In both rural and urban areas small and scattered outbursts against the government were quickly and harshly put down. With decreasing wages and increasing population, peasants struggled to find remunerative employment, as exemplified by Isidro Apolinar's story in the previous chapter. Coincidentally, in the early 1950s foreign laboratories and Syntex announced the discovery of cortisone derived from barbasco. This seemingly foreign and irrelevant development created and then reinforced ties between the scientific world of steroidal chemistry and unemployed Mexican peasants desperate to find jobs.

Despite these overall national trends, Syntex's strong-arm tactics to restrict the actions of its competitors in Mexico were precisely what led to the July 1956 hearings in the United States. It became clear that the "removal of obstacles" to obtain the cheapest source for the manufacture of cortisone, among other hormones, was only one reason for investigating a Mexican company.[22] The U.S. Senate wanted to keep tabs on Syntex in particular because the company was producing something of vital importance to the United States. As one witness grimly told the subcommittee members, "The total number of victims [of rheumatic diseases in the United States] is greater than the combined populations of Chicago and Los Angeles, and of those 10 million sufferers . . . 1 million are permanently disabled."[23] Physicians who testified presented a list of at least 40 different diseases that could be treated with steroids.[24]

To further underscore the importance of barbasco to science and medicine, physicians discussed the latest medications derived from the yam. By 1954 the unwanted secondary effects of cortisone were already becoming apparent in the general population. Patients found that with time they required increased doses of the drug to attain similar results. But larger doses of cortisone led to muscle-mass loss, water retention, and high blood pressure, among other health problems. Clinicians at the National Institute of Arthritis and Metabolic Diseases found that "two chemical cousins" of cortisone and hydrocortisone—prednisone and prednisolone—were four times more potent and "did not cause some of the undesirable side effects which

FIGURE 18 Syntex headquarters in Palo Alto, California, circa 1979, when Russell Marker was invited to visit. Photo from Marker's personal album. Pennsylvania State University Archives, Paterno Library.

had brought about some of the disenchantment with cortisone."[25] The leading source for these two new drugs was still the Mexican yam, barbasco.

The history of the rise of Syntex from a small Mexican laboratory to one of the most powerful pharmaceutical companies in the Western Hemisphere has fascinated several researchers over the years. Referring to the company's move to the United States, the sociologist Gary Gereffi concluded:

> The case of Syntex shows that original research of the highest quality was not only feasible in Mexico but had actually been carried out successfully for over a decade. Once Syntex became a foreign based TNC [transnational corporation], however, Mexico lost a key opportunity to keep a strong foothold in the international industry.[26]

Mexico would try to regain this foothold two decades later under the auspices of the populist president Luis Echeverría Alvarez (1976–82).

The government of the United States attempted to work around its reliance on barbasco. For example as early as 1951 Congress allocated $200,000 to the Agricultural Research Service for the "discovery, propagation, chemical composition, and utilization" of plant material as a source for cortisone.[27] Plant explorations were undertaken in Africa, the West Indies, Mexico,

Central America, and South America. By 1956 scientists had chemically screened 5,800 collections with the familiar results that "unquestionably the most productive source of cortisone precursors is the genus *Dioscorea*, which is the wild yam or what has been called barbasco root."[28] In the years after that discovery, more than 200,000 dioscorea plants were transported to different sites in Georgia, Florida, Louisiana, Texas, and Puerto Rico in the hope that they could be grown as profitable crops.[29] None of these experimental sites was successful enough to warrant a switch from Mexican yams. The single source for this raw material became a greater issue as science found further uses for steroids.

With an increased demand for prednisone to treat arthritis, Syntex "almost overnight found itself unable to acquire the quantities of root necessary" to meet the demand.[30] According to Irving V. Sollins, a former barbasco buyer for Syntex, the global demand for steroids forced Syntex to pay "higher than normal market prices," not only for solvents but also for "larger quantities of roots."[31] Syntex and other companies would later use this last argument to justify the low prices paid to campesinos for barbasco. Nevertheless, the goal of all companies was to pay the least for the roots and to process barbasco into its first and basic derivatives, then export these materials to their laboratories outside of Mexico, where they would be transformed into medications. These medications, in turn, were imported back into Mexico. This setup, described as triangulation, allowed companies to "[avoid] paying taxes on final products," while maintaining their technology at home.[32] The triangulation of profits would become the crux of future battles against transnational companies. By the early 1960s Syntex was an established American company with headquarters in Palo Alto, California. In 1982 Syntex celebrated its first one billion dollars earnings in a single year.[33]

Permits and Barbasco

To obtain barbasco, pharmaceutical companies were required to obtain government-issued permits. In June before the beginning of the barbasco-harvesting season, companies would consider their standing orders and any new requests for diosgenin and calculate how many tons of barbasco they would need to buy from local gatherers. They reported that number to the Subsecretario Forestal (Forestry Undersecretary), who issued them a permit for that amount. However, there was no systematic control to ensure that companies did not exceed the permitted amount. In 1959 the permit total for all companies was approximately 12,000 tons of dry barbasco, or roughly 60,000 tons of fresh barbasco. Assuming that an average plant weighed about two kilograms, approximately 30 million barbasco plants were collected *in a single year*.[34] As the permits over time reflected an increasing tonnage of barbasco being extracted from the jungle, individuals within the Mexican government began to voice concerns about the future supply of barbasco and potential loss of profits.[35]

Barbasco was far from the only natural resource exploited during the "Mexican Miracle," the nation's period of unbridled industrialization. Many politicians believed that this was Mexico's opportunity to modernize; the government promoted business by lowering tariffs and, as in the case of Syntex, protecting domestic companies from foreign competition. But the belief that conservation was antithetical to progress led to the rapid devastation of many Mexican natural resources. For example, by 1948, the destruction of the nation's forests was such that President Miguel Alemán attempted to "stop the exportation of unprocessed timber and to eliminate the use of charcoal" in an effort to protect them.[36] Regulation was a constant problem. The government could do little, for example, when there were only twelve forestry students in all of Mexico in 1950.[37]

Shortly after the U.S. Senate investigation into Syntex, the new Mexican Undersecretary of Forestry Resources and Wildlife Enrique Beltrán, a biologist, conservationist, and historian of science, realized that, remarkably, very few Mexican biologists knew anything about barbasco.[38] It was obvious that to regulate exploitation of the plant one needed, beyond the manpower, certain basic knowledge: where it grew, how it grew, how many plants existed, whether it could be cultivated, and whether it had any local uses. The U.S. Senate hearings held in 1956 had illustrated that foreigners knew a substantial amount about Mexican barbasco and had already made several attempts to wrest its control from Mexico through domestication.

Stinging comments from the director of another forest agency, Luis Macías Arellano, during Alemán's administration, were apt not only for forests but also for barbasco: "Mexico was less concerned with the taxonomic classification of trees than it was in learning what forest products could be obtained from trees."[39] Mexican scientists would later prove him wrong by establishing one of the most important and influential scientific commissions, one focused almost exclusively on the study of barbasco.

Barbasco: A Diminishing Commodity?

In the history of conquest and expansion, plants—in particular plant science—have played a remarkable part. The well-documented role of, say, Britain's Kew Gardens shows how colonial plant-collecting and plant-classifying institutions played a crucial part in disseminating information and changing the global balance of trade.[40] For example when Kew Gardens published the "secrets of the carefully guarded" sisal industry, German agronomists were able to replicate and improve that industry in their East African colonies.[41] Similarly, until the 1930s it was often foreigners' scientific accounts that detailed the natural wealth of Mexico.[42]

Foreigners' increasing demand for barbasco permits must have played a role in the Mexican government's decision in 1950 to inaugurate National Chemical Laboratories, or Farquinal, a domestic laboratory responsible for manufacturing diosgenin. One could argue that Farquinal was the only "true Mexican[-owned] laboratory" in the late 1950s in Mexico.[43] But Farquinal's origins were not Mexican: the company's creation was rooted in the expropriation of German laboratories during the Second World War. Farquinal's manager, a Spanish biologist named Francisco Giral, approached professor Faustino Miranda of National Autonomous University of Mexico (UNAM) and urged him to look into the diminishing supply of barbasco.[44] By 1957, less than fifteen years after the exploitation of the wild yam began, biologists were already musing over its finite supply and considering how to uncover the secrets of its growth cycle.

Of particular concern, for obvious business reasons, was the "varying quality in the lots of barbasco": some yielded a relatively high percentage of diosgenin whereas others were "bad lots" with very low diosgenin content. Farquinal hired Arturo Gómez-Pompa, a newly graduated biologist, to find out why the quality of barbasco varied so significantly. He considered several possibilities: Were there various species of barbasco? Was there variation within a single species? Did when and where barbasco was picked affect the diosgenin yield? For nearly two decades these and other questions would engage Mexican scientists. Indeed, it was the root itself—and not the campesinos who picked it—that first enticed politicians and bureaucrats to examine the economic and political potential of the southern jungles and to heavily invest in understanding how to manage the yam.

A Mexican Scientist and Barbasco Pickers

During an interview in 2005, Arturo Gómez-Pompa, chronicled how in 1956 he, a mere twenty-five years old and a wholly inexperienced recent graduate, was overwhelmed by his first professional job—to find out as much as possible about barbasco. Because not one of his professors was familiar with the root, Gómez-Pompa headed to an herbarium, where he observed and drew pictures of a dried sample. Armed with this scant information he then traveled to Tabasco to the home of a colleague's parents. The following day he bravely entered the jungle only to realize within minutes of having stepped off the footpath that he could not distinguish individual plants from what seemed to be hundreds growing all around him. Discouraged, he made his way back to the ranch where he was a guest. That evening, his host suggested that Gómez-Pompa ask the foreman, a local man named Abraham, about barbasco. This simple act would shift how future generations of urban-trained Mexican ecologists would relate to rural people.

The following day Abraham led Gómez-Pompa directly to barbasco and, over the course of a few days, the foreman pointed out that there were multiple varieties that could be identified by the color of the yam, as well as different leaf characteristics and vine widths. Abraham also explained that the plentiful wild yam was a crucial source of income for locals.

Learning from Campesinos

Listening to Abraham, Gómez-Pompa quickly grasped what earlier generations of Mexican agronomists, often vocally disdainful of rural Mexicans, had missed. In the 1930s and 1940s agronomists were urged by the president to "undertake a patriotic educational task," and "as advisors and guides teach the man of the fields" the elementary principles of economics.[45] They would accomplish that task by bringing campesinos up to date in agricultural techniques, expanding cultivated fields, and organizing labor in the countryside with the goal of production, rather than for the well-being of individual farmers.[46] For some observers, however, it seemed that Mexican agronomists preferred not to be in the countryside. As the historian Joseph Cotter remarked, in describing the attitude of many agronomists, who "seemed to feel that agriculture was a science best learned in the laboratory and classroom rather than the field, and a social stigma was apparent toward fieldwork generally."[47] This attitude would have to change if the diggers of barbasco were to be perceived as more than mere gatherers of "weeds."

In the 1940s people in Mexico believed that outsiders were bringing botanical and agricultural knowledge to rural Mexico. But as Gómez-Pompa explained years later, the study of ecology in Mexico actually "was built on the back of the many Abrahams," meaning that campesinos would lead a new generation of ecologists into the field.[48] The goals of Mexican scientists, not unlike those of Russell Marker a generation earlier, were to track down barbasco. In addition, however, they sought to understand and catalogue the surrounding vegetation and its effect on the yam, to experiment with cultivation, and to document the varying levels of diosgenin content.

Gómez-Pompa, his curiosity piqued, began to track what happened to the yam when it left the jungles. He would sit with a notebook and observe the loads of barbasco trucked to collection sites, which by 1959 numbered several hundred in southern Mexico.[49] Occasionally, and especially when an interesting dioscorea caught his eye, he would stop a barbasquero who was walking to the Catemaco or Orizaba (Veracruz) *beneficios* (barbasco-processing plants) with a load of barbasco on his back. Engaging these men in conversation, Gómez-Pompa sometimes convinced them to take him to where they had found their barbasco and, once there, he "took samples and notes" of the location. Through these conversations, Gómez-Pompa meticulously recorded the distribution of dioscorea, learning how to track, dig up, and identify the various types of barbasco, and eventually becoming the leading expert on dioscoreas in Mexico. Today many consider Arturo Gómez-Pompa to be the one of the fathers of modern Mexican ecology. In what other scholars have explained as "giving plants a civil status," Gómez-Pompa counted yams (as one would in a census) in order to heighten the visibility of barbasco in Mexico.[50] Although the wild yam was crucial to the livelihood of many campesinos at this time, a scientist needed to legitimize its presence and its worth so that it would warrant further action by the Mexican government.

Other researchers have explored how "scientists, like other men and women, are shaped by the social values of their times,"[51] but I add that in postrevolutionary Mexico scientists such as Gómez-Pompa also quite capably aided in refocusing the industrial potential of the nation.[52] The historian Gregg Mitman explored the social dimension of ecology and its significant and defining role in the early twentieth-century United States. For, as Mitman argued, "by studying animal and plant societies, many ecologists hoped to bring biological understanding to problems confronting human society in what seemed to be an acutely troubled time."[53] In a similar fashion knowledge about barbasco and its pickers would be used to reframe social problems in Mexico.

When Gómez-Pompa returned to Mexico City, his supervisor, pleased with the work that had been accomplished, introduced him to Beltrán, the undersecretary. Beltrán immediately grasped the implications of the report: without a detailed assessment of or control over barbasco, Mexico was losing a significant level of revenue. Beltrán then called a meeting of all companies extracting barbasco in Mexico; Gómez-Pompa, as a representative for the domestic company Farquinal, attended. Beltrán stated that his main concern was that a company, or even an individual, needed only a permit to extract barbasco, but there was no governing body that could oversee the exact quantity harvested and, more important, how much was left. As Gómez-Pompa later explained, companies could "come and ask for a permit for 10 or 100 tons," and no questions were asked.[54] This meeting made it clear that Mexican officials not only understood the financial value of controlling barbasco outflow but also were concerned that the raw material could potentially be exhausted.

During that meeting Beltrán gave the heads of the pharmaceutical companies some options. Transnational companies could fund their own studies on barbasco and its reproductive cycle and share the findings with the Mexican government. However, they would face fines if the amount of barbasco they had previously harvested exceeded the amount allowed in their previous permits. Alternatively, the companies could opt to use their significant profits to fund the creation of a Mexican commission to study the dioscorea. The latter option would give Mexican scientists complete control of all the studies to be performed.

Commission for the Study of the Ecology of Dioscoreas

At that time barbasco's reproductive cycles, its pests, and its other uses had been studied by the transnational pharmaceutical companies, which kept the information for their own efficient exploitation of the wild yam. Potentially facing fines, the companies readily agreed to fund the Commission for the Study of the Ecology of Dioscoreas, the first collaborative effort between transnational pharmaceutical companies, Mexican scientists, and the Mexican government.[55] Arturo Gómez-Pompa would be named the commission's first director. The partnership yielded unexpected results.

The arrangement between the companies and the Mexican government was quite simple. The total number of tons of barbasco that a company extracted in a year determined how much money it would "donate." That money went directly to the commission, which in turn used the funds to hire researchers and buy supplies. With these vast financial resources, it was able to recruit and retain some of the most talented and rising stars in biology and botany and, as a result, soon gained a reputation as a model for science research in modern Mexico. The guaranteed source of nongovernmental funds transformed the commission into a top-rate scientific community with high-tech equipment, travel funds, per diems, money for research assistants, vehicles equipped to tackle the almost nonexistent roads, fully stocked laboratories, and stable and decent salaries—an oddity in Mexico's scientific community in the 1960s.[56] Furthermore, with the steady flow of funds and concentration of talent, barbasco was one of the most-studied plants in Mexico for several decades. The wild yam's reproduction, natural pests, propagation, domestication, and so forth were all meticulously studied in the various experimental camps set up to monitor the life of a barbasco plant in southern Mexico. The Dioscoreas Commission would set the standard for research on medicinal plants. By 1970, after eleven years, the commission had trained twenty-seven agronomists and twenty biologists in the methods of ecological research using barbasco as their case study.[57]

Clearly the pharmaceutical laboratories understood that establishing a commission to regulate and amass information on barbasco was crucial. Also in favor of the Mexican government's initiative was the enticement that funneling funds to the commission would guarantee a supply of barbasco through permits and lower or eliminate any potential tax on future barbasco collection. Initial studies centered on the ecology and geographic distribution of the root, but later studies focused on its potential cultivation.[58] For the following fifteen years the agreement of 1959 fostered cooperation between companies and the government, as well as competition among the various laboratories in their search to derive new patented medications from barbasco. Furthermore, it also cemented the idea that Mexico could produce science.

Partnerships between the Mexican government and foreign institutions intent on developing the countryside were not new. Perhaps the most studied of these has been the United States–based Rockefeller Foundation, which had a dizzying agenda to improve medicine and public health in Latin America from 1913 to 1962. For example the foundation tackled yellow fever in Latin America purportedly to reinforce national security in the United States. In the 1950s the initial health-based goals expanded to include support of agriculture and thus relied heavily on the nation's agronomists. Among these Rockefeller Foundation programs was the Mexican Agricultural Program (MAP), which sought to find "technical solutions to the problems of Mexican agriculture."[59] To solidify their credibility as experts, agronomists "continued to invalidate the *campesinos'* agricultural knowledge by defining it (and the *campesinos* themselves) as backward, debilitated, and inferior to their own expertise."[60] In contrast, members of the Commission for the Study of the Ecology of Dioscoreas were encouraged to follow Gómez-Pompa's lead and learn from local people. As rural Mexicans aided scientists in understanding and tracking down barbasco, the commission flourished.

In 1970 a special National Institute of Forestry Research (INIF) publication lauded the commission's significant accomplishments that had resulted from this unprecedented collaboration between the government and the pharmaceutical laboratories. Summarizing the dire conditions for the study of botany in Mexico in 1959, the publication emphasized that despite many hurdles, in just 11 years, commission members had collected 24,162 plant specimens for the National Herbarium, including several new species and a complete new plant family.[61]

Although plant classification and herbariums were not new to Mexico, the commission was accomplishing something novel. As illustrated by the Florentine Codex and Cruz-Badiano Codex, among others, plant collecting and knowledge about medicinal plants were extensive and systematic before the arrival of Europeans who, in turn, continued to classify and translate the knowledge of former Mesoamerican botanists. The commission, for its part, trained researchers to all follow the same parameters of study, classification, and scientific language for the study of medicinal plants, using

FIGURE 19 The Mexican chemists at the Institute of Chemistry at UNAM, 1950. Chemists, botanists, ecologists, and biologists produced hundreds of articles, studies, and dissertations on the study of dioscoreas. Courtesy of the Miramontes Family.

local knowledge as a key source. Within a short time, Mexico came to dominate dioscorea studies, and works from the commission were widely and internationally cited. Mexico became known in scientific circles as a crucial center for studies on the wild yam, and in 1970 Mexico City was the site of the International Symposium for the Ecology of Dioscoreas. Representatives from the world's leading research institutions, as well as directors of leading pharmaceutical companies, attended.

The commission also played a critical albeit less direct role in aiding the government in determining which areas of southern Mexico should receive "attention" in the form of funds for barbasco cultivation. Moreover, just as the Green Revolution "did not target campesinos or make them more prosperous" but, rather, "contributed to their political and economic disempowerment";[62] so too did the well-intentioned Commission for the Study of the Ecology of Dioscoreas. By channeling funds into areas with potential for barbasco cultivation, the government gave unequal attention to the countryside.

Just as scientists were learning more about the dioscorea, Mexican peasants were also learning about the yam. The immediate goal of scientists was to report to the Mexican government about the potential for industrialization of the barbasco trade, but for campesinos a better understanding of the particularities of the root translated into better pay for their labor. Despite their crucial role in the collection of knowledge concerning the plant, campesinos who extracted barbasco were conspicuously absent in most of the scientists' reports.[63]

"Barbasco Was Like Gold"

Although pharmaceutical money breathed new life into Mexican science and burnished its international reputation, these funds did not bring any national awareness about the people harvesting barbasco in the jungles.[64] Ironically, had it not been for domestic political and social developments in Mexico that forced more campesinos to seek barbasco, the increasing demand for the root might not have been met. For some campesinos barbasco picking kept them from going hungry, but for others it made their fortunes and allowed them to enjoy more of what modern Mexico had to offer.

Many urban Mexicans in the 1950s felt that, indeed, the "modern era had arrived."[65] By the mid-1950s 42.6 percent of Mexico's population was urban, with nearly 38 percent of the nation's population employed in the service and industrial sectors.[66] The Mexican urban middle class prospered, but the situation was starkly different for those living in the countryside. As Nathan Wetten remarked in the 1950s, "Mexico City is a completely different world than that known by most Mexicans. To understand this country you must leave the capital and visit isolated towns where life tranquilly flows by, without newspapers, telephone, roads, or radios."[67] It was estimated that "43 percent of families in the countryside earned less than six hundred pesos a month," about fifty dollars.[68] Consequently an increasing number of peasants were forced to seek temporary employment in order to subsist. The situation was exacerbated because fewer peasants owned land. By 1960, out of 7.6 million "economically active" peasants, fewer than 4 million had access to land.[69] The increased demand for barbasco brought men who were unable to migrate, like Isidro Apolinar, some relief from their grinding poverty. The rising demand for the yam also redefined the value of both barbasco and those who worked with barbasco—at all levels.

The beneficio owner hired salaried assistants (*chalanes*) from nearby communities, some of whom eventually learned the trade so well that they discovered a way to "purify" the root to yield higher percentages of diosgenin. Since the laboratories paid both for quantity and for quality, these men became indispensable "practical chemists."

Processing-plant owners also relied on local men to oversee the operations. These men decided where future beneficios might be located, so they needed to understand all aspects of the industry—the basic steps that scientists and engineers used to determine the annual yield of plants, the area's ecology, the risks in establishing a beneficio in a conflict zone, and even basic accounting. As Lorenzo León Felipe, who successfully managed the barbasco trade in nearly three dozen communities in the 1950s and 1960s, recalled:

> If I saw that there were more towns around this one, I asked the town *patrones* for permission to make a beneficio. I would give them all the information. For example, I would square an acre [make a grid] and then count the roots on each square of each acre to see, more or less, how much [barbasco] there was to make a beneficio. All those interesting things I did. The engineers, the chemists would ask me, "How is this year going to be?" and I would say, "We will make it." Other times I would say, "No, we won't."[70]

Outsiders often questioned the accuracy of campesinos' knowledge. For example, an American botanist insisted that one could not "ask natives" to correctly report the number of yams because "[these people] have a mixture of hometown pride and greediness that can be very misleading."[71] In his view rural Mexicans could not follow proper scientific methods because greed or self-importance clouded reason. In a 1964 publication he described the steps a scientist would take to accurately count barbasco:

> Using the quadrant method, we grid a region on cardinal compass points. In each corner of a square kilometer, we mark off smaller squares of 400 meters, called a quadrant. By counting all the plants in the quadrants, we can convert this sample into the total for the entire area.[72]

Despite the obvious similarities between that description from 1964 and León Felipe's recollection three decades later, the campesino's narration underscored the mutual dependence between knowledge provided by local people and nonlocal laboratories. In other words the chemists depended on "all the interesting things" he did. By having outsiders—chemists no less—seeking his opinion, León Felipe was able to challenge local power hierarchies by making future laboratory research dependent on his predictions of yam yields. When chemical knowledge that European and American researchers had jealously guarded was dispensed in the Chinantla, it acquired a different tone and currency. Knowledge of barbasco, its collection, and its transformation conferred a certain status that could elevate unemployed campesinos to the ranks of knowledgeable and valuable workers. The knowledge and the wealth amassed by some campesinos involved in the barbasco trade would challenge the rigid social boundaries that had been in place for centuries in the Papaloapan.

Learning a New Language

For nearly three decades (1950–70s), León Felipe—who in 1999 was white-haired and an established shopkeeper in Valle Nacional—was employed by owners of beneficios to walk to isolated communities to initially spread the word that people wanted to buy the root and that they would later return to purchase barbasco with cash. When he arrived at some of these far-flung places, he would find campesinos already waiting with small piles of barbasco. Initially surprised at how fast the news was spreading, he grew to understand that "the campesinos have much better communication [networks] than we do."[73] In the early 1950s his first job was in a beneficio near Catemaco, Veracruz. His employers, two Spaniards named Daniel Montellano and Angel Rodríguez, taught him about barbasco and how he could best make money off it.[74] In great detail León Felipe explained that barbasco was "a beloved (*muy querida*) plant of laboratories." He clarified that there were several types of barbasco—"yellow, pink, white"—and that it grew throughout the region's sierras. When asked why laboratories bought barbasco, he said that it was because of its diosgenin, "the most important liquid" contained in the root. Together with chemists, he said, "we were able to experiment with barbasco for eight months" and find different purities. He recalled that "diosgenin was part of what before was penicillin that as the chemists told me, to get one kilo or gram of penicillin, they had to gather ten tons of mare urine or ten tons of pregnant women's urine, or ten tons of bull testes." León Felipe's story contained many of the key components in the history of the discovery of barbasco, but it was also sprinkled with local perceptions. In contrast, the middlemen gave the most varied of stories concerning the external need for barbasco.

The urban, middle class of Tuxtepec harbored their own beliefs. They commented on the inordinate amount of gay men residing in Jalapa de Díaz. "Se debe a lo del barbasco" (it's because of barbasco) stated an eighty-three-year-old former store owner. He explained that when one digs up barbasco the tuber's outer layer breaks, releasing a sappy substance. This was the same substance that former root pickers recalled would burn the skin beneath their nails. To emphasize the veracity of his claim, the man called over his eldest child who gravely confirmed that indeed homosexuals thrived in Jalapa de Díaz, and the son also attributed it to "esas cosas del barbasco." Tuxtepecanos rationalized that when pregnant women harvested barbasco, the substance entered their bodies and affected the growing fetus. Subsequently, the children of these mothers became gay. I would hear this version countless times while in Tuxtepec.[75] It seems that in Tuxtepec people's understanding that barbasco's end product was a medicine (perhaps even grasping that it was a precursor to oral contraceptives) led to their developing an explanation that the plant caused the apparent demographic concentration of homosexual men. But the town of Tuxtepec was the only place where people openly discussed Jalapa de Díaz's alleged homosexual reputation and its links to the root picking. When I mentioned this story in other parts of the region I was greeted with confused stares.

Individuals seemingly created myths about barbasco when they felt they had the creative license to do so, or believed that they had to. Most pickers accepted that barbasco was the precursor for the detergent Fab. In addition, in a region where masculinity is a source of pride, fear of feminization might affect the size of the barbasco-harvesting labor force, and hence the number of tons extracted. Another possible explanation for this lack of stories about barbasco in the countryside is that the end product, medication, was so removed from campesinos' everyday existence that it was impossible for them to conceive of barbasco as anything other than soap, which, in a way, they could perceive when they submerged the root in water.

In his analysis of commodity fetishism in South America the anthropologist Michael Taussig argues that "societies on the threshold of capitalist development necessarily interpret that development in terms of precapitalist beliefs and practices. This is nowhere more florid than in the folk beliefs of the peasants, miners, seafarers, and artisans who are involved in the transition process."[76] Following this logic one would expect that campesinos of the Papaloapan, responsible for the weekly removal of tons of yams,

Links: Mit Moreno (Friedrich Schütter, links) zieht Professor Marker (Rudolf Wessely) durch den Urwald, auf der Suche nach der ›Riesenwurzel‹

Die Spur führt nach Mexiko

Unten: Professor Marker hat ›Progesteron‹ gefunden. Mit seinem Assistenten (Lutz Mackensy) beobachtet er die Umwandlung der Pflanze

Geschichte einer umwälzenden Entdeckung

21.15

Professor Marker macht eine sensationelle Entdeckung: Er findet in den Wurzeln von Lilien ›Progesteron‹. Ein seltenes und sehr teures Präparat, mit dem Frühgeburten bei Zuchtstuten verhindert werden können.

Marker will das Mittel für Menschen nutzbar machen. Er gibt seinen Job auf, reist in den mexikanischen Urwald und findet die geheimnisvolle Riesenwurzel ›Cabezza de Negro‹. Auch sie enthält ›Progesteron‹, das heute zur Herstellung der Anti-Baby-Pille dient.

FIGURE 20 On September 2, 1974, the German television network ZDF aired "Die Spur führt nach Mexiko," a film about Marker's discoveries. On the left, Marker and Moreno, played by German actors, look for dioscoreas in Veracruz. Pennsylvania State University Archives, Paterno Library.

would speculate or create "myths" about the eventual fate of the product they removed from the jungle. But the consistent answer among those who only picked barbasco but never moved up the labor ranks created by the barbasco trade was that "they say that it is used for soap." When one contrasts this answer to that of campesinos who worked in beneficios or who purchased the yams, the differences are striking. Interviews with campesinos who had worked in beneficios inevitably yielded explanations and recollections, as wrong as they may be, that alluded to the chemical origins of the yams. For this group of campesinos, barbasco was no longer a simple plant sought by ecologists and pharmaceutical companies. Instead, they connected it to molecules, fermentation processes, and, ultimately, their own social mobility.

Today throughout the Chinantla men, like Delfino Hernández, confidently explain their interpretation of diosgenin. As Hernández remarked, one must "throw out barbasco's *penogenina* to obtain *diosgenina*, an intermediary, until you get to the *terminado* (finished product). This can then be sent off to make medications."[77]

Some campesinos even began to experiment on their own. Eduardo Domínguez of Amatepec explained that his dry region yielded a poor quality barbasco, and hence he and his neighbors were paid less than most barbasqueros. After observing the process and independently experimenting they discovered that they could manipulate the percentage yield of diosgenin content by adding what Domínguez shrewdly described as "something."[78] Laboratory representatives were astounded when a purer diosgenin content began to emerge from the Amatepec beneficios. These campesinos were experimenting with basic steroid hormones.

Conclusion

In 1956 American interests bought Syntex. Although the world's leading steroid-producing company was no longer Mexican, barbasco-derived diosgenin continued to be the most sought-after raw material for steroid hormone production. For this reason individuals within Mexico's scientific community became concerned about future supplies of the yam. Initial inquiries led to the formation of the Commission for the Study of the Ecology of Dioscoreas, a research group wholly funded by transnational pharmaceutical companies but staffed and controlled by Mexican scientists. The research and botanical discoveries it achieved placed Mexico on the international map. No longer was the country simply a supplier of raw material: it was also producing science. As the nation's reputation grew in the field of dioscorea studies, changes were also taking place within the countryside. Mexican campesinos were selectively choosing yams that could yield more diosgenin and, more notably, were beginning to demonstrate their specific skills using scientific terms. Not only were they mimicking scientists in laboratories and workers in beneficios, but were also, like the peasants of Amatepec, experimenting to produce higher quality diosgenin.

In early 1970, five classmates from the National Polytechnic University in Mexico City left school, hoping to spread some revolutionary zeal in their home state of Chiapas.[1] Disillusioned by the Mexican government's failed social promises and its strong-arm tactics in the 1968 student uprising, they were determined to heed a "call for social change" and ideological revolution, the rallying cry of many university students of their generation. Taking the name Los Pañales (the diapers)—because they ranged in age from seventeen to twenty—they ventured into the Chiapanecan jungle in search of, in their own words, communities to *concientizar*, or enlighten. Víctor Mayer, now an engineer, summarized this goal in a 1999 interview, "We were [studying to be] economists, biologists, technicians, and we had a vision that if they [the campesinos] were owners [of their land and individual labor], why, then, did they have to be peons in their own land?"[2]

Mayer's explanation may not surprise anyone familiar with Mexican peasant studies of the 1970s. For many Latin American intellectuals the pressing question of the time was: Why had capitalism not transformed the agricultural sector in the region?[3] As university students in the late 1960s and early 1970s, Los Pañales were certainly familiar with the terminology of Marxist ideology that became part of the agrarian question of the time.

Despite their theoretical knowledge of rural mobilization, in Chiapas the students were surprised to find a web of scattered jungle communities connected by barbasco-buying middlemen who served as a link to transnational laboratories. Members of the indigenous community harvested the tubers and sold them to an *acopiador*, who in turn waited for a middleman to come with a truck or *chalupa* (raft) to transport the roots.[4] Uncertain of what the tubers contained but intrigued, the students sent samples of the root to classmates and professors at the Polytechnic Institute.[5] News came back that the yams were rich in diosgenin, a precursor to all synthetic steroid hormones. At the height of the barbasco trade few outside of the yam-growing areas knew that Mexico produced steroid hormones, and even fewer barbasqueros knew what steroid hormones were. The students had found their project to enlighten the locals.

As a result of their efforts Mexico would see barbasco make a symbolic leap from its position in the scientific world to a political apex, in which the nation's goals for rural development would turn on the wild yam. This chapter explores the varied social and political reasons that made barbasco an important symbolic and material tool for the nation. It explains the events and factors that made the story of barbasco a crucial part of the populist ideals of the Echeverría administration. Public awareness of barbasco during the populist era of Echeverría's reform ensured that the poor who picked the root would be thrust into the center of a much larger debate regarding the price of medication, overpopulation, and the role of the countryside in Mexico's quest to modernize.

Barbasco collection was so common in the nation's jungles that when overtaken by the Mexican Army or questioned by locals, guerrilla organizations coalescing in southeast Mexico would use it as a pretext. Two investigative journalists researching the roots of the current EZLN (Zapatista Army of National Liberation) in the 1970s, noted that "so as not to raise suspicions, the recently arrived tell the indigenous campesinos that they are searching for lands to domesticate a plant called barbasco."[6] The perceived links between barbasco and guerrilla organizing would later prompt the Echeverría administration to organize restless yam-picking peasants. Barbasco not only yielded medications, but the government believed the yam could act as a social salve to combat Mexico's growing unrest in an increasingly impoverished countryside.

Finding Barbasco on the Front Page

In November 1974 readers of the popular Mexico City daily *Excelsior* discovered the story of barbasco on the front page. The article explicitly depicted the plight of those who collected the root as "peasants who had never reaped any profit" from the raw material for oral contraceptives. It singled out six foreign pharmaceutical companies as the source of their exploitation.[7] The article was only the first of nearly 800 that would pepper the nation's leading publications in the following years. In a curious twist the scientific achievements linked to barbasco, once a source of Mexican pride, were not mentioned at all.

By 1974 an estimated 100,000 men, women, and children had participated in emptying the jungles of barbasco.[8] Between 1955 and 1974, according to government sources, 956,569,465 tons of fresh barbasco had been gathered throughout southeastern Mexico, with a reported 7,652-ton yield of diosgenin.[9] Despite the heavy involvement of peasants in harvesting these enormous quantities of barbasco, Mexicans were largely unaware of the story of the wild yam, even though the American press had covered it widely. There are two possible explanations. First, as Ernesto Miramontes, the chemist and co-discoverer of the Pill pondered, at that time "no one in Mexico cared about chemists."[10] Pressed to explain that, Miramontes elaborated that science did not seem to be so important in Mexico, and individual scientists and their work did not garner the kind of attention that scientists in other countries received.[11] A second reason may be that in the minds of most Mexicans it was difficult to link the image of filthy peasants digging up muddy yams with the image of the cutting-edge pharmaceutical end product.

So, why were urban Mexicans suddenly interested in barbasco and its pickers in 1974? After decades of virtual obscurity, domestic and international forces led the government to shift its focus from the science of the yam to the men and women known as *barbasqueros*, pickers of barbasco. Several factors precipitated this convergence: the price of medications, Mexico's technological dependence on pharmaceutical companies, growing urban unrest, increasing concern with overpopulation, and expanding rural discontent. Taken together they lay bare an attempt by the Mexican government to gain control over a recalcitrant citizenry while outmaneuvering a strategically powerful foe: pharmaceutical companies. In addition, the rise of barbasqueros as a rural issue worthy of state intervention speaks to the diminishing power of the Mexican government and its inability to contest local and established power structures in the countryside. Quite simply, without the rhetoric and promises of a populist regime, the history of barbasco would have most likely remained in the footnotes of chemistry textbooks. An examination of President Luis Echeverría's populism helps explain the convergence around barbasco of four seemingly unrelated issues.

Social Unrest, Rural Discontent, Medicines, and Dependence à la Echeverría

Luis Echeverría Alvarez ushered in a Mexican welfare state which, by definition, necessitated the renegotiation of the relationship between the state and the peasantry. For Echeverría's administration barbasco came to symbolize how his political ideology could materialize into change for Mexican society. Thus, as barbasco became front-page news and the public's familiarity with it grew, the perception of those associated with the root—the barbasqueros—was also, by necessity, transformed.

Echeverría came to power on the coattails of one of contemporary Mexico's most disturbing and defining moments: the 1968 massacre of an unknown number of student protesters (estimates range from a couple dozen to more than three hundred deaths).[12] In Mexico at the time, as in most of world, university students were the most visible and vociferous sector of urban discontent, demanding state accountability for increased unemployment, persistent social inequality, and decreasing standards of living for the middle class. Similar to the physician strikes that had occurred barely four years earlier, the student movement spoke to the deteriorating status of the educated class and the diminished ability of the government to co-opt a growing middle class with traditional enticements, in many instances, a bureaucratic job. The student movement was, in effect, both the culmination of a state project gone awry—after nearly three decades—and the beginning of a more cautious, but no less co-optive, state.

Although the countryside had borne the weight of Mexico's accelerated industrialization, urban youth in Mexico demanded what they had been raised to believe: that the revolutionary government would provide for them. Echeverría's administration was determined to show that the promises of the Mexican Revolution—land, education, labor rights—were still very much alive, and that the state could still provide and protect the well-being of peasants, workers, the indigenous, and, certainly, Mexico's youth without sinking into erstwhile paternalistic patterns. Echeverría's approach or as his contemporaries called it, his "personal style of governing"—

with, for example, meetings with peasants that stretched into the predawn hours—was a response to the dire social conditions of his time. However, he usurped his ideology and projects from the populist administration of Lázaro Cárdenas (1934–40).[13] Echeverría in many ways personified a populist head of state in that he used an appeal to nationalist sentiments, a "charismatic leadership, mass media blitzes, promises of reform, and avocation of the common people's interest."[14] But the populist formula which brought the promises of the 1910 Revolution to fruition would be more difficult to implement in a vastly different Mexico.

In 1970, when Echeverría began his campaign, Mexico's population was 48.3 million; by the end of his term in office, six years later, it had grown to more than 70 million.[15] Mexico City alone had 6 million residents at the beginning of Echeverría's presidency. A mere six years later, it was teeming with 13 million. In addition to this dramatic demographic change, which brought the inevitable social problems of unexpected and unregulated population growth, the economic failure of heavy industrialization—the Mexican Miracle (1940–68)—manifested itself in growing rural unemployment; mass migration to capital cities, especially Mexico City; and more incidents of organized violence perpetrated by peasants, whom the government expediently labeled guerrillas. The nation, it was apparent, needed a drastic change in its path toward revolutionary development. During his campaign Echeverría had shocked all, especially his mentor, President Gustavo Díaz Ordaz, when he transformed himself from an efficient bureaucrat into a tireless orator. At any moment he was ready to pose with, grin at, and embrace campesinos, widows, and workers. During his candidacy he had advocated for change and called for a new financial order that would benefit developing nations with Mexico leading the way. Instead, in August of his last year in office, the government had to let the peso exchange rate float, and the currency rapidly plummeted to an unprecedented 25 pesos per dollar from a stable (since 1954) 12.5 pesos. In early 1970, however, none of these failures were yet known and, indeed, it seemed possible to achieve change with hard work, visionary plans, and speeches that rallied the nation's disillusioned, unemployed, and underpaid.

In 1968, during the height of the student protests, Echeverría served as Secretario de Gobernación (Secretary of the Interior) and hence was directly responsible for the military. Two years later, as president, he deftly placed the blame for the student massacre on his predecessor, Díaz Ordaz, and tried to distance himself from the previous administration's political agenda. Analysts of the time have remarked that Echeverría's late and erratic form of populism was a direct link to his involvement in the massacre, a mea culpa and an act of atonement.[16] Regardless of the motives for his actions, Echeverría became an ardent supporter of peasants, workers, and students. His behavior, often described as megalomaniacal or mercurial—he publicly and openly embraced peasants and bowed his head in deep sorrow at stories of land-tenure abuse—confounded political colleagues and angered investors, but it charmed Mexico's unemployed and landless.

His actions convinced many, especially campesinos, that *this* president would finally listen to them. One was Miguel Valdés, a self-defined *agricultor* (farmer). In a letter to President Echeverría he extolled the fact that never before "have we seen a multiplication of efforts and direct focus on the countryside"—but it should not stop there: campesinos should also be guaranteed "buying power."[17] In other words the rural poor should also enjoy the material goods that defined so many middle-class Mexicans. By the third page of his letter an emboldened Valdés offered concrete suggestions that these social reforms be accomplished "with the perfection with which the Olympics were organized," clearly or purposefully forgetting the social cost of the 1968 Olympic Games.[18] Moreover, Valdés urged that campesinos be seen as one body, rather than continuing the state's imposed rural divisions based on land-tenure status, consisting of *ejidatarios, colonos, pequeños propietarios*, or *grandes agricultores* (owners of communally held lands, tenant farmers, smallholders, and owners of large properties). He also acknowledged the importance of interregional communication and suggested that the state fund conferences where peasants could come together to discuss their crops and the maintenance of their lands.

Finally, if peasants felt that there was real support—with, of course, the proper manifestations such as the "national media taking advantage of radio, television, newspapers, magazines, etc."—Valdés concluded, then "there would be a new mindset of progress and not one of backwardness and demoralization." However, even a populist government needed time to restructure the countryside and alter society's perceptions of it and its inhabitants.[19]

Three years later, in 1974, Valdés wrote another missive, this time to the

Secretary of Agriculture and Livestock (Secretaría de Agricultura y Ganado, SAG), Oscar Brauer Herrera. Although Valdés praised Echeverría's regime for bringing "justice to the campesino,"[20] he still implored the government to listen to the voice of the rural population when devising plans for the countryside because *they* "are the most qualified to provide [such plans]."[21] In those three years the state's view had matured; taking into account the voices of campesinos was now more plausible. Valdés did not specifically mention barbasqueros, but his demands could be interpreted as being representative of similar groups. In 1974 barbasqueros would not only be listened to. They also would have a chance to meet with the heads of transnational corporations and demand better prices. What had occurred in those three years? The answer harks back to the 1968 student demonstrations. Many students, especially student leaders, as wanted individuals by the nation's security forces, had few reasons to remain in the cities. An unknown number headed for the mountains, the jungles, and other remote areas. If they could not begin a social revolution in the urban environment that was so familiar to them, then they would travel to encounter what in history class they had learned was the core of the Mexican nation, the indigenous campesino.

Writing about peasant struggles in Colombia, the sociologist Leon Zamosc stated that the rise of peasant movements requires "the existence of allies who support and help the peasant mobilization."[22] The barbasqueros' ideological allies would be emergent student and worker organizations reacting to the authoritarian, repressive tactics used against the student movements of 1968 and 1971. These groups highlighted the government's loss of legitimacy among middle-class sectors of society and also underlined the decline of real wages, the lack of government-sponsored subsidies for small landowners, and increased unemployment.[23] This new urban consciousness, as the historian Héctor Aguilar Camín termed it, was a type of national consensus in which urban Mexico realized that it could not continue to ignore rural decay without eventually bearing the weight of its consequences.[24] By helping to restore order to the countryside middle-class activists additionally assured their own privileged position in society.

This was the case for Los Pañales who stumbled across barbasco in Chiapas while helping to evacuate indigenous communities that would be flooded once the Malpaso Dam was completed in the early 1970s. These students unknowingly set in motion a series of events that would lead to the nationalization of the barbasco industry. The vehicle that would take them out of the jungles was Echeverría's populism, and the medium would be the national press.

Mexican Students Discover Barbasco

After discovering that barbasco contained diosgenin, as one of Los Pañales explained, "we managed to define a project. The project was a *beneficio* to dry, grind, and ferment barbasco. In that way we, ourselves, could obtain barbasco flour and sell intermediary products to the industry."[25] Taking production into their own hands, bypassing local hierarchies, certainly seemed like the most appropriate thing to do, although none of the students had a background in the sciences, let alone in chemistry.

By early 1974 Los Pañales had decided to call themselves the Confederación de Estudiantes Chiapanecos. Their next step was significant: They opted to contact peasant organizations instead of scientific ones for help. This choice would redefine the relationship between barbasco and rural Mexicans. They contacted the National Fund for Ejido Development (Fondo Nacional de Fomento Ejidal, FONAFE) and got help drafting a plan to create a Mexican-controlled barbasco-processing plant that cut out middlemen.[26] However, the construction of the Malpaso Dam, near where they were based, would flood much of the area's barbasco-rich land. The wild yam was so vital to the community that the students along with members of the town of Vega del Chalchi began to hurriedly dig up the roots in the place that would become a lake when the dam was completed. Rafael Ceballos, one of the original Pañales, and in 1999 an official in the National Peasant Confederation (Confederación Nacional de Campesinos, CNC), described the evacuation:

> Guillén, the engineer, went with us to a little town that was being evacuated. There was nothing there because the water was coming. We were there with the campesinos trying to get what we could of barbasco and then taking it to the town's church. We transformed the church into a warehouse because there wasn't any infrastructure.[27]

But as pickers before them had learned, barbasco tends to rot quickly if it is not dried within hours of having left the ground, so shortly after collecting the roots, campesinos and students—who were still learning the rudiments of processing diosgenin—negotiated with teenagers from a nearby village for use of their basketball courts as a drying area. The arrangement was a compromise at best: for some, basketball was more important than barbasco.

> First we ground it and fermented it in old [gasoline] tanks and dried it on the basketball courts, but only in the mornings because . . . at three in the afternoon we had to pick it up and put it in a corner so the kids could play basketball; if not, they wouldn't let us [ferment barbasco].[28]

From this single rustic beneficio the students claimed they saw results within a few months. The first noticeable effect was visible when residents began buying food and goods with five-peso bills that they had received when they sold their barbasco to the student-run beneficio: "the money [that] circulated in fairs, in the CONASUPO centers" was clear evidence to the students of how crucial barbasco was to the local economy.[29] Ceballos explained, "Barbasco oxygenated dying communities' economy." And giving themselves credit, he added, "We reactivated a region."[30] With such quick and conspicuous results the students chose to propose their plan to Echeverría because "this was a group with a vision. Since we already had some knowledge we understood that as a company we could go beyond the Angostura, farther than Malpaso." He continued: "Why? Because barbasco was an essential primary resource for transnational companies. There was no substitute."[31] In their minds all they needed to do was inform the president and Mexico. As soon as the nation understood the extraordinary value of barbasco, change—in the form of just payment—would be swift.

But the world's reliance on barbasco had significantly diminished by 1974. It seemed that young Mexicans had belatedly grasped the importance of the wild yam. This, however, would not deter a populist president in search of a product and a story that could promise to transform Mexico. Taking advantage of a trip the president made to Chiapas the students found a way to speak to Echeverría. During this conversation Echeverría promised them that he would "look into it." He spoke with such fervor that the students were convinced that he would take action.

During his campaign, Echeverría, who insisted that the Mexican Revolution had been interrupted with Manuel Avila Camacho's presidency (1940–46) and had remained stalled for thirty years, swiftly became known as the "man of promises."[32] He exuberantly promised hospitals, land, roads, schoolhouses, technical universities, potable water, and respect for the marginal and indigenous.

A speech he gave on March 17, 1970, while campaigning in Tlaxiaco, Oaxaca, provides an example of his sometimes concrete promises. Before an audience that was demanding more educational choices closer to Tlaxiaco, he responded:

> This very night I will study the requirements needed for a center for technological studies which next year will be inaugurated. I leave you with my promise that in precisely one year the first students will register [there] to pursue their studies with an emphasis on technical and practical . . . degrees that will bring more economic activity to this area. This will be a center of study for the children of campesinos and workers and of this middle class in dire need of financial stimulus.[33]

Lest audience members begin to think that this was a blueprint speech repeated countless times, he sought to bring it closer to the people of Tlaxiaco by adding, "Degrees will be planned so that they can be applied in this area and [these degrees] will contribute to stimulate the riches of this area. . . . May this bear witness to my firm determination to cooperate with *el pueblo* to enrich it at a physical and spiritual level."

Once in power his populist manifestations only increased. On a trip to Campeche in 1973, a reporter noted how people flocked to him waving pieces of paper, letters, and notes. The reporter asked, "Is such a paternalist system adequate for governing a modern State?" Echeverría's response is quite telling for as he explained:

> It is a tradition. People complain about abuses, injustices, they demand things. Many of those pieces of paper I look at personally, while others find their way to the *dependencias*. Even if the State becomes modern, we must not do away with that type of communication. . . . People feel that they have placed their problems in the hands of the president and they need that hope. Moreover, it is a way for the president to find out about a lot of things that otherwise might never come to his attention.[34]

It was not long before the Pañales began to see that barbasco was going to be linked to the Echeverría administration. By the end of that year the newspaper *Excelsior* ran a series of articles on the students and the remarkable barbasco root.[35] Specifically, the articles demanded that President Luis Echeverría curtail the number of permits given to transnational laboratories that "for decades have exploited" Mexican peasants.[36] Coincidentally, editorialists of the time were arguing that Mexico needed to create a domestic pharmaceutical industry that could be independent of foreign laboratories. The demands for patented medications, it later proved, were timely.

The High Cost of Importing Medication

The change in attitude toward barbasqueros was linked to research that revealed that the health of the Mexican people was dependent on medications produced in foreign laboratories. These companies raised prices seemingly on a whim. These concerns were not new, however. As early as 1947 president Miguel Alemán issued a decree creating a federal commission to study the price of medications.[37] As late as 1977, as the newspaper *El Día* reported, "ninety percent of material" used in Mexican laboratories had been imported. This article also revealed that for some time, most Mexican laboratories had "devote[d] themselves to making pills, mixing, packing, and labeling the products"—endeavors for which no actual chemical science or pharmacological knowledge was needed.[38] The implication was that Mexico did not have the necessary technology to produce its own medicines.

The 1970s ushered in a period of renewed interest in health issues in Mexico. More people began to explore alternative healing practices, particularly the methods of traditional healers using medicinal plants. These alternatives were considered a viable option for achieving Mexico's pharmaceutical independence. The search for these plants was linked to the growing awareness of the "rapacious" nature of transnational pharmaceutical laboratories. The 1975 mission statement of the newly created Mexican Institute for the Chemical Vegetable Industry (IMIQUIVE) would pinpoint transnational companies as the bane of Mexico's stunted domestic pharmaceutical industry:

> They spoke of the plant's pillage by transnational companies that quietly arrive in our country, locate the vegetable species that interest them, and then replicate them in their countries or in the natural regions of Mexico, establishing norms of destruction for the plants and paying derisive amounts to the inhabitants of these rural areas.[39]

The IMEPLAM (Mexican Institute for the Study of Medicinal Plants) and the IMIQUIVE promoted the study of these medicinal plants in one attempt to find a way to free the country from its dependence on foreign pharmaceutical companies. The realization that Mexico's inability to care for its sick was linked to the high cost of medicines, most produced by foreign laboratories, was exacerbated when in early 1974 pharmaceutical companies raised the price of basic medicines in Mexico. Although the Ministry of Industry and Commerce "did not authorize the general raise, in nearly six months more than 400 medicinal products have increased significantly in price."[40]

National laboratories, domestic pharmacies, and even doctors began to call for swift presidential action against "this fondness for obtaining exorbitant earnings from minimal investments." Most disturbing in the opinion of the newspaper *El Día* was that "the health of the entire population" was being bartered for that miniscule investment.[41]

A series of studies emerged that presented, in easy-to-read tabular form, the enormous price disparity in basic medications. For example vitamin B lozenges offered at 34.45 pesos to the general public sold for a mere 2.95 at the IMSS (Mexican Institute of Social Security). The price for another popular medicine, tetracycline, had increased by 87 percent and sold on pharmacy shelves for 31.85 pesos.[42] With this price gouging occurring at all levels of the pharmaceutical chain, Mexican analysts definitely had cause for alarm. The studies concluded a mere 7 percent of "national" laboratories controlled 75 percent of all sales. Foreign investors had bought out thirty of the seventy-five laboratories that made up the National Association of Medicine Manufacturers (Asociación Nacional de Fabricantes de Medicina). In other words the profitable "Mexican" companies were in reality subsidiaries of foreign companies. Indeed, foreign pharmaceutical corporations sold 80 percent of all medications purchased in Mexico.

Full-page advertisements—paid for by Mexican pharmacies, laboratories, and medical institutions—demanded that Luis Echeverría do something.[43] Some of these advertisements called for social justice: "an industry as important as the pharmaceutical one should not exist simply for financial gain. It has to be beholden to Mexican interests and the State has to procure ways to produce and distribute medicines at low prices."[44] Meanwhile, studies continued to appear that revealed the extent of the disparity between production costs and the price of medicines. Under the heading "The Business of Medications" a newspaper article explained:

> A product coming out of the laboratory, including the use of raw material and production costs, is 100 units. This is sold at wholesale for 111.98, the pharmacies buy it at 168.24 and then sell it to the public at 201.88. It means that from the laboratory to the hands of the sick the [cost of the] product has increased 110%.[45]

First among the solutions offered was one involving the National Company of Popular Subsistence (Compañía Nacional de Subsistencias Populares, CONASUPO), the state-subsidized food distribution network and a string of low-cost grocery stores. People demanded that CONASUPO sell, at or below cost, basic medicines in marginal areas. Additionally, several pharmacies agreed to stock social service units with medications acquired at "symbolic" prices.[46] Another proposal called for the creation of a Mexican Institute for Medications, which would function as a watchdog and comparison shopper for key medicines.[47]

Among other potential solutions one clearly stood out given the political climate: the creation of a domestic pharmaceutical industry. As the newspaper *El Día* declared in July 1975, "It is obvious that the increasing cost of basic items needed for survival confirms the opinion held for some time"— quite simply, "the Mexican State needs the advantages derived from a domestic industry for pharmaceutical products."[48]

Recent findings supported this proposal. For example research compiled by the Banco de México revealed that raw materials used in medicines made under patent were purchased cheaply in Mexico and then imported as finished and often excessively priced products. An oft-mentioned example was oral contraceptives, which used Mexican barbasco as their starting material and returned to the country neatly packaged and unavailable to the majority of the population. This example caused particular unease in political circles preoccupied with overpopulation. During a 1972 conference in Mexico City, sponsored by the Dioscoreas Commission, yam experts concluded, "[we] have the responsibility to see that our special expertise on yams is utilized to enhance the production of this important root crop—to feed the hungry, on the one hand, and to help curb the frightful population explosion, on the other."[49] *Dioscoreas*, in particular barbasco, were swiftly emerging as part of

Mexico's solution to attain pharmaceutical independence. Battling against private foreign capital, Echeverría's populist state took aim at the steroid hormone industry. This stance is evinced in a fragment from his speech on March 27, 1974, at the inauguration of the National Population Council (Consejo Nacional de Población, CONAPO):

> I understand that only a few transnational companies sell oral contraceptive pills; those companies that cannot produce them are losing capital [*desdolarizan*] because of their high cost. . . . With that in mind I would like to urge Mexican researchers to discover Mexican pills so that they can curb the commercial influence of large transnational pharmaceutical companies that sell these pills.[50]

Seemingly, the work of Miramontes, Rosenkranz, and Djerassi on oral contraceptives had already been forgotten in Mexico.

In September 1974 Mexico hosted the Fourth International Congress of Hormonal Steroids. The person making the opening remarks applauded the president and the country in general for hosting the congress: This should be celebrated "since there is hardly any other city on earth that has had such an important historic role in the development of the steroid field."[51]

With those opening remarks the Congress of Steroidal Hormones inaugurated an intense week of dialogue among the world's scientific community. It was no coincidence that Luis Echeverría presided over the event. At a time when population control was viewed as a global concern it seemed only appropriate that the leader of the country that "had such an important historic role" in bringing oral contraceptives to the world should also attend the meeting. Many of the scientific papers presented discussed the role of steroid hormones in oral contraception, a theme that by then had captured the attention of many leading Mexican institutions. It was on the heels of this congress that social demands concerning barbasco were first voiced.

Barbasco and Echeverría

Given these events, it was not surprising that in the fall 1974 Echeverría invited the group of students from Chiapas to Los Pinos, the presidential residence. He announced that a government commission would study the barbasco problem.[52] This time, however, the question was not the root but rather the people associated with the yam—and neither the students nor the peasants had a concrete plan. As these activists explained years later, they only wanted to make government aware of the abusive payment practices in the barbasco trade. But for Echeverría's administration, barbasco had come to symbolize the first step toward an independent Mexican pharmaceutical industry. So, although students offered barbasqueros an ideological foundation, the funds to finance the project came from an unlikely source — the Mexican government. After the student activists drew attention to the plight of the barbasqueros, it became necessary for Echeverría to make the peasants' and the students' demands appealing to all Mexicans. The idea for linking the needs of all Mexicans to those of peasants and transnational corporations needed a hook. It would be *salud*—health.

A group of scientists and economists headed by a recent college graduate, Alejandro Villar Borja, claimed that Mexico was ready and capable of producing *all* its pharmaceutical needs. In a report presented to Echeverría on July 1, 1974, Villar Borja and his team outlined the solutions to the problem of overpriced medications. Among the six points was the suggestion to develop, coordinate, and control the exploitation of barbasco as a strategy for building up the country's own pharmaceutical industry.[53] They argued that more than 300 medicines could be extracted from barbasco alone. This argument made for a simple solution: nationalize the steroid hormone industry, create domestic medicines, shore up the Mexican healthcare system, *and* curtail foreign dependence. This challenge would be taken up as a call to finally establish Mexico's own pharmaceutical industry—but it would have a very *Mexican* touch because it would be based on a medicinal root.

"Health for All by the Year 2000"

Present-day enthusiasm in the Americas for the systematic study of medicinal plants and indigenous forms of curing can be traced to the 1970s, according to Dr. Xavier Lozoya, director of the Biomedical Research Center in Traditional Medicine and Natural Products. It was then that Western medicine "'discovered' that the People's Republic of China, with a human population of millions, had a high degree of success in solving its primary medical necessities through the use of traditional procedures and therapies, at that time unknown to Western science."[54]

These primary-care options appeared to be a plausible solution to the problem of deficient or nonexistent medical assistance in other regions of the world, primarily Asia, Africa, and Latin America. The World Health Organization (WHO) employed the term *traditional medicine* to mean any indigenous medicines and medical practices that, until then, had been considered backward, primitive, and unscientific.[55] After the WHO's nod of approval researchers and medical professionals set about to systematically study and develop these previously disdained practices. Because these practices fit within the WHO's mission of "Health for All by the Year 2000" the 1970s and 1980s witnessed a surge of that organization's collaborative centers whose main goal was to achieve scientific validity for the use of local plants and remedies.[56] These efforts created connections between European companies and other regions of the world, particularly Asia, with promising herbal remedies.

In the Americas, however, the study of traditional medicine was not as politically accepted as it was elsewhere. Burdened with a historical legacy of government disdain for traditional forms of healing, there was a marked lack of interest in the WHO's initiative.[57] According to Lozoya, this apathy was due to the attitude of United States health institutions, which fostered little respect for alternative or plural forms of healing, and the influence of pharmaceutical companies. These companies, Lozoya argued, still followed a 1950s economic botany model in which Western science—not indigenous knowledge—was perceived as legitimate.[58] Nevertheless, with independence from the pharmaceutical companies, researchers in the fields of anthropology and biology began to conduct studies focusing on plants that heal. In the case of Mexico the government's strong desire to establish a successful domestic pharmaceutical industry prompted Mexican scientists to search for domestic solutions as well as nondependent venues of contact with foreign institutions in order to address Mexico's particular health and cultural needs.

The Social Security Law of 1943 aimed to cover the health needs of wage earners in a country where a significant portion of the population had minimal or nonexistent healthcare. However, the law was passed when Mexico's population was predominately rural and the country had only begun to industrialize. Subsequent amendments reflected the true nature of society and tried to underscore the need to encompass the largest sector of Mexican society without health assistance, namely, the peasantry. Under the 1960 Farm Workers' Obligatory Social Security Regulation campesinos received the same benefits as city dwellers. However, the geographical dispersion of the population in the Mexican countryside not only made administrative matters (inspection, registration of patients, quotas, etc.) difficult but also made it hard to quantify seasonal employment, part-time labor, and work in subsistence agriculture into measurable units on which to base social insurance benefits.[59] So, in reality, very few peasants actually received any coverage. In 1973 Echeverría decreed an amendment to the law stipulating that residents in the tobacco-growing regions of Nayarit; the Comarca Lagunera in the states of Coahuila and Durango; the Henequen-growing zones of Yucatán; the Chontalpa in Tabasco; and areas of Oaxaca, Puebla, and Guerrero be granted a modified form of social security.[60] Despite these random measures adequate healthcare continued to be a faint promise for those in rural areas. It appeared that Mexico desperately needed an inexpensive and abundant primary resource with which it could jump-start a pharmaceutical industry to improve the domestic healthcare system, particularly in rural Mexico.

The sluggish bureaucracy made it more difficult to obtain even basic medical equipment. A 1976 letter, drafted during Echeverría's administration and written by the leader of a recently created organization consisting of "1,000 heads of family . . . 90 percent indigenous Mixe, Mixteco and Masahuas" from the jungle region of the area of the Isthmus of Tehuantepec, described the community as having been "exposed [to] and weathered hundreds of fatal tropical maladies."[61] Alarmingly, it stated, women and children "continually die" because of the "lack of medicines" and medical assistance.[62] However, the petitioners had recently become aware that an abandoned supply of medical equipment, including ambulances, was "rotting without giving any human service."[63]

Speaking for his community, the letter writer beseeched the director general of the IMSS to grant him and his compatriots access to these supplies based on his "human quality and his love for the country."[64] These fine qualities, however, were not enough to convince the director. In a curt response the director denied permission and cited that the supplies would be taken and used elsewhere in Mexico City. Ironically, the slogan above the IMSS's signature read, "Security and Social Solidarity."

As a leader in touch with the masses President Echeverría recognized the importance of the lack of medications and the limited access to healthcare, and he vowed to provide healthcare for all. He would create hundreds of state-funded industries, and in his eyes, the solution was quite simple: a domestic pharmaceutical industry that would allow Mexicans to address the health issues of their fellow Mexicans.

But what medicinal plants could Mexico use for its industry? Prior to the 1970s there was not an exhaustive study of medicinal plants, with one exception: a set of studies on diosgenin-yielding *Dioscoreas* (barbasco). These studies would consequently become the blueprint for all future studies of medicinal plants. In 1975 IMEPLAM was created by presidential decree to unite botanical, chemical, and pharmacological knowledge on Mexican flora and attempt to save (and catalogue) popular knowledge on the medicinal uses of plants. The government-funded institute was later incorporated into the IMSS under its current name, Biomedical Research Center in Traditional Medicine and Natural Products.[65] By building on existing knowledge, the government believed, it could make barbasco the cornerstone of future pharmaceutical development based on medicinal plants. Key to this search for medicinal plants was public awareness of the "greedy" nature of transnational pharmaceutical laboratories. And, if the sentiments expressed by national newspapers were any indication, Mexico seemed ready to nationalize the industry to both shore up its medical system and provide affordable pharmaceuticals for the citizens of Mexico.

However, there were several problems. Although Mexico possessed the technology to produce basic steroid hormones, vitamins, and certain antibiotics, it could not produce specific or complex medicines. In a letter to a member of Echeverría's administration the former director of the Commission for the Study of the Ecology of Dioscoreas, Arturo Gómez-Pompa—arguably one of the individuals most knowledgeable about the social repercussions of barbasco—wrote on behalf of Mexico's scientists that the president should rethink nationalization.[66] As Gómez-Pompa presciently argued:

> The nationalization of barbasco can have serious consequences for Mexico. Some steroid hormone companies have complete control of barbasco cultivation and as of next year they will attempt to domesticate it so as to become self sufficient. The process of growing the wild yam, then, will no longer function independently of the companies. Those who will be harmed are the campesinos who collect the wild yam.[67]

In spite of Gómez-Pompa's warning it appeared to the Echeverrista government that Mexico had what it needed to create a successful steroid-hormone industry—barbasco, a willing labor force, the need for domestic pharmaceuticals, and public support.

Conclusion

In September 1974 President Luis Echeverría decreed that the government would no longer issue permits to steroid manufacturers for barbasco extraction. He claimed that the demands of students and barbasqueros in Veracruz, Oaxaca, Puebla, Chiapas, and Tabasco guided his actions. Their complaints, he explained, were prompted by the "exploitative price which they received for their natural resource" *and* "the systemic fraud" from middlemen who bought barbasco for the steroid manufacturing companies.[68]

While few outside of Mexico's scientific community had heard of barbasco and its importance to the nation, the national press swiftly set about putting the wild yam in the public spotlight. By 1976 Mexico City residents were repeatedly treated to newspaper articles dealing with steroid hormones, transnational pharmaceutical companies, and barbasco. Through a sampling of headlines, one can clearly trace how the story evolved from one of steroids—"Barbasco from Mexico Produces the Pill" (January 14);[69] "If Transnationals Pressure, We Will Nationalize Steroids" (March 11);[70] "Mexico Will Once Again Dominate the World Production of Hormones" (March 11)—to one centered, no longer on chemistry, but on Mexican peasants—"They [campesinos] Asked Echeverría to Nationalize Chemical Steroid Laboratories" (March 13);[71] "With State Funds Barbasco Will No Longer Be a Source of Exploitation of Peasants" (March 13).[72] By the 1970s it seemed clear that to get barbasco out of southern Mexico, one had to make a detour and deal directly with the Mexican government.

Barbasco was becoming a public and symbolic Mexican commodity: the wild yam held the promise of liberating the nation from pharmaceutical dependence, technological backwardness, and unrestrained population increase. The root would be the source from which Mexican medicines would be derived—and not just any medications, but oral contraceptives which guaranteed Mexico's image as a developing nation in control of its population growth. It was also tactically convenient for President Echeverría to link the need for national medications with ignored campesinos. Basing his regime on reforms that would benefit all Mexicans, he specifically showcased the plight of landless peasants struggling to make ends meet.

Barbasqueros would replace chemical and botanical issues as a focus of public attention. However, one obstacle remained: Campesinos would have to come to identify with the root if a social struggle were to be constructed around barbasco. Interest in the root had been, up until then, purely economic: Quite simply barbasco aided their survival. Consequently, the government had to mold barbasco into a peasant issue, just as Los Pañales had done on a smaller scale in a region of Chiapas. Ultimately, what Echeverría was seeking in the case of barbasco was to resolve the social contradictions that had plagued barbasco-harvesting regions for years—contradictions that had become entrenched with the involvement of pharmaceutical companies in the rural barbasco trade.

To achieve Cárdenas-like reforms, Echeverría relied heavily, as had Cárdenas himself, on the notion of a national patrimony—which, loosely translated, claimed certain industries, natural resources, lands, monuments, and even people as the inalienable property of the Mexican nation and its citizens. Before attempting to nationalize the pharmaceutical industry, however, there had to be recognition that its raw material was the state's property to exploit. But foreign corporations would not quietly step aside and let Mexico take over barbasco exploitation.[73]

As a populist regime portraying itself as an ally of the countryside, Echeverría's government welcomed the chance to openly battle for control of what then grew to be termed for Mexico "*our* barbasco." Notwithstanding this stance, the battle would not be led by Echeverría's government. The fight would fall to the barbasqueros, who would passionately and sometimes violently lay claim to what, before 1975, had no owner. To prove ownership, government actions would introduce a new and powerful discourse as well as economic resources into previously ignored regions of Mexico. A handful of campesinos, using this language, would contest their place as Mexican peasants. The following chapter will describe the goals and the hope for Proquivemex, the new company based on barbasco production.

THE STATE TAKES CONTROL OF BARBASCO ⬤6
The Emergence of Proquivemex (1974–1976)

By the early months of 1976 newspaper articles both fostered and reflected the opinion that it was the government's duty to publicly protect barbasco *and* the barbasqueros. This protection was needed because barbasco represented "an important opportunity to unite the [steroid hormone] industry with agricultural production."[1] For a president who cast himself as capable of reviving Mexican nationalism by using a populist formula, the protection of vulnerable peasants was crucial to his plan.[2]

By 1975 barbasco would no longer simply be within the domain of science. It would be a tool to transform rural society. For years, public policy regarding barbasco focused nearly exclusively on the yams' association with laboratories, but under Echeverría peasants, not scientists, had social currency.

When one speaks of the late populism of Echeverría, or for that matter of Latin America, we seldom analyze how the fiery rhetoric was perceived and reshaped by those who fueled the nationalistic inspiration. Specifically, this chapter explores how the populist rhetoric of the 1970s infiltrated the goals of the state-owned company Proquivemex, created to manufacture medications from barbasco, and radicalized the parastatal beyond the intended goals of the administration. By focusing on Proquivemex one can see how the state's attempt to restructure the countryside formed both arenas of inclusion and also, inevitably, exclusion for those rural Mexicans associated with barbasco. By infusing the company with the populist ideals of the time, its leaders unwittingly established practices that would lead to its eventual demise. Echeverría's populism—in the guise of a state-owned, steroid-producing company—"looked" to those in the countryside, as this chapter and the next will show.

The State Takes Control of (Dwindling) Barbasco

After thirty years of producing steroid drugs for the rest of the world, the steroid hormone industry became politically valuable in the 1970s because a domestic industry capable of supplying Mexican needs was still nonexistent.[3] Scholars have shown that the need for a national industry spurred Echeverría's administration to action, but it is essential to consider the social pressures challenging his administration. Examining those pressures can help explain Mexico's wholehearted embrace of the barbasco industry as a tool for generating progress in the countryside.

By 1975 barbasco was losing ground to alternative synthetic materials in the world market. Whereas in the late 1950s diosgenin from Mexico's barbasco accounted for 80 to 90 percent of the world production of steroids, by the early 1970s, this portion had dropped to 40 to 45 percent.[4] Mexico, it seemed, was unable to increase its production of diosgenin to keep pace with world demand. According to the sociologist Gary Gereffi, who studied the Mexican steroid industry as a model of economic and technological dependency, from 1963 to 1968 the world demand for steroid hormones doubled, but Mexico only increased its diosgenin output by 33 percent. In addition, from 1968 to 1973 world demand increased another 50 percent, but Mexican diosgenin production increased only 10 percent.[5]

Several reasons internal to Mexico explain why the country was unable to keep up with the world's demand for diosgenin. As the history of barbasco grabbed hold of the nation's imagination, ironically in many regions of Mexico the root was already becoming scarce. Land fit for barbasco production was being converted to commercial agriculture and cattle ranching. Mexico's National Institute for Forestry Research (INIF) reported that 7.6 million hectares were suitable for barbasco production, but by the 1970s 80 percent had already been converted, leaving fewer than 1.5 million hectares in the six leading barbasco states—Veracruz, Tabasco, Chiapas, Puebla, Oaxaca, and México.[6] The concentration of diosgenin in Mexican barbasco had also decreased alarmingly. As the number of barbasqueros rose, they were forced to harvest smaller, younger plants, which had lower percentages of diosgenin.[7] Some areas were particularly hard hit, with diosgenin content declining from 6 percent to under 4 percent. In addition, barbasco began to disappear completely from certain regions, especially around Los Tuxtlas in Veracruz.[8] Destruction of its habitat was caused by grazing and conversion to commercial agriculture, coupled with increasing numbers of peasants who, determined to get the most barbasco, no longer left a piece in the ground so that it could regenerate. These were the sources of Mexico's declining market share for diosgenin.

Most pointedly, despite its enforcement of permits, the state still did not have a regulatory body to watch over barbasco extraction, and it could only assume that the number reported by companies was accurate. In 1973 the Ministry of Water Resources (SARH) reported the annual extraction of 60,000 tons of barbasco *verde* (green, meaning "fresh"). Despite these official numbers, other agencies—such as the National Fund for Ejido Development (FONAFE)—estimated extraction at least five times the reported amount for that year alone.[9] Despite these disheartening statistics, the Mexican government promised that, with "the creation of a state-controlled pharmaceutical industry," the "irrational exploitation" of both plant and man would end.[10]

Realizing that decreasing levels of barbasco production were weakening Mexico's position as the world's supplier of steroid hormones, the Echeverría administration used its remaining "sovereignty over barbasco" to force a negotiation with transnational companies.[11] The Mexican government made a wrong assumption, however. Because Mexican barbasco was the most versatile and sought-after primary resource for synthetic steroid hormone production, the administration believed that transnational corporations would readily comply with its demands and expectations. Its solution, Proquivemex, a state-run company, would effectively displace middlemen and become the link between barbasco pickers and transnational corporations. By decree of a populist president Mexico would have a successful pharmaceutical industry.[12] For the administration the will to succeed in taking control of the raw material was enough to trump an industry that had been perfected over a three-decade span. This turned out to be a serious miscalculation.

The Emergence of Proquivemex

The government's response to the demands of both barbasqueros and, it claimed, students came on January 20, 1975. Proquivemex, or Productos Químicos Vegetales Mexicanos S.A. (Mexican Chemical Vegetable Products), would regulate barbasco prices, control barbasco extraction, process diosgenin, and sell diosgenin flour directly to pharmaceutical companies. Interestingly, however, more than just an attempt to curtail the foreign stranglehold over the steroid hormone industry, the company claimed to have a predominantly social goal: "the progress of campesinos."[13] Hence, Proquivemex also promised to eliminate middlemen, encourage barbasqueros to diversify their labor, teach campesinos about their rights, foster agrarian organizations where none existed before, and educate barbasco gatherers about the plant and the steroid hormone industry.

The name Mexican Chemical Vegetable Products implied that barbasco would be the first raw material for a pharmaceutical industry based on medicinal plants, or as some chemists of the time derisively pointed out, "vegetables." According to Proquivemex's founding charter, beyond its other far-reaching objectives, it was specifically planning to funnel *a minimum* of one-third of all barbasco sales back into the ejidos, foment the organization of *uniones de ejidos* (ejido collectives), with the ultimate goal of making ejidos *owners* of the company, develop areas where barbasco was found so that campesinos would not depend solely on barbasco, encourage further research into other exploitable plant resources. All these goals would be achieved through the explicit mission of producing affordable medications for the Mexican people.[14]

It is worthwhile to briefly analyze the meaning of these goals. There is no record of what Russell Marker paid for the dioscoreas he obtained in 1942, but by 1975 some campesinos were receiving between ten and thirty centavos per kilo of barbasco. The recruiter of barbasco-selling communities, Lorenzo León Felipe, recalled that in the early 1950s he was paying ten centavos per kilo of barbasco. This may imply that since the time of Marker, the price had not changed.[15] Before 1975 it may have been obvious to many people that profits from the sale of barbasco were disproportionately low to the pharmaceutical companies' profits from the sale of medications. However, this was the first time that the Mexican government had addressed this inequality. The Echeverría administration hinted that locals were the de facto owners of the natural resource and hence deserved a higher percentage of the profits. Two other goals—organization of unions and development of alternatives to monoculture crops—spoke directly to the need to diversify the Mexican countryside.

The founding charter also guaranteed that legally Proquivemex would be the only exploiter of barbasco sanctioned by the state.[16] Unlike the episode with foreign oil companies in 1938 the government would not expropriate transnational pharmaceutical corporations, but it would subordinate them to Proquivemex by government mandate. The charter also stipulated that after ten years, Proquivemex could produce its own barbasco-based medications, but in the interim, the top priority would be organizing campesinos. As newspapers proclaimed, the ultimate beneficiary was *el pueblo de México* (the Mexican people).[17]

Transnational companies took the notion that Proquivemex could successfully produce its own medications in fewer than ten years to be a clear indication that neither the president nor those involved in Proquivemex's creation understood the pharmaceutical industry. Research and development for a new drug can take upward of fifteen years and cost as much as US$250 million (that estimate is presumed to be closer to US$500 million today), so the idea that a bare-bones industry with little technology, few trained professionals, and a skeletal domestic infrastructure could eventually compete with transnational pharmaceutical companies was unfeasible.[18] But under Echeverría the unfeasible and farfetched often acquired a quality of the mundane.

To achieve its multiple goals, Proquivemex would be divided into two main areas —(1) pharmaceutical: for research, development, and eventual production of medications; and (2) agroindustrial: to organize barbasqueros into productive units in rural Mexico. For better control of the yam-producing areas, six leading barbasco states would be divided into five zones.[19] The Region of Tuxtepec comprised seven ejido unions and two "poblados." This area was designated as Zone 1 because Proquivemex's first processing plant and laboratory would be built on the outskirts of Tuxtepec since that region's barbasco contained higher percentages of diosgenin than other areas. Proquivemex's administration would team up there with representatives from the Secretariat of Agrarian Reform (SRA) and the National Peasant Confederation (CNC) to better "transform" the communities. But there could be little or no reform in barbasco-producing areas if Proquivemex did not make money. Consequently, Proquivemex's administration did not wait long to make drastic changes in barbasco production.

Proquivemex's Leadership

Key to Proquivemex's social commitment were the people who led the company. These employees, from the chemists to the director, were young, idealistic, and full of energy, and for most of them, it was their first venture into the world of steroid hormones. For example, the director, Alejandro Villar Borja, was an economist in his mid-twenties whose previous experience consisted almost entirely of having written his undergraduate thesis on the triangulation of prices by pharmaceutical companies in Mexico. In addition he had worked for nearly five years in the IMSS (Mexican Institute of Social Security). A proposal he had drafted, with research from his thesis and with the aid of doctors from IMSS, sought to find alternate and more affordable ways to purchase medications. The proposal reached the presidential residence, Los Pinos, in 1974—at the same time that students were mobilizing root pickers in Chiapas and peasant leaders in Veracruz were complaining about the price of barbasco. Eventually, Villar Borja's proposal and the nation's needs merged into Echeverría's vision of Proquivemex. Echeverría chose Villar Borja to head Proquivemex and design its administrative strategy.[20]

Driven by Echeverría's vision and enthusiasm and a need to, as he remembered, "change Mexican society," Villar Borja surrounded himself in 1974 with equally young and committed professionals who lacked work experience but made up for it with their eagerness to "make a difference."[21] One such person was the secretary, Emma López, who in a 1999 interview recalled how the entire staff of "Proqui" was expected to go into the barbasco zones to understand how difficult it was to harvest the tuber. Remembering these exhausting treks twenty-five years later, she explained that the staff kept their spirits up by singing the ballad of Proquivemex, which recounted the "vileness" of transnational pharmaceutical companies. To illustrate the power of the ballad, she spontaneously began singing verses as she pulled out pictures of the outings to *beneficios*, mills, and processing plants. After more than two decades, she was still able to recall:

On January 20
Of 1975
We saved barbasco
from transnational companies

Proquivemex was founded
As a company of the People
and in this way we defended
plant resources.

Oh Diosynth and Syntex moaned
Ciba and Proquina whined
Searle and Beisa screamed
And the coyotes [middlemen] howled.[22]

López reflected that after witnessing the poverty of the indigenous people she felt a "moral obligation" to make Proquivemex work, even if one had to forsake a salary as she did for nearly four months in 1976.[23] Convictions such as López's were apparently not as uncommon as one would suspect. Still gripped with the memory of 1968 and now under the sway of a populist government that fostered a patriotic adherence to Mexico, it was normal— according to those associated with Proquivemex—to place the needs of the community before one's own. This practice, however, would not translate as easily into the countryside. Pharmaceutical companies at that time, and later, would heavily criticize Proquivemex's young staff, and their inexperience, lack of basic chemical training, and "common good" attitude.[24] Enthusiasm—often seen as naiveté—and patriotism were not enough to effectively win a battle against transnational corporations.

Villar Borja had a concrete idea of the role Proquivemex should play in the steroid hormone industry. In a newspaper article of 1976 he outlined his vision. "What we want is to compete, under a mixed economy regime, on equal terms with those big companies. We are the owners of barbasco: they, of the technology, and each one must defend themselves however they can."[25] Villar Borja's words are quite telling, for they illustrate that from the start for him and other Proquivemex employees any partnerships with transnational companies were out of the question. Instead, each would battle and negotiate with what they possessed: the one possessing the commodity and the other the technology to transform it into something of value. This antagonistic attitude would permeate all the initial dealings between the pharmaceutical companies and Proquivemex. But, first, the company had to be jump-started.

Proquivemex Takes Control

Proquivemex administration's first act—after selecting letterhead, setting up a city office, and hiring Mexican chemists—was inventorying all the processing plants, beneficios, machinery, mills, trucks, and other means of transporting barbasco. Proquivemex then speedily expropriated it from local middlemen and pharmaceutical companies, and ceremoniously handed them over to their "rightful owners," the barbasqueros.[26] By the end of 1975, Proquivemex reported 25,000 campesino families as dependent on the root for their survival, 600 campesinos in charge of *acopios*, 210 beneficios with 2,520 workers, 92 trucks, 4,000 mills, 500 rakers),[27] 22 boats, and a small army of bureaucrats who worked in Proquivemex's central office in Mexico City.[28]

These numbers and their impact acquire a different meaning when we place them within the context of the people of Tuxtepec. For example, Gabriel Cué, a native of Tuxtepec and the patriarch of an influential political family, solidified his fortunes and landholdings by, according to various locals, becoming one of the largest barbasco buyers in the region in the 1950s. Proquivemex targeted precisely this sort of person—a resident of a semi-urban area, landed, wealthy, and at the top of an established labor hierarchy. Not surprisingly Cué has unfavorable memories of Proquivemex. As he recalled, "Proquivemex came to destroy everything and took everything away from us."[29] Similarly, the beneficio owner from Catemaco, Emilio Fortín, echoed these thoughts: "The great times were before 1975 when we [supplied] nearly six foreign companies and some independent ones, too, but in 1975 President Echeverría nationalized barbasco and, I don't know if you are from the PAN or the PRI, but everything the government takes into its hands ends in certain failure."[30]

Even those who did not own beneficios but had profited directly from their association with transnational laboratories, such as Lorenzo León Felipe, were skeptical of what Proquivemex could accomplish. León Felipe had worked from 1955 until the early 1970s in the barbasco trade; in an interview he confessed: "I still sometimes dream about barbasco. I dream that the work is about to start, and I have to go to the beneficios, and go seek out the people."[31] He had overseen beneficios from Catemaco in Veracruz to faraway Valle Nacional at the height of the barbasco trade, and though he had fond memories, when Proquivemex tried to hire him, he declined the offer. With transnational laboratories he had always made one peso more than the local minimum per-day wage, but he viewed the state-run Proquivemex as disorganized and unstable.

But Proquivemex meant something very different for some campesinos, such as Isidro Apolinar. In 1975 Apolinar was in his mid-forties and in the process of raising ten children. In the communities surrounding Chiltepec, he had gained a reputation for being honest and hard working but also a hard drinker. As he had for most of his life, he still woke up at dawn to work in his milpa and took on odd jobs to make ends meet. He played his marimba on the weekends at weddings, parties, and other social events, and he also still dug up barbasco.

Adhering to its social goals, and using a nearly one million peso subsidy from the Secretariat of Agrarian Reform, Proquivemex targeted its first obstacle. The company helped establish new drop-off points, which barbasco pickers—not established middlemen—would control.[32] To make these changes happen it sent out promoters to instruct community members how they could elect the purchaser of barbasco and the liaison with Proquivemex. Each ejido was to have two representatives who would attend national meetings and who would control the purchase, sale, and collection of barbasco in their region.

When representatives from both Proquivemex and the Secretariat of Agrarian Reform arrived in the region, they called an assembly and targeted men such as Apolinar, who were perceived as honest though they might never have held social or political positions of power within their communities. In the specific case of Apolinar his small hut was near the main road, he spoke Spanish, and because of his marimba playing, he was well known in the area. Others who were approached initially resisted a nomination to be a Proquivemex representative. Apolinar's own hesitation was partially due to the presence of the Agrarian Reform promoters. As he plaintively stated, "Before Agrarian Reform would come here, but they wouldn't organize us; they would charge us, but they wouldn't organize or counsel us."[33] For Apolinar, however, growing up in postrevolutionary Mexico, the dictates of the state had surely been well absorbed. In addition he also recalled his father's final advice—to always follow the PRI—and so he also complied.

But fulfilling one's role as a dutiful citizen was not easy. As he explained, "You can't imagine how much we suffered. We continued on sheer courage, without any help. We functioned for a year without any support. We would even walk twenty kilometers to Agrarian Reform in Tuxtepec."[34] Apolinar also had to walk often an entire day to various communities to explain that barbasco could only be sold to Proquivemex-sanctioned buyers. He later spent hours in bureaucratic meetings with representatives from the SRA and the National Peasant Confederation, much of the time learning from manuals about peasant organization.[35] But he also understood that "the first union in the area was the one based on barbasco. Before they [Proquivemex] came, we had no organization. We had nothing. There was no one to organize us because this [barbasco] used to belong to the transnational companies, and they [companies] gave no money to the ejido."[36] Proquivemex would try to change this.

Tackling the Middlemen

By the end of its first year, Proquivemex had spent nearly 5 million pesos organizing barbasqueros into collective units, each comprising approximately twenty-five ejidos. Each unit would deal directly with Proquivemex without using middlemen.[37] In one stroke Proquivemex attempted to remove middlemen and replace them with barbasco-picking local ejidatarios, who in many instances had never occupied positions of power in the former agrarian structure. The parastatal sought to eradicate a complex system of exploitation which, perfected over the years, had given important social roles to middlemen. Most of these middlemen also functioned as moneylenders in times of emergency; references for possible jobs; go-betweens for migrants; and *padrinos* (godparents) for baptisms, communions, and weddings. Overlooking these reciprocal ties, which were crucial for the survival of each community, Proquivemex zealously sought to eradicate what Echeverría himself termed the bane of the countryside—the middlemen— and thus increase the ejido's self-reliance.[38] The company would target four areas usually controlled by middlemen: transportation, sale of discounted food, credit, and processing plants.

First, Proquivemex granted a number of ejidos freight trucks with the promise that eventually all ejidos would get one. The trucks were meant to directly undermine middlemen, who often owned the means of production and controlled distribution and transportation. In the first year Proquivemex helped twenty ejido unions purchase trucks at a discounted price.[39]

FIGURE 21 A Proquivemex beneficio worker in Veracruz, circa 1976. Note the swollen feet. Courtesy of Mariana Yampolsky.

The significance of owning a truck in these areas cannot be understated. A lack of credit and saving potential made it virtually impossible for most ejidos to purchase their own means of transportation. Unions would repay Proquivemex for the trucks, given as credits, from the profits they made transporting their own barbasco and crops.

Second was the role of CONASUPO, the state-subsidized grocery stores that sold basic commodities at discount prices. Since barbasco-transporting trucks returned empty to the ejidos, Proquivemex established agreements with nearly 210 local CONASUPO outlets in the region to have the trucks haul in the stores' basic staples, such as corn, rice, cooking oil, and beans, once again curtailing the previous influence of local middlemen.

In terms of credit the official ejido-lending institution (BANRURAL) vowed to extend small loans to barbasco-picking ejidos.[40] Proquivemex promised to conduct in-depth studies in each zone so that aid would be compatible with the differing needs of each community.[41] This revolutionary approach contradicted decades of governmental assistance which, in cookie-cutter form, applied one solution to the entire countryside.[42]

Finally, a diosgenin-processing plant was slated for the outskirts of Tuxtepec, and the Proquivemex board argued, that it would be "the first step in the complex chain needed to produce steroids."[43] The symbolic power of building a processing plant, and later a laboratory, in what many considered a "financially depressed" area was extraordinary. This act alone suggested that the Papaloapan region could be perceived as more than a monoculture region. It also meant that locals would have to reexamine their views of campesinos for it would be the barbasco pickers who would be working inside Proquivemex.

However, to successfully implement these reforms, Proquivemex needed to teach barbasco pickers about barbasco, which takes us back to its founding charter.

Teaching Root Pickers about Barbasco

The guiding principle for Proquivemex's social goals was that pickers had to understand the uses for barbasco before they could have complete autonomy over their labor process. In the words of Proquivemex's first administration, transnational pharmaceutical companies took advantage of barbasqueros ignorance to pay them less than they deserved. Hence, if they knew that barbasco contained diosgenin, the campesinos themselves would demand a better price. Teaching campesinos about barbasco would be a grassroots movement of social mobilization—ironically propelled by the government—to empower campesinos against middlemen and, ultimately, pharmaceutical companies. But to be empowered, barbasqueros needed to understand what happened to barbasco after they dropped it off at the home of the *acopiador*.

Determined to reach even illiterate campesinos the state-subsidized company published a booklet simply entitled "Proquivemex." From cover to cover the booklet illustrated Proquivemex's mission in drawings. Superimposed over an outline of Mexico is a glass vessel, which contains the chemical configuration characteristic of steroids (four rings) with a mortar lying

MEXICO OCUPA EL PRIMER LUGAR ENTRE LOS PROOVEDORES DE HORMONAS ESTEROIDES EN EL MUNDO...

FIGURE 22 Proquivemex distributed pamphlets to educate rural Mexicans about barbasco. They were meant to instruct, as suggested by this illustration and message (Mexico occupies first place in the world among steroid hormone producers), beyond the chemical value of dioscoreas. Proquivemex instruction booklet, circa 1976. Courtesy of Alejandro Villar Borja.

to its side. Placed discreetly above this is the heart-shaped leaf of barbasco. The first page is affectionately dedicated to "Barbasco-gathering campesinos" who "with great effort extract barbasco from our tropical jungles."[44]

The booklet's quasi-feel of a coloring book is striking. In the first couple of pages a campesino holds a root in one hand while he smilingly lifts a triumphant fist in the air and in a cartoon bubble shouts, "¡Arriba, el Sureste!" (Go, Southeast! [Mexico]). Despite its childlike quality, the message is clear: "la unión hace la fuerza" (union makes for strength); campesinos must band together to fight for their rights. More importantly, as the text insinuates, campesinos are the ones who will bring progress to Mexico, and Proquivemex will protect their interests. For that reason Proquivemex pledged to uphold a fair price for barbasco, a whopping 1.50 pesos per kilo compared to an earlier maximum of fifty centavos. In addition it would impose a mandatory ten centavos per kilo "tax," which would be saved in a communal fund, and each ejido assembly would decide how best to spend their portion. The booklet also explains that eventually all campesinos will be legal associates of the company, meaning that all ejido unions would own stock in Proquivemex. Finally, the booklet also speaks about how best to protect the areas where barbasco grows—for example, by filling in the holes after they dig up the root and leaving a portion of the root in the ground.[45] The message at the end includes a mailing address where campesinos are encouraged to send suggestions for making Proquivemex a better company.

Some areas were so remote and inaccessible that even the most determined of the SRA and Proquivemex staffers were unable to get to them with the educational outreach programs. In instances where individuals could not reach distant communities, the assemblies at which the price for barbasco was discussed became opportunities to explain the historical "roots of exploitation." One of these lessons, written out but presumably read aloud, was entitled "Orientation Bulletin No. 1." It narrated the story of the "Niños Héroes" (Boy Heroes). On September 13, 1847, during the Mexican-American War, a group of young Mexican soldiers defended Chapultepec Castle from the invading American Army. Seeing that they were surrounded, the boys wrapped themselves in Mexican flags and leapt to their deaths. To this day a national holiday commemorates their sacrifice. The bulletin continued by recalling the French invasion of 1863, which "after the loss of Mexican blood, they [Mexican forces] briefly held off those intruders who looted our natural resources for the benefit of European countries."[46] The bulletin added that in the twentieth century exploitation no longer took the form of invading armies but of unreasonably low prices for natural resources. It concluded with the following valiant call to patriotic citizens: "For these reasons, it is necessary that we become aware that we ourselves can exploit, transform, and sell all these food and medicinal products that until now have served to generate wealth and well-being for other countries, [in so doing] we begin our independence."[47] In an incredible interpretative leap once-lowly root pickers were equated with heroes of Mexico's past who had defended Mexico from foreign hands. Slowly, Proquivemex was attempting to empower a powerless group.

In these meetings Proquivemex workers displayed maps of the barbasco

FIGURE 23 "And as to contraceptives, Mexico produces close to half of the world market's total (though it consumes very little)." The woman, holding a barbasco, states, "They should have told me before." From one of the pamphlets educating peasants about barbasco. Proquivemex instruction booklet, circa 1976. Courtesy of Alejandro Villar Borja.

regions, specimens of barbasco, different types of machinery and implements used in the beneficios, and, most importantly, medications were also prominently displayed. Barbasqueros were encouraged to walk among the displays to get a sense of the important role that they played in the manufacture of medications.

On the walls, maps of the nation indicated key barbasco zones, and ejidatarios could locate thriving barbasco organizations. Also on display was small machinery used to either ferment or finely chop barbasco. With the goal of increasing the campesinos' sense of connection to the end product Proquivemex also circulated another pamphlet that illustrated with drawings and photographs the transformation of barbasco from root to beneficio, to Proquivemex, and then to an export product. Finally, barbasco—often displayed with its heart-shaped leaves elegantly draped over a map—could be admired, touched, and talked over during the meetings.[48]

Representatives from Agrarian Reform (SRA) were also sent to rural areas to teach campesinos about "organization." Silvio Delgado, then a *promotor* for the SRA, recalled that in the 1970s he would organize elections in an ejido to select the two representatives who would manage funds derived from barbasco. Once selected, all the delegates would assemble in an act that constituted the formation of their union. SRA representatives such as Delgado had to be present to lend authenticity to the act. These government representatives carried with them letterhead, copies of decrees, and books of laws and regulations; in a sense they controlled what was recorded about these meetings and how it would be preserved. During these meetings ejidatarios learned about their rights and obligations as members of an SRA-sponsored organization. Campesinos, as a part of what was duly identified as a government-approved organization, were consequently encouraged to pay dues, attend meetings, and abide by the rules and regulations. Although the SRA encouraged the campesinos to get together to discuss things, a meeting was legal only when an SRA representative was present.

Notably, to take part in these meetings, barbasqueros had to be ejidatarios, or in other words, landed campesinos. Despite Echeverría's rhetoric of bringing progress to *all* campesinos while eliminating the vices of paternalism, the very structure of his reforms excluded those who could benefit the most from innovative reforms—landless root pickers. Moreover, the terrain once again worked against barbasqueros. For example most remote ejidos were not incorporated into a union because SRA representatives deemed these communities inaccessible.

According to Delgado, however, the biggest obstacle to organization was not the remoteness of communities—campesinos sometimes walked twenty kilometers to attend a meeting—but the social structures of the region: "There were power groups, individuals who opposed any measure that would benefit the entire community."[49] He also pointed out that "when we went in [to a community] to offer orientation, there was always a clash." Nevertheless, Delgado explained that the SRA was if not respected at least feared because "It could take away their [middlemen's] agrarian rights."[50]

In a region where people lived a marginal existence, struggling to clothe and feed themselves and their families, Proquivemex assumed that yam gatherers would enthusiastically welcome its project. But the company's administration failed to fully consider the complex relationships that had developed over decades.

Zone Chiefs, the New "Approved" Middleman

Hoping to remove middlemen from power, Proquivemex instituted a measure to create zone chiefs (*jefes de zona*) and unwittingly re-created ancestral forms of exploitation. To combat local caciques Proquivemex brought in outsiders from different states to act as a system of checks and balances for each region. These men would oversee a web of buyers, sellers, and beneficio workers. They would receive payments from Proquivemex and distribute them in the countryside. However, Proquivemex did not consider the amount of power the company bestowed on individuals who had no formal restraints or affective ties in the area. Not bound by honor or respect it was often the case that once having abused their position they would return with their pockets full of money to their, customarily, faraway hometowns.[51] For example the jefe de zona of Tuxtepec convinced representatives to sign blank checks (each *unión de ejidos* had a bank account) and hand them over to him. It was not until campesinos noticed that he was building a palatial house on the outskirts of town that they realized the extent of the amount of money that was flowing out of their organization. As will be shown in chapter 9 these patterns of corruption would eventually erode Proquivemex from the bottom up. Nevertheless, within months of the company's creation, the region of Tuxtepec began to see some benefits from working with it. The ejidatarios of Valle Nacional acquired a *molino de nixtamal* (corn mill) and a tortilla-making facility, and other ejido unions near Tuxtepec used the money to buy cattle.[52] For these transformations to continue, Proquivemex needed to be successful. The next chapter addresses how the state-owned company created more problems than solutions for campesinos.

Conclusion

It would be the work of a first generation of campesino organizers, such as Isidro Apolinar, and a brigade of Proquivemex employees who tenaciously taught barbasqueros about the fate of the root once it left the jungle. In these meetings, during teach-ins, and in pamphlets, the oft-repeated message was that Proquivemex wanted campesinos to live better. To achieve that, it would pay more for barbasco (a substantial, one peso increase). It would eradicate the middlemen and challenge transnational companies. And most importantly, it would struggle to make the campesinos the owners of Proquivemex.

Contrary to what newspaper articles intimated, the state did not seek to eliminate foreign capital from the steroid hormone industry. Despite Echeverría's rhetoric about freeing Mexico from commercial dependence, he sought to redefine the terms of dependency rather than *breaking* ties with the transnational pharmaceutical companies.[1] In this chapter we briefly discuss the problems Proquivemex encountered when it attempted to push its populist agenda on pharmaceutical companies.[2]

In contrast to the tactics of Proquivemex's young administration, the state's more measured approach was visible in how the company was financially subsidized. For example, of the initial infusion of 15 million pesos, a fifth came from the six leading pharmaceutical companies in Mexico that used barbasco-based diosgenin: Proquina, Searle de Mexico, Steromex, Diosynth, Beisa, and Syntex, the last of which had been sold to American interests in 1956. Nacional Financiera, a Mexican bank, provided nearly 6 million. The remainder was provided by the Secretariat of the Treasury and Public Credit (Secretaría de Hacienda y Crédito Público, SHCP), and the National Fund for Ejido Development (Fondo Nacional de Fomento Ejidal, FONAFE).[3]

Proquivemex's board of directors also reflected the government's expectations for the steroid hormone industry. Its eighteen members (including the director) had vastly different professional backgrounds, but they were appointed to fulfill Proquivemex's social, economic, and medical objectives. For example, representing the interests of campesinos, two members were from the Secretariat of Agrarian Reform (Secretaría de Reforma Agraria, SRA). One member each came from the Office of the President (Presidencia), the Secretariat of Agriculture and Livestock (Secretaría de Agricultura y Ganadería, SAG), the Ministry of Finance and Public Credit, the Ministry of Commerce and Industry (Secretaría de Comercio y Fomento Industrial, SECOFI), the Ministry of Health and Assistance (Secretaría de Salud y Asistencia Social), the National Fund for Ejido Development (FONAFE), the Nacional Financiera (National Finance Coompany), the National Peasant Confederation (Confederación Nacional Campesina, CNC), and the National Confederation for Small Property (Confederación Nacional de la Pequeña Propiedad, CNPP), and also a representative from each of the transnational pharmaceutical laboratories Beisa (Beneficiadora e Industrializadora S.A. de C.V.), Proquina (Productos Químicos Naturales, S.A.), Searle (Searle de México, S.A. de C.V.), Steromex, Syntex, and Diosynth.

Changing the Price of Barbasco

Despite transnational laboratories' significant capital investment in Proquivemex, they had little power in determining the course it would take. Why did the companies agree to fund the state-controlled company, which was technically a competitor? Proquivemex was the means to bring together a varied workforce.[4] For decades the transnational companies had worked with hundreds of independent beneficio owners with variable results. Now they could deal directly with one supplier—and it would be the government. Of specific interest to the companies was their new ability to demand a consistently high percentage of diosgenin with fewer impurities. Thus, initially, they saw Proquivemex not as competition but as a regulator of barbasco supply.

The companies, however, were wary of the social measures imposed by Proquivemex and upheld by Echeverría's government. Proquivemex sought to swiftly eradicate the social contradictions that had emerged during the initial decades of the barbasco trade, which had allowed the companies to make their fortunes. The pharmaceutical industry's objective (enhanced barbasco), in contrast, was not altruistic and nationalistic but economic and private. This would clash with Proquivemex's mission. The transnational companies' initial reaction, as they waited to see how things would develop, was apparent compliance with new government mandates. Of these, the first measure, price, would become one of the most contentious.

Determining a Fair Price

Proquivemex's first issue with the companies was to regulate the price paid to campesinos. To pay a better wage Proquivemex's administration reasoned it would have to increase the price at which barbasco was sold to transnational companies. Mexican scientists warned Echeverría that at this stage it was impossible to compete technologically with transnational companies and so it was not prudent to alienate them.[5]

Despite the warnings, in April 1975, three months after it opened its doors, Proquivemex began selling barbasco flour at 20 pesos per kilo, an increase of 8 to 10 pesos.[6] In its "Política de Ventas" (Sales Policy) report of March 1976, Proquivemex justified its actions by claiming two things. First, the price increase was intended to generate the most revenue possible while barbasco still had value in the global market so that excess funds could be funneled back into the barbasco zones. Second, the cost of barbasco flour would not surpass that of the end product, medications, but it would instead reflect their price. Consequently, the price for barbasco with a 3.9 percent content of diosgenin (less than the 4.2 percent diosgenin-purity level demanded by transnational companies) was set at 20.28 pesos.[7] The initial allocation would be 1.50 pesos to the barbasquero, forty centavos to the ejido where the root was picked, and ten centavos to the barbasco buyer.

Less than a year later, in January 1976, Villar Borja raised the price from 20 pesos to 70 pesos per kilogram.[8] Of that, 2.50 pesos would be for the picker, 1.80 pesos for the ejido, and twenty centavos for the buyer. Villar Borja requested that companies use 20 percent of their total capacity to process diosgenin into steroids for Proquivemex, so that the state-run company could begin commercializing its own medications.[9] Claiming that the demands were unreasonable, the companies canceled all purchase orders.

Newspaper headlines proclaimed that the "primary resource for birth control pills had increased 800 percent" (in reality it was closer to 250 percent), but Villar Borja, despite the cancellation of orders, insisted that this was only the first step and that Proquivemex would not stop until it "saw that justice was done."[10] While Villar Borja's actions seem unduly extreme, to understand Proquivemex's actions in 1976 we need to turn back a year earlier to when it was created.

FIGURE 24 This *beneficio*—where barbasco was bought, fermented, processed, and packaged in sacks bound for laboratories—opened in the early 1980s. During the height of the barbasco trade, beneficios operated three eight-hour daily shifts processing tons of yams every day. Courtesy of Pedro Ramírez.

In January 1975, when Proquivemex opened for business, the six leading transnational companies requested 17,000 tons of fresh barbasco for the year. Added to the 5,000 tons that they reportedly already had in stock, the order seemed perplexingly high.[11] According to their representatives, however, the companies were uncertain of Proquivemex's ability to produce diosgenin of a quality that the private beneficio owners supplied.[12] In September, when the barbasco harvest was at its peak, the companies rescinded their request or asked for less diosgenin—only 7,000 tons had been sold of the original 17,000 requested. Proquivemex, consequently, had three options: lower prices to motivate demand, stop the purchase of barbasco from peasants during the peak of the season, or ask for further loans that would eventually drive the price up.[13]

These considerations led Proquivemex to reevaluate the price of barbasco. A report it issued determined that it was impossible to know the root's intrinsic value or to gauge its value based solely on the labor of the peasants who extracted it. The price had to reflect the infrastructure needed to remove barbasco from the jungles and, most importantly, the fact that it was a resource that nature had given Mexico "since the times of the

Olmecs."[14] The report concluded that the only way to set a price was to determine the value of the end product—medications. In other words steroid medications *could not* be obtained without barbasco, so the price paid for raw barbasco should be based on the price of these medications. For many this reasoning was contradictory.

As an example of how Proquivemex had derived barbasco's "fair price" the company reported that a kilo, which would be processed into approximately 40 grams of diosgenin, was sold for 36.00 pesos. Buyers, however, had paid the pickers between ten to sixty *centavos* per kilo of barbasco. A starker difference in price was obvious when those 40 grams of diosgenin were synthesized into pregnenolone, its first derivative, and the value rose to 72.00 pesos per kilo; later, as progesterone, it sold for 87.00 pesos per kilo. A finished product, such as fluocinonide acetonide, the example used by Proquivemex, cost 4,250.00 pesos.[15]

Another example used to justify the price hike was the quantity of finished products that could be obtained from 250 kilos of barbasco. From that amount, one kilogram of the starting material acetonide fluocinonide was obtained and yielded 300,000 tubes of Synalar, a topical skin cream, which averaged 30.00 pesos per tube at Mexican pharmacies, for a total of 9 million pesos.[16] The report explained that this was only one product of many produced by the transnational laboratories. While the numbers were striking, as a final note the authors added that the report was not intended to "condemn" transnational pharmaceutical companies despite the fact that their actions "created barriers to national development and [affected] the weakest sectors of the population."[17] Since barbasco's dominance in the world market had deteriorated from 80 percent to less than 50 percent by 1975, Proquivemex concluded that the only way to guarantee work for the 100,000-plus campesinos connected to the barbasco trade was by increasing as much as possible the price of raw barbasco.[18] In spite of the fact that Mexico was being edged out of the world market Proquivemex did not shift its stance. This "irrational" behavior in the eyes of the pharmaceutical companies revealed to them that the Mexican company clearly did not understand the steroid hormone industry.[19] Ironically, Mexico might have successfully created a domestic pharmaceutical industry if Proquivemex's goals had been implemented in the 1950s, when Mexico did indeed control steroid production.

"Victims of Transnational Companies"

Merging its social agenda with its need to control the barbasco market, Proquivemex contrasted the already familiar situation of barbasco peasants with the lucrative pharmaceutical industry. Using 1970 national census data, Proquivemex concluded that compared to the rest of the nation, the six primary barbasco states had a higher illiteracy rate (45 percent compared to 23 percent), nearly 24 percent did not eat meat (a standard poverty measure), and between 50 and 68 percent did not consume milk (except in the state of Veracruz) and of that total from six states, less than 6 percent had access to patented medicine. Thus, the Mexican states "that produce the raw material to supply 50% of the world market for hormonal medications do not have access to any type of medications."[20] Newspaper articles reported that for nearly three decades campesinos had been the "victims of transnational companies, of pharmaceutical laboratories, [which] have dedicated [themselves] to the iniquitous exploitation of the campesino picker of barbasco."[21] By the end of 1975 the companies, with one exception, had not bought barbasco.[22]

As an ultimatum, the parastatal set February 15, 1976, as the deadline for pharmaceutical companies to accept the price increase, or, it warned, there would be a 2 percent monthly increase in the price of barbasco-derived diosgenin. Following in the nationalist vein a call was made to all "directors, functionaries, and workers in the steroid hormone industry, of which 99 percent are Mexican" that it was time to recognize that they were all indebted to the "workers of the countryside."[23] Hence those Mexicans who wanted to build "a freer, more just and more humane nation" would stand by Proquivemex and its planned strategy.[24] The transnational companies did not budge, and Proquivemex continued to buy barbasco at the advertised prices, storing processed diosgenin in ever-fuller hangars.

Left with few options and an increasing debt Proquivemex obtained a government subsidy so that it could continue to purchase barbasco. Sensing that the nation would back the appeals of exploited barbasqueros, the board of directors at Proquivemex convened a general assembly of barbasco unions in Papantla, Veracruz, and invited the local and national press. According to Proquivemex, the transnational corporations' stance was a tactic driven by their main fear, that Mexico would become technologically, and hence, economically independent.[25]

First National Assembly of Barbasco Pickers

On March 12, 1976, nearly fifteen months after Proquivemex opened its doors, more than two thousand campesinos gathered in the Livestock Association's auditorium in Papantla, Veracruz, to loudly demand the nationalization of the steroid hormone industry. Twenty-five representatives of barbasco-based unions took to the stage and publicly showed their support for Proquivemex. In passionate speeches which alluded to their exploited condition, the abuse of Mexico, and the need to preserve a valuable natural resource, they all echoed their support for Proquivemex.[26] That meeting set the tone for the "battle" against transnational corporations.[27]

At that meeting campesinos were publicly and legitimately acknowledged as the protectors of Proquivemex. The secretary of ejido organizations in the Ministry of Agrarian Reform, Helio García Alfaro, stated that it was the campesinos' "responsibility [to ensure] that Proquivemex continue, without conceding to the corruption of transnational corporations."[28] The secretary admonished the campesinos: "Whenever one of your representatives fails or when one of your own weakens before the temptation of transnational corporations, you yourselves should run and denounce them."[29] The pressure to protect barbasco was suddenly a governmental mandate.

Despite this call to action and the ensuing newspaper articles that blamed transnational corporations for the abuse suffered by Mexican peasants, the companies did not budge. The presence of such a large contingent of campesinos clamoring for their rights vis-à-vis the steroid hormone industry had nonetheless taken the companies and the government by surprise. Proquivemex, it seemed, was going beyond its role of simply educating campesinos.

Interestingly, the newspapers covering the meeting reported that the campesinos had demanded that steroid companies uphold a fair price, and that these peasants called for the nationalization of the industry. However, if we examine the perspectives of the campesinos from the region of Valle Nacional, the portrait we see is quite different. Most campesinos in Región Tuxtepec were unaware of the price war, never learned that barbasco was used to make products other than soap, or understood that the union had demanded rights for barbasco pickers. The campesinos, such as Apolinar, who attended local meetings and traveled to national assemblies, were not representative of most barbasqueros.

National Images of Exploitation

By early March a series of cartoons began to accompany newspaper coverage of the barbasqueros and the pharmaceutical companies. Invariably transnational pharmaceutical companies were depicted as vultures, pirates, snakes, or a vicious-looking Uncle Sam (figures 25 and 26). The newspaper articles referred to the companies as octopuses, rats, or empires.[30] In one image a robust-looking barbasco root desperately runs from the clutches of a sinister Uncle Sam, who carries a bulging sack of barbasco.[31] The transnational companies had slowly morphed into Mexico's image of pillage and plunder by the United States. Below that particular cartoon an article entitled "The History of Barbasco" details in a melancholic tone how barbasco had given the world the primary resource for nearly 500 chemical combinations and hundreds of medications. It also laments that a series of awards and honors in the chemical field, to say nothing of profits, had been bestowed on others but not on Mexicans. It marvels at a "small-time" company trying to beat the powerful pharmaceuticals.

In another image labeled "Recipe: Nationalization!" Proquivemex appears as a nervous mouse that valiantly swings a punch at an enlarged snake sinisterly wrapped around a chemist's mortar. The snake wears a stars-and-stripes top hat. At this point, March 1976, it appears that transnational pharmaceutical companies were not going to release their hold on the industry and that Proquivemex, which once appeared so strong, was in reality much weaker than it wanted to accept. For all its boasting (a surplus of state subsidies), it could not hide the fact that it was, in fact, a puny mouse (technologically deprived). Despite these images there were those who still believed that nationalization was the healthy option for Mexico.

The Companies Respond

As verses from Proquivemex's ballad suggested, the presence of the state-subsidized company produced a series of reactions in the established pharmaceutical companies. In a letter signed by the six pharmaceutical laboratories and addressed to Echeverría's chief of staff, Hugo Cervantes del Río, the companies expressed their belief that quite simply "the price paid for barbasco has always been remunerative."[32] The representatives of the companies arrived at this conclusion by comparing the price for barbasco against minimum wages in the barbasco regions.

FIGURE 25 By 1976 an intense campaign was waged in Mexico City's daily newspapers, where barbasco pickers were depicted as victims of "rapacious" transnational corporations. Source: *Excelsior*, March 16, 1976.

FIGURE 26 A common target of these cartoons was the United States or U.S.-based transnationals, depicted here as Uncle Sam chasing a barbasco that shouts, "Help, I'm being robbed!" Source: *El Día*, circa 1976.

In 1974 the companies paid up to 1.50 pesos per kilogram. Accordingly, a man could earn more than 100 pesos daily, which was well beyond the minimum wage in southeastern Mexico, which ranged from 17 pesos in Oaxaca to nearly 28 pesos in Veracruz. Moreover, the companies explained, they bought directly from root pickers. The clever omission of local middlemen revealed how well the companies understood the goals of the state company. However, as a response to the new 70 peso-per-kilo price for barbasco, the companies simply opted not to buy any barbasco from Proquivemex. Companies were able to hold this strategy because, anticipating the creation of Proquivemex, they began to hoard barbasco and allegedly had enough to tide them over until the end of 1976 and, they hoped, into a more corporation-friendly presidential regime. In certain areas, particularly Veracruz, companies had also previously increased the price of barbasco by as much as three pesos per kilo, propelling a frenetic gathering of barbasco.[33] Both the pharmaceutical companies and the directors of Proquivemex understood that the presidential changeover, which would occur on December 1, 1976, would be crucial for the parastatal's survival.

If the pharmaceutical companies stood firm through the end of the year, then it was unlikely that Proquivemex could maintain its inflexible position. If this did happen Mexican steroid production would fall to the point that external economic pressures would force the parastatal to make a decision. But most detrimental to Proquivemex's goal, campesinos would be the most affected if Proquivemex could not sell barbasco; then it would not be able to continue to buy the root from the campesinos. To maintain its firm stance against transnational companies, Proquivemex needed government subsidies, but as the presidential term came to an end, it was unclear if that support would continue. Echeverría did not respond to the demands for nationalization, and to study the problem of barbasco prices, the government commissioned a task force that pointedly excluded Proquivemex. Gary Gereffi speculated in his 1983 book that both the government and the companies were caught off guard by Proquivemex's galvanization of such immediate and massive support.[34] Both oral histories and archival research demonstrate that it was not the government's intention to give Proquivemex such a visible and powerful role as protector of campesinos' rights. For many middle-class and urban Mexicans the image of angry and organized campesinos was disquieting. In fact, their concern revealed an apparent frustration with Echeverría's vision for the countryside.[35] Despite this, Proquivemex once again turned to the peasants instead of backing down. This time no longer seeking simply a price increase, Proquivemex explicitly attacked the transnational companies on two counts. First, they did not pay a *derecho de monte* (land tax) to the campesinos, and, second, they committed tax fraud. In both instances Alejandro Villar Borja came up with concrete numbers to illustrate the degree of exploitation. This time the meeting was held in Mexico City.

Derechos de Monte

The foundation for campesino support was the alleged abuse of the derechos de monte, the payment for commercial exploitation of the forests: "the men of the countryside are tired that others exploit natural resources which legally belong to the campesino and whose profits belong to them but are instead enjoyed by foreigners."[36] This discontent would be the basis for their demands. According to the Agrarian Reform Law, the campesinos owned the land (or leased it from the state). Accordingly, if a third party realized any monetary gain from the land, they owed the campesinos something for that use. The practice of not paying for the use of natural resources would become the key argument to illustrate the "voracious" nature of transnational corporations.

On August 13, 1976, each pharmaceutical company received a letter from a newly minted barbasco union, Ejido Unions of the Southeast, represented by Proquivemex, demanding reparation for the use of land where barbasco had been extracted from December 12, 1954, to the date of the letter. Proquivemex noted that according to Article 115 (the third clause) of the internal regulations of Agrarian Reform (SRA) the companies had thirty days to respond. Each company was quoted a different overdue balance based on the reported amount of barbasco and the years that each company had exploited the root. The total debt was a staggering 470 million pesos.[37] If the companies did not pay reparation to the campesinos, the unions would sue them. As Villar Borja explained years later, "What was contracted was the labor to extract a product from nature. The communities were never paid a derecho de monte or any other claim."[38] The companies successfully countered that the government had never before requested such a payment. In spite of continued demands by campesinos, letters to Echeverría, and newspaper articles, the companies never paid the campesinos the derecho de monte tax. Years after this initial argument, however, letter writers in barbasco regions continued to insist that they be paid their derecho de monte.

Tax Fraud and Transfer Pricing

In addition to derecho de monte violations, Villar Borja claimed, companies avoided paying taxes by relying on transfer pricing.[39] Transfer pricing is used when trying to lower a company's tax burden, so "exports to an affiliated company are often undervalued, whereas imports from an affiliate have a higher than normal price."[40] In other words, companies transferred funds out of a country without paying taxes on them. Concretely, this meant that the six transnational companies had defrauded the Mexican treasury at a rate of nearly 1 billion pesos per year. An example written in a 1980 article to underline the continued abuse by transnational companies noted that Syntex exported *etinil-estradiol* at 11,250 pesos per kilo while Organon (an affiliate of Diosynth, based in Holland) imported it at 1 million pesos, an 88 percent increase over the value cited by Syntex.[41] According to Villar Borja, the value of steroid hormone exports from Mexico was 1.4 billion pesos yearly (based on quoted global prices for their products) and not the reported 400 million pesos that they were charging.[42] Thus, the Mexican government was losing 420 million pesos, and workers were losing another 80 million pesos in shared profits. Overpricing by pharmaceutical companies was neither new nor insignificant in Mexico.

In his study of the steroid hormone industry Gereffi selected five random products and determined that for these five products alone, the total overpricing was nearly 5 million pesos. He concluded, "When you consider that there are sixty-five different import codes for steroid hormones products entering Mexico and that there is evidence of overpricing in almost every one, the concerns about fraud expressed by Proquivemex certainly appear justified."[43] The companies, recognizing that this evidence was sufficient to demand nationalization, masterfully pitted Mexico's domestic laboratories against Proquivemex. It was determined the companies had never been informed of their alleged offenses by either Agrarian Reform (*derechos de monte*) or the Secretary of the Treasury (tax fraud). In spite of this overwhelming evidence Proquivemex was unable to garner sufficient support from Mexico's private sector.

Mexican Laboratories Respond

In newspaper articles throughout the country different groups began to voice their support for barbasqueros, and many added their particular demands. For example medical students met with José López Portillo, then the PRI presidential candidate, and demanded that the government nationalize the pharmaceutical industry and initiate constitutional reforms to ensure that each citizen receive health coverage.[44] The presidential candidate responded by linking the goals of health for all as a final tenet of the Mexican Revolution: "Our government is on the difficult path that leads to health as part of social justice, with it [health] we will attain a vital goal of the Revolution."[45] Overall, the future president remarked, it was necessary that Mexico overcome "gigantic" obstacles in order to bring health to all Mexicans, not just those who could afford it. Intertwined with the demands of the future doctors was a clear yearning or concern that was emerging throughout Mexico, which was echoed by attendees at a conference on medicinal plants, who argued it was time for Mexico to gain control of the products derived from its medicinal plants.[46]

The state's increased participation in various economic entities, as can be expected, generated a series of conflicts and confrontations with the private sector, which saw it as an "invasion" of the areas it traditionally controlled.[47] One of these was, of course, the steroid hormone industry. Transnational corporations would find unexpected support from private businessmen, especially members of the National Chamber of Chemical-Pharmaceutical Laboratories, who feared that if the government successfully took over the steroid hormone industry, then their profits would plummet. A concrete fear was that Proquivemex's finished products might be sold directly to government institutions, which comprised 25 percent of all pharmaceutical sales in Mexico at the time.[48] Consequently, Proquivemex was accused of "disloyal competition."[49] The government and not surprisingly the pharmaceutical companies found support in institutions such as the Confederation of Trade Organizations (CONCAMIN), which defended the companies' interests. As its leader, Jorge Sánchez Mejorada, explained in a March 17, 1976, interview, from the CONCAMIN's point of view, all industries operating in Mexico were Mexican.[50] He further stated that Proquivemex's claims had no legal foundation and that transnational corporations had never been aware of a derecho de monte tax. Reflecting the opinion of many industrialists, he heavily criticized Proquivemex's demands to nationalize the steroid hormone industry, stating that if the companies were not correct then, "they should be bought or nationalized, but it should be done by the authorities."[51] When the reporter clarified that it was not Proquivemex but peasants who were demanding the nationalization, Sánchez Mejorada curtly asked, "If we do everything that campesinos ask us to do, then, where will we end up?"[52] He also believed that it was impossible for a group of campesinos to independently demand the nationalization of the steroid hormone industry. As he saw it they simply were "being manipulated."[53] Sánchez Mejorada additionally argued that it was impossible to compete against the government, because "the odds are to lose, because the rules followed are not the same."[54] Given the rise in rural unrest, these accusations were detrimental to Proquivemex's case.

Even more alarming to transnational corporations and to privately owned Mexican laboratories was Proquivemex's apparent success at producing various products derived from barbasco. Not only was Mestril, the Mexican contraceptive, ready to go on the market but fungicides and rat poisons allegedly were also ready for commercial sales.[55] Mestril was rumored to cost 4 pesos, well below those pills sold by transnational corporations, which at 18 pesos were significantly more expensive. A price difference that was not overlooked by local businessmen. This diversification and ability to replicate some pharmaceutical products sent ripples of concern throughout the pharmaceutical world.[56] But time was on their side.

On December 1, 1976, José López Portillo, an ardent supporter of transnational capital as a means to bring development to Mexico, replaced President Luis Echeverría, the "protector of campesinos." At the time of the transition Proquivemex—then one month short of its two-year anniversary—still had not sold barbasco to pharmaceutical companies. Negotiations continued well past Echeverría's term, but few of Proquivemex's original social goals would survive beyond Villar Borja's tenure. Nevertheless, the lessons taught to campesinos in the first years would leave a lasting legacy. It would be up to barbasco leaders and not government representatives to continue the struggle for a fair price for barbasco.

In spite of the previously mentioned warnings uttered by scientists such as Arturo Gómez-Pompa, the government's hopes for what could potentially—financially and socially—be achieved further compounded Proquivemex's dire situation. In sum, the Echeverría administration's flawed expectations were that transnational companies would contribute technologically and economically to the development of a domestically controlled Mexican steroid hormone industry. Instead just the opposite happened.

The current director of the institute for the study of medicinal plants, Dr. Xavier Lozoya, agreed that Mexico's last opportunity to create its own pharmaceutical industry came in 1974–75.[57] Mexico had the natural resource, and the transnational companies had the technological know-how. Hence, the first step in building a domestic industry was to regulate the access to the root.[58] To understand the mission of Proquivemex it is necessary to take a closer look at the state's assumptions.

Echeverría built his regime on addressing the needs of the disenfranchised and increasing state funding to the countryside.[59] In his inaugural address on December 1, 1970, he stated, "The mixed regime established by the Constitution presupposes that public investment has enough strength to direct growth. A public company can only be prolific if the government has enough resources to ensure the successful carrying out of national objectives."[60] In this fashion fomenting industry would be added to the state's traditional role in the private sector. Between December 1, 1970, and November 30, 1976, the number and types of industries in which the state participated generally increased.[61] The state created such varied companies as those dealing with the automotive industry, fish, poultry, fertilizer, tobacco, and citrus products. Some contemporaries expressed concerns, as did Armando Bartra in his book *Notas sobre la cuestión campesina* (Notes on the Campesino Question). It was not enough to invest more money in the countryside, but rather, as Bartra argued, the state had to change *how* it participated in that sector.[62]

A new form of state participation entailed a more aggressive stance concerning the commercialization of agriculture and an increasingly active role in the promotion, education, and organization of the agrarian sector. In this context the SRA was created and replaced the Department of Agrarian Affairs and Colonization (DAAC). The state's new agenda was reflected in the creation of the Agrarian Reform Law established by presidential decree on May 1, 1971.[63] As was reported in the peasant publication *Organización*, the Agrarian Reform Law granted ejidos "legal capacity, and a truly revolutionary approach to organization grounded on democratic decision making, self-management, and an integral and rational planning of resources at the ejido level as a unit of production and also higher forms of organization."[64] An example of this form of organization was the notion of *uniones de ejidos*, a collective unit of ejidos. The need to push for such organization was premised on the idea that the source of all problems in the countryside stemmed from campesinos' inefficient organization. Explicitly, "their isolated effort increases costs, impedes the access to modern technology, increases the need for services and agricultural assistance and exposes them to a voracious intermediation."[65]

Hence, Echeverría's ultimate goal, reminiscent of reforms by the former president Cárdenas, was to empower campesinos by making them self-sufficient. No longer wishing to have a "paternalistic model" reign in the countryside, he instead sought "collective exploitation of the land that would put an end to the unproductive minifundio."[66] Furthermore, he promised to respect the "patrimonial rights of communities," a move he claimed would ultimately lead to rural development. In his definition respect of patrimonial rights encompassed more than "common values" and "respect for other forms of life." It also involved an acceptance of the campesinos' ability to "bring development" to the countryside.[67] The key to ending perceived roadblocks to campesinos' development, in Echeverría's vision, was a complete restructuring of the countryside. Concretely this meant more equipment; easier-to-obtain credits; collective marketing arrangements; and direct access to the government through the newly created SRA, which would regulate and administer the countryside. This task, however, "would not be easy," because the transformation of Mexican agriculture necessitated a shift in agrarian credit and lending institutions that would reflect the new vision of the Agrarian Reform. New ways of funding the countryside would have to be created, including, for example, multipurpose companies such as Proquivemex.

The new Agrarian Reform Law attempted to give peasants more autonomy, but it was a *regulated* autonomy, in which the state was an active player in the production process. In other words by organizing into collective units campesinos could become independent of middlemen in the countryside, but they would have to abide by the rules and regulations of the Secretariat of Agrarian Reform. The state's structural initiatives in the countryside were increasingly aimed at gaining command over independent peasant and indigenous organizations. The National Peasant Confederation

(CNC) had initially monitored them, but now they were straying from state control at a time of rural crisis and popular discontent.

The attempt to organize the growing numbers of unemployed rural Mexicans was not new to this administration. On June 6, 1973, the undersecretary to the president, Ignacio Ovalle, received a curious report from the National Laboratories to Foment Industry.[68] Months earlier, chemists had been asked to compare two fiber samples of lechuguilla, an agave that grows in the Sonoran and Chihuahuan deserts and is used to make ropes, mats, and brushes. The report compared the rigidity results of lechuguilla polished by hand and by machine. Interestingly, machine-polished fibers lost nearly 44 percent of their rigidity, a discovery that raised concerns.[69]

Curiously the letter did not focus on this loss, but rather it echoed worries expressed in an earlier letter. If Mexico adopted the new polishing machines, the letter writer argued, each machine would "displace 20 to 30 heads of family," a move "which would not be advisable to make."[70] So instead of replacing men with the proposed machines, the goal was to "organize the polishers of *ixtle* [fiber] into financially viable communities."[71] The author of the letter, Manuel González, contended that it was crucial to remember that "ixtleros lack any agricultural knowledge, a fact which requires intensive training in practical [farming] techniques since the ixtleros are experienced gatherers [of ixtle] and not farmers."[72] González also warned that the apparent insufficient labor force in the ixtle-producing region—in the arid zones of the states of San Luis Potosí, Nuevo León, Tamaulipas, Coahuila, and Zacatecas—was due to recent and transitory work for government-led road construction as well as the drain of men working at other sites as *braceros*, and hence it would be wrong to bring in machines for a temporary need.[73]

What is striking about this letter is that the government is warned of adopting any advances in technology that could displace hundreds of campesinos. Similar to the case of lechuguilla, in the eyes of the government, barbasco was a regional solution to poverty and lack of employment opportunities.

Seen from this perspective control of barbasco was one in a series of state attempts to regulate natural resources and optimize their output while at the same time attempting to control (co-opt) the campesinos who provided the associated labor. Proquivemex was just one of the dozens of state-subsidized companies created by Luis Echeverría to meet this end.[74]

Conclusion

After nearly thirty years of barbasco extraction the state—now under a populist regime—took control of the root and used a nationalist agenda to bring relief to the barbasqueros. A cadre of young professionals, such as Alejandro Villar Borja, had taken up Echeverría's goals and had swiftly and enthusiastically rallied peasants to confront their own exploitation by the transnational companies. Despite its revolutionary zeal Proquivemex fully depended on transnational pharmaceutical companies to continue with its reforms in the barbasco regions. Without transnational support Proquivemex's power in the steroid hormone industry began to wane barely two years into the company's existence. It was unable to compete against transnational companies that had successfully controlled the market since Mexico lost control of Syntex. Even if barbasco belonged to Mexico, the knowledge and technology to transform it into something beyond a root still belonged to others.

By bringing the knowledge of barbasco to the countryside—allowing peasants to walk among exhibits and trace with their fingers the trajectory from jungle to laboratory—Proquivemex unwittingly began to transform the self-perception of many barbasqueros. For, by repeating that barbasco was *theirs* and that without their help the world would not know many of the medications derived from the wild yam, the parastatal opened a venue previously out of bounds for Mexican campesinos: domestic and international laboratories.

In spite of Proquivemex's initial *social* intentions—creating an organization that would strengthen peasant relationships and which would act as the foundation for a new type of peasant union—a true peasant organization did not emerge at this time. What did emerge was a flow of information about their labor and the product of their labor, and an understanding of the place of campesinos in the manufacture of steroid hormones. These campesinos, to the surprise of the government, would carry Proquivemex into its next phase: a consolidated peasant organization.

I remember how we had nothing. Nothing.
The only thing we had was barbasco.
There were no jobs. Times were hard.

Eusebio Jiménez, interview, July 1999

BARBASQUEROS INTO MEXICANS ⬤8

Eusebio Jiménez shook his head as he recalled in July 1999 the not-
so-golden years of the 1950s and 1960s.[1] To emphasize his claims of
hardship, he pulled out three tattered photographs that showed him
and his family standing barefoot outside a thatch hut, blankly peering
into the camera lens and sheepishly holding up a number. The plac-
ard revealed the Jiménez family's relocation number, given to them
shortly before they and thousands of other campesinos were forcibly
removed from Veracruz to Ojitlán, Oaxaca, to make way for construction of the Cerro de Oro Dam.[2] The peasant in the photograph
physically resembled the man who now sat contemplating his rich
acres on the border of the Tonto River, but the resemblance stopped
there. As he called his daughter, a recently graduated chemical engineer, to put the pictures away, it was difficult to imagine him decades
earlier trudging barefoot into the jungle and clawing at the earth,
desperately searching for a wild yam. Jiménez was one of a handful
of former *barbasqueros* who used their knowledge of barbasco as the
means to forge an identity beyond that of campesino and, as in his
case, lead a life that was far removed from that of a twentieth-century
Mexican peasant.

This chapter explores the emergence of a collective identity centered on the barbasco trade. It also provides the context within which
to examine how identification with a medicinal plant of interest to the
government played out in 1970s peasant organizations in the Mexican countryside. Contrary to other campesinos associated with commodities such as, say, cane or rubber, some barbasco pickers altered
their self-definition from simple gatherers of barbasco to *owners* of

the tubers and, specifically, of the chemical compounds held in the roots. Terms such as *belonging, national patrimony*, and *progress* took on a meaning of their own when used by root pickers and reflected how nationalist rhetoric of the period trickled into the everyday lives of rural Mexicans. Campesinos' reinterpretation of their role in the history of the barbasco trade illustrates how some locals shaped national processes to further their own agendas. Because Proquivemex, the state-subsidized laboratory, was conceived of as an alternative to the foreign-controlled steroid industry model, the peasants who were linked to barbasco would also be conceived of as distinct from historical perceptions of campesinos.

Producers of Barbasco

Key to the formation of the barbasquero identity were the associations that the picker could make with the root and, more important, with the end product, diosgenin. Pickers, thus, needed to link themselves with the steroid hormone industry; with Proquivemex; with transnational corporations; with the need for patented medications, which most had no access to; and with their *essential* role in the commercialization of barbasco. To garner public support, a romanticized version of the root pickers' daily existence and their battle against transnational corporations would have to emerge in the daily press. To change national and international perceptions of who they were, root pickers' multiple identities as peasants, day laborers, citizens, and agricultural workers would have to be overshadowed by that of *barbasquero*, or yam picker. Although the above began as a government-sponsored project, later political transitions, namely a new president, forced campesinos to continue their social transformation as barbasqueros without government backing. In the late 1970s rural Oaxacans, and not the government, were redefining and challenging what it meant to be a campesino in Mexico.

Despite barbasqueros' crucial role in the steroid hormone industry, it was not until the creation of Proquivemex in 1975 that root pickers were officially recognized not only as steroid-industry workers but also specifically as *producers* of barbasco. Later, in 1978, the National Union of Producers and Gatherers of Barbasco (UNPRB), would emerge to represent barbasco pickers on a national level.[3] The misnomer of "producer" reflects the success that Echeverría's rural program had in molding public opinion. Although every major laboratory involved in the steroid industry had a dioscorea experimental and research camp in southern Mexico, there were few concrete successes with actually cultivating barbasco in commercial quantities.[4] In other words, barbasco was not domesticated for production. Campesinos did not cultivate the plant, but rather gathered or picked them wild.

Access to government-approved venues—banks, Secretary of Agrarian Reform (SRA), and teach-ins—expanded the root pickers' self-definition and identity as they embodied different roles associated with their labor, identified with other root pickers across regional and linguistic barriers, joined an organization in places where none had existed before, and learned about their role in the world market.[5]

Tracing Changing Self-Definitions

To trace the transformation from peasant yam pickers to self-named barbasqueros, much of this chapter relies on letters from barbasco leaders to President Luis Echeverría. This material is uncommon, due in part to the illiteracy rate among root pickers and also to the destruction of many barbasco files.[6] Driven in part by well-founded suspicions that the end of Echeverría's presidential term would also mean the end of state subsidies for Proquivemex's socialization project, its staff members encouraged and took part in a frantic letter-writing campaign. They also saw to it that dozens of newspaper articles appeared, alluding to the pressing need to nationalize the industry. These letters, in particular, let us discern peasants' conceptualization and understanding of their position vis-à-vis the nation and of their role as barbasco pickers. The similarities between some letters—style, content, use of key terms—suggest that either the SRA or Proquivemex employees were actively, if not coaching, then suggesting the issues to be addressed and the phrases to be used. Arguably, then, the letters may not offer concrete proof of a barbasco picker's agency in selecting certain terms or focusing on certain issues. I argue, however, that even in copying a possible template, campesino leaders made a conscious choice to align with a state company whose bent, when compared to other state-supported endeavors, was decidedly radical.

Root Pickers Represent the Nation

On March 13, 1976, the front page of the national daily *El Sol de México* reported that "Twenty-five thousand peasants demand that [Luis Echeverría] nationalize the steroid hormone industry." The article went on to explain that for the past twenty-five years, transnational corporations had "bled the country's economy and had grown rich off the hunger of thousands of peasants."[7] The article also reported on an embargo by transnational laboratories against purchasing barbasco from Proquivemex, and thus singled out the foreign companies as those responsible for Proquivemex's inability to function at full capacity.[8] The fact that Mexican exports of diosgenin had plummeted when Proquivemex opened its doors was discreetly omitted.

Instead, the newspaper portrayed peasants as the immediate victims of the companies' machinations, claiming that the transnationals exploited campesinos and the nation by not paying the derechos de monte to peasants in Oaxaca, Veracruz, Puebla, Tabasco, and México. The derecho de monte refers to a Mexican law that demands remuneration for a landowner when a third party exploits natural resources (especially minerals and timber) on the person's land. As the representative of an ejido lamented, the companies "grew rich off our sweat, we who work in the fields, because they never gave us our derechos de monte for exploiting our nation's subsoil."[9] The petition for restitution of ejidos' money was based on the claim that barbasqueros, as ejidatarios, were the immediate owners of the land where barbasco was gathered and, consequently, it was the companies' responsibility to pay the nation for use of the subsoil. Transnational corporations, however, claimed that these demands had no legal foundation because no requests for payment for the exploitation of dioscorea plants had ever been made.[10]

But on both sides, these creative arguments were full of holes. First was the notion of ownership. Due to the very nature of barbasco gathering, there was never an official tally of the number of peasants who harvested the root. The unofficial estimate, circulated among the press, ranged from 25,000 families to 100,000 individuals. No firm record existed because the government considered barbasco collection an ancillary means of subsistence since it grew wild and had few uses locally. Due to the root's lack of tangible *value* in the eyes of those who collected it, it did not lend itself to discussions of ownership. Even those who relied exclusively on barbasco gathering felt "it belonged to no one," whether they dug it up in the jungle or on ejido lands.[11] The loaded meaning of land ownership in the area and the view that barbasco was part of the *acahual* or *monte* (brush) where crops were not planted meant that no single ejido or ejidatario laid claim to the land where the root grew.

By the mid-1970s, however, the perceived value of barbasco had dramatically increased. On a national level, unbeknownst to most pickers, the act of barbasco gathering also gained value. Newspaper headlines echoed this association when they reported that "[CAMPESINOS] DEMAND THAT THE [STEROID] INDUSTRY BE NATIONALIZED,"[12] or "CAMPESINOS ASK THAT THE INDUSTRY BE GIVEN OVER TO MEXICAN HANDS,"[13] or "TWENTY-FIVE THOUSAND CAMPESINOS ASK THAT SIX STEROID PLANTS BE EX-PROPRIATED."[14] In the national imagination the chasm between illiterate campesinos and the world of chemistry had been breached. Campesinos now had every right to demand that which was *theirs*—barbasco—and by extension and surprisingly, they could also call for the nationalization of the steroid hormone industry. A draft of Proquivemex's charter made explicit that it was created to provide more hormone-based products and "*to bene-fit the owners of the land where barbasco grows.*"[15] Consequently the state recognized ejidatarios, communal landholders, as the owners of the tuber, unintentionally creating a future divisive wedge between two groups of root pickers: those who owned land and those who did not.

The Changing Meaning of Land: Owning Barbasco

Barbasco grew on both communally held and private land. Because barbasco was an opportunistic plant, it quickly and easily spread. It appears that dur-ing the early years—especially before the late 1950s' barbasco boom—land-owners did not object to people coming on their property to harvest bar-basco since it was considered part of the surrounding acahual. However, by the late 1960s some campesinos remember that ejidatarios began to charge pickers to enter their lands in search of barbasco. This signifies three things: first, barbasco and its value were now well known in these areas; second, by the 1960s the commercial power of barbasco prompted new and entre-preneurial ways of making money; and third, it might also signal that bar-basco was already becoming a scarce commodity, which undoubtedly gave it more value. By the late 1970s ejidatarios began to buy barbasco from the landless peasants and resell it to the union's buyers at a higher price. There are, unfortunately, no clear studies of how much the ejidatarios paid for this barbasco, but anecdotal evidence suggests that it was a small percentage of what was paid in the collection sites.

This trend also reflects a larger issue, that of the power and privilege linked to land ownership in rural Mexico. Although the 1910 Revolution had ostensibly been about land, the question of who owned Mexican land in the late twentieth century would determine who in the countryside could benefit financially from the steroid hormone industry.

Historical Context

The significance, in 1975, of acknowledging the owners of barbasco is greater when we recall the place that pickers occupied in Mexican society. As mostly indigenous, illiterate, rural, and poor, root pickers were in essence the image of all that modern Mexico had been moving away from. In the decades after the Second World War—in particular the decades of the push for increased industrialization based on agricultural production (1940s–70s)—campesinos had been systematically co-opted into government-controlled organizations. The rural population had borne the brunt of unemployment and had reaped few benefits from the government's plan to bring development to Mexico. Most attempts at independent organization—through which campesinos sought to escape the paternalism and corruption extant in government-subsidized peasant collectives—were swiftly and violently resisted. Problems in the countryside were euphemistically labeled as "the agrarian problem," but few solutions were offered. As a researcher of the time explained, from 1941 onward the authorities did not care about organizing Mexican agricultural workers, because "agricultural products were growing, exports were increasing, we were developing: people spoke of the 'Mexican miracle' and they ignored the misery in which a great part of the peasantry lived."[16] It was not until Luis Echeverría's regime that the president pointedly blamed his predecessors' unwillingness to open the Pandora's box of discontent which the countryside had become.[17]

In describing the effects of the Mexican Revolution (1910–17), the historian Judith Hellman stated, "Mexican political mythology has it that the peasants and workers are the heirs of the Mexican Revolution."[18] Nevertheless, postrevolution development policies implemented in Mexico reflected the interest of those in power and not the revolutionary "heirs." Nearly twenty years after the creation of the 1917 Constitution—which, at least in writing, proclaimed rights, protection, and justice for *all* citizens—President Lázaro Cárdenas's (1934–40) political agenda finally promised to fulfill those rights. Cárdenas's project of political renovation included the promotion of labor unions closely associated with the state, attempts at a rapprochement with marginal sectors and long-awaited agrarian reform. In essence his project for agrarian reform consisted of the allotment of communally owned plots of land (*ejidos*) partitioned from larger tracts of land expropriated from landowners, domestic and foreign. In less than six years he distributed nearly 45 million hectares, compared to the less than 19 million in the nearly twenty years since the revolution's end.[19] But in addition Cárdenas cleverly and successfully gave both peasants and workers a channel through which to express their discontent. However, it was limited to organizations subsidized and controlled by the government. A true political genius, Cárdenas assuaged general discontent in the countryside and urban factories without fully alienating the moneyed business elite, who, cautious of his socialist reforms, threatened to tighten their purse strings on the capital, badly needed for road construction, raising schools, literacy programs, and other socially minded projects the president promoted.

Cárdenas understood that a large portion of Mexico's problems stemmed from its inability to manufacture essential goods, so he injected government subsidies into the industrial sector while making concessions to owners of factories (in the form of mandating low wages for workers, making it unlawful to unionize, and allowing ten- to twelve-hour workdays) with the goal of producing cheap products accessible to all levels of society. Initially, profits would only be enjoyed by the core industrial sector, which in theory would reinvest part of their profits for the welfare of the nation. Indeed, Cárdenas hoped that the push for development would come from the trickling down of the industrial sector's largesse. In Cárdenas's plan, however, there was an implicit acknowledgment that the government would have to subsidize the countryside even after he left office. If the next administration continued the plan, the countryside could potentially produce plentiful and inexpensive crops that would be available to all in Mexico, especially those who earned artificially low wages. In effect the formula partially worked. The business elite got richer, but few funds managed to reach those occupying the lower social strata, in particular campesinos.

Foreseeing this potential flaw Cárdenas planned to redistribute wealth by allocating land to peasants. His hope was that land transfer would transform the peasantry into a productive sector of Mexican society. But the land reforms of the 1930s had an unexpected result. As some scholars noted, ejidos which produced much of Mexico's food "had no overarching organization independent of the state, and, by holding down the prices of agricultural products, the state used its control of peasant organizations effectively to subsidize industrial and urban growth."[20] This strategy also sustained a somewhat marginal self-reproducing reserve labor force that subsidized industrialization by depressing wages. Implemented as a response to the specific demands of the Cárdenas era, this economic approach became a permanent fixture of Mexican agrarian life. Subsidizing industrial growth with cheap agriculture products, however, would sap the countryside. The consequence would be the explosion of the peasant movements of the 1960s and 1970s.

The other significant act of Cárdenas's regime was arguably the expropriation of seventeen foreign oil companies in March 1938. The expropriation was an economic and political tactic which temporarily united a nation still physically and emotionally torn by the effects of the Revolution two decades earlier. It was a public-relations coup when the media captured humble peasants dropping coins into an awaiting collection can that would help Mexico "buy" back the companies from foreign investors. Hence, Mexico, once sold, now *belonged* to these peasants and to all Mexicans who would rally to protect the natural resources within its borders. In the act of "purchasing" the oil companies the disenfranchised sectors of Mexican society momentarily belonged—*were part of*—a nation which constantly and insistently pushed them to the fringes of society. Future presidents would take note of this national fervor and mythical sense of ownership of natural resources to orchestrate political support for decades to come.

Cárdenas's successor, Manuel Avila Camacho (1940–46) put the brakes on this reformist agenda and thus changed the course of the Revolution. By bowing to the interest of business capital and commercial agriculture, he effectively ended the social and political reforms begun by Cárdenas. As historian Stephen Niblo described, the Avila Camacho administration "saw a dramatic shift to the right by which the Mexican Revolution abandoned much of the radical nationalism of the early Cárdenas era and moved toward the adoption of a far more orthodox development program."[21] Avila Camacho used the Cardenista organizational structures to promote growth and to "redistribute income away from the popular sectors that the organizations had been designed originally to favor."[22] Consequently, the rural population existed at a bare subsistence level, unable to accumulate any savings. Alternative employment to agricultural jobs was nonexistent, and there were no venues for organizing other than the state-approved ones.

The above contradiction would characterize much of Avila Camacho's administration but was seen at the time as crucial for the progress of Mexico at war. Taking advantage of the world war raging in Europe, the president implemented a program of *carestía*, or scarcity, which slashed existing public works projects and subsidies for workers and campesinos. These cuts affected programs which had been in place for less than a decade and many of which would never be reinstated, even after the war. The situation in the countryside, exacerbated by the world war, became tense as increasing numbers of men were relegated to the role of day laborers. A partial solution to cope with the increasing number of unemployed peasants came in the guise of the Bracero Program (1942–64), a labor agreement between the United States and Mexico. During the duration of the program, an estimated 12 million Mexican men worked as braceros in the textile, agricultural, manufacturing, and service sectors.[23] The need for employment in the countryside was so palpable that reports tell of riots breaking out among the hundreds of hopeful campesinos at rural bracero-contracting stations when labor quotas were reached.[24] Russell Marker came to Mexico for the first time in the midst of all of this rural upheaval.

The later administration of Adolfo López Mateos (1958–64) commanded an increasingly repressive state, which dealt with force against any sector that chose revolt as a means to manifest growing urban and rural inequalities. However, his administration attempted to continue land reform, handing out a quantity of land that was second only to what Cárdenas had distributed. López Mateos's zeal was driven less by a desire for social justice than by the need to respond to pressures from a growing rural population. Population in the countryside would increase from 14 million in the 1940s to 23 million by 1970.[25] Moreover, land redistribution helped guarantee greater supplies of food for a growing urban population.[26] A problem arose, however. Rather than producing the staples (beans and corn) consumed by most of Mexico's rural population, the focus was on production of commercial crops, consumed by middle-class Mexicans or exported to the United States. Peasants were left with few options as the situation deteriorated in the countryside. The most popular choices were to migrate, join alternative peasant organizations, some of which became armed insurgencies, and undertake land invasions.

During the 1950s an increased number of peasants migrated to Mexico's urban areas, mainly Mexico City, in search of employment. Once in Mexico City most peasants discovered that thousands had come before them and that housing, basic necessities, and government assistance were hard to come by. As more and more people crowded into the city, the living conditions worsened. The government's safety valve continued to be the Bracero Program. In the countryside, however, the situation did not change quickly enough: the salary for campesinos in 1970 was on average 64 pesos a month.[27]

As a second survival strategy, campesinos began to create organizations independent of the state-sanctioned National Peasant Confederation (CNC). Men like Rubén Jaramillo and Lucio Cabañas, frustrated with the corruption of state-sponsored organizations, began a series of land invasions reminiscent of the rural leaders during the Mexican Revolution. This offered an alternative venue through which peasants could finally obtain land, fair wages, and other rights. The final option for peasants frustrated with the Mexican government's inability and unwillingness to meet their demands was armed insurgency.

The Mexican government was gravely concerned about retaining control of the rural population. Campesinos were increasingly left outside of the state's social fabric, which meant they had fewer ties and obligations to the larger society—such as paying land taxes, organizational dues, income tax. Unable to find employment or get access to land, many relied on barbasco collection or other informal employment as their main source of income. Regions of high unemployment not surprisingly began to manifest signs of subversive movements, and the Mexican government became increasingly concerned with quelling the rising unrest, which had been slowly spreading since the 1940s.

Barbasqueros represented a potential solution for a populist government intent on maintaining control over those who remained in the countryside and lived off *el campo*. After three decades of championing industrial and technological growth, in the early 1970s the PRI, led by the recently elected populist president, Luis Echeverría, began to question the cost of the country's progress. As the "Mexican Miracle" sputtered to an end, migration from rural to urban areas increased as did inflation. The countryside had more landless peasants than there had been when President Lázaro Cárdenas implemented his reforms.[28] The demands of a landless, underemployed, or unemployable peasantry were reflected, for example, in more than 600 land invasions in 1973 alone, the intensification of rural guerrilla movements, and the creation of autonomous peasant organizations throughout

Mexico.[29] Between 1969 and 1973, according to a scholar of rural movements, more than 600 campesinos were killed by government forces.[30] The sociologist Gloria Zafra, who wrote about land invasions and repression against the peasants of the Chinantla in the 1970s, stated that between Tuxtepec and Valle Nacional, unrest literally followed "the highway."[31] The areas where barbasco grew most abundantly were among the most volatile.

Echeverría and the Environment

Many of Echeverría's references to barbasco were made from the perspective of environmental protection. Unlike his American counterpart, Richard Nixon (1969–74), however, Echeverría did not enact environment-friendly legislation to appease an increasingly powerful environmental movement. Instead he acted "principally because he feared that the severity of environmental problems in Mexico would result in more political and social unrest."[32] Echeverría's 1973 speech to the Mexican Chamber of Deputies reinforced that:

> The development of technology and industry along with demographic pressures have given rise to great urban concentration without services; moreover erosion, the deterioration of the atmosphere, the contamination of water, the depletion of flora and fauna, malnutrition, low productivity, and illness produce political instability and social unrest. This reality obliges us to avoid danger.[33]

Mexico's ruling party, the PRI, still espoused the notion that rapid industrialization was the answer to the country's development problems. But Echeverría asserted that environmental protection and industrialization could go hand in hand. He argued that multinational corporations were to blame for most of Mexico's environmental problems and were partly responsible for the country's poverty since they, and not Mexico, benefited from the international system of trade.[34] To survive, the impoverished were driven to exploit local natural resources. The creation of Proquivemex was a direct expression of the nation's need for "sovereign control over a natural resource," a right that Echeverría explicitly asserted during his address to the third United Nations Conference on Trade and Development (UNCTAD III). Proposing an attachment to the Declaration of the Universal Rights of Man, he underlined that each nation-state should work to guarantee world peace and respect for human rights. The proposed Article 2 dealt with regulating foreign investment, arguing that each nation-state should have complete control over its natural resources. Consequently, each country had the right to nationalize, expropriate, or transfer any of its natural resources.[35] More importantly, the proposal mandated that a nation-state regulate the activities of transnational companies functioning within its borders to ensure that they fulfill their social and legal responsibilities in that country.[36] Although global in scope and arguably needed the world over, this proposal, as so many associated with Echeverría, did not come to fruition.

State-Backed Campesino Organization

Echeverría's response to campesino mobilization was to publicly transform himself into the ally of the dispossessed and an active promoter of change through increased state intervention in the countryside. Less publicly his administration intensified the search for, incarceration, and killing of subversive peasant leaders. But a letter signed by fourteen barbasco unions enthusiastically embraced the presidential rhetoric of allegiance to campesinos:

> From one corner of the nation to the other, the President of Mexico, Luis Echeverría, shows his deep affection for us, the peasants. We are aware of his unending battle to protect us, we are loyal to his policies, and we are aware that he is a patriotic president who only wants the best for Mexico, because Mexico is the countryside, because peasants are the subsistence of our country.[37]

By the 1970s, however, a 1930's Cardenista approach of parceling out the land was no longer viable, since little arable land was left; nor was it likely to work at a time when the government needed outside investment for its industry and foreign loans to mitigate social problems.[38] Consequently, one of the strategies employed by Echeverría was to increase government spending in the countryside, funneling money to make small ejidos more productive. The creation of the National Fund for Ejido Development (FONAFE) in 1971 increased public funding for agricultural development from 2,628 million pesos in 1970 to 17,595 million pesos by 1976.[39] More important than financial backing, however, was the administration's proposal to reorganize the countryside, taking the ejido as the basic unit for change.

The goal of the so-called Master Plan for Organization and Peasant Training was to organize 11,000 ejidos into successful "economic units" in just two years.[40] On July 8, 1975, in letters addressed to Mexican governors, Echeverría urged them to play a more active role in their states' rural areas. The objective, he argued, was to "stimulate the country's economic and social progress and create a more equitable distribution of wealth among Mexicans."[41] Echeverría's reforms criticized the landed elite and the power of foreign companies in the countryside. In the past, these groups had acted as the government's regional enforcers of national policy. Now, the federal government also proposed to increase its presence in the commercialization of Mexican agriculture by further funding the creation of more state-owned companies: Cordemex for henequen, Tabamex for tobacco, Inmecafe for coffee, and so on, as well as Proquivemex for processing medicinal plants. These parastatals were not exclusively for the countryside. Several hundred were established in urban areas including some producing tile and one, Bicimex, producing bicycles.

Key to the government's success in the countryside was the creation of unions of disparate ejidos, organized by and under the Secretary of Agrarian Reform and the National Peasant Confederation. The unions united ejidos in similar ecological regions and that produced similar crops. Presidential advisors believed that changing how campesinos conceptualized their role in the production process would alleviate the economic problems facing ejidos.[42] For example, a barbasco picker who envisioned himself as a part of a larger group—say, of an ejido, or, better yet, of a collection of ejidos—was no longer as vulnerable or dependent on local social and financial hierarchies. Additionally, the Mexican government would be better able to monitor the ejidos' activities since they would become part of the SRA and the CNC.

An SRA manual (1978) for organizing peasants discusses the benefits of the associations created among ejidos: "With the implementation of these organizational forms there has been a change in the peasant's mentality. He is more active in the ejido, he is achieving optimum use of his resources, and there is a noticeable increase in the economic value of these organizations."[43] Moreover, this restructuring of the countryside presupposed that middlemen would be eliminated from the production cycle, leaving more profits for the producers. The barbasco regions hailed the government's unprecedented proposal. As a coalition of fourteen barbasco ejidos noted: "Problems are getting worse, and it is sad to note that we are in part responsible for our misery. Among us there is misunderstanding, disorganization, selfishness—all of which makes us easy prey to the despotic exploiter who has gotten rich off our ignorance."[44] But Echeverría's promises, purportedly addressed to all campesinos, would come true only for some barbasqueros.

Belonging to Barbasco Unions

According to former barbasco officials, the first ejido organizations established in eastern Oaxaca were based on barbasco.[45] Peasants' previously unsuccessful attempts to organize in the region of Tuxtepec, as well as in many of the other barbasco-producing areas, illustrated the hold of anachronistic local strongmen (*caciques*), the land-tenure systems, the lack of roads, and the unreliable communications system. By June 1976, throughout Mexico the Echeverría administration had established 164 unions (nearly two dozen of them based on barbasco). These comprised 3,000 ejidos, 12 colonias, and 54 communities in 400 municipalities, with more than 225,000 members who received more than 742 million pesos in government credits.[46] These numbers, however, only hint at the importance of the unions for local peasants, especially those who, like barbasqueros, had limited previous contact with state institutions.

At a time when progress in the countryside was increasingly defined by peasants' ability to organize into successful economic units, barbasco unions became the means for bringing change to the countryside around Tuxtepec. The ability of disparate peasants to come together under state-sanctioned unions signified a major triumph for an administration seeking to validate its efforts in rural areas.[47]

After the March 12, 1976, national-level meeting of barbasco unions in Papantla, Veracruz, newspaper articles had succeeded in re-creating the story, making root pickers, and not the wild yam, the leading protagonist. As one article detailed, in Mexico's history "one of the most exploited groups in terms of their labor and their natural resources were the barbasco pickers,"[48] because, as another article explained, they had never been paid "the true value" for the "invaluable element needed for hormone production."[49] The latter article explained that chemists had failed to "reproduce barbasco" in a laboratory setting, making Mexico critical to the steroid hormone industry. Mexican campesinos were still "exploited victims" of transnational corporations because they were paid a mere fraction of the value of the root. Consequently, as the members of the Unión Hilario C. Salas from Mecayapan, Veracruz, wrote: "If we don't nationalize these companies we will forever

FIGURE 27 Teach-ins, such as the above image, allowed members of the National Union of Producers and Gatherers of Barbasco (UNPRB) to walk among maps showing where barbasco grew, look at samples of medications derived from barbasco, and see diagrams of the multi-step process for deriving steroid hormones. Courtesy of Pedro Ramírez.

be victims of foreigners and *coyotes* [middlemen] who exploit the products of our countryside and our natural resources which have no price tag—and yet foreigners have grown rich off of us, the peasants."[50] Hence the exploitation of barbasco, Mexicans now believed, went hand in hand with peasant exploitation. But this battle against abuse was not new. As the letter stated, the source of the problem was the "undeniable fight of campesinos against modern forms of invasion."[51] Many former barbasqueros, when referring to the unions, stated that "the blindfold was removed," and they expressed a deeper understanding of their position in society. As some barbasqueros wrote, "a lot of the things that happen to Mexico are due, in great part, to the lack of general knowledge about things."[52] It was this alleged persistent lack of general information in the countryside—such as the price of products, how to buy a truck, or where to sell one's harvest—that prompted the SRA to push for a different relationship between the Mexican government and campesinos.

Functioning as a form of political control, the peasant unions effectively linked otherwise independent ejidos to the government structure. By belonging to the barbasco unions, peasants became part of a machine that consisted of the CNC's National Executive Committee and official state banks or other credit organizations, such as FONAFE. The barbasqueros benefited from this official recognition. Belonging to a government-sanctioned union lent them much needed credibility in dealing with lenders, bureaucrats, and local leaders. Although they now had to use official channels, it meant they had a means to file complaints, ask for loans, pay permits, and so on.

This was particularly important because many of the better-off residents in the barbasco regions did not consider yam gathering to be work.[53] The barbasqueros were poor even by peasant standards, and because they had to crawl, squat, and dig with their hands in the mud, they were perceived as being dirty. Worse yet, beneficio owners and middlemen fostered the image of a lazy yam picker who came back as early as "noon with sacks full of barbasco," a sign that pickers simply "don't like to work."[54] With the creation of state-sponsored unions, however, barbasqueros' labor was given importance, and local middlemen were supposedly eliminated. With subsidies from the government and advice from the SRA and CNC, pickers envisioned improving their lives. Nevertheless, for a regime that sought to romanticize the plight of campesinos, the poorer, the dirtier, and more exploited the pickers were in the eyes of the nation, the better. Yam pickers' poverty made them appealing to the rest of the country because it represented the country's extreme exploitation at the hands of foreigners.

The incorporation of these peasants into the government's institutional structure revealed how persistently the state sought to establish itself in politically volatile zones. Nevertheless, peasants managed to assert themselves independent of the state. In Tuxtepec, for example, they appropriated the organization, turning it into an institution that would represent their claims. The designation of barbasqueros united the peasants of the Papaloapan under a common banner that could easily be understood throughout Mexico because of its connection with the promise of more affordable medications for all. The newly assigned identity of "barbasquero" ensured that these peasants would be seen as *more than simple campesinos.*

Proquivemex and Barbasqueros

The creation of Proquivemex was "a step closer for peasants' vindication and attainment of economic independence in the Mexican countryside."[55] The relationship between the parastatal and the barbasco unions was officially described as a "contract of association and participation." It would gradu-

ally move barbasqueros from being simple root gatherers to actual participants at all levels of barbasco production, including processing the yam and
negotiating with transnational corporations.[56] During Proquivemex's initial
years (1974–76), however, peasant organization was still limited, and most
barbasqueros continued their routine labor, gathering yams and bringing
them to the company.

Indeed, the rhetorical foundation for the creation of Proquivemex had
been to empower local campesinos by allowing them to control production of barbasco at all levels, to "economically and politically strengthen
the organizations which are central to peasants, pushing to the fore their
true leaders."[57] This proposed social reconstruction was possible because
in Proquivemex's view all peasants were barbasqueros and all barbasqueros
were peasants, with no differences among them. This perception, however,
was quite different from reality.

The government's decision to create unions only for those barbasqueros
who owned land or were ejido members created a rift among the yam-
gathering population. When Proquivemex sought to teach peasants about
barbasco this divisive wedge became more apparent. For the government
and Proquivemex, it was imperative that an imagined identity, embodied in
a coherent group of barbasco pickers, persist. This identity was an imaginary
one, however, because a barbasquero *community* as such did not exist even
though the myth of the unifying power of barbasco persists to the present.

The response of a campesino expresses this division eloquently. When
I approached him on the side of the road outside of Jacatepec in 1999 and
asked him about Proquivemex and barbasco, he hesitantly responded, "I
don't own land, so I don't know anything."[58] When pressed with simpler
questions (for example, what is barbasco), the man continued to repeat that
as a landless campesino, he knew nothing. A former barbasco leader explained this response:

> Somewhere they told us that barbasco was used for soap, because it was
> easy for poor people to grind it and with the soap wash their clothes. Our
> big problem, and it continues to be between the poor and the rich, is that
> there are a lot of things that we don't know about or we don't know the
> appropriate use of the thing. We don't know what they're worth.[59]

Despite what he said, this barbasco leader knew more than many of his
fellow campesinos would ever know about the process and the end prod-

ucts of barbasco. He explained that "our fellow campesinos were cheated," because even though they knew all about barbasco's growth patterns and minute distinctions between types of plants, they never grasped the plant's commercial potential.

The fact that campesinos did not understand the commercial uses of barbasco was attributed to an active effort on the part of companies, who "knew exactly what it was worth" to keep them in the dark."[60] Ironically, in seeking to remedy the inequality created by transnational corporations, the peasant unions created new ones.

Root pickers who attended local and national meetings were told about their rights and about venues for achieving specific goals in their communities; government representatives and barbasco leaders constantly repeated that the campesinos were the rightful owners of barbasco. In a handwritten letter to Alejandro Villar Borja, the director of Proquivemex, the campesinos of Villa de Tapijulapa from the *municipio* of Tacotalpa in Tabasco clearly identified barbasco as theirs: "We join you to demand the nationalization of barbasco from the transnational companies [that are] producers of hormones who have been exploiting us for such a long time by paying a miserable price for *our* product."[61]

More importantly, the meetings were a forum for remote ejidos to become familiar with peasants from other barbasco-producing regions. Members of other national unions discovered, as did Juan Francisco Jacobo, president of the Unión de Ejidos Lázaro Cárdenas,[62] that the union formed a common bond among men and women who previously would not have had a reason to come together. "It is because of the organization that we have all formed a brotherhood and when we land in an ejido we know that we are among our own and that is another advantage."[63]

Finding Identities beyond Pickers

In 1977, Crispo Pérez, a campesino from Veracruz, wrote a letter to a barbasco consultant. With an unsteady hand, he carefully crossed out many words and rewrote them before continuing the letter. After stating his reason for writing, "the need to bring teachers to the Ejido Fernando López Arias School," Pérez added an interesting detail: "I am writing the History of the beneficio where I work and for which I am responsible as well as [taking] photographs of the [it.] I will send them by mail."[64]

As it turns out, Pérez was a *delegado* (representative) for the barbasco union 23 de Junio La Toma de Zacatecas,[65] an elected position he shared with one other ejidatario. As delegado, he represented his ejido at the National Assembly of Barbasqueros and had the added responsibility of conveying to his fellow ejidatarios all the information pertaining to barbasco that he gathered. The beneficio he ran most likely had been expropriated from one of the six transnational pharmaceutical companies.[66] He probably oversaw the purchase of fresh barbasco, the fermentation and drying process, and the loading of barbasco onto trucks bound for either the Proquina or Syntex laboratories. During the high season (June through September), if this particular beneficio was an average-sized one, as many as ten tons of fermented barbasco could be carefully laid out on hot concrete slabs each week. There, the heat would transform the pasty substance into grainy, earth-brown "flour," rich in diosgenin.

It was not uncommon for an ejidatario to hold this position of power in a beneficio. As we have learned, all six companies had always employed local men as overseers in the diosgenin-producing process. The difference, however, was that ejidatarios now *owned* the beneficio and all its machinery.

Fortunately, in his letter, Pérez, a self-defined peasant, explained why he intended to record the history of the place where he worked in words and pictures: "I know that you are going to formulate a book about the product Barbasco." He said he wanted to contribute both his experience and knowledge. By offering to write a narrative of barbasco, Pérez was refiguring the history of the root in Mexico from the *perspective* of a campesino.[67] In a region where campesinos' workplaces were historically associated with abuse, rights violations, and little legal recourse, Pérez's effort to extol his beneficio was definitely a rarity.

Belonging to the uniones de ejidos created new spaces for campesinos to voice their concern, and some individuals, such as Crispo Pérez, used their newly acquired knowledge to question their position as campesinos. It is worth noting that in the letter mentioned above, Pérez adds a historical analysis. He proposes a new analysis of oppression filled with revolutionary heroes, but adds the crucial element that transnational corporations were the bane of peasant life. As his letter states, in meetings when "everyone speaks of history they mention Revolutionaries but no one is capable of telling the truth because Zapata was like villa [*sic*] but no one mentioned the transnationals."[68] His explanations echo Proquivemex's teachings and urge others to analyze the role of transnationals in Mexico's past.

Pérez was not alone in his quest to educate outsiders about barbasco pickers. Others within the ranks of barbasqueros began to express their concerns from peasants' points of view. In coming together, barbasco ejidatarios discovered that they had more in common than barbasco. Poverty, unemployment, injustice, and oppression were not localized but spread evenly throughout Mexico's barbasco lands. As this realization united them, the general assemblies began to demand more than a just better price for barbasco.

Moving Beyond Echeverría's Vision

In conversations with other ejidatarios, barbasqueros discovered that transnational corporations owed ejidatarios the *fondo común* (a common fund),[69] which according to newspaper articles amounted to 470 million pesos. After learning of the amount due them, the president of the Unión Emiliano Zapata Salazar, Mario Sentís López, wrote in 1976 to President Echeverría, "Imagine, Mr. President, if they had paid us that common fund, today . . . we would have . . . not only cattle, but schools, industries, roads, and plenty of other things to live in better conditions."[70]

In a series of letters referring to the fondo común, the transnational corporations and their agents, the local caciques, are depicted as the clear culprits. The government, or President Echeverría, needed to be informed of these injustices so that he could put a stop to it. Campesinos' letters revealed the hope that when Luis Echeverría became aware of their plight, he would castigate the wrongdoers and reward the patriotic barbasqueros by getting a fair price for their product. Campesinos hoped that by aligning themselves with the president, their project would be furthered. As members of an ejido explained:

> We are aware of the problems with barbasco, but we also know how much you want the commercialization of this project and the well being for our families, our colonists, and the men of the countryside who form this union, all of us are with the Union and with you, Mr. President. Our great President Luis Echeverría Alvarez we are firmly with you and against those transnational companies who have exploited us for so long.[71]

From the point of view of root pickers, the achievement of recognition as barbasqueros through the creation of barbasco unions was due to *their* struggle or battle against transnational corporations, against caciques, and against middlemen:[72]

> We understand the creation of Proquivemex to be not a great triumph, but the beginning of a great battle and we need to understand that there are some great powers that would have preferred that the battle end here and that our Organization would have acted, as one of peasant leaders said, as a springboard to strengthen the interests of the large transnational companies.[73]

By the first months of 1976, those who spoke for the barbasco unions announced how they, as campesinos and specifically as barbasqueros, could contribute to the country's well-being, such as when campesinos explained who should profit from the barbasco trade: "We don't want these funds to benefit only a small group of campesinos. We hope to contribute to Mexico, to our Mexican nation, where laboratories that produce medications that we so desperately need and which are so expensive, can be Mexican laboratories."[74] By that time, barbasco leaders had appropriated the nationalization of the steroid hormone industry as their *own* battle because, they asserted, "a Mexican product, such as barbasco, must benefit the Mexican peasantry."[75]

The state project—to organize a dispersed band of root pickers into recognizable campesino unions—had subtly veered out of control. Campesino barbasco pickers were told of their worth by state institutions and, encouraged by a young and enthusiastic Proquivemex staff, they went beyond the state's projected change. Once having understood the importance of barbasco to Mexico and to the world, some yam pickers would not stop until they had seen the industry nationalized.

Fighting for Chemists

To form a collective identity, barbasqueros needed a common enemy or antagonist. In their immediate reality, it initially was the middlemen or caciques who controlled the land and consequently their options for self-employment. But for the organization to gain national recognition, barbasqueros also needed to address a national enemy to which the rest of the Mexican population could relate: transnational pharmaceutical companies.

The campesinos stated, "While they have a right derived from coercion, we have the strength that the law gives us."[76] The companies became, as had the oil companies in the 1930s under Cárdenas, the emblem of what was wrong in Mexico. The presence of pharmaceutical companies absolved the government of mismanagement and corruption in the countryside and of an inability to understand the health crisis, because it was the pharmaceutical companies that in the end controlled the profits from medications. Consequently, a battle plan for nationalization was set in motion. A letter from the Unión Lic. Adolfo López Mateos in Hidalgotitlán, Veracruz, details the reasons for waging battle:

> May we fight together so that transnational companies, which still exist in Mexico, exploiting not only our products but our chemists and also ourselves, be nationalized so that we, as Mexicans, fix the price for those pharmaceutical products extracted from Barbasco and not the transnational laboratories which have always lived off our resources and our sweat. That vast capital belongs to us.[77]

Before demanding a price for fresh barbasco that would earn them a subsistence-level wage, these ejidatarios first listed the needs of chemists, other Mexicans, and the nation as a whole, to underscore that nationalization would benefit everyone in the country.

For campesinos in the barbasco regions and for the national press, barbasco became the banner for seeking independence from foreign domination.[78] As one newspaper noted, "The struggle over barbasco is a struggle which summarizes our deepest and oldest desires for the Mexican people. The battle for liberty and for independence."[79] This nationalist rhetoric echoed the speeches of Luis Echeverría and reflected the desires of Mexican society to rid themselves of the economic exploitation by transnational pharmaceutical companies.[80]

Clearly, the barbasqueros were leading the battle. The newspaper articles described them as *ejércitos* (armies), and in their assemblies they were rallied to battle against the amorphous transnational pharmaceutical companies.[81] Campesinos chosen to lead the barbasqueros moved to the national headquarters in Mexico City, and with the change in residence came a transformation of the individual. Delfino Hernández remembered that during the first general assembly in Chiapas (1976), where he was elected national president for the barbasqueros, he was too shy to speak up. Belonging to the organization, however, "opened my eyes."[82]

The Change in Barbasqueros

The struggle over barbasco was subtly changing campesinos' self-perception: "We must offer them [transnational companies] our hand, as the gentlemen that we are, before taking drastic measures. That is the right of all Mexican peasants."[83] Campesinos were suddenly transformed from uncouth rural laborers to gentlemen. Peasants, however, would be acting like gentlemen not because they were benevolent toward their oppressors but, as they explained, "because with modern communications the entire world is watching what is happening in our country, and we must show the world that Mexico is not a country of barbarians."[84] Progressive barbasqueros were bringing their modern way of debate to the countryside. It appeared that root pickers, contrary to other peasants, would not rely on uprisings; instead, if we believe the writer of the quotation above, discourse and diplomacy were to be the modes of battle.

In addition, attitudes toward what campesinos could accomplish, reminiscent of Crispo Pérez's actions, also shifted. "This area was once run by a chemical engineer, but now the leader is an ejidatario Professor Mario Vianey Malpica Bernabé[;][85] this leads us to believe that we, the peasants, are capable of organizing, leading, administering and executing activities that until recently were considered to be the domain of a specific group."[86]

When barbasco gatherers asserted their identity in new social surroundings with meetings in Tuxtepec, in Mexico City, and with transnational corporations, they inevitably transformed the identity of the *barbasquero as a root gatherer* to that of the *barbasquero as protector of Mexico's natural resources*. By these actions, the campesinos asserted that they *were* different from other campesinos. They were not opposed to a project of modernity they could embrace—but on their own terms: they would appropriate barbasco as their own because, as they put it, barbasco grows in "in the mountains that belong to us."[87]

In another example of campesinos' growing assertiveness, a group of ejidatarios from Minatitlán, Veracruz, wrote to protest a newspaper article printed in 1976 in *Excelsior* that reported that the same people who once worked in transnational corporations were now working at Proquivemex.[88]

However most newspaper coverage was quite positive, portraying Proquive-mex's potential as so powerful that if the company functioned at its full capacity, it would curtail migration to the cities and end the international labor migration to the United States. The hope was that "transnational companies will understand that the exploitation of the men of the countryside is a thing of the past."[89]

Despite claims of self-sufficiency, campesinos readily acknowledged that Echeverría had "opened the door" for them. "This theft lasted until you as a Mexican and with your desire to serve all of Mexico, without distinction of classes, managed to control the large returns derived from barbasco."[90]

> Mr. President, as you say "up and keep going" in the Nationalization of transnational laboratories. . . . Since they never gave us the *derecho de monte* after they exploited our country's subsoil, and grew rich with our sweat, we want to give the decisive step by your side in this battle, Go Home Transnationals![91]

> We now know that [price increase] does not affect the enormous profits made by those companies but poor planning for the exploitation of barbasco would create a crisis in which more than a hundred thousand campesinos would be affected.[92]

Empowered by political and economic backing, letters from barbasco unions changed in tone. Phrases such as "we demand" (*exigimos*) and "we deserve" (*merecemos*) noticeably replaced more subservient vocabulary, such as "we beg" (*rogamos*) and "we ask" (*pedimos*):

> We insist and demand if necessary *the nationalization of the chemical steroid industry*, a transcendental act which would mark the end of our shameful dependence on transnational companies.[93]

> We acknowledge that our struggle has not been easy, but definitely just, and that is why through this medium we want to tell the exploiters of our people that we will no longer buckle in the face of the exploitation of which we have been victims for more than 25 years.[94]

After the first National Congress of Barbasqueros, the root pickers' demands solidified.[95] In the event that transnational corporations would not pay a "just" price, barbasqueros offered a solution: the companies would withdraw from Mexico and "as payment to the root pickers leave behind the well-equipped laboratories."[96] In that way, the campesinos argued, "Mexico will be the one to industrialize its natural resources linked to the steroid industry."[97]

The implicit message was that Mexicans did not need foreign technology, specifically foreign chemists, because the nation was equipped to process steroid hormones on its own; it had barbasco and campesinos who would pick it. In reasserting their status as "producers" and "pickers," barbasqueros were also overcoming the negative stereotypes associated with barbasco collection. By gaining membership in institutions such as the SRA and the CNC, barbasqueros were becoming the public face of the campesino. And in their own minds, if only by association, they were acquiring the technological know-how to develop the steroid hormone industry.

National Security and Barbasco

Alejandro Villar Borja's actions and his popularity among campesinos triggered close monitoring by the government. As Echeverría's administration came to an end, Villar Borja was replaced but fought to retain some role within the barbasco trade. To the chagrin of the government, he eventually became an independent consultant to the barbasqueros. Declassified national security accounts of the time report that this "minor functionary" with "Marxist ideas and possibly a member of the Mexican Workers' Party with whom he surely sympathizes" considers himself "a guide to campesinos," with whom "he adopts messianic attitudes."[98] Especially problematic for the government was that Villar Borja "insists that Proquivemex belongs to them [campesinos]," and he attempted to remain at the helm of Proquivemex, despite having been replaced, by distributing "nearly 1 million pesos" to campesino unions.[99] Even more disturbing for Mexican national security was that according to a report in a section labeled "intentions," Villar Borja, if left to his own devices could gain control of the "cane and tobacco workers, the producers of coffee, cacao, and other Southeastern [Mexico] groups."[100]

By 1977 twenty-nine barbasco unions were representing hundreds of barbasco-picking ejidos. Given that rural organizations were thought to be simmering with plans for revolt against the government, a popular agitator, such as the director of Proquivemex, needed to be controlled. The government concretely detailed its response to this potential threat: "Provide funds and people to the Mexican Workers' party," and create "a smokescreen" (*cortina de humo*) regarding the "serious faults" committed by Villar Borja during his administration of Proquivemex. Newspaper reports of the time, strongly critical of Villar Borja and his role in Proquivemex, illustrate that the government smokescreen succeeded.

Beyond barbasco's obvious financial importance, the reason for keeping a national-security file on barbasco and Proquivemex was explained in an earlier report, which noted that a substantial number of barbasco pickers lived in such remote areas that it was extremely difficult to distribute government aid there. Consequently and in conjunction with CONASUPO (the government-subsidized grocery store chain), the government sponsored a floating store near the Raudales Dam in Malpaso, Chiapas. The floating Conasupo store would travel to "the most remote zones and supply provisions and clothes to campesinos producers of barbasco who may request [the aid]."[101] The interest in barbasco pickers clearly went beyond the need to keep remote campesinos clothed and fed but, as mentioned earlier, some guerrilla groups had on occasion claimed to be barbasco pickers or students searching for areas to cultivate the yam. Thus, it was in the government's interest to provide subsidies to those who could become targets for existing or future groups critical of the government.[102]

The new administration at Proquivemex turned its focus from campesinos back to chemistry with the apparent approval of a new presidential administration. So even as news was spreading about specific government subsidies for root pickers and though many campesinos enthusiastically believed new promises, the new presidential administration had moved away from Echeverría's established goals. In the next chapter, we briefly explore how Proquivemex's vision could not survive with the country's changing economic and political priorities.

Conclusion

The hopes and demands expressed in peasants' letters are testimony to their understanding of the increasing importance of Proquivemex and barbasco in their daily lives. At a time when peasant upheavals and repression were increasing in the countryside, peasant organizations sanctioned by the state lent legitimacy and brought much-needed funds to rural areas. To gain control of the steroid industry, the Mexican state needed root-picking campesinos to embrace a barbasquero identity and demand their rights as pickers. In turn, to get subsidies from the state, campesinos became barbasqueros.

Taking their cue from the state, some pickers merged multiple social roles—farmer, community member, day laborer—to highlight their role as barbasqueros. In other words, the state offered them the label of "barbasquero" to lend legitimacy to their organizational project, and campesinos molded it to represent what was important to them. From barbasco union letters, we glimpse how barbasqueros embraced the identity and began to define themselves in terms of their role as root pickers. But what does this barbasquero identity reveal about rural Mexico?

At a broad level, it illustrates how malleable the term *campesino* truly was by the 1970s in Mexico. A barbasquero did not cultivate the land or produce crops (despite the fact that barbasco unions were labeled "producers of barbasco"); nor did they in most cases *own* land, the battle cry of the Revolution. Most were day laborers, recent migrants to the area, widowed women, young children—in short, marginal members of rural society. That the CNC and other state institutions courted and eventually sanctioned them as peasants also illustrates just how necessary it was for the state to be able to group scattered individuals into easily controlled social units by giving them a particular designation.

Moreover, the emergence of the barbasqueros illustrates that Lázaro Cárdenas's shadow had faded but was still present in the Mexican countryside in the 1970s. For example, the state's ability to create an organization based on the medicinal root illustrates the state's continued importance to the countryside. Without the participation of the SRA, the CNC, or Nacional Financiera (the economic link), the barbasco organization and the movement would not have been possible. Peasant letters also reveal a basic tenet: it did not matter how funds were labeled or what they were expressly used for as long as peasants *had* funds.

Likewise, the actions of barbasqueros help us to understand how campesinos in the mid-twentieth century struggled to have their voices heard. We learn just how effectively peasants were able to manipulate words, concepts, and nationalistic sentiments to benefit their own agendas. The venues through which they could voice their discontent were all government-sponsored ones. In order for campesinos to be heard, they had to use the language of those in power. Certain individuals—such as Crispo Pérez or Eusebio Jiménez at the beginning of this chapter—not only used the language, they also acted on those words by writing their own history.

Historians argue that despite the vast economic, technical, and bureaucratic resources showered on the countryside during Echeverría's term, a change in power structures—similar to that witnessed during the Cardenista years—never occurred in the countryside in the 1970s. On the contrary, according to the historian Gustavo Gordillo, the high point of transformations did not belong to peasant organizations but to government agencies that brought these organizations into being. The government did not change the countryside because the way in which it entered the countryside reinforced existing forms of oppression. The historian Fernando Rello argues that in the 1970s the "modern cacique" did not isolate himself geographically but rather welcomed the flow of government projects as a means to become the essential mediator between the region and the nation. The cacique, Rello explains, "did not oppose modernization as long as it did not undermine his power base.[103] Soon dominant groups came to understand that government-subsidized programs could be used as a source of wealth and power.

Del barbasco no nos quedó nada
[Of the whole barbasco affair, nothing was left for us].
Campesino from Cinco de Oro, interview, Oaxaca, June 1999

ROOT OF DISCORD ● 9

By the early 1980s, Proquivemex's initial and, some believed, naive inflexibility toward pharmaceutical companies had instead given way to a resigned understanding that Mexico simply could not compete on a global scale without transnational pharmaceutical companies. Proquivemex's earlier promises—inexpensive medications and self-sufficiency for root pickers—were recalled as quixotic goals as a new director traveled the globe in search of clients. As the state company struggled to compete at an international level, barbasco production systematically decreased in Mexico, and by late 1979 diosgenin was being *imported* into the country.

The primacy of Mexico had so swiftly deteriorated that in February of 1980 the new director of Proquivemex, Manuel Puebla, wrote to the director general of the Department of Plant Sanitation (Sanidad Vegetal), to try to find out what permits were required to import 350 tons of barbasco from Guatemala.[1] This action was more surprising because a mere two weeks earlier, Puebla had written to the undersecretary of Forestry and Fauna, Cuauhtémoc Cárdenas, to request permission to obtain 2,700 tons of dried barbasco from the six main barbasco-producing states in Mexico.[2] In his request for a permit, the director stressed that all Proquivemex contracts be made with participating barbasco unions sanctioned by Agrarian Reform. Though the search was on for more barbasco from other countries, the orders for diosgenin were significantly lower than in previous years.

A few months later, in May, the Oaxacan representatives of Proquivemex met with the gubernatorial candidate to guarantee that the more than 50,000 Oaxacan peasants who depended on barbasco could count on a harvest of 35 million kilos of barbasco.[3] The lower demand was a result of medical and chemical advances in patent medication made possible, ironically, by earlier work using barbasco for research.[4] For example, the boom in steroid hormone production of the 1960s was connected to the discovery of oral contraceptives high in estrogen—which necessitated larger quantities of diosgenin—but with intense secondary effects. By the 1970s traditional dosages were perfected and reduced; consequently, the need for steroids from diosgenin diminished.[5] Science had perfected steroid hormones to the degree that instead of larger quantities of raw materials, better, more potent hormone synthetics were available. By 1980 the drop in diosgenin content in barbasco and the decline in orders for more diosgenin warranted alarming editorials in Mexico City daily newspapers, which predicted the closure of Proquivemex.[6] Competing directly with barbasco were other natural products, such as soy and henequen, which yielded compounds similar in chemical structure to barbasco's diosgenin.[7]

Furthermore, the political atmosphere, which had fostered and catapulted the needs of barbasco pickers to the fore in the mid-1970s, was very different by the 1980s. The mood was reflected in newspaper headlines which, this time, gave voice to businessmen who demanded that President José López Portillo (1976–82) "privatize state-owned companies."[8] Business demands were buoyed by the new administration's attitude toward campesinos. As a politician put it, the government could no longer pretend to "do the work of agricultural producers"—training campesinos and offering large subsidies—because then the country would "stagnate instead of moving forward."[9]

Finally, by the early 1980s the financial crisis, which prompted neoliberal reforms that would culminate in the eventual closure of many of Mexico's state-owned companies, was already under way. As a result Proquivemex no longer enjoyed the large subsidies that had kept it afloat during its turbulent initial years. Plus, in a strange reversal of its former policies, the Mexican government allowed national companies to go above Proquivemex and import Chinese diosgenin directly into the country.[10] With the latter practice the Mexican government effectively brought to a close a period that had linked barbasco to the nationalist and protectionist tendencies of an earlier era.

As the awareness of Proquivemex's lost priority sunk in, its role changed at all levels. For example, Proquivemex attempted to diversify its "vegetables" and include other medicinal plants in its manufactured products. Among these were *toloache* (Jimson weed), vinca, *higuerilla* (castor oil plant), papaya, and jojoba. Ironically, this was also the period when, for the first time, campesinos actually met some of the initial and fanciful goals of Proquivemex: a successful and autonomous organization and the completion of a laboratory in the Papaloapan run by campesinos. This chapter explores the brief rise and eventual disappearance of the peasant-controlled barbasco trade set up in the countryside. What these peasant organizations reveal is that by the mid-1980s, barbasco had become a mere vehicle for guaranteeing continued government support and a means of preserving rural organization.

International Market Redefines Barbasco Supply

In contrast to Alejandro Villar Borja—who had made the root pickers central to the mission of the company—for the new director of Proquivemex, Puebla, it was crucial that Proquivemex establish itself as a competitive international company. Puebla in some ways achieved this goal and showed that a small state-owned company in the developing world could be taken seriously in an industry dominated by transnational corporations. For example, by early 1980 Proquivemex signed accords with companies in Hungary, Germany, and the United States to process barbasco and began to actively publicize its business on a global scale.[11] Many foreigners found information on Proquivemex in the commercial directory of the Mexican embassies of their respective countries. Such had been the case of a managing director of Bluebell, a cosmetics company in Tokyo, who contacted Proquivemex in his quest to find cactus juice for Bluebell's beauty line.[12] While the fate of that particular business connection is not known, that same year one of Proquivemex's administrators took a fifteen-day business trip, selling "products" and "initiating conversations" with the leading European steroid manufactures in Portugal, Germany, and Italy.[13]

Letters reveal the itineraries followed by Proquivemex employees as they circled the globe in search of buyers. Their quest was likely connected to earlier complaints by Puebla to the undersecretary of commerce about the, again, serious "dumping of Chinese diosgenin" into Mexico.[14] The flooding of the international market with Chinese diosgenin, according to the letter, was worrisome for two reasons. Proquivemex was at "a critical juncture" because alternative raw materials were displacing barbasco and second, Proquivemex was attempting to recapture the steroid market by making intermediate and advanced steroids in its plant in Tuxtepec, Oaxaca. To this end Proquivemex had ended its commercial partnership with the Upjohn Company of Kalamazoo, Michigan, and had taken over Upjohn's Guatemalan experimental camps. This single move, Proquivemex's director hoped, would give the state-company a profit of nearly 9 million pesos and the upper hand in the market. But with cheaper Chinese diosgenin available, these plans were seriously derailed.

Adding to the uncertainties of dwindling barbasco supply and alternative products replacing the yam on the market, a state company such as Proquivemex faced an increasingly tense domestic climate as Mexico's economy worsened. Evidence of how deeply the national economy affected Proquivemex's daily activities was apparent in its most mundane decisions. For example, in the summer of 1980 the organizers of Tuxtepec's regional fair and exposition wrote asking for use of a truck to transport locals to the event; the building and expansion of a diosgenin-processing plant had shown locals that "Proquivemex is one of the federal parastatals with the most impact in the region." Although Proquivemex was promised one of the largest stands at the fair because, as the organizers proudly added, Tuxtepec and its surroundings "were the leading areas in Oaxaca where the root" was produced and gathered in large quantities, Puebla denied the use of the vehicle.[15] The reason behind the denial is quite revealing. Puebla wrote that while the zone chiefs would gladly participate in the expo, they did "not have any funds because of the financial crisis" and so suggested that the organizers contact the Papaloapan Commission instead.[16] Gone were the times when the previous director had used 1 million pesos to appease restless barbasco pickers. As Proquivemex struggled to find its footing in a new political and commercial atmosphere and the market for barbasco declined, what was happening to root pickers?

National Economy Affects Barbasco Regions

The immediate aftermath of the decline of the barbasco market was captured by a German researcher, Sigrid Diechtl, who in early 1980 traveled to various ejidos to document any social changes for a special report commissioned by the Ministry of Agriculture and Hydraulic Resources (SARH). Diechtl formed part of a binational research team, Mexico-Germany Accord on Forests, housed within the SARH in Mexico City. The single question driving her inquiry was: How important had barbasco been in this area? The evidence was staggering.

With an obvious eye for detail, Diechtl described the extreme poverty in the barbasco region surrounding Papantla, Veracruz. For example, she noted that Ejido Gildardo Muñoz was so "very poor" that it did not even have a store: "all merchandise is trucked in through intermediaries at exorbitant prices."[17] While the ejido's commissioner had at one point collected barbasco, it had been three years since any yams had been purchased. Not only had supplies of barbasco drastically diminished but, more disturbing, the Proquivemex owed the ejido 50,000 pesos. The only money received from the barbasco trade, four years earlier, had gone toward purchasing two young calves and some medicine. The commissioner added a curious detail: he cautioned that it was not worth it to purchase barbasco, because locals would rob any stored yams at night and resell it to the same buyer in the morning. Moreover, Proquivemex refused to purchase rotted or rotting barbasco, which was, as we learned in chapters 3 and 5, nearly impossible to avoid.

A similarly desperate situation was reported in Ejido Plan de Hidalgo, a mere twenty kilometers from the majestic ruins of El Tajín. Though ethnically Totonaca the ejido dwellers were all bilingual, and Diechtl was able to interview some of them. Proquivemex, it appeared, also owed this ejido money, and though the campesinos had been told that barbasco would once again be bought, most of the yams had been lost when surrounding lands were transformed into pasture for cattle. The same situation was observed in nearby Ejido San Diego, prompting several campesinos to ask Diechtel, "When are they going to buy barbasco again?" Not surprisingly, the situation was not any better in the *beneficio*.

The largest beneficio in the region, one called, appropriately, El Tajín, was completely abandoned but for two watchmen who alternated between the day and night shift. This was quite dramatic given that a mere three years earlier El Tajín reportedly operated twenty-four hours a day in eight-hour shifts, and employed nearly a thousand campesinos.[18] The situation was more dire in Beneficio San Escobal, also abandoned and with two resident watchmen. Though the warehouse had been filled with dry barbasco the previous year, it had not operated in four years. Diechtl observed fifteen sacks of barbasco, partially eaten by rats. Moreover, signs of graft, which would plague later officials, were widely apparent. The researcher noted that the highest price, "paid fast and easy," was two pesos per kilogram of barbasco, but Diechtl added that if this was indeed right it was fifty cents below the official price established by Proquivemex in the area.[19] This discrepancy meant that a buyer, or buyers, were skimming fifty cents off each kilogram of barbasco.

In 1999, when I interviewed Diechtl in her home in Catemaco, Veracruz, she vividly recalled that earlier research trip despite her many years working for the Mexico-Germany accord. As a recently arrived German national in Mexico, Diechtl had never heard of the dioscorea but was astounded by the number of people involved in the barbasco trade.

But campesinos were not the only ones affected by changing policies within Proquivemex. A beneficio owner from Catemaco, Veracruz, recalled working in his beneficio as an employee for the state company, and, "On one occasion they forced me to pay seven tons' worth for a truck that was filled with three tons of yams and four of dirt. When I saw [what they were doing] I realized that the company was going head first into failure."[20] With Proquivemex's reputation in swift decline, fewer roots, and decaying beneficios, the new generation of general managers at Proquivemex would have the difficult task of gaining the trust of the only ones capable of harvesting barbasco and who had been made so many promises: the campesinos.

Laboratories in the Jungle

In 1978 construction of two planned diosgenin-processing plants in rural areas had been halted.[21] What this meant, aside from the obvious point that the state company was having difficulty accomplishing its original goals, was that the mission of transforming campesinos into white-coated workers in laboratories was also shifting. But the populist project was not completely dead. The construction of a plant for the production of intermediary steroids was begun in 1980 in the outskirts of Tuxtepec, Oaxaca. A federal subsidy of 25 million pesos was allocated for the Oaxacan plant with the expectation that it would process a minimum of fifty tons of diosgenin per year.[22] Two years later, in 1982, all construction was stopped while an audit of Proquivemex was conducted. Proquivemex's fate now rested within the Secretariat of Energy, Mines and State-Owned Industries. After months of reviewing financial records, the ministry temporarily shut down the Tuxtepec plant. The audit found that Proquivemex Agroindustrial, the division devoted to the production of medications, had only four clients, one of which, Proquivemex's other branch, represented 63 percent of sales.[23]

There were various attempts in 1983 to restart processing barbasco in Tuxtepec, but most failed because of lack of funds to fix or replace damaged or aging equipment.[24] While the documents do not detail what these dwindling funds meant to the region, former employees, local people, expressed their disappointment that the processing plant had shut down. One of these, Fidel Santiago Hernández, son of a former barbasco union chapter president of Valle Nacional, proudly described how he had been hired to work there. His pride stemmed from the fact that, as he explained, "not just anyone could work there" because "chemistry" (*química*) was done there.[25] When asked to elaborate, he described his duties in the following terms: "There they used to weigh 500 kilos [of barbasco] in a reactor. . . . They added hot water and then *sosa*. Sosa is sulfuric acid. That reaction took two and a half hours at 160 degrees, after that you added cold water, then hot and cold again." Recalling another task in the laboratories, he added, "Diosgenin came from there. It was white like flour, like cocaine; yeah it looked like that. Diosgenin was then shipped to the laboratories in Mexico [City]."[26] Despite the fact that Santiago Hernández had just detailed part of his labor, when questioned if he was surprised to see a root transformed into medicine he shrugged and stated, "Maybe the chemist performed an 'exorcist' [*sic*] on it" (a la mejor el químico hizo un exorcista). To this day the shell of what was to be a literal jungle laboratory staffed by locals is in the outskirts of Tuxtepec.

The Need for an Independent Union

In 1986 an unpublished document assessed the role of campesino organizations involved in barbasco collection. It argued that although it took thirty years (1945–75), root pickers had indeed won the right to organize into ejido unions.[27] But a recurring problem for the organization was the difficulty in controlling an association whose members were geographically dispersed, and who were dependent on a plant that grew in the wild and with deep market price fluctuations. In spite of these drawbacks and with substantial difficulty, between 1978 and 1986 the national organization known as National Union of Producers and Gatherers of Barbasco (UNPRB) consolidated.

Although barbasco unions were characterized by a complicated and thorny maturation period, they had achieved many of their initial goals. As we saw earlier, many campesinos *did* gain awareness or general understanding of their role in the production process, and of the opportunities to organize around a product, make demands, and maneuver within a changing bureaucracy. This knowledge, however, was not evenly distributed but instead was vertically divisive, transforming some campesinos into power holders. In spite of the all-encompassing rubric the UNPRB was also not uniform. Oaxaca, for example, contained six regional unions representing sixty municipalities in the Chinantec, Mazatec, and Mixe zones. The 450 ejidos, communities, *colonias*, and "new population centers" totaled more than 50,000 campesinos who gathered barbasco.[28]

Future Proquivemex administrations—typified by their directors, Manuel Puebla (1977–82) and Manuel Calderón de la Barca (1982, only six months)—were characterized by a series of relapses in the countryside to the time before Proquivemex: local strongmen, low prices for barbasco, and stronger affinity between Mexican business interests and transnational companies than between Mexican business and campesinos. During these periods campesinos appeared mainly in official documents, but were rarely given priority within the organization.

In the first months of 1977 Proquivemex attempted to weather the change of a presidential administration. President López Portillo had declared that the only practices from transnationals which he would not condone were abuse and exploitation, but he added that his tenure would not be hostile to foreign investment because, "We want foreign investment that will help our country develop its natural resources."[29] Initially undeterred, Proquivemex continued with its plan to manufacture domestic medications for use in Mexico's public healthcare system, the IMSS. But Proquivemex's project was short lived.

As we saw, within months of López Portillo's taking office, Villar Borja was unceremoniously removed as director of the company and was replaced with the chemical engineer from Sonora, Manuel Puebla.[30]

Under Puebla's command, Proquivemex manifested a decidedly commercial bend that reflected the new administration's goals—more emphasis on economic progress and less on a social agenda. But, unwilling to release his hold on Proquivemex and its ideals, Villar Borja would remain an independent consultant to the *uniones de ejidos* through most of 1978.[31] From this position, he battled against the new Proquivemex administration, arguing that the campesinos had been forgotten in the administrative shuffle. What campesinos now had, however, was an incipient organization from which *they* could voice their opposition to national decrees. The ejido unions were quick to declare their concern with the new administration, and they also issued the following warning in the press: "Proquivemex is not the owner of barbasco and consequently we all, in solidarity, are in agreement that we will not commercialize a single kilo of barbasco if it is not at the agreed price of 70 pesos per kilo."[32]

In April 1977, barely two months after that newspaper article, the ejido unions, which emerged because of Proquivemex, were violently attacking the state company in the press. Their complaints were varied but specific. For example, the divisions that Proquivemex's new administration was creating among the pickers alarmed them. Proquivemex allegedly bypassed the unions and instead offered individual campesinos more money for their barbasco. In addition, there were reports that some unions felt their existence threatened if they persisted in their demands for a higher price for barbasco.[33] When Proquivemex cancelled a meeting where prices for barbasco would be discussed, campesinos declared that the company's intent was to destroy the campesino organization. More alarming, campesinos reported that "we do not understand why a policy that has cost so much, even lives, is being changed. With your actions you are forcing us to believe that transnationals are being favored and forcing Proquivemex to go bankrupt. We will not allow it."[34] The death most likely referred to the killing of Mario Vianey Malpica. A former teacher and organizer of vanilla pickers, Vianey Malpica began to organize barbasco pickers in his home state of Veracruz but was found stabbed to death in November of 1975 in what the newspapers reported as a homicide linked to his work with barbasco pickers.

A portion of the Proquivemex ballad, quoted in chapter 6, honored his memory in the following lines: "Defending the rights of our brother campesinos, Malpica was eliminated by a cowardly assassin."[35] The murder broadened the organization's actions by forcing barbasco leaders to reflect on the depth of peasant problems in the countryside.[36] Making reference to the murder in a newspaper article, the Unión de Ejidos de Producción Agropecuaria Ursulo Galván wrote that "if the [transnational] companies, the caciques, and the large landowners thought that we would feel threatened, they are mistaken because we are fired up in our struggle which begins and ends with . . . Proquivemex."[37] But campesinos were also reinforcing their move beyond Proquivemex. As described in the previous chapter, Crispo Pérez, a beneficio worker, had written in a letter to Villar Borja, when he saw that Malpica had replaced a chemical engineer hired by the transnational companies to run the beneficio, acknowledging that this shows that "we as campesinos are capable of organizing, leading, managing, and performing activities which until recently were only allowed for a specific group."[38]

To clarify their position within Proquivemex, campesino leaders drafted a letter which they presented to Puebla and in which they demanded that the minimum 2.50 pesos per kilo paid to pickers be respected; unions control the process of barbasco; Proquivemex pay the unions 5 pesos for each processed kilo; Proquivemex openly discuss its administrative decisions with the unions; and, finally, all profits be transparent so that the unions could have a say in how the money would be spent.[39] Campesinos also referred to Proquivemex's original document in which, supposedly, 80 percent of all profits would be for the development of self-sufficient campesino unions.[40]

If these demands were not met, union leaders warned, then stored barbasco would not be sold nor would the barbasco unions sign checks. The threat was not an idle one: To cash checks Proquivemex needed the union's signature. In spite of these bold claims, without the administrative support of a progressive Proquivemex administration, the unions slowly began to lose momentum. But the withdrawal of support had an inverse reaction in terms of campesino organization.

The UNPRB separates from Proquivemex

On July 30, 1978, a government-backed National Union of Producers and Gatherers of Barbasco came into being, founded by the first generation of Proquivemex-supported campesinos. No longer a disperse collection of unions controlled by Proquivemex, the national union had a different, independent agenda. Although the union came into existence after Echeverría's populism had smoldered in the countryside, its origins are rooted in the populist promises of that era. The UNPRB brought together all regional barbasco unions, with complete membership in the SRA and the CNC. Root pickers finally had national support and *legitimacy* within state institutions and, more important, representation at all levels. In spite of concerted efforts to the contrary, the UNPRB would not gain a stronghold until 1983, when the union finally and completely disassociated itself from Proquivemex, claiming that the state-owned company no longer sought the welfare of the campesinos.

One of the first acts of the UNPRB was to negotiate a standard price for barbasco. After negotiations between barbasco pickers, Proquivemex, and the heads of transnational companies reached an agreement of US$1.39.[41] However, in 1985, a kilogram of barbasco flour was being sold for one dollar.[42]

The UNPRB would represent a new era of campesino organization, with financial credits to the barbasqueros. But persistent corruption and power struggles between established middlemen and Proquivemex-backed ones continually thwarted the organization's efforts.

ARIC Libertad

In 1982 Proquivemex's administration, in fulfillment of the founding chapter, passed complete control of the state company's beneficios to the barbasco unions. This meant that the national union—campesinos—would have absolute control of the initial chemical process.[43] It was the first time in the history of barbasco in Mexico that campesinos were autonomously responsible for what they produced. According to Eduardo Domínguez, a union leader at the time, it was the first time that campesinos were accepted as the owners of the means of production.[44]

In 1982 the UNPRB incorporated an independent credit union, Asociación Rural de Interés Colectivo (ARIC), as part of the barbasco enterprise and named it *Libertad* (Freedom). The ARIC option was to combat the pervasive corruption among the Union administration, specifically among the zone chiefs who had replaced traditional middlemen as local strongmen. The ARIC Libertad comprised 20 unions totaling 470 diverse ejidos and 750,000 hectares.[45] While the ARIC's role was purely administrative and financial, its founding contract warned that it was "dangerous to base the future of the organization solely on the root."[46] Consequently, the ARIC encouraged the incorporation of coffee, cattle, pepper, and pineapple products, though ejidos still used the title "gathers and producers of barbasco" to describe themselves. But, indeed, the erstwhile barbasco-only unions were branching out into other areas. It appeared that barbasco would function as the springboard from which ejidos had learned to negotiate with other organizations and the government and how they incorporated themselves into state structures. Once a part of an institutional arrangement, it was easier for ejidos to move horizontally and expand their interests. In sum, the ARIC would be the financial branch, and the UNPRB would have the campesino and government connections. The allure of barbasco was still strong enough to garner financial credits.[47]

New Management, Return of the Campesinos

In 1983 Guillermo Wilkins Chapoy, an economist, took the helm of the company and surrounded himself with a different staff. Unlike Villar Borja's group—which, though driven, was often inexperienced and impulsive— members of Wilkins's staff, also socially conscious, had gained their experience before joining Proquivemex and often broke with stereotypes. A case in point was Barbara Caughlin.

Caughlin was hired as the liaison between campesino unions and transnational companies. Caughlin had worked in various financial institutions in Mexico and the United States before joining Proquivemex. But it was again the potential of what could be achieved in the countryside which prompted her to join Proquivemex. When asked how Caughlin faced stereotypes pertaining to her gender (she was the only female in most meetings) and her *gringa* nationality, she immediately interjected, that campesinos "understood that I am more Mexican than American."[48] Explaining the continuing vision of Proquivemex and that of Mexico, Caughlin asserted that many of the problems stemmed from the idea that "Mexico was bent to become instantly modern." This drive toward modernity often trampled over traditional forms of coexistence, which, in Proquivemex's case, continued to hamper its more altruistic goals. One of these persistent problems was the inability to monitor individuals from geographically and socially disperse locations, specifically, the zone chiefs. So before any steroids could be processed, the company needed to tackle the social problems created by the barbasco trade in the countryside.

Before accomplishing that, campesinos needed to assure transnational companies that they would be able to continue without the problems that had plagued them in the past. As Wilkins remembered the events, it was success for campesino representation:

> In the first year [1983], we took the Unions to the negotiating table [with transnational companies] and they sat behind the table. In the second year they sat with us at the table. In the third year they sat at the table and we sat behind them. In spite of all their limitations, illiteracy, inexperience . . . I never met a dumb [barbasco] leader. It was natural selection. Some were, frankly, too smart.[49]

The following anecdote, recounted on two different occasions, serves as an example of barbasqueros' understanding their role, or rather the role that they had to play before the heads of Proquivemex. Both Wilkins and Silvio Delgado vividly recalled the actions of a man named Loreto, the union president of Arroyo Negro. Loreto, one of the most vocal barbasco leaders, usually sat at the head table during the weekly meetings with Proquivemex representatives. When he had to give a report on the seasonal yields of barbasco and diosgenin, he would slowly take out his reading glasses, reach into his pocket, and pull out a piece of paper. He would then read in a loud voice the production levels, making sure to read from his piece of paper or glance at it while he made comments. After several meetings in which Loreto followed the same procedure Wilkins, who was sitting next to him, noted that the paper was blank. Similarly Delgado remembered this same delegate as "reading" from a paper which he could see was upside down, was a scrap of newspaper, or had squiggles on it. Both Delgado and Wilkins were astounded by the man's prodigious memory, given that he could correctly recite the yields of barbasco and terms of agreements that he clearly had not written down.[50] This example also illustrates that though campesinos were taken away from their everyday tasks in the countryside and were ill prepared to function within the rigid schedule of weekly or biweekly meetings, or the sometimes tedious protocol of maintaining meeting minutes, some managed to thrive in the setting in which they were thrust. For, according to Wilkins, it was different when campesinos bargained with transnational corporations. "We practically became their consultants and nothing more." Campesinos gained, as Wilkins put it, a sense of property, even if communally held, that barbasco was their property.

What we see in this anecdote is the change in some root pickers' relationship to government and transnational companies. The UNPRB had managed what Proquivemex began in 1975: organize, educate, and let those who pick barbasco control the trade. How was the UNPRB able to attain these goals? It did it in conjunction with a new and different Proquivemex.

There were many local practices which Proquivemex could neither control nor stop and which ultimately contributed to the demise of the company. The case of the barbasco unions of Arroyo Negro y Anexas in Veracruz is revealing of the problems, both social and business in origin, that Proquivemex faced. During Proquivemex's final administration, it became common to provide transcripts of meetings with campesinos. These often lengthy documents provide the reader with the details to understand how campesinos negotiated, confronted, and evaluated the company and the chemical process. Discussed were issues as varied as tensions between ejidos and the company, the differing quality of barbasco, and the future of the company.

One such transcript, of a Mexico City meeting that took place on July 1, 1985, between seven employees, discusses how the company should deal with a shipment of low-quality barbasco sent to various companies.[51] In attendance were the director, Wilkins, and the president of the union Arroyo Negro y Anexas, the previously mentioned Loreto Castañeda Aviles. As we recall, certain dioscoreas contain higher concentrations of diosgenin. Roots with a lower diosgenin content tend to have a higher concentration of impurities, chief among these a substance called *penogenina*. If high traces of penogenina were found in any particular shipment, the entire lot was degraded because the presence of penogenina required an additional chemical process which affected the yield of diosgenin. Consequently, it had been the practice to reward those areas whose roots contained fewer impurities.

The problem of low-grade barbasco also raised other issues. It reveals how difficult it was for Proquivemex to control what thousands of pickers dug out of the jungles. Although more experienced pickers tended to know that barbasco skin tones meant different grades of barbasco, Proquivemex could not control what the earth yielded any more than the companies could.

Poor-quality barbasco posed a particular business problem for Proquivemex. If companies ordered, say, 100 tons of barbasco, they would prepay, at most, 75 percent of their order to Proquivemex at a fixed price. But when Proquivemex requested 100 tons from its unions, there was no guarantee that it would receive this amount. Some unions started picking barbasco too late, some of the money earmarked for payment locally went to purchase other items, or the picked barbasco was of such poor quality that more would have to be ordered to complete the shipment. This meant that Proquivemex needed to request double, in this case 200 tons, of barbasco to guarantee that it would have 100 tons ready for delivery. But it still paid for 200 tons and thus absorbed the costs. In the end, this meant that Proquivemex would have to store any excess barbasco, sometimes for two or three years, in the process losing money. The money lost was due to two reasons: first, Proquivemex was paying out of pocket for the excess barbasco that would guarantee its shipment and, second, it paid a specific amount for barbasco with no guarantee that it would be able to sell it at that price in the future. In some cases, the level of penogenina was so high that the lot was discarded as trash. In those instances Proquivemex would penalize an individual union by not buying barbasco for a few months. But how did this translate to those pickers who rarely if ever had any dealings with Proquivemex's administration or their own representatives? This was a serious problem.

When the representative of Arroyo Negro y Anexas met with Proquivemex officials on that July morning, they discussed a typical problem that arose from this arrangement: pickers who turned against Proquivemex, demanding they be paid for their barbasco. As campesinos saw it, they were being cheated by not receiving a payment. They had picked barbasco and should be paid by the company. By 1985, and one of the reasons this meeting took place, all attempts to send Proquivemex technicians to or teach classes to problematic unions had been rejected.

Another more general problem in dealing with government officials charged with campesino issues was the "bureaucratese" used by CNC representatives, which confused and often derailed any constructive decisions in the transcripts of five different meetings.[52] The wordplay became more obvious when we contrast it to the direct requests of the representative of barbasco pickers or even Proquivemex's administrators. It leaves one to wonder what role, if any, the CNC played in bettering the condition of barbasco pickers.

Problems Plague the UNPRB

The UNPRB's and Proquivemex's last administration initially removed those *jefes de zona*, who had siphoned off much of the initial profits. Instead, the union heads installed supervisors who would tour the areas, sometimes unexpectedly, and placed a permanent "leader" in each zone. Moreover, each zone would have more control of its area and not be so beholden to a central administration as during the initial years of Proquivemex. As the UNPRB gained more power, Proquivemex's role was limited to handing out the *adelanto* (advance) and accounting. Weekly meetings of the Committee for Production and Finance, held on Friday in Mexico City, determined how much barbasco was currently being processed. This information came from weekly meetings of the Committee for Production (held each Tuesday in each regional zone). What these meetings theoretically accomplished was a deeper understanding of what each zone could potentially produce, the quality of each region, and the particularities of each union. With this detailed knowledge, the UNPRB could then tailor its financial and technical assistance to each specific union and not to the entire region. For example in its 1986 annual report, the UNPRB committee described the Unión Región Tuxtepec (Zone 1) as one with many internal problems. Reportedly, the president of the union had paid each delegate between 1,000 and 10,000 pesos to vote him into office. Moreover, the general assembly meetings, which were supposedly held in each community, were only held in Tuxtepec, making it impossible for all ejidos to be fairly represented. The twenty-eight delegates who represented the fourteen ejidos were only called upon when the price of barbasco was raised or to elect a new president. Among those ejidos in the union, Nueva Málzaga was described as being far removed from any decisions made by ejido authorities. Delegates were assigned, not voted, into their positions.

Another problem emerged regarding Arroyo Zacate in Playa Vicente, Veracruz, which allegedly belonged to the Unión de Ejidos Alberto Cinta. When members of the UNPRB traveled to the area, they were surprised to learn from a Zapotec family that neither the UNPRB nor the union had been heard of before. Other barbasco-producing ejidos such as Ojitlán, while claiming to be part of the UNPRB, denied any ties to the CNC and instead advocated membership in the CCI (Confederación Campesina Independiente).

Reports from other zones were not much different. One of the largest unions, with the most ejido members, the Unión Hilario C. Salas, was also one of the most problematic. For example, in 1984 it did not fulfill its barbasco orders; two shipments of barbasco were deemed of "very bad quality," not accepted for purchase, and labeled debts of the union. Consequently all financial help to that union was denied for the fiscal year 1985. Similarly, the Unión de Ejidos Helio García Alfaro was termed troublesome, mainly because its president was not an ejidatario but had managed to serve three consecutive terms (a practice not allowed by the UNPRB). As if this were not enough, the union president had collected but not given out the common fund to any of the ejidos in his jurisdiction. It was unclear what had happened with this small fortune. The UNPRB-installed infrastructure was still unable to combat the excessive power given to those who purchased barbasco. The large amounts of cash given to these men often led to corruption and abuses.

As another example, again in the Unión Arroyo Negra y Anexas, a union perceived by Proquivemex as having significant problems (see earlier discussion), had a former zone chief who, despite being removed from his position, still controlled the purchase of barbasco and would sell directly, independently of any organization, to pharmaceutical companies.[53] Wilkins, the former director of Proquivemex, summarized the difficulty of dealing with the power of the jefes de zonas in the following description: "[They] would get funds, call a union president, and make him sign a paper saying that he had received money [without giving it to them]. Afterward we [Proquivemex, ca. 1983] tried to put many of these jefes de zona in jail but they had proof that they had given money to the ejidos. Why did they [ejidatarios] sign? They were in desperate need."[54]

Wilkins was quick to add that that was only at the beginning. After these initial practices, Proquivemex decided to directly deposit each individual subsidy into a bank account held in each union's name. The signatures of the treasurer, president, and *jefe de vigilancia* were then needed to take out any money. Subsequently, each union was encouraged to hire an accountant and administration consultant so that it could better complete its job. Each new complaint or regional problem needed to be dealt with on an individual basis. For each region had a specific history, particular social relations, and explicit needs that could not be solved or addressed in sweeping reforms. This practice, of course, delayed any dramatic changes in the barbasco zones.

The internal structures of the Mexican countryside also functioned against the union. For example, in the Gabarrino Barria Union, the outgoing president in 1983 tried to break all ties to the UNPRB, saying that they had "organized a separate ARIC." To get the ejidos to join his organization, he threatened not to purchase any coffee from ejidos that opted to join the UNPRB. Six of the total eight unions opted to leave the UNPRB to ensure a buyer for their coffee.

Newer unions also experienced problems. A union from Guerrero went directly to Agrarian Reform to demand that they be taken seriously after the UNPRB labeled them as *revoltosos* with many internal problems. Also in the state of Guerrero, there were some ejidos that were incorporated into the UNPRB but which lacked even the basic knowledge of how to gather barbasco. As the report detailed, "Don Seferino's [the president of the Unión de Ejidos] people gathered in a general assembly to find out about barbasco, people don't know how to dig up the root." The union consequently requested that someone teach them how to gather barbasco. The UNPRB eventually sent someone to speak to the union.[55]

Speeches by UNPRB representatives were sprinkled with loose references to chemical compounds, and they still emphasized the important role of barbasco pickers for the nation. For example during a distribution of barbasco profits in 1984, the UNPRB leader Eduardo Dominguez, with obvious delight and palpable satisfaction, explained the following to an audience eager to receive the money derived from their participation in the barbasco trade:

> Diosgenin is a powder [*polvito*] that is no longer black. Like flour it is completely white, more like ivory, and this powder still requires twenty-eight more chemical steps . . . here, in Mexico, we can go up to step eight and we refine it, refine it, refine it until oral contraceptive pills come out and [one can also get] Synalar, used for cuts, and an additional eighteen to twenty products used for medicine. But these final steps are no longer done here in Mexico, the powder goes abroad [*al extranjero*] and they buy [the powder] in dollars and so Mexico receives its payment in dollars and however you want to put it, gentlemen, but that is the currency that rules the world. So those dollars come here and help Mexico buy many things that it needs. . . . We are part of the process that lets our country have money.[56]

After years of depending on government subsidies, rural inhabitants heard that it was possible, through their association with barbasco, to move beyond stereotypes and function as full-fledged citizens. This issue of belonging to a larger society was the constant theme in the recollections of former UNPRB members.

But for some root pickers, years of illiteracy, acute poverty, and lack of opportunities translated into insurmountable obstacles for social inclusion. For example, Isidro Apolinar, twice a treasurer of the local UNPRB, recalled one particularly vivid image of how barbasco was not a miraculous panacea for deeper social problems. In the early 1980s two brothers asked to accompany Apolinar on his next trip to Mexico City. Apolinar resisted because the brothers were "very humble people," (*gente muy humilde*), extremely poor campesinos from the sierra. They had nevertheless heard barbasco described as belonging to all and that as pickers they should benefit equally. Despite Apolinar's initial protests the adult brothers accompanied him. It was their first time out of the Región Tuxtepec. On the bus Apolinar tried to explain what they would see, but there was no way of preparing the brothers for the bustle of Mexico City. After walking around in a daze a brother mentioned that he needed to use the restroom. Apolinar found a public facility but the man took a long time to return. Telling this story in 2004 a visibly moved Apolinar explained that when he went in search of the man, "there was the poor guy staring at the sink and toilet."[57] The brother had not known where to defecate.

As individual campesinos struggled to take advantage of the opportunities that interest in barbasco had generated, so to did some unions struggle to attain basic rights promised to them. For example, ejidatarios from Rubén Figueroa in Guerrero discovered that they were not recognized by Agrarian Reform only after they tried to establish some credit with the official bank, Banrural. Apparently, the delegates from their union had lost the assembly papers, which guaranteed their membership and which determined who among them was the union president.[58] Wilkins succinctly explained the problem within the barbasco zones as "it is very different how things are seen from the perspective of a [city] desk and how one sees them in the countryside."[59]

Unbalanced monetary compensation was also a concern for the UNPRB. Acutely aware of the social problems occasioned by high commissions to buyers and by the disproportionately high salaries to overseers, in comparison to what was paid to root pickers, the UNPRB attempted to create a general minimum wage based on the national minimum averages. This proposal, however, did not get very far. Once again the geographic dispersion, unequal barbasco production, and irregular diosgenin percentage between regions were too contentious to attempt to regulate the trade.

A Female Barbasquera

Given the absence of women's responses in the archives, it was noteworthy to find a series of letters accusing a female beneficio owner of misdealings in the barbasco trade in Veracruz. But the case of Eva Domínguez Valdez, president of the Unión de Ejidos Helio García Alfaro of Las Choapas, Veracruz, is an example of the power that a few females managed to attain within the ranks of the barbasco complex.

On November 26, 1984, a typed letter from Domínguez was sent to Proquivemex's main offices addressed to the director Wilkins.[60] In the correspondence she implores Wilkins to investigate what has happened to 7 million pesos missing from the union's coffers. Adding that the union "had some problems," both political and administrative, about "which you can't even imagine," she continues, "so I am asking you, not as the head of the company, which you so capably represent, but as a friend," to look into this matter.[61] As a closing detail, she states that she could "no longer live knowing that we will have to work again as we did last year during a sad and bitter Christmas." As an afterthought, she reminds Wilkins that she is still expecting funds to be sent to better the beneficio and install a drying bed and fermentation tins. She ends by slyly writing "I bid you farewell wishing you all the goodness that God may give you so that you, in turn, can then help me." Domínguez, however, could not be helped; nor was she a stranger to Proquivemex.

As other documents reveal, Domínguez was not a meek woman struggling to make "this Christmas different from the last"; rather, she appeared to be a quite savvy and shrewd businesswoman. A year earlier the leaders of the National Peasant Movement Alfredo V. Bonfil had already written a scathing letter denouncing her unorthodox practices in the barbasco trade. While Domínguez had only "been seen when the [barbasco] union was formed and the contract [with Proquivemex] signed," she ran the union as she wished.[62] She acquired "two trucks, hired consultants, and spent the money" without informing the other members of the ejido. Her actions had bothered the members of three ejidos—Guadalupe, Constitución Mexicana, and Ignacio López Rayón—enough that they held an assembly and demanded that Proquivemex start an inquiry into her practices. Not only should her "handling of money" be questioned, they contended, but also her legal identity as an ejido member. As the private owner of more than 100 hectares, Domínguez was technically not a member of an ejido. This letter was the second time that ejidatarios had requested that Proquivemex and the National Union of Producers and Gatherers of Barbasco (UNPRB) look into her dealings, but even by 1984 the issue had not been resolved.

Some Successes

The UNPRB served as an effective protective body for the root pickers, but offering protection in the financial sense. Its obligations were described as representing the goals of each union, bettering their current functions, stimulating their production, and curtailing their economic vulnerability. For example, when Unión Hilario C. Salas found that halfway through its term it was running out of money to complete the barbasco harvest, the UNPRB was allowed to use the future harvest as credit toward a loan. In this fashion, those who relied on barbasco picking could continue their labor undeterred.

Crucial, once again, to the success of Proquivemex's goals was that the leaders fully understand the chemical process. This generation, however, went a step further than previous administrations had. They not only sat campesinos at the negotiating table with transnational companies; they also flew several to Europe to see the pharmaceutical plants during the years 1984–86.[63] Wilkins admitted that the latter practice was to release some of the pressure that Proquivemex felt from those campesinos who were anxious, based on previous rhetoric, to build a domestic pharmaceutical industry. When they came back from touring Schering in Germany, these same leaders realized how much was needed to get the project going. After returning from their tour, campesinos were, according to Wilkins, more forceful in their negotiation, but they were also more aware that barbasco itself was not going to solve their problems. At that point, many of the campesinos who spoke in chemical terms and could predict yields began to suggest that the organization should diversify its interests. One such proposal, for example, was to begin to produce jams in jars.

In 1985, according to estimates by the UNPRB, approximately 2,000 root gatherers were employed and an additional 1,200 employees worked in the beneficios. This was a dramatic decrease from the more than 100,000 estimated a mere decade earlier.[64] This sudden drop in root collecting was partially due to the changing demand for barbasco, but also a changing attitude toward Proquivemex. As Guillermo Wilkins stated, "We saw that there was no future when Proquivemex was being passed from Secretariat to Secretariat." The company that had once fostered populist dreams had become undesirable.

Privatization—Dissolution of Proquivemex

Dissolving Proquivemex would turn out to be more difficult than starting it without chemists. In December of 1982 the Mexican government controlled more than 1,100 parastatals: 724 had majority state participation, 75 had minority stake, 103 were decentralized companies, and 223 were considered trusts.[65] Between December 1, 1983, and November 30, 1988, 741 parastatals were unincorporated but, surprisingly, 61 others created. The majority of those forced to close their doors were from the industrial sector, among those Proquivemex. While the roster of companies described as parastatals slotted to be closed reveals much about the hopes and ambitions of former administrations, they also have an initial random quality to their demise or transformation. Among these were Cementos Anahuac del Golfo, S.A. (cement); Cloro de Tehuantepec (Clorox and sosa); Bicicletas Cóndor (bicycles and bicycles parts); and even an airline, Compañía Mexicana de Aviación, the latter of which was privatized. But upon closer inspection of the products or services to be cut—bricks, tractor engines, sodas and mineral water, synthetic rubber, compressors for refrigerators, and shingles—one can gauge the political ambitions and dreams of those who thought that something like Mexican "shingles" could bring progress and economic independence to the nation.

In a futile attempt to force President Miguel de la Madrid to reverse the fate of Proquivemex, Valdemar Cabrera, the president of the UNPRB, wrote a lengthy letter to him on February 19, 1986. Exemplifying how deeply the barbasco union understood the changing fiscal and political tides, the letter noted that with a "swipe of the pen" peasant conquests not only with barbasco production but in the countryside would be summarily "erased."[66] Referring to workers who were petitioning that Proquivemex meet its obligations, the union leader asserted, "It would be regrettable that those responsible for Mexico's mortal coup would be disoriented workers," and referring to the continued import of Chinese diosgenin, he concluded, "Liberalizing our internal market and sabotaging Mexican peasants with Chinese ones is not the best position that as Mexicans we should take. . . . [We] totally reject the disappearance of state involvement in the guise of Proquivemex."[67]

These ardent letters would not change a new economic plan. On March 24, 1986, the *Diario Oficial de la Nación,* the government's official daily newspaper of resolutions and events, announced that the pharmaceutical branch of Proquivemex (known as DAISA—División Agroindustrial, S.A.) was going up for sale. The announcement suggested that individual states would be given preference over private investors, but still the UNPRB argued that campesinos, as stockholders of the company, had the right to bid.[68]

The dissolution process of Proquivemex began on May 27, 1987, and would continue for more than a year until October of 1988, when the order was revoked.[69] Ironically, the stumbling block to dissolution and liquidation turned out to be funds. Proquivemex did not have enough liquid assets to carry out its closure. What remained of Proquivemex was handed down from one secretariat to the next. The company, which a decade earlier had been the pride of a presidential administration, was swiftly shuttled, as unwanted as rotting barbasco, until it ended up under the Secretariat of Agrarian Reform (SRA). A memo from November 1988 mentions the fallen value of Proquivemex, when it suggests that "given that the company was virtually not functioning from the day dissolution was ordered, mainly due to the lack of fiscal support, there has been no auto-evaluation for the six year period nor the following one for 1988."[70] The company's value was not even worthy of an analysis for two years in a row. Proquivemex was rapidly sliding out of fiscal and political awareness.

Surprisingly, given the above memo, another memo was also found in the official transfer and liquidation analysis. Referring to the time of the actual transfer, "the directorship of the company as well as the Secreteriat of Agriculture and Hydraulic Resources (SARH) guarantee that the transfer of the entity [Proquivemex] will take place under the assumption that it is a healthy and working business to avoid the unease of producers and consumers, as was the case in 1988."[71]

On September 15, 1989, the *Diario Oficial* reported the closure of Proquivemex. The social experiment had come to an end. Or maybe not. The announcement reported that Proquivemex's profits from the sale of barbasco would be turned over *in its entirety* to campesinos.[72] It also added, however, that government subsidies would be crucial for the continuance of Proquivemex. This seemingly insignificant fact would be the end of Proquivemex as a state-owned enterprise. The "producers and consumers" mentioned above, who would receive the remnants of the company, were the barbasco unions.

That final memo made clear why Turco, the barbasco buyer from Jacatepec, Oaxaca, had saved a tattered piece of paper with an original date of November 12, 1976. It was a clear photocopy with the intriguing words "I present an original copy, May 25, 1983." What makes this paper interesting is that it is a copy of the certificate of Unión Región Tuxtepec's stock holdings in Proquivemex; 48,795 stocks with a designated value of 33,314,000.00 pesos.

By 2001, when Turco gave it away, together with all his remaining papers about the union and Proquivemex, it was clear that any remaining hope of retrieving money from the union's participation in the defunct company was gone.

The campesino-run version of Proquivemex, INBASA, only survived for a couple of years. In those years, according to anecdotal evidence, the same abuses linked to lack of oversight, which had previously plagued Proquivemex, would come to the fore. Today, ruined and abandoned beneficios, cement blocks used for drying barbasco, and stories of a time when barbasco pickers went into the jungles with empty sacks and returned with wild yams that sometimes transformed lives are all that remain in the Chinantla. But, according to some locals, barbasco, the hope of thousands of campesinos, of students, and of a president lies scattered underground waiting to be dug up again.

Conclusion

Why did campesinos take INBASA when the company was not profitable? In order to understand, this we can turn to the case of henequen in the Yucatán. As Ana Paula De Teresa vividly illustrates, land distribution at the height of Cárdenas's land reform, in the late 1930s, was no gift. First because "they received ruined harvests that had previously been abandoned by hacendados," and second because the lands were officially designated as henequen-only lands.[73] Campesinos were given lands at a time of declining

FIGURE 28 This Proquivemex-processing plant on the outskirts of Tuxtepec lay abandoned in 2000. Populist hopes from an earlier era were that this "jungle laboratory" would one day be staffed by peasants who would replicate the work of erstwhile technicians and chemists. Photograph by author.

henequen prices and world depression, without the adequate machinery for removing the agave fibers which was critical to agave harvesting. In addition campesinos were not given subsidies to competitively enter the market. After initially declining to take the land, they finally relented under force. As in the henequen case, campesinos were given the remains of the barbasco industry only when it was clearly no longer profitable.

What is remarkable about the barbasco trade is that despite the documented loss of Proquivemex, the dissolution papers state that to avoid any risk of failure, the peasant organization had to be *trained* as businessmen— with healthy finances, no debts, and capital that will allow it to "immediately and successfully" compete—yet there is no mention of a market analysis revealing whether diosgenin was still a viable commodity.

The dissolution of Proquivemex was part of the larger economic trends of Miguel de la Madrid's government, which continued under Carlos Salinas de Gortari (1988–94). Born in a time of populist largesse, Proquivemex was the shining promise of what could be achieved with government funds. The company also became an example of what could happen when that patronage evaporated or when funds went unchecked. By 1986 the political climate was no longer friendly to peasant capital as it had been at Proquivemex's inception under Luis Echeverría. In that brief period, policy had changed from a *campesinista* one that tried to solve campesino problems to one focused more on ethnicity of those campesinos, be they Chinanteco, Maya, or Mixtec.

Whereas barbasqueros could at first gain the sympathies of a nation by calling attention to the deep divide between their labor and the profits made by transnational companies, by the late 1980s this argument was drowned by the thousands of similar ones made at that time. In other words, the barbasqueros were no longer unique in their insertion and understanding, no matter how limited or sophisticated, of global markets. As protests and demands began to incorporate the rhetoric of human rights, barbasqueros lagged behind in their ability to appeal to a changing government and society. Not nimble enough in their language to procure the sympathy nor the money of an ever slimmer neoliberal government, barbasco pickers began to fade from national memory.

Cada quien cuenta como le fue en la feria
(Everyone tells the story as they lived it).

Popular Mexican saying

"Everyone has a different story to tell about their time at the fair,"
goes a popular Mexican saying expressing the infinite and multiple
perspectives of each participant. This saying could also be applied to
the vastly different experiences of rural Mexicans in the period when
state-sponsored barbasco projects dominated eastern Oaxaca's rural
development.

Although many campesinos of the Región Tuxtepec continue to
eke out a subsistence existence, for some the barbasco trade introduced significant social change. As some barbasqueros gained an
increasing knowledge of what they were doing with barbasco, they
expanded their conception of their role in the countryside and in
Mexico more broadly. As members of the National Union of Producers and Gatherers of Barbasco (UNPRB), among others, gradually
became conscious of their political value, they used this awareness
to gain public, and in some instances private, capital. The men and
women involved with the barbasco trade who managed to alter their
social condition in a major way, as opposed to those who did not,
had one conspicuous thing in common. When asked about the dioscoreas, they invariably used a chemical term. This simple linguistic
difference proved to be a crucial element in how people shaped their
memories of the barbasco trade and crafted the narratives of their
participation.

Perhaps more telling of this inconsistent character of barbasco production was the hesitant answer, "I don't own land, so I don't know anything," offered in 1999 in response to my questioning a former picker
about his experience. How was it possible that at the close of the twen-

tieth century such a dramatic difference in responses still persisted among those who had gathered barbasco? These answers are indeed more curious given that the government and Proquivemex ran several development and teaching programs for the pickers of the wild yam.

The history of barbasco in rural Mexico reveals how local realities conflicted with nationalistic projects and, in the 1970s, with the goals of sweeping populism. This divergence came about partly because in the mid-twentieth century many politicians and urban Mexicans were unable to fully understand the Mexico that lay beyond semi-urban areas. This lack of comprehension led to a series of quick fixes or unsustainable projects. Barbasco in Mexico, then, epitomizes a national scheme or project—in this case science, through the manufacture of synthetic steroids—that was embraced as the fastest means to bring modernization to people and regions which had long languished neglected. Some well-intended, rural-development administrators, however, were unable to grasp that the hundreds of thousands of people who gathered barbasco across southern Mexico exhibited some starkly different traits: some could speak Spanish whereas other could not, some could read but others were illiterate, some were landholders and some were landless, among other characteristics. Barbasco could have certainly served as a unifying banner for disenfranchised rural Mexicans but, as this book illustrates, the region's history precluded these yam pickers from being lumped under a single category of *barbasqueros*, or concomitantly, campesinos. A new *name* alone could not erase existing hierarchies and prejudices.

Given this, it is quite significant that in far-removed pockets of rural Mexico, places like Chiltepec and Valle Nacional, new ways of conceptualizing the value of this local plant that arose in the early 1970s still persist among some locals. Although Proquivemex and the foreign laboratories are long gone, a select group of people formerly involved in the steroid hormone trade still speaks at length and in detail about their experiences. It is noteworthy that when former barbasqueros from the Región Tuxtepec were questioned about barbasco, they invariably listed the same, small group of people as the individuals capable of talking about the history of the yam.

As the case of the barbasco trade illustrates, some savvy campesinos were not passive recipients of government aid. Some were able to use their affiliation with barbasco to refashion their role in the countryside. For those who may still question if Mexican peasants used scientific terms as a tool for social mobility, it is worth revisiting some of these men, singled out by their neighbors, who took the time to answer questions about their experience with barbasco.

For example, Melquíades Santiago, a former member of the UNPRB, is now an established coffee buyer who also owns one of Valle Nacional's popular cantinas. He lives in a spacious two-story cement home, and he is considered one of the wealthier residents of the town. During one of our interviews I noticed sacks of coffee piled to the ceiling in his living room. He explained that he purchased coffee from locals, but the going rate was too low for him to resell so he was waiting until prices climbed and he could make a larger profit. He no longer identified himself as a campesino, though he described his childhood as one of extreme rural poverty. Santiago, who was mentioned in a vignette in this book's introduction, in addition to teaching other campesinos about barbasco, was charged with keeping a tally of the total amount of barbasco purchased in the Valle Nacional region. His broad knowledge of the quantity and types of dioscoreas needed to yield more potent diosgenin made him a crucial link between laboratories and yam gatherers. He also traveled to Mexico City, made a tour of several pharmaceutical companies, and as he said in passing, "met the President of Mexico."[1] These were remarkable achievements for any single individual, but an almost unheard of outcome for an erstwhile campesino with barely a grade school education. As many pointed out, he had ascended into Valle Nacional's closed circle of established residents by climbing the rungs of the barbasco trade.

The most remarkable social transformations, however, were seen in the cases of people, such as Eduardo Domínguez, who left rural communities of origin during the Proquivemex and UNPRB years and immersed themselves fully in an urban existence. During an initial interview with Domínguez in Toluca, I was struck, not by his gleaming VW bug, but by his immaculate sports coat and political pin on his lapel. For years he had represented the barbasco pickers of Amatepec, and he still spoke passionately and eloquently about the rights of campesinos to equal citizenship. He had spent part of his time in the barbasco trade experimenting alongside other members of his local union to find ways of bettering the poor diosgenin content found in the yams of his region. Though not a chemist by training he had successfully learned to work in a laboratory and to manipulate barbasco's chemical output.

Others abandoned the countryside completely. One was Pedro Ramírez, who over many years had relied on barbasco picking for survival and who recalled learning about it from purchasers who came to Minatitlán with samples of the yam. A current employee of Mexico City's subway system, he explained that after years with the UNPRB fighting for the rights of barbasco pickers, and campesinos in general, he had burned out. As the president of the UNPRB for several years, he had negotiated with representatives of transnational laboratories, had obtained Citibank loans for his union, and achieved the respect of former bureaucrats of the National Peasant Confederation (CNC) and the Treasury Secretariat (Hacienda y Crédito Público). He still remembered his experiences with barbasco as a "beautiful time," and he lamented the economic reforms that had led to the closure of Proquivemex and the eventual dismantling of its processing plants and the discontinuation of plans to build laboratories. He, like so many others, had firmly believed that barbasco could have been the vehicle to bring prosperity to *el campo*.

In 2004 Isidro Apolinar still lived on the land he had inherited from his aunt in Chiltepec. Surrounding his house were several homes where his now-married children lived (with the exception of two who had migrated to North Carolina in search of work). As treasurer of the UNPRB he had traveled farther than he had ever imagined possible. He had attended meetings in Mexico City, received per diems to stay in hotels, and when he spoke at national CNC meetings, people listened. None of this, he acknowledged, would have been possible without barbasco. Indeed, all of those interviewed insisted at some point that "before barbasco we had nothing."

It is no coincidence that those who spoke confidently about the chemical processes that yielded diosgenin were also those who also voiced different opinions about what campesinos could accomplish.

In the past, explorers, colonizers, travelers, and scientists alike have used their own words and categories to explain the world around them. In this book, I suggest that in a similar fashion, some barbasqueros took, if even briefly and often incorrectly, the foreign language of chemistry and made it their own. By "making it their own" I mean that they used the barbasco trade to carve out new positions for themselves in the countryside or all together leave their place of origin. It was not just the language but also, concretely, their appropriation of the practice of "chemistry" that challenged local and national notions of what it meant to be a peasant in mid-twentieth-century Mexico. Just as scientists had borrowed from campesinos knowledge about local flora and their uses to discover steroid synthesis, in turn, Mexican barbasco pickers borrowed scientific terms that offered to magically bring respite from poverty and unemployment. In so doing, a handful of success-ful barbasco collectors accomplished what President Echeverría's populist agenda had set out to do: transform the Mexican countryside by redefining what a peasant was capable of accomplishing.

Under a populist regime, science became the "most powerful and most positive tool" to bring about change.[2] In other words, barbasco's molecules became the talisman that would bring peasant organization, capital, and respect to areas long forgotten by previous presidential administrations. This book has explored what happens when science travels in the modern world, affecting both individuals and nations in unexpected ways. Specifi-cally for the case of Mexican barbasco pickers, we are forced to acknowledge that familiar narratives of global science take particularly odd turns when we include the histories of men and women normally not associated with scientific discovery.

The transformative power associated with modern science allowed Mexi-can politicians to assert that they, too, could alter social conditions, and so a processing plant and a laboratory in rural Oaxaca were built as the means to cure poverty and underdevelopment. Rather than blaming centuries of abusive behavior in Mexico's countryside, politicians succeeded in linking rural Oaxacan exploitation to greedy transnational laboratories. Many poli-ticians conflated protection of barbasco with protection of Mexicans but in so doing, they disassociated themselves from the country's historical poli-cies that allowed campesinos to be exploited in the first place.

The global scramble for dioscoreas and the subsequent synthesis of ste-roid hormones from Mexican yams lasted less than fifty years. But these events, which involved European and American drug houses, scientists from around the world, Mexican and American politicians, and, notably, rural Mexicans, occurred at a time of fast-paced scientific and medical dis-coveries. Among these, the synthesis of steroid hormones was certainly one of the most compelling. Often billed as life-saving and life-altering medica-tions, synthetic steroids allowed many to live a life without pain by taking, say, cortisone or permitted others to control reproduction by taking a daily pill. But, as this book has shown, the histories of these remarkable discoveries are not complete without the story of the participation of Mexico and especially rural Mexicans.

Although the events surrounding barbasco represent a brief moment in Mexico's history, their significance is extraordinary. The history of barbasco in Mexico touched directly or indirectly on nearly every major aspect of the country's climactic 1940–80s period: the battle to nationalize natural resources, the shifting rural landscape, the social upheavals of the 1960s, the rising power of rural guerrilla groups, Echeverría's 1970s populist rediscovery of indigenous peasants as "equals," technological development, and the closure of state-owned companies driven by the neoliberal reforms of the 1980s. These are only a few of the themes that encompassed the world of barbasco in Mexico. But the search for synthetic steroids' peculiar impact on rural Mexicans, who were caught up in a frenzied attempt to "modernize by any means," forces us to pause and think.

Locally the tuber was sought without regard for its medicinal or chemical properties. Then in the 1970s teaching brigades entered the dense thicket of Mexico's southern jungles to challenge peasants to "see" barbasco as scientists might envision the tuber. The intentions, grounded in the Mexican Revolution, of the young, idealistic bureaucrats of the 1970s redefined barbasco and became part of the daily lives of rural Mexicans. When locals were permitted to ponder barbasco's chemical transformation, many realized that they, too, could be transformed into model citizens. Just as the white lab coat became a global symbol of the pristine spaces occupied by doctors, scientists, and researchers, the mythical lab coat of progress linked to barbasco became in rural Mexico an emblem for potential rural metamorphosis.

By the late 1970s the evidence of barbasco's impact in the countryside was quickly accumulating. People today recite how a community's access to electricity, a paved road, or potable water first became possible because barbasco capital flowed into cash-strapped regions. Most telling, however, were repeated claims that the barbasco trade had kept many from migrating to Mexico City and the elusive "El Norte" by providing comparatively easy access to cash. While anecdotal testimony was substantial, specifically in the Papaloapan region, these developments were more difficult to quantify in the archives. A possible explanation may be that many of these communities were so far removed from government aid that for decades they had relied on their own ingenuity to obtain what other communities received through subsidies.

The study of dioscoreas also opened up a completely new way of examining medicinal plants in Mexico. As Arturo Gómez-Pompa, first director of the Commission for the Study of the Ecology of Dioscoreas, explained, in their daily fieldwork, biologists needed to acknowledge the participation of rural Mexicans because modern Mexican biology, botany, and ecology were built "on the backs" of these people. The search for barbasco led field scientists to acknowledge the valuable participation of their field guides, so it was not a far leap for politicians to reconceptualize peasants' services as a practice of science. But this association could never be so simple.

In the 1970s some championed the changes that barbasco could bring to Mexico, while others remained skeptical. Among these were Mexico's scientific elite, which questioned politicians' rationale for allowing peasants to take over the means of steroid production and warned of the possible pitfalls of allowing rural people to believe that they could perform the tasks—measuring, analyzing, and cataloguing—that had long been the exclusive domain of the nation's research elite. Ultimately, these debates revealed that the history of barbasco speaks of the often-baffling interactions between a government desperate to push its rural citizens into the modern world and these same citizens, who willingly transformed themselves into puzzling guises ("owners" of a state laboratory and practical "chemists") in order to continue to receive scarce subsidies.

By 1975 the fate of more than 100,000 barbasco-picking families depended on redefining the barbasco trade as a nationalistic battle that would end Mexico's dependence on transnational pharmaceutical companies. The government's projected gains in this endeavor were twofold. First, by nationalizing foreign laboratories, it stood to gain control of the extremely lucrative industry based on patented medication derived from steroid hormones and with that, the means to produce Mexican oral contraceptives. Second, in edging out foreign laboratories, the government planned to deal directly with root pickers who, as disproportionately poor, indigenous, and underemployed or unemployed Mexicans, might become the restless feeding grounds for organized discontent. The government's broader goal of regaining control of the steroid hormone trade, which had been controlled by foreign companies since 1956, was often described as foolish. Placed within the history of expropriation, the Mexicanization of key industries, and populist designs the creation of state-owned Proquivemex was not re-markable. These were all attempts to control Mexican resources. But the social goals of Proquivemex certainly were unusually ambitious.

As we learned, Proquivemex would manufacture domestic steroid hor-mones and produce patented medications that would bring "pharmaceuti-cal independence" to Mexico. But the company's social mission of peasant organization and rural self-sufficiency was in conflict with its more prag-matic, profit-centered goals. As Proquivemex Agroindustrial—the branch of the company devoted to manufacturing medications—foundered the de-velopment of peasant organizations in areas with historically little govern-ment support and even fewer funds surprisingly flourished.

Spurred on by the populist rhetoric of the Echeverría regime, a hand-ful of campesinos exceeded the planned goals of Proquivemex. By the end of 1975, when it was obvious that transnational laboratories would not be cowed into relinquishing their hold on the Mexican steroid industry, Mexi-can peasants launched protest marches. But as months passed, campesinos no longer simply demanded a fair price for barbasco; they also voiced ex-plicit demands about expropriating laboratories, manufacturing steroids, and the need for an independent pharmaceutical industry in Mexico. Slowly, formerly grubby, uneducated, and unemployed peasants became the emblem for the nation's struggle against an "increasingly greedy" world which "hungrily" sought Mexican raw materials. By incorporating phrases, chemical terms, and actions reserved for the educated elite, root-picking peasants subverted their traditional social role. As Proquivemex employees had preached, lowly peasants held the key to controlling the steroid trade because barbasco grew in their lands.

An affiliation with Proquivemex became the launching pad for some campesinos to question anachronistic social hierarchies in the Región Tux-tepec and throughout southeastern Mexico. Letters, as well as individuals' memories, are filled with the use of uncharacteristic words that became useful tools in asserting their new social positions. Although some contem-poraries argued that root-picking campesinos were simply manipulated, as the CNC and the ruling party had done countless times before, peasants' growing awareness of their role in the steroid hormone industry prompted some to consciously insert themselves into new social spaces. But their in-sights did not stop there. Negotiations with transnational pharmaceutical companies, a national peasant organization, and meetings with chemists were all new experiences for rural Mexicans. Root pickers were no longer symbolic of the rural poverty that was the bane of Mexico. Instead, they now symbolized the march toward the nation's independence in the area of patented medicines.

Although most pickers never knew what became of the barbasco once it left the Papaloapan, the actions of a few barbasqueros were truly remarkable. As the financial crisis deepened in the countryside, some tried to use the government's interest in manufacturing synthetic steroids to improve and transform a decaying rural lifestyle. Under these circumstances, I have argued that campesinos' sophisticated explanations of their role in the search for barbasco and their actions in the steroid hormone trade contested roles often attributed to them throughout the twentieth century. Instead of allowing a political rebaptism of their identity as peasants, barbasqueros transformed the image of the root picker and made it their own. Association with the root evolved into a group identity that in some cases transcended ethnicity, class, and the jagged geography of the Papaloapan, former classic deterrents for organization in rural Oaxaca.

The administration's emphasis on campesinos as the crucial link for understanding the steroid hormone industry persisted in the waning months of Luis Echeverría's presidency. But his project, Proquivemex, revealed that even his administration's peasant-friendly attitude had persisted in lumping all rural Mexicans into a nebulous category of "campesinos." From divisions created by the government's intervention, we learn that regardless of presidential mandates the deeply entrenched rural social networks determined who learned the true nature of barbasco and who did not.

Once the knowledge of barbasco's chemical makeup was circulating, new subgroups of power formed, but these did not completely displace the former landed elite nor was this knowledge, as we saw, evenly spread throughout the region. When questioned about Proquivemex and barbasco unions, answers poignantly revealed that many former gatherers never escaped the rigid social divisions nor did they live out the expectations of Echeverría's populist dreams.

Analyzing how barbasco was understood by presidential administrations allowed us to gauge the political and social atmosphere of Mexico. For example, a 1955 presidential decree issued by Adolfo Ruiz Cortines and a 1960 decree by Adolfo López Mateos both mandated the subsidization of the "exploiters of barbasco," in other words, the transnational corporations.[3] These subsidies consisted of 50 percent to 75 percent of the tariff price. As a tariff, companies were asked to pay two hundred pesos per ton of *dry* barbasco, which amounted to *five* tons of fresh barbasco. At this time, newspaper headlines boasted that Mexico "dominated the market for steroid hormones," yet articles made only passing reference to the root itself, emphasizing instead the chemical compound diosgenin derived from it.[4] Barbasco was important not in its own right but because it was a precursor to steroid hormones. The focus, then, was specifically on the diosgenin-yielding chemical properties of the yam, and not the actual tuber itself. This distinction was crucial for later groups that would be involved in the barbasco trade.

By 1961, however, the attitudes about the root had shifted. Newspaper headlines repeated that special measures had been taken to preserve the "vital plant for the asteroid [*sic*] hormone industry," which by now was termed "a valued natural patrimony for the nation."[5] This attitude was most likely a reflection of the creation of the Commission for the Study of the Ecology of Dioscoreas in 1959, which focused exclusively on studying all aspects of barbasco production and reproduction. It was also at this time that *Life* magazine named barbasco "the most important drug-yielding plant ever discovered."[6]

During the early 1960s the number of tons of barbasco gathered per year remained at high levels, decreasing significantly only after 1974. Permits, regulations, and tariffs increased in the 1960s, but so did the subsidies to transnational corporations. At this time, any mention of barbasco tended to be linked to the discoveries made by the Commission regarding possible cultivation, the reproductive qualities of dioscoreas, and experimental projects to increase diosgenin production. Articles rarely mentioned the peasants who were crucial for bringing the plant to the laboratories.[7] For journalists, campesinos were *not* important to the final chemical product diosgenin. Mexicans viewed barbasco as a domestic plant for export, though later regulations prohibited exporting barbasco, requiring instead that the diosgenin first be synthesized into some other chemical substance. It was not until the late 1960s and early 1970s, that politicians deemed barbasco to be important to Mexican institutions because of its new classification as a domestically grown export product *and* a traditional medicinal plant.

In the early 1970s Echeverría and others pinpointed foreign companies as the cause of Mexico's stunted domestic pharmaceuticals industry. The creation of institutes to study domestic medicine promoted medicinal plants as a viable option to achieve national pharmaceutical independence. These actions were fueled by the rising cost of medications and a realization that Mexico's inability to care for its sick was connected to foreign laboratories' control over the production of most medications for domestic sale. By 1975 barbasco had become a public, prized Mexican commodity because it held the promise of liberating Mexico from pharmaceutical dependence. It also became tactically convenient for Echeverría to link the need for nationally produced medications with the long-ignored campesino population. Basing his regime on reforms that would benefit all Mexicans, Echeverría showcased the plight of landless campesinos struggling to make ends meet. Consequently, his populist agenda helped connect root-picking peasants to a forgotten tenet of the Revolution: healthcare.

The creation of Proquivemex was a first step in achieving pharmaceutical independence for Mexico, but by bringing the laboratories to rural areas in Tuxtepec, and to other places in Puebla and Chiapas, and staffing them with local residents, the government radically, and most likely unwittingly, demystified the image of the type of individual who could work in a scientific setting. The presence of a laboratory in the jungle implied that even campesinos could and should do science. And some did. As this book showed a handful of campesinos were able to learn enough key chemical processes to manipulate diosgenin yields. These individuals benefitted financially and socially from their association with the root. But in the end, Proquivemex—with its lofty goals of eventually handing over all the installations to campesinos—could not survive an increasingly hostile market for barbasco-derived steroid hormones. Advances in science had made barbasco irrelevant.

At least three of Proquivemex's former directors agreed that the state-subsidized company would have survived and thrived if it had been funded for a few more years.[8] When interviewed fifteen years after the company's closure, they all agreed that the problem had been time: Proquivemex opened its doors too late in Echeverría's administration to fully benefit from the populist reforms. Some Proquivemex officials also blamed a corrupt political system. For their part, certain *beneficio* owners blamed Proquivemex mismanagement and its reliance on Marxist ideals which clashed with its role as a profit-seeking company. Many within the company blamed corrupt campesinos who exploited their own communities and some campesinos, in turn, blamed Proquivemex mismanagement and graft. And, of course, transnational laboratories blamed a government with no knowledge of chemistry for getting involved with pharmaceuticals in the first place. As was shown, this finger pointing reflected the varied groups and multiple interests—social, political, medical, and economic—that claimed barbasco as their own.

Most documentation pertaining to the barbasco trade from 1985 onward is a pessimistic recounting of failed attempts to make the industry work. That makes campesinos' fond memories of Proquivemex so much more extraordinary. That the Mexican government decided to create a domestic laboratory *in the jungle* with the end goal of competing on an international scale with transnational laboratories is, in hindsight, significant for its folly. The foolishness for some, however, lies in the government's inability to carry its financing of the company beyond the end of one presidential term. Still, a lesson of the barbasco trade is that former employees and bureaucrats heatedly insisted years after its closure that Proquivemex's social-commercial experiment might have worked if campesinos had been allowed to continue. It is in their fervent memories that we can begin to question who is allowed to have a historical memory and who is also allowed to, in this case, synthesize steroids. As peasants metaphorically and symbolically donned white laboratory coats, they challenged the nation to see them in a role beyond that of rural dwellers. In a similar fashion, as Mexico contested the rights of transnational pharmaceutical companies, it challenged the world to see it as a producer and not simply a consumer of science. But in the case of barbasco no institutional or national memory of its impact on Mexico would survive.

On May 21, 1997, the Secretariat of the Environment, Natural Resources, and Fishing (SEMARNAP) received a letter from a chemist outlining a project for the "integral use" of barbasco.[9] The first proposed step was to promote the organization of potential barbasco pickers. The second proposal made the reader stop and ponder. It suggested that campesinos might be taught how to best gather and "transform" barbasco and, in partnership with chemists from the UNAM, "increase diosgenin content" for sorely needed pharmaceutical products.[10] But a somber note attached to the letter dispels any eagerness for future projects. Ironically, it concludes that barbasco gathering is unfeasible in rural Mexico because campesinos do not know the yam nor do they know how to harvest it.

Today diosgenin-filled barbasco continues to grow in southern Mexico.

1. Name

2. Age

3. Town where you were born? Town where you now live?

4. Occupation

5. Have you heard of barbasco?

6. What is barbasco?

7. Did you ever pick barbasco? How do you dig it up?

8. How old were you when you started to pick barbasco?

9. What tools did you use?

10. Did you need special clothes or shoes to pick barbasco?

11. How much did you dig up in one day?

12. Was it hard or easy to pick barbasco? Why?

13. Were there any dangers in picking barbasco?

14. Where did you pick barbasco?

15. How far was it from your home?

16. What time did you leave your home? What time did you come back?

17. What days did you pick barbasco? Why on those days?

18. Where did you sell your barbasco?

19. How did you get it there?

20. How much did they pay?

21. Why were they buying barbasco?

22. Why did you gather barbasco?

23. Did you hear of the Unión Nacional de Productores y Recolectores de Barbasco?

24. Were you a member?

25. Did you hear about Proquivemex? What was it?

26. Did you go to school? What grade did you complete?

Translations of all Spanish-language quotations are my own.

Introduction

1. Melquíades Santiago, personal interview, Valle Nacional, Oaxaca, April 1999. The story was corroborated by Pedro Ramírez and Guillermo Wilkins, former president of the Barbasco Union and former director of Proquivemex, respectively. I sat in on two National Peasant Confederation (CNC) meetings in Mexico City and Valle Nacional. In addition, Pedro Ramírez shared photographs of barbasco meetings, which helped shape the above description.

2. Though weeds are understood as "a plant growing out of place" (Elmer Grant Campbell, "What Is a Weed?," 50) or wild plants which grow in "habitats markedly disturbed by human activity" (J. C. Chacón and S. R. Gliessman, "Use of the 'Non-Weed' Concept in Traditional Tropical Agroecosystems of South-Eastern Mexico," Agro-Ecosystems 8 [1982]:1), weeds, as such, are socially constructed. In southeastern Mexico the idea of "nonweed" is closely associated with the concept that certain plants that are noncrops still perform a valuable role in the agroecosystem.

3. Some notable examples of recent scholarship that urges us to rethink Latin America's role in modern scientific endeavors are Julyan Peard, *Race, Place and Medicine*; J. Rodriguez, *Civilizing Argentina: Science, Medicine and the Modern State* (Durham, N.C.: Duke University Press, 2006); N. Leys Stepan, *Beginnings of Brazilian Science* (Watson Pub. International, 1981); and Juan José Saldaña, *Science in Latin America* (Austin: University of Texas Press, 2006).

4. Cited in Carl Djerassi, *Steroids Made It Possible*, 34.

5. "Mexican Hormones," 162.

6. The quote continues by asserting "a statement that is not meant in any way to denigrate Searle's commitment to the contraceptive field and that company's successful drive to be the first on the market with a steroid oral contraceptive."

Earlier, Djerassi had clarified this point by explaining that "Searle deserves full credit for reaching the market first with an oral contraceptive, norethynodrel, under the trade name Enovid, but its repeated claim to have synthesized the substance independently and concurrently with Syntex's norethindrone constitutes a blatant misrepresentation of the facts." Djerassi, *This Man's Pill*, 58 and 53, respectively.

7. *Harper's Magazine* reported, "The cortisone production problem was solved . . . it should be noted that the leader in the race was a chemical manufacturer in presumably backward Mexico." Leonard Engel, "ACTH, Cortisone, & Co," 25.

8. D. Freebairn, *The Dichotomy of Prosperity*, 38.

9. Gary Gereffi's *The Pharmaceutical Industry and Dependency in the Third World* uses the steroid hormone industry as an example to illustrate dependency theory in Latin America.

10. At the inauguration of the National Population Council (CONAPO), Echeverría explicitly called for Mexican scientists to produce Mexican oral contraceptives. Act of the Solemn Founding of the National Population Council, March 27, 1974.

11. D. Borges, "'Puffy, Ugly, Slothful and Inert': Degeneration in Brazilian Social Thought, 1880–1940," *Journal of Latin American Studies* 25 (1993): 235–56; A. Stern, "Responsible Mothers and Normal Children"; N. Stepan, *The Hour of Eugenics*.

12. As Stepan reminds us, Latin American intellectuals "embraced science as a form of progressive knowledge, as an alternative to the religious view of reality, and as a means of establishing a new form of cultural power." *The Hour of Eugenics*, 41.

13. K. Bliss, *Compromised Positions: Prostitution, Public Health and Gender Politics in Revolutionary Mexico*; Diego Armus, *Disease in the History of Modern Latin America: From Malaria to AIDS*; E. Zolov, *Refried Elvis: The Rise of the Mexican Counterculture*; W. Anderson, *Colonial Pathologies: American Tropical Medicine, Race and Hygiene in the Philippines*.

14. Lara Marks, *Sexual Chemistry*; L. Briggs, *Reproducing Empire: Race, Sex, Science, and U.S. Imperialism in Puerto Rico*.

15. L. Schiebinger, *Nature's Body*, 185.

16. David Wade Chambers and Richard Gillespie, "Locality in the History of Science," 224.

17. Steven Feierman, *Peasant Intellectuals*, 18.

18. Paul Gootenberg, "Cocaine in Chains," 322.

19. Steven Topik, *From Silver to Cocaine*; C. Walsh, *The Social Relations of Mexican Commodities*.

20. Vandana Shiva, "Bioprospecting as Sophisticated Biopiracy," *Signs: Journal of Women in Culture and Society* 32, no. 2 (2007): 307; W. Reid et al., *Biodiversity*

Prospecting: Using Genetic Resources for Sustainable Development (Washington, D.C.: World Resources Institute, 1993).

21. C. Hayden, *When Nature Goes Public: The Making and Unmaking of Bioprospecting in Mexico*; M. Goldman, *Privatizing Nature: Political Struggles for the Global Commons*; A. González, "Biopiratería o apoyo al desarrollo comunitario? La Guerra por los microorganismos," *La Jornada* (January 10, 2000); J. Goodman and Vivien Walsh, *The Story of Taxol: Nature and Politics in the Pursuit of an Anti-cancer Drug*; V. Shiva, *Monocultures of the Mind: Perspectives on Biodiversity and Biotechnology*.

22. Studies on the neem tree, for example, broadly paint the main uses of the plants before the arrival of pharmaceutical companies. Studies of commodities in Latin America—particularly sugar, coffee, tobacco, and bananas—serve as interesting models for how specific ethnic groups determined labor and land use.

23. Anderson, *Colonial Pathologies*, 110; B. Latour, *"Give Me a Laboratory and I Will Raise the World,"* and *The Pasteurization of France*; S. Shapin, "The House of Experiment in Seventeenth-Century England."

24. Latour, *"Give Me a Laboratory and I Will Raise the World,"* 159.

25. Kohler, *Landscapes and Labscapes*, 2.

26. Djerassi, *This Man's Pill*; Jean-Paul Gaudilliere, "Better Prepared than Synthesized," 612–44; Gereffi, *The Pharmaceutical Industry and Dependency in the Third World*; Marks, *Sexual Chemistry*.

27. Myrna Santiago, *The Ecology of Oil*; Christopher Boyer, "Modernizing the Monte"; Stuart McCook, "Giving Plants a Civil Status."

28. Florencia Mallon, *Peasant and Nation*; Boyer, *Becoming Campesinos*; Gilbert Joseph and Daniel Nugent, *Everyday Forms of State Formation*.

29. Boyer, *Becoming Campesinos*, 79.

30. Roy McLeod, "Nature and Empire."

31. In exchange for this privilege, I left a detailed log of which boxes were contained in each room. This rudimentary log, with my handwritten annotations, was still being used in early 2007 by the archivists in Galería 3.

32. Francisco Rosas, Cerro Concha, 1999.

33. Isidro Apolinar, Chiltepec, 1999.

34. Melquíades Santiago, Valle Nacional, 1999.

35. Francisco Rosas, Cerro Concha, 1999.

36. Alejandro Weber, Jacatepec, 1999.

37. Isidro Apolinar, personal interview, Chiltepec, 1999.

38. L. Engel, "Cortisone and Plenty of It," and "ACTH, Cortisone, & Co."

1. Papaloapan, Poverty, and Wild Yam

1. The author conducted interviews with Isidro Apolinar of Chiltepec, Oaxaca, in November 1998, April 1999, November 2001, and July 2004. The text regarding Apolinar is based on transcriptions from these interviews.
2. In 1952, the population of San José Chiltepec was 2,219 inhabitants, compared with a recorded 1,108,915 total for the entire Papaloapan River Basin. Alfonso Villa Rojas, *Las obras del Papaloapan, 1947–1952*, 20.
3. After the Lacandon in Chiapas and Los Chimalapas. Julia Carabias, Enrique Provencio, and Carlos Toledo, *Manejo de recursos naturales y pobreza rural*.
4. Ibid., 57.
5. Quoted in Paul Garner, *Regional Development in Oaxaca during the Porfiriato (1876–1911)*, 8.
6. Ibid.
7. *Fondo Mixto Revolvente para Estudios de Preinversión.*
8. Villa Rojas, *Las obras del Papaloapan*, 9.
9. Villa Rojas, *El Papaloapan, obra del Presidente Alemán*, 9.
10. Ibid., 8.
11. Ibid., section V.
12. Ibid.
13. Ibid.
14. Ibid.
15. Birn, *Marriage of Convenience*, 86, 146.
16. Mixe, Mixteco, Zapoteco, Triqui, Mazateco, and even some Nahuas from the state of Puebla were just some of the ethnic groups that passed by or settled in the areas surrounding Chiltepec.
17. Villa Rojas, *Las obras del Papaloapan*, 21.
18. Villa Rojas, *El Papaloapan, obra del Presidente Alemán*, section V.
19. Ibid., 7.
20. Though Apolinar referred to them as plantations, their description more readily fits that of Mexican haciendas.
21. *Etnografía contemporánea de los pueblos indígenas de México*, 26.
22. Before the Aztec conquest, the area of the Chinantla was divided and ruled by three independent *señoríos*, but the communities of the Chinantla did not vary significantly from other Mesoamerican settlements. The towns were centers for the ruling class, priests, and nobles, and clustered around these population centers were disperse *rancherías*, or smaller human settlements. Chinantecos were not, despite their remote location, isolated from the rest of what is now central Oaxaca. Active commerce existed between other ethnic groups, such as the Mixtecos, Popolucas, and Zapotecos.
23. *Etnografía contemporánea de los pueblos indígenas de México*, 29.

24. Ibid., 29.

25. Ibid., 34.

26. Ibid., 31.

27. Ana Paula de Teresa, *Población y territorio en la región chinanteca de Oaxaca*, 17.

28. Chassen-López, *From Liberal to Revolutionary Oaxaca: The View From the South, 1867–1911*.

29. Matías Romero, *El Estado de Oaxaca*, 83 ss, and cited in Tomás García Hernández, *Tuxtepec ante la Historia*, 210.

30. Cited in *Recursos naturales de la cuenca del Papaloapan*, 864.

31. John Kenneth Turner, *Barbarous Mexico*, 54.

32. Turner's reports were initially serialized in *American Magazine* and were a huge hit. After the third installment, however, the series abruptly ended. Turner would charge that President Díaz himself had intimidated the magazine's staff. The following year *Barbarous Mexico* made its appearance and was popular both in the United States and in England. In the preface to the original, Turner explained that "the term 'barbarous' which I use in my title is intended to apply to Mexico's form of government rather than to its people." Though certainly written to outrage, Turner's book is often credited with winning the sympathies of the United States population in support of the Mexican Revolution. Turner is painted over the left shoulder of Karl Marx in David Alfaro Siqueiros's mural in Chapultepec Castle. See the introduction to the 1969 edition for further details.

33. Once skeptical about Francisco I. Madero, the leader of the revolution, Turner would eventually meet the Mexican president; upon meeting him, Turner expressed some hope for change. Turner was, however, briefly imprisoned after Madero's assassination. He returned to the United States at the start of the Mexican Revolution to denounce the partisan hand of Henry Lane Wilson, the U.S. ambassador. Turner, *Barbarous Mexico*, xi–xxix.

34. Turner, *Barbarous Mexico*, 68–90.

35. Ibid., 72.

36. "Margarita ¿por qué lloras? Porque tengo que llorar. Si a mi negro se lo llevan/Para el Valle Nacional." (Margarita, why do you cry? Because I have to. They are taking my negro/to Valle Nacional.) Mexican Corrido, quoted in Arellanes Meixueiro, *Oaxaca*, 89.

37. Turner, *Barbarous Mexico*, 72.

38. García Hernández, *Tuxtepec ante la Historia*, 92.

39. Charles David Kepner Jr. and Jay Henry Soothill, *The Banana Empire*, 305.

40. Shortly thereafter the building was torn down and a cultural center was built.

41. Joseph Cotter, *Troubled Harvest*, 126.

42. Ibid., 125.

43. Manuel Avila Camacho, "Address to the Mexican Agronomists," National and International Problems Series, no. 8 (Mexico City: Talleres Gráficos de la Nación, 1941), 12.

44. John Mason Hart, *Empire and Revolution*, 418.

45. Ibid., 412.

46. Nine rivers—Grande (also known as Alto Papaloapan), Salado, Santo Domingo, Tonto, Valle Nacional, Usila, Obispo, Tesechoacán, and San Juan Evangelista— flow into the Papaloapan River. The Blanco River, which flows independently, also leads into the Laguna de Alvarado.

47. Thomas Poleman, *The Papaloapan Project*, 89.

48. Ibid., 89. Mariano Espinosa, *Apuntes históricos de las tribus chinantecas, mazatecas y popolucas (Papeles de la Chinantla III)* (Mexico City: Museo Nacional de Antropologia, 1961), 89. For references to Tlalocan, see Villa Rojas, *El Papaloapan, obra del Presidente Alemán*, 7.

49. Quoted in Mariano Espinosa, *Apuntes históricos de las tribus chinantecas, mazatecas y popolucas (Papeles de la Chinantla III)*, 90.

50. Delfino Hernández Salazar, personal interview, Tuxtepec, Oaxaca, 1999.

51. To this day, a prisoner is traditionally set free on September 23. García Hernández, *Tuxtepec ante la historia*.

52. Villa Rojas, *El Papaloapan, obra del Presidente Alemán*, 45.

53. *Fondo Mixto Revolvente para Estudios de Preinversión*, 38.

54. *Todos con México, Reuniones nacionales de estudio, discursos de Luis Echeverría, 1970*, 128.

55. Villa Rojas, *Las obras del Papaloapan*, 36.

56. There is some dispute over this number. According to the Subcoordinadora of Tuxtepec, the actual number was 26,370 hectares. The official number provided by the then Secretaría de Recursos Hidráulicos was 20,000.

57. Miguel Alberto Bartolomé and Alicia Mabel Barabas, *Presa Cerro de Oro y el Ingeniero el Gran Dios*.

58. *Etnografía contemporánea de los pueblos indígenas de México*, 40.

59. Roger Bartra, *La jaula de la melancolía*, 56.

60. Though scholars have explored how increased drinking and homicide after the conquest should not be interpreted as a sign of demoralized despair among indigenous communities but rather as a form of adaptation and survival, Apolinar explained that his "bad path" to drinking was because times were so hard. Though he did not use the word *despair*, his descriptions of attempting to get by and provide for his family are riddled with frustration. See Taylor, *Drinking, Homicide and Rebellion in Colonial Mexican Villages* (1979).

61. The Chinantecos are the fourth largest indigenous group of a total of eighteen groups in the state of Oaxaca.

62. De Teresa, *Población y territorio en la región chinanteca de Oaxaca*, 15.

63. As a point of comparison, in 1900 there were 491 population centers through-out the Chinantla, but by 1997 there were only 256 left, suggesting that the probability of survival for population centers was extremely low. Ibid., 19.

64. Valle Nacional with 1,067; Yolox with 1,059; Ojitlán with 3,131; and Usila with 2,430. Ibid., 21.

65. Many locals claim it was the end of the barbasco trade that forced people who no longer had the barbasco safety net to look elsewhere, either in other states within Mexico or even farther afield in the United States. Although some biologists also noted this correlation between the decrease in barbasco trade and an increase in migration out of the area, no studies, to my knowledge, have shown this relationship.

66. Juan Ballesteros, Matthew Edel, and Michael Nelson, *La colonización del Papa-loapan*, 57.

67. "Explotaciones forestales en la cuenca del Papaloapan."

2. Peasants, a Chemist, and the Pill

1. Russell E. Marker, interview by Jeffrey L. Sturchio at Pennsylvania State University, April 17, 1987 (Philadelphia: Chemical Heritage Foundation [CHF], Oral History Transcript #0068): 21. From this point forward referred to as Marker interview.

2. Ibid., 21.

3. Norman Applezweig, *Steroid Drugs*, x.

4. Ibid., x, and also quoted in Albert Maisel, *The Hormone Quest*, 52–53.

5. Marker interview, 1.

6. Unless otherwise noted, all the details from Marker's earlier years are taken from transcripts of the Marker interview and an autobiography of him provided by the CHF and information found in Russell Earl Marker's personal papers in the Pennsylvania State University Archives in College Station, Pennsylvania.

7. R. E. Marker and N. E. Gordon, "Effect of Hydrogen-Ion Concentration on Compound Formation and Absorption of Dyes by Mordants," 1186–88.

8. Marker interview, 11.

9. Supposedly, a friend of the endocrinologist Ernst Starling first used the term to describe the chemical messengers secreted in the glands but producing effects elsewhere; see Paul Vaughan, *The Pill on Trial*, 8.

10. Albert Maisel, *The Hormone Quest*, 9.

11. For obvious political reasons Kennedy's condition was kept out of the press. It would have been difficult to be elected with a deteriorating health condition. At a time when cortisone was prohibitively expensive, treatment was accessible only to a wealthy few. Richard Reeves, "John F. Kennedy." I thank Sarah Cline for pointing out this fact to me.

12. "Diabetes: Dreaded Disease Yields to New Gland Cure," *New York Times*, May 6, 1923.

13. Ernst Henry Starling first publicly introduced the word *hormone* in his 1905 lecture titled "The Chemical Correlation of the Functions of the Body." This lecture put forth the idea that hormones were chemical messengers produced at one point in the body that acted at other specific sites in the body. All hormones together form the endocrine system, and the study of this system and its disorders is called endocrinology. See Lawrence Crapo, *Hormones*, 11; and Maisel, *The Hormone Quest*, 20.

14. The other type of hormones are peptides, which differ from steroids not only in how they are made but also in how they act in the body. Composed of amino acids bound together, peptides work on the surface of receptor cells, promoting reactions via secondary messengers. On the other hand, steroids, which are made from cholesterol, have the characteristic four-ring structure, work by binding to internal cell receptors, and are regulated by the genetic code in DNA. Both peptide and steroid hormones are essential for the proper function of human life. To understand how differently these two hormones act, see Crapo, *Hormones*, 26.

15. Ibid., 25.

16. Gary Gereffi, *The Pharmaceutical Industry and Dependency*.

17. Seyhan Ege, *Organic Chemistry*, 710. I borrowed this layman's explanation of the steroid nucleus from Margaret Kreig, who succinctly lays out the problem in her chapter on wild yams in *Green Medicine*, 257.

18. Shelly Oudshoorn, *Beyond the Natural Body*, 67.

19. "Mexican Hormones," 161.

20. In 1941 the U.S. Justice Department ruled that American branches of Ciba, Schering, and Organon could not carry on their monopoly, price fixing, and manipulation of patents of sex hormones in the United States. "Mexican Hormones," 161.

21. Oudshoorn, *Beyond the Natural Body*, 73.

22. This chemical discovery altered the Victorian conception of biological determinism, which held that nature had determined men's and women's social roles and that these roles could neither be equal nor compatible with each other. See Adele Clarke, "Controversy and Development."

23. Quoted in Oudshoorn, *Beyond the Natural Body*, 29.

24. Ibid., 68, n. 10. The problem, then, became how to obtain comparable amounts of male sex hormones. In the 1920s no institution or clinic existed that could aid in the collection of male urine, and urine collected from hospital patients contained noticeably lower amounts of hormones than that of healthy males. Consequently, to obtain men's urine, scientists were forced to look for other

places where men gathered regularly. A solution was found in 1931, when the German biochemist Adolf Butenandt reportedly "collected 25,000 liters of men's urine in the police barracks in Berlin, from which he isolated 50 mg of a crystalline substance." Quoted in Oudshoorn, *Beyond the Natural Body*, 76. Believing that this substance was the essential male hormone, he called it "androsterone." Despite researchers' advances in obtaining male urine, it remained virtually impossible to maintain a constant supply from prisons and military barracks. The only real solution was to rely on pharmaceutical companies which, as explained earlier, regulated the supply of other source materials for hormones. Researchers now assert that the lack of available male urine and testes affected the study of endocrinology to the degree that andrology would not be institutionalized as a medical specialty until the late 1960s. Moreover, the knowledge of the development of reproductive research would lead to astounding advances in female hormone production, culminating in the creation of the Pill, whereas delayed knowledge about male reproduction socially affected how people conceptualize birth control. See Adele Clarke, "Controversy and Development of Reproductive Sciences," 18–37.

25. Oudshoorn, *Beyond the Natural Body*, 80.

26. Ibid., 74. Regarding the interspecies equivalence of steroid hormones, according to Dr. Barrie Grant of the San Luis Rey Equine Hospital, "progesterone is progesterone"—the progesterone structure is the same in mares as it is in women. The main qualitative difference is the level of acidity in mares' urine compared with women's urine.

27. To collect urine, a special campaign to target horse owners was begun. As Oudshoorn wrote, "Farmers and even the Ministry of Agriculture were most surprised to discover that they could sell the liquid waste products from their mares for prices equal to those of cows' milk." *Beyond the Natural Body*, 75.

28. Ibid., 98.

29. Ibid., 93; also see Clarke, "Research Materials and Reproductive Science in the United States, 1910–1940."

30. Women suffering from dysfunctions attributable to the ovaries—such as melancholia, schizophrenia, psychoses, depression, eczema, joint disorders, epilepsy, hair loss, diabetes, hemophilia, obesity, rheumatism, irritability, tension, and even eye disorders—were all treated with female sex hormones. Since then, other social and medical factors have debunked these earlier prognoses. Oudshoorn, *Beyond the Natural Body*, 92–95.

31. The hesitancy of his supervisor, P. A. Levene, was most likely a reaction to recent work by a Rockefeller Institute colleague, Walter A. Jacobs, who had used sarsaparilla roots to show that hormones could not be derived from the sapogenin contained in those tubers. However, Marker, with what would become

a familiar doggedness, insisted that he wanted to focus on hormones; despite his colleague's findings, Marker was certain that the hormone supply problem could be solved using vegetable material. On the same day that he made public these desires, Marker's supervisor took him to see Dr. Flexner, the director of the institute. Several histories of Marker have commented on the heated discussion that ensued: Flexner, befuddled as to why someone who was completing satisfactory work at the Rockefeller Institute would want to jeopardize his appointment by working independently of the principal investigator, allegedly insisted that Marker could stay only if he continued to work on what had been assigned to him. Marker then simply commented, "I'll find somewhere else to work on my own." Marker interview, 11. Lara V. Marks, in her book *Sexual Chemistry*, also comments on Marker's abrupt departure from the Rockefeller Institute.

32. Maisel, *The Hormone Quest*, 258.
33. Marker, E. L. Wittle, and E. J. Lawson, "Sterols. XLIX. Isolation of Pregnanediols from Bull's Urine," 2931–33.
34. Vaughan, *The Pill on Trial*, 10.
35. At the same time, researchers from the National Institute for Medical Research (NIMR) in England were searching for plant sapogenins in West Africa. In addition, NIMR researchers had also discovered that hecogenin, the main substance in sisal fiber, could serve as starting material. "Early English Steroid History," 57. For Marker's work on yucca and agave plants, see Kreig, *Green Medicine*, 259.
36. Vaughan, *The Pill on Trial*, 11.
37. Ibid.
38. Sarsaparilla, a popular treatment for syphilis in the sixteenth century, was also used to treat rheumatism and other ills. In the 1800s sarsaparilla tonics claiming to "purify the system of all leftover infelicities of winter" could be found nationally throughout the United States. Moreover, it was believed that sarsaparilla tonics could cure "lost manhood" (presumably impotence) ailments. See Kreig's chapter "It Started with Sarsaparilla," in *Green Medicine*, 255–71.
39. "Sarsaparilla Root Yields 3 Hormones: Price Slash Predicted through Discovery at Penn State," *New York Times*, December 18, 1939.
40. Ibid.
41. The following sources mention Marker's search throughout the southwestern United States and northern Mexico: Vaughan, *The Pill on Trial*, 10; Gereffi, *The Pharmaceutical Industry and Dependency in the Third World*, 82; Pedro Lehmann, "Russell E. Marker," 197; Kreig, *Green Medicine*, 255–71; and Lehmann, "Early History of Steroid Chemistry in Mexico." Other accounts of the initial testing on steroids that eventually led to the search for *Dioscoreas* were part of a series in *Steroids* 57 (1992) recalling the origins of steroidal research. These articles included Ewart Jones, "Early English Steroid History"; Seymour Bernstein, "Historic Reflections on Steroids"; Arthur Birch, "Steroid Hormones and

the Luftwaffe"; Josef Fried, "Hunt for an Economical Synthesis of Cortisol"; and Konrad Bloch, "Sterol Molecule."

42. Lehmann, "Early History of Steroid Chemistry in Mexico," 407.

43. Ibid.; Marker interview, 19.

44. Gordon Schnedel, *Medicine in Mexico*, 76.

45. Marker interview, 21.

46. Ibid.

47. Marker was not allowed to import "avocado seed, sugarcane (all parts of the plant), citrus stock including scions and buds, Musa spp., all general and species of the tribe Bambuseae, all species of sweet potatoes." In "Letter from the In Charge of the Laredo Area to Frank Whitmore," November 10, 1941. Russell Marker Papers, Paterno Library, box 1, folder 18.

48. Russell E. Marker. "The Early Production of Steroidal Hormones," autobiographic notes, 2 (Philadelphia: Chemical Heritage Foundation [CHF], archives).

49. Marker to Frank Koch, July 5, 1983. Russell Marker Papers, Paterno Library, box 1, folder 18.

50. "Letter from Frank C. Whitmore to Whom It May Concern, November 5, 1941." Russell Marker Papers, Paterno Library, box 1, folder 1, Paterno/GST/A001.13.

51. Hart, *Empire and Revolution*, 420.

52. *Dioscorea mexicana Guillen* grew in San Luis Potosí, Veracruz, Oaxaca, Tabasco, Chiapas, and Guerrero. Its diosgenin content oscillated between .3 and .8 percent. Luis González Leija and Ana Cecilia Mañón, "Estudios ecológicos sobre el barbasco," 9.

53. Marker interview, 21.

54. Marker to Frank Koch, July 5, 1983. Russell Marker Papers, Paterno Library, box 1, folder 18.

55. Marker interview, 21.

56. Ibid.

57. According to an often-repeated tale, while in Veracruz, Marker observed how local fishermen chopped up a wild root and flung it into a lake. Moments later, fish would float to the surface, stunned but alive. What Marker the chemist noticed, however, was that when the root touched the surface of the water, it produced a soapy foam, a clear indication of the presence of saponins. Despite this highly popular version of the cunning-scientist story, Lehmann also alludes, correctly, to the Moreno connection. Moreover, in the summer of 1990 the then aged Russell Marker traveled from Penn State to Veracruz and, accompanied by an entourage of Mexican chemists, presented a plaque (made in Marker's honor by Penn State) to Adolfina Moreno, Alberto Moreno's daughter. See Lehmann, "Early History of Steroid Chemistry in Mexico," 403–8.

58. Marker's personal papers at Penn State have several photo albums filled with

pictures that Marker took during his various trips to Mexico. One of them is of the storefront with Moreno's family in the foreground.

59. Marker interview, 22.

60. Ibid.

61. Russell E. Marker, "The Early Production of Steroidal Hormones," autobiographic notes, 3 (Philadelphia: Chemical Heritage Foundation [CHF], archives).

62. Marker interview, 23.

63. Marker repeats this exact line, "nothing could be done in Mexico," in two different sources: his autobiography and a 1987 oral history conducted by Jeffrey Sturchio.

64. Lara Marks noted in her book *Sexual Chemistry*, 66, that Parke-Davis believed that the hormone market was somewhat limited. However, as Oudshoorn alluded to in *Beyond the Natural Body*, and newspapers of the time revealed, hormones and the glands from which they derived were believed to be linked to crime rates and even world peace: "Glands as Cause of Many Crimes," *New York Times*, December 4, 1921; and "Glands Held Key to Peace in World," *New York Times*, December 3, 1937, respectively.

65. As quoted in Marker interview, 23.

66. Vaughan, *The Pill on Trial*, 13.

67. Of seventeen oil companies, fourteen were held by United States interests.

68. Kreig, *Green Medicine*, 265.

69. Ibid., 262.

70. Maisel, *The Hormone Quest*, 45.

71. Marker had already explored the area around Mexico City and discovered that Parke-Davis had a new packaging place in Mexico City with "a lot of land and . . . buildings." Hence, Marker thought that Parke-Davis would be willing to invest what he called a "mere" US$10,000 and allow him to use the existing facilities. Marker interview.

72. Letter from F. C. Whitmore to Russell Marker, December 16, 1942. Russell Earl Marker Papers, Paterno Library, box 1, file 18.

73. Djerassi, "The Making of the Pill." See also Kreig, *Green Medicine*, 263.

74. As quoted in Djerassi, *This Man's Pill*, 22–23.

75. Lehmann, "Russell E. Marker," 196.

76. Gereffi, *The Pharmaceutical Industry and Dependency in the Third World*, 83.

77. Marker interview.

78. Vaughan, *The Pill on Trial*, 15.

79. "Mexican Hormones," 90.

80. As late as 1966, however, steroid hormone researchers were still using animal organs as a means of research. For example A. V. Schally received a generous

donation from Wisconsin meatpacker Oscar Mayer for his research on pig hypothalami. Oscar Mayer employees slaughtered approximately 10,000 pigs a day and, over time, donated more than 1 million pig hypothalami to Schally's laboratory. Crapo, *Hormones*, 45.

81. Marker had also done this when he left the Rockefeller Institute.

82. George Rosenkranz, "From Ruzicka's Terpenes in Zurich to Mexican Steroids via Cuba," 409–18.

83. Marker interview, 27.

84. Marker interview; Bernard Asbell, *The Pill*, 101.

85. Marker recalls one of his assistant's being threatened with a gun by someone who commanded him to stop collecting wild yams. Marker interview, 27.

86. Letter from Russell Marker to Frank Koch, July 7, 1983. Russell Earl Marker Papers, Paterno Library, box 1, folder 18, Paterno/GST/A001.13.

87. Ibid.

88. Rosenkranz, "From Ruzicka's Terpenes in Zurich to Mexican Steroids via Cuba."

89. Pennsylvania State Archives, letter from Russell Marker to Frank Koch, May 4, 1983. Russell Earl Marker Papers, Paterno Library, box 1, folder 18, Paterno/GST/A001.13. In this letter, Marker also mentions a painting he commissioned (of the original coffee-drying spot in Veracruz) in 1974, when he returned to Mexico for the IV International Congress.

90. The most cited work is that of Pedro Lehmann, "Russell E. Marker," which originally appeared in Spanish but was reprinted in abridged form in *Chemical Education* in 1973. Lehmann himself sent reprints of the article to more than seventy chemists, including Ruzicka and Percy Julian. In a letter of May 16, 1983, Marker complained to Frank Koch that the version of the creation of Syntex told by Lehmann, son of Marker's original partner in Syntex, was not entirely correct. Marker instead recommended the version written years later by Carl Djerassi, entitled *Progestins in Therapy*, to which he himself contributed two paragraphs. Marker to Koch, May 16, 1983. Russell Earl Marker Papers, Paterno Library, box 1, folder 18, Paterno/GST/A001.13.

91. Letter to Frank Koch, June 7, 1983. Russell Earl Marker Papers, Paterno Library, box 1, folder 18, Paterno/GST/A001.13.

92. Cited in Penn State, Russell Earl Marker Papers, Paterno Library, box 5, GST/A001.15.

93. Marker's life was interesting enough to be considered for cinematic treatment. In 1974 a German crew shot the story of Marker's discovery on location in Playa Vicente, Mexico, with the German actors Friedrich Schütter (playing Moreno) and Rudolf Wessely (as Professor Marker) in *Die Spur führt nach Mexiko* (*The Trail Leads to Mexico*). Marker and his wife were in Veracruz

for the filming of the made-for-television movie, which was well received in Germany.

94. Penn State, Russell Earl Marker Papers, Paterno Library, box 1, folder 28.
95. Marker interview, 17.
96. Rosenkranz, "From Ruzicka's Terpenes in Zurich to Mexican Steroids via Cuba."
97. "Mexican Hormones," 90; Gereffi, *The Pharmaceutical Industry and Dependency in the Third World*, 84.
98. Gereffi, *The Pharmaceutical Industry and Dependency in the Third World*, 84.
99. Ibid.
100. However, because mostly students worked at Syntex's laboratories, Syntex was soon nicknamed "University of Steroids." Rosenkranz, "From Ruzicka's Terpenes in Zurich to Mexican Steroids via Cuba," 414.
101. Dr. Ricardo Reyes Chilpa, personal interview, UNAM Instituto de Química, Mexico City, March 1999; also mentioned in Rosenkranz, "From Ruzicka's Terpenes in Zurich to Mexican Steroids via Cuba," 414.
102. Maisel, *The Hormone Quest*, 62–63.
103. Ibid., 63.
104. Ibid., 66.
105. Ibid., 65–69.
106. "Cortisone from Giant Yam," 75–77.
107. Maisel, *The Hormone Quest*, 69.
108. Ibid.
109. Reeves, "John F. Kennedy."
110. Kreig, *Green Medicine*, 267.
111. Ibid.
112. Cited in Djerassi, *Steroids Made It Possible*, 34.
113. Letter from Francis. S. Brown to Russell Marker, September 26, 1949. Russell Earl Marker Papers, Paterno Library, box 1, folder 18.
114. Ibid.
115. Engel, "ACTH, Cortisone, & Co.," 25–33.
116. "Mexican Hormones," 87; "Cortisone from Giant Yam," 75.
117. Gereffi, *The Pharmaceutical Industry and Dependency in the Third World*, 86.
118. Vaughan, *The Pill on Trial*, 20.
119. *Life*, June 6, 1949. According to the article, rheumatoid arthritis surpassed even polio in number of cases.
120. "Mexican Hormones," 168. In addition to Syntex, by 1961, Searle & Co.; Smith, Kline & French Laboratories; the Schering Corp.; Wyeth Laboratories' Division of the American Home Products Corp.; and German Schering were also exploiting Mexican wild yams. Maisel, *The Hormone Quest*, 54.

121. Gereffi, *The Pharmaceutical Industry and Dependency in the Third World*, 125.

122. Ing. Luis Ernesto Miramontes, personal interview, Mexico City, July 2004. For more information on Mexico's role in oral contraception research and a history of the Pill global in scope and not centered on the United States, see Marks, *Sexual Chemistry*. For an autobiographical account of the research taking place in Syntex laboratories in Mexico City, see Djerassi, *This Man's Pill*. For the health risks associated with earlier versions of the Pill, see Vaughan, *The Pill on Trial*.

123. Djerassi, *This Man's Pill*, 22–35; Marks, *Sexual Chemistry*.

124. Ing. Luis Miramontes, personal interview, Mexico City, July 6, 2004. The inadequate production of or inability to generate progesterone and other essential pregnancy hormones, which some women experienced, was believed to be one of the leading causes of miscarriages. The use of synthetic hormones, which became available on a large scale after the 1950s, guaranteed a reduction in miscarriages caused by hormone deficiency.

125. Ibid.

126. "Intervención del Dr. Rodolfo Tuirán."

127. The General Hospital of Zone 1 of the IMSS of Tepic, Nayarit, Miramontes's home state, was named the Luis Ernesto Miramontes Cárdenas Hospital in 1992.

3. The New "Green Gold"

1. J. C. Chacón and S. R. Gliessman, "Use of the 'Non-Weed' Concept in Traditional Tropical Agroecosystems of South-Eastern Mexico," 9; Lance Van Sittert, "The Seed Blows about in Every Breeze"; Elmer Grant Campbell, "What Is a Weed?"; Tim Cresswell, "Weeds, Plagues, and Bodily Secretions," 330–45.

2. Carlos Tello, personal interview, SEMARNAP, Mexico City, November 1998.

3. Heladia Portugal Guadalupe, personal interview, Jacatepec, Oaxaca, November 1998.

4. Ibid. Although female, Portugal used the male form of "killer," *asesino*, to describe herself.

5. A woman would drink the beverage and present signs of hemolysis, in which red blood cells dissolve in the plasma and cause bruising and blotching of the skin and possible death. I was unable to confirm this story, but for an account of the "creative" fashion by which women in the Mexican countryside were tested for adultery, see Steve Stern, *The Secret History of Gender*.

6. In 2006 Mowbe, a leader of the Nukak of Colombia, committed suicide by ingesting local barbasco, a fish poison used for fishing. "Suicide as Resistance," *Counterpunch*, December, 13, 2006. Though Colombian barbasco (a loncho-

carpus) is not similar to the Mexican barbasco, it illustrates that some local people were and are familiar with barbasco's potent properties.

7. Kreig, *Green Medicine*, 270. I found no mention of this story in Marker's personal papers.

8. Kreig, *Green Medicine*, 270.

9. Villa Rojas, *Las obras del Papaloapan*, 21.

10. Ibid.

11. Vaughan, *Modernizing Patriarchy*, 199.

12. Ibid.

13. I want to thank Professor Francie Chassen-López, who, in a brief e-mail exchange, explained the possible connection between Apolinar's interchangeable use of Liberal Party and PRI. According to her research, she suspects that this was the PRI's successful incorporation and association of Juárez's liberal beliefs.

14. Words pronounced by Edward S. Ayensu at the First International Symposium on *Dioscoreas* in Mexico City (1972), "Comments on Old and New World Dioscoreas of Commercial Importance," 77–81.

15. Vaughan, *The Pill on Trial*, 12.

16. Gustavo Zamora, "Del barbasco a la progesterona," 179.

17. The main commercial varieties found in Mexico are *Dioscorea speculiflora*, *Dioscorea composita* (known as barbasco), *Dioscorea mexicana* (known as cabeza de negro), and *Dioscorea floribunda* (known as barbasco rosado).

18. The Cruz-Badiano Codex depicts the Chichic Texcalamatl, which resembles other images of barbasco in Martín De La Cruz, *Libellus de Medicinalibus Indorum Herbis*. I am grateful to Sarah Cline for also pointing out the similarities in the description of illustration 441 of the Florentine Codex as what might be, potentially, barbasco. *Florentine Codex*.

19. Howard's *Botanic Medicine* (1836), quoted in Kreig, *Green Medicine*, 261–62.

20. Kreig, *Green Medicine*, 261–62.

21. Ibid.

22. Popol Vuh, *A Sacred Book of the Maya*, 151.

23. Rotenone from nekoe was also used as a biodegradable pesticide, and American soldiers used it during the Second World War to kill mites in their clothing. Plotkin, *Medicine Quest*, 169.

24. Applezweig, *Steroid Drugs*, 25.

25. Pedro Ramírez, personal interview, Mexico City, April 1999.

26. M. Santos, personal interview, Tuxtepec, Oaxaca, July 1999.

27. Kreig, *Green Medicine*, 288.

28. M. Santos, personal interview, Tuxtepec, Oaxaca, July 1999.

29. The following description is based on interviews with forty-nine former male root pickers and two female pickers. Please refer to the bibliography. Interviews

were conducted between November 1998 and November 2001. The process was verified by a Proquivemex report titled "Proceso del Barbasco." AGN, Proquivemex Archives, caja 22.

30. J. S., personal interview, Mexico City, 1999.

31. In July 2004 I was invited to join a group of UNAM scientists led by Dr. Ricardo Reyes Chilpa to collect plant samples near Catemaco, Veracruz. The day before I arrived, a man had been bitten by a nauyaca and, though the man's fate was uncertain, the local guide refused to take the group beyond the well-carved footpaths for fear that the snake was still in the area.

32. Based on interviews conducted in Cinco de Oro, Cerro Concha, Jacatepec, Chiltepec, La Gran Lucha, Tuxtepec, and Valle Nacional, all in Oaxaca, between November 1998 and July 1999.

33. Between 1979 and 2003 there were 2,728 deaths in Mexico linked to bites from snakes and poisonous lizards. The majority of victims were from the southeastern states, with Oaxaca coming in second only to Quintana Roo; the majority were male; and the largest group were sixty and older. M. Frayre-Torres et al., "Mortalidad por contacto traumático con serpiente y lagarto venenoso, México 1979–2003," *Gaceta Médica de México* 142, no. 3 (2006): 209–13.

34. Alejandro Weber, personal interview, Jacatepec, Oaxaca, April 1999.

35. Ibid. This last clause is extremely important because of the lack of roads in rural Oaxaca. In 1994, Jacatepec finished building a cement bridge wide enough for cars; until then, the only means of getting from the main highway to town, and the dozens of communities beyond it, was by rafting or crossing a hanging foot bridge.

36. Beneficios are where the root was finely chopped up, allowed to ferment, then placed to dry on cement slabs before it was shipped in sacks to laboratories. The entire process took about eight days.

37. "El Turco no dejaba que se fueran a vender a Valle." Personal interview with campesino from Jacatepec, Oaxaca, July 1999.

38. "¡Casi yo ganaba más de los que iban a sacar!" Alejandro Weber, personal interview, Jacatepec, Oaxaca, February 1999.

39. Ibid.

40. Lorenzo León Felipe, personal interview, Valle Nacional, Oaxaca, June 1999.

41. Alejandro Villar Borja and Eduardo Domínguez, personal interviews, Tlaxcala, Tlaxcala, February 1999; Pedro Ramírez, personal interview, Toluca, Estado de México, February 1999. Silvio Rodríguez, personal interview, July 1999, Mexico City.

42. Lorenzo León Felipe, personal interview, Valle Nacional, Oaxaca, June 1999.

43. Ibid.

44. Ibid.

45. "Proceso del barbasco." AGN, galería 2, Proquivemex, caja 22.

46. Francisco Rosas, personal interview, Cerro Concha, April 1999.

47. Alejandro Villar Borja, personal interview, Mexico City, 1999.

48. Folleto Proquivemex, ca. 1975. AVBP.

49. Emilio Fortín, personal interview, Catemaco, Veracruz, November 1998.

50. This fact was repeated by two beneficio owners, several dozen former pickers, and some former employees of Proquivemex.

4. Patents, Compounds, and Peasants

1. United States Senate, *Wonder Drugs*.

2. Ibid.

3. Gereffi, *The Pharmaceutical Industry and Dependency in the Third World*, 90.

4. Ibid., 90.

5. Ibid., 89.

6. Ibid.

7. Kreig, *Green Medicine*, 288.

8. The six nonsubsidiaries included General Mills (1956); Ogden Corporation (1956); Syntex (1958, when it became a private company again); G. D. Searle and Company (1958); American Home Products (1959); and Smith, Kline, and French (1961). Janka, *Relacionario del barbasco*, 9; Gereffi, *The Pharmaceutical Industry and Dependency in the Third World*. The European companies that established themselves in Mexico were the same ones that earlier in the century, in the 1930s and 1940s, controlled the global steroid hormone industry, among them Schering AG in Mexico in 1963 (German), Organon in 1969 (Dutch), and Ciba-Geigy in 1970 (Swiss).

9. Gereffi, *The Pharmaceutical Industry and Dependency in the Third World*; Felipe León Olivares, "Syntex, origen, apogeo y pérdida de una industria estratégica para México." For dependency theory, see F. H. Cardoso and E. Faletto, *Dependency and Development in Latin America* (1979; orig. pub. 1971).

10. United States Senate, *Wonder Drugs*, 52.

11. Ibid.

12. Ibid., 83.

13. Marker interview.

14. Hart, *Empire and Revolution*, 414.

15. Loyola Díaz, *Una mirada a México*, 46.

16. Hart, *Empire and Revolution*, 414–15.

17. Michael Meyer, William Sherman, and Susan Deeds, *The Course of Mexican History*, 569.

18. J. Romero, "Crecimiento y comercio," 175.

19. Meyer, Sherman, and Deeds, *The Course of Mexican History*, 569.

20. Miguel Ramirez, "Mexico's Development Experience, 1950–1985," 41.

21. *Diario Oficial,* Monday, May 7, 1951.

22. United States Senate, *Wonder Drugs,* 52.

23. Ibid., 5.

24. Ibid., 12.

25. Ibid., 8.

26. Gereffi, *The Pharmaceutical Industry and Dependency in the Third World,* 109.

27. United States Senate, *Wonder Drugs,* 17.

28. Ibid., 19.

29. Ibid., 19.

30. Ibid., 44.

31. Ibid., 44.

32. "Informe sobre situación actual y perspectivas."

33. Syntex, Stockholder's report, 1982.

34. (Emphasis mine.) Faustino Miranda and Efraím Hernández Xolocotzi, and Arturo Gómez-Pompa. "Un método para la investigación ecológica de las regiones tropicales," 102.

35. Arturo Gómez-Pompa, personal interviews, UC Riverside, Calif., June 2005.

36. Lane Simonian, *Defending the Land of the Jaguar,* 124.

37. Ibid.

38. Arturo Gómez-Pompa, personal interviews, June 2003 and June 17, 2005. This fact must have been more disturbing upon further inquiry because most transnational companies had independent experimental camps scattered throughout Mexico and understood more about the plant than any Mexican scientist before 1959.

39. Simonian, *Defending the Land of the Jaguar,* 124.

40. Lucile Brockway, "Plant Science and Colonial Expansion," 49–66. See Stuart McCook's use of plants as "citizens" of nations in "Giving Plants a Civil Status," 513–36.

41. Brockway, "Plant Science and Colonial Expansion," 51.

42. Alexander von Humboldt's *Political Essay on the Kingdom of New Spain* detailed not only the political system but agrarian administration and the natural wealth contained in Mexico.

43. As Gereffi underlined, "Syntex, Diosynth, and Protex were all founded by Hungarian Jews . . . who became naturalized Mexican citizens. Labs. Julian and Pesa were established by U.S. citizens." *The Pharmaceutical Industry and Dependency in the Third World,* 97, n. 2.

44. This was not the first time that a presidential decree ordered the creation of a state-owned pharmaceutical company. On December 17, 1949, President Miguel Alemán decreed that "developing a domestic pharmaceutical industry"

was needed to "produce medicines for all sectors of society" (para que desarrollando la industria químico-farmacéutica pueda producir medicamentos al alcance de las clases populares). Departamento de Gobierno, *Empresa de participaciones estatal para el desarrollo de la industria químico-farmacéutica, Decreto 1903*. Volumen 122. expediente 20, folio 3, AGN, Mexico City.

The foundation for the pharmaceutical industry came, not from domestic industry, but from German laboratories confiscated as a result of the outcome of the Second World War. The following laboratories were affected by this decree: Casa Beyer, S.A.; Merck México, S.A.; Química Schering Mexicana, S.A.; Reick Félix y Cia.; Instituto Behring de Terapéutica Experimental; S. de R.L.; Carlos Stein y Cia.; Laboratorios Codex, S.A; Gran Droguería del Refugio, S.A.; and Droguería Stein, S.A. Departamento de Gobierno, *Decreto 1903*. Agosto 16, 1950. "A la junta Intersecretarial Relativa a Propiedas y Negocios del Enemigo," Volumen 122. expediente 20, folio 3, AGN, Mexico City. Also seized with the physical property were the name brands, patents, and rights linked to these companies. Outlining the goals for the industry, the new company was to (a) produce medications that "alleviate illness endemic to our nation" at prices accessible to all, (b) increase the production of medicines in general, and (c) act as an impetus for the development of all pharmaceutical products in Mexico, especially those derived from "the use of the nation's natural resources, in particular medicinal plants which grow in Mexico and which up until now have only been used at a reduced scale." Ibid.

45. Departamento de Gobierno, *Decreto 1903*, 16–17.
46. Ibid., 19.
47. Fitzgerald, "Exporting American Agriculture," 460.
48. Arturo Gómez-Pompa, personal interviews, June 2005, UC Riverside, Calif.
49. Janka, *Relacionario del Barbasco*.
50. McCook, "Giving Plants a Civil Status."
51. Brockway, "Plant Science and Colonial Expansion," 49.
52. Not since the days of Miguel Angel de Quevedo during Cárdenas's administration had botanists and biologists had such sway in national proceedings. But the conservationist goals of Cárdenas would clash with the goals of the revolution, land distribution. Simonian, *Defending the Land of the Jaguar*, 124.
53. Gregg Mitman, *The State of Nature*, 1.
54. Gómez-Pompa, personal interview, UC Riverside, Calif., June 2005.
55. Creating commissions was not new. A commission brought together leading scholars from various disciplines, sometimes in conjunction with entrepreneurs, to ponder and solve scientific or technological questions facing the nation. For example, the government had on previous occasions called for the formation of a commission to study the borders with the United States (1827–50, reportedly the first commission); one to study the Isthmus of Tehuantepec as

part of a larger United States commission to determine the potential location of an interoceanic canal (1879); and one to examine the limits with Guatemala. The commission about Guatemala resulted in large quantities of plant, fruit, and seed samples being brought to Mexico for study.

56. Arturo Gómez-Pompa, personal interview, UC Riverside, Calif., June 2005.

57. Efraím Hernández Xolocotzi, Arturo Gómez-Pompa, and Javier Chavelas Polito, "Contribuciones de la Comisión de Estudios sobre la Ecología de Dioscóreas, en México 1959–1970"; Arturo-Gómez Pompa, personal interviews, UC Riverside, Calif., June 2003 and June 17, 2005.

58. This agreement between the government and pharmaceutical companies fell under circular 5–61, which went into effect on January 14, 1961, and was published two months later, on March 13, in the *Diario Oficial*.

59. Cotter, "The Rockefeller Foundation's Mexican Agricultural Project," 97.

60. Ibid., 8.

61. Efraím Hernández Xolocotzi, Arturo Gómez-Pompa, and Javier Chavelas Polito, "Contribuciones de la Comisión de Estudios sobre la Ecología de Dioscoreas, en México 1959–1970." The history of the commission contrasts, however, with the illustrious career of the School of Botany.

62. Cotter, *Troubled Harvest*, 324.

63. As an interesting side note, the central offices of SEMARNAP (Secretariat of the Environment, Natural Resources, and Fisheries) in the southern section of Mexico City house a tiny, cluttered library where two workers have in the last two decades devised a catalogue system for retrieving information, which is known only to the both of them. Despite this ingenious method of establishing job security, both women have also created an informal economy of sorts in which they lay out, on top of some piles of books, hard candy, assorted soft drinks, potato chips, gum, and other snacks. In their desk drawers, they keep an array of pantyhose in various sizes and colors, feminine products, and even men's socks. This functioning library and vending machine of sorts is well known in the various ministry offices. What is not well known, however, is what became of the barbasco files or whether anyone remained who could remember the importance of barbasco to the development of the ministry—facts that bring us back to the small library in the center of the large office complex. The tiny library, as well as several buildings surrounding it, were created with the money that flowed in from the Commission for the Study of the Ecology of Dioscoreas; the library had been, in a previous manifestation, a drying room for barbasco. Ing. Javier Polito Chavelas, personal interview, Mexico City, April 1999.

64. The quotation in this section's heading is from Lorenzo León Felipe, personal interview, Valle Nacional, Oaxaca, November 1999.

65. Moguel, "La cuestión agraria en el periodo 1950–1970," 103.

66. Ibid., 103.

67. Wetten, "México rural."

68. García, *Problemas campesinos México, 1977*, 11.

69. Ibid.

70. Lorenzo León Felipe, personal interview, Valle Nacional, Oaxaca, April 1999.

71. Kreig, *Green Medicine*, 287.

72. Ibid., 287.

73. Lorenzo León Felipe, personal interview, Valle Nacional, Oaxaca, November 1998.

74. In 1999, when Emilio Fortín proclaimed himself "the oldest barbasquero in Mexico," he insisted that his Catemaco beneficio, which previously belonged to his father, was the first in the country.

75. Allegedly an American doctor had written an article documenting this phenomenon, but none of those interviewed recalled where it had appeared.

76. Michael Taussig, *The Devil and Commodity Fetishism in South America*, 11.

77. Delfino Hernández Salazar, personal interview, Tonto Ranch, Oaxaca, February 1999.

78. Eduardo Domínguez, personal interview, Estado de México, 1999.

5. Yam, Students, and Populist Project

1. This information was obtained through a series of oral history interviews with Tito Rubí, Rafael Ceballos, Alejandro Villar Borja, and Carlos Huerta, all of whom were active participants in the events described. All, except for one, whom I shall call Víctor Mayer, accepted that their real names be used. Their stories were corroborated with newspaper articles and documents found in the Archivo General de la Nación (AGN). For their first appearance in the press, please see José Reveles, *Excelsior*, November 1, 1974. Interviews were conducted between October 1998 and July 1999.

2. Víctor Mayer, personal interview, Mexico City, January 1999.

3. R. Harris, "Marxism and the Agrarian Question," in R. Bartra, *Notas sobre la cuestión campesina, Mexico 1970–1976*.

4. In many communities inaccessible by road, peasants used *chalupas*—a raftlike boat of tied wooden boards—to transport barbasco down the rivers and to the beneficio. In much of the Chinantla, barbasqueros used the Tonto, Nacional, and Papaloapan Rivers to float their goods close to beneficios or to roads where truckers could pick up barbasco.

5. Rafael Ceballos, personal interview, Mexico City, 1999.

6. Bertrand De la Grange, and Maite Rico, *Marcos*, 133.

7. José Reveles, *Excelsior*, November 1, 1974.

8. Due to the nature of barbasco collection, the labor force was never accurately

tabulated. This is a rough estimate compiled from newspaper articles which cite 25,000 *families,* and from interviews with Alejandro Villar Borja, Eduardo Domínguez, Andrés Correa, and Pedro Ramírez, who list the number as high as 150,000 campesinos.

9. These numbers, of course, reflect what was reported by the pharmaceutical laboratories and, because of their practice of underreporting, can only be taken as a rough estimate. *Asociación rural de interés colectivo* (Mexico City, 1986).

10. Ernesto Miramontes, personal interview, Mexico City, July 2004.

11. Some Mexican researchers tended to agree with Miramontes. For example, on their study of Mexican scientists, Lomnitz and Fortes concluded that "the socialization of scientists in peripheral countries occurs in 'adverse conditions' compared to those that exist in advanced countries." *Becoming a Scientist in Mexico,* 160, They explained that these conditions were mainly a lack of scientific traditions and consequently a lack of scientific ideology; hence, "science did not result from internal development; it is an imported cultural product." Ibid., 161. Hopefully, the cases of Arturo Gómez-Pompa and Ernesto Miramontes demonstrate that this is far from the case. Recent and emerging literature on science production in Latin America also contests these initial findings. The answer may have more to do with the availability of tangible funds than with, as the authors suggest, authoritarian regimes that reward those who do not contest authority.

12. The official and public number was 27, but extra official estimates have always placed it at more than 300. For more information, see Julio Scherrer García and Carlos Monsiváis, *Parte de Guerra*; and Elena Poniatowska, *Fuerte es el silencio* (Mexico City: Ediciones Era, 1980). Recent archival work by Angeles Magdaleno, appointed by then president Vicente Fox to organize and classify the 1968 files, corroborates the low number of civilian deaths. She suggests that the higher numbers were of fallen sharpshooters, army soldiers, or both. Angeles Magdaleno, "Papelito habla: El Fondo de Gobernación. Sección DFS," paper given at the "Cárdenas, Echeverría and Revolutionary Populism Conference," University of Arizona, Tucson, April 7–8, 2006.

13. Daniel Cosío Villegas, *Estilo personal de gobernar.*

14. Clayton and Conniff, *History of Modern Latin America,* 495.

15. J. Castañeda, *Perpetuating Power: How Mexican Presidents Were Chosen* (New York: New Press, 2000), 133.

16. Cosío Villegas, *El estilo personal de gobernar.*

17. Miguel Valdés Castillo, letter to Luis Echeverría Alvarez, February 7, 1971. AGN, ramo "Presidentes, Luis Echeverría Alvarez," vol. 637, acervo 96, Mexico City.

18. Judith Adler Hellman, *Mexico in Crisis,* 105. Mexico hosted the Olympic games in 1968, ten days after the October 2 assault on students.

19. Miguel Valdés Castillo, letter to Luis Echeverría Alvarez, February, 7, 1971. AGN, ramo "Presidentes, Luis Echeverría Alvarez," vol. 637, acervo 96, Mexico City.

20. Miguel Valdés Castillo, letter to Oscar Brauer Herrera, November, 28, 1974, ibid.

21. Ibid.

22. Other factors are "organizational links uniting the peasants, a strong legitimation of contentious attitudes, and the existence of allies." See Leon Zamosc, "Peasant Struggles in Colombia," in *Power and Popular Protests* (Berkeley: University of California Press, 1989), 111.

23. Víctor Raúl Martínez Vásquez, *Movimiento popular y político en Oaxaca (1968–1986)*, 16.

24. Héctor Aguilar Camín, *Después del milagro*, 96.

25. Rafael Ceballos, personal interview, CNC Headquarters, Mexico City, March 1999.

26. Ibid.

27. Ibid.

28. Ibid.

29. Ibid.

30. Ibid.

31. Ibid.

32. Enrique Krauze, *El sexenio de Luis Echeverría* (Mexico City: Clío, 1999), 26.

33. *Ideario Luis Echeverría March 11, 1970–April 4, 1970*, Vol. 4 (Mexico City: PRI, 1970), 1042.

34. L. Suarez, *Echeverría Rompe el Silencio* (Mexico City: Editorial Grijalbo, 1979), 186.

35. José Reveles, *Excelsior*, November 1, 1974.

36. Transnational laboratories could not harvest barbasco without a forestry permit given by Secretaría de Agricultura y Ganadería, SAG, today SAGAR. At the beginning of the harvest, each laboratory requested and was issued a permit for a determined number of tons which they planned to extract that year. The value of the permit varied according to the amount of tons requested and authorized. The permit was issued in triplicate. One copy remained at the tollbooth that served as checkpoints for barbasco, another was kept by the beneficio that received barbasco, and the third was given to the laboratories. It was fairly easy to extract more tons than those specified in the document.

37. "Comisión Consultiva para la Fijación de Precios de los Productos Medicinales. Noviembre 24, 1947." AGN, Departamento de Gobierno Sr 1, Decreto Presidencial no. 1718, exp. 32, caja 114, folio, 7, Mexico City.

38. "El 90 por ciento del mercado de las medicinas, en manos de transnacionales," *El Día*, August 4, 1977, 7.

39. Jesús Uribe Ruiz, "El Instituto Mexicano de Investigaciones para la Industria Química Vegetal A.C. (IMIQUIVE)," in *Estado actual del conocimiento en plantas medicinales mexicanas*, ed. Xavier Lozoya (Mexico City: IMEPLAM, 1976), 227.

40. *Excelsior*, August 1974.

41. *El Día*, July 6, 1975.

42. "Resumen de productos farmacéuticos—Adquisiciones del sector público." AVBP, files, ca. 1974.

43. "Señor Presidente de la República: Consideramos que ya es necesario que Usted intervenga en el problema de las medicinas," *Excelsior* May 2, and August 1974.

44. "Una industria tan importante como la farmacéutica no debe servir simplemente para lucrar. Debe estar bajo el control de intereses mexicanos y el Estado debe buscar las formas para que se produzcan y distribuyan las medicinas a precios populares," *El Día*, January 4, 1974.

45. "El negocio de los medicamentos," *El Día*, July 6, 1975.

46. "Medicinas baratas," and "Los laboratorios venderán medicina barata vía Conasupo," *Novedades*, June 18, 1975.

47. "Resumen de productos farmacéuticos—Adquisiciones del sector público." AVBP, files, ca. 1974.

48. *El Día*, July 6, 1975.

49. Edward S. Ayensu, "Comments on Old and New World Dioscoreas of Commercial Importance," 1.

50. Acta de la sesión solemne de instalación del Consejo Nacional de Población, celebrada en la Ciudad de México, D.F., el día 27 de Marzo de 1974 (Mexico City: CONAPO,1974).

51. "Opening Remarks: 4th International Congress on Hormonal Steroids, September 2–7, 1974, Mexico City," *Journal of Steroid Biochemistry* 6 (1975): 1.

52. Rafael Ceballos, personal interview, Mexico City, March 6, 1999.

53. "Señor Presidente de la República, Señores Funcionarios. . . ." AVBP, folder 7, "Jefatura de Coordinación."

54. Xavier Lozoya, "Two Decades of Mexican Ethnobotany and Research in Plant Drugs," in *Ethnobotany and the Search for New Drugs*, ed. G. T. Prance, Derek J. Chadwick, and Joan Marsh, in *Ciba Foundation symposium* series 185 (Chichester, N.Y.: J. Wiley, 1994).

55. Lozoya, "Two Decades of Mexican Ethnobotany and Research in Plant Drugs," 131; Lozoya, personal interview, Mexico City, July 19, 1999.

56. Lozoya, "Two Decades of Mexican Ethnobotany and Research in Plant Drugs," 130.

57. Ibid., 131.

58. Lozoya further argued that this perception of inferior knowledge was also re-

sponsible for why North American companies were "late" in the search for new plant drugs. Ibid.

59. *Mexico 1976: Facts, Figures, Trends* (Mexico City: Banco Nacional de Comercio Exterior, 1976), 303.

60. Ibid.

61. Horacio de la Sierra, letter to Jesús Reyes Heroles, director general del IMSS, May 12, 1976. AGN, ramo "Presidentes: Luis Echeverría Alvarez," vol. 637, acervo 96, no. 14342, Mexico City.

62. Ibid.

63. Ibid.

64. Ibid.

65. Lozoya, "Two Decades of Mexican Ethnobotany and Research in Plant Drugs," 133.

66. Gómez-Pompa later became the first director of UC MEXUS and a faculty member at the University of California, Riverside.

67. Dr. Arturo Gómez-Pompa, letter to Lic. Gerardo Bueno Zirión, December 6, 1974. AGN, ramo "Presidentes, Luis Echeverría Alvarez," caja 562, 96, Mexico City.

68. AVBP, folder "LEA: Creación Proquivemex," Mexico City, n.d.

69. "Sale de México el barbasco para hacer la Píldora," *Excelsior*, January 14, 1976.

70. "Nacionalizaremos los esteroides, si presionan las transnacionales," *El Universal*, March 11, 1976.

71. "Pidieron a Echeverría la nacionalización de laboratorios químicos de esteroides," *Ovaciones: El Diario de México*, March, 13, 1976.

72. "Con capital del Estado, el Barbasco dejará de ser fuente de explotación del campesino," *El Día*, March 1976.

73. Please see Gereffi, *The Pharmaceutical Industry and Dependency in the Third World*.

6. The State Takes Control of Barbasco

1. "Mexicanización de los esteroides," *El Universal*, March 13, 1976.

2. "Sale de México el barbasco para hacer la píldora," *Excelsior*, January 14, 1976.

3. Gereffi, The Pharmaceutical Industry and Dependency in the Third World, 136.

4. Ibid., 133.

5. From 500 to 550 metric tons. Ibid.

6. *Excelsior*, October 30, 1974. "La superficie actual productora de barbasco se reduce actualmente a 1.5 millones de hectáreas, esto lo dijo Ing. Fiacro Martínez del INIF."

7. Barbasco achieves its mature stage between four and six years. Companies paid not only for the amount of diosgenin flour but for its percentage of diosgenin

content, 4.2 percent being the minimum diosgenin content allowed for in purchase contracts.

8. *Excelsior*, October 30, 1974.

9. According to Roberto Peña Razo from FONAFE the number was difficult to calculate, but closer to 300,000. *Excelsior*, October 10, 1974.

10. "El ingreso de una empresa paraestatal a la industria farmacéutica, permitirá reducir precios de productos derivados del barbasco: La explotación irracional estaba reduciendo la capacidad productiva de nuestro país," *El Heraldo de México*, March 12, 1976, 15.

11. Gereffi, The Pharmaceutical Industry and Dependency in the Third World, 137.

12. See chapter 5, n. 43, above. Also seized with the physical property were the name brands, patents, and rights linked to these companies. Outlining the goals for the industry, the new company was to (a) produce medications that "alleviate illness endemic to our nation" at prices accessible to all; (b) increase the production of medicines in general; (c) act as an impetus for the development of all pharmaceutical products in Mexico, especially those derived from "the use of the nation's natural resources, in particular medicinal plants which grow in Mexico in varied and which up until now have only been used at a reduced scale."

13. Alejandro Borja Villar, personal interview, Tlaxcala, Tlaxcala, February 12, 1999.

14. "Productos Químicos Vegetales Mexicanos, S.A. de C.V." AGN, ramo "Presidentes, Luis Echeverría Alvarez," vol. 625, exp. 95, Mexico City.

15. Personal Interview, Lorenzo León Felipe, Valle Nacional, Oaxaca,1998.

16. Proquivemex also hoped to commercialize medical extracts from papaya and the vinca plant.

17. "Proquivemex fue creado para beneficiar al pueblo de México," *El Tuxtepecano*, February 6, 1977.

18. Stephen S. Hall, "Prescription for Profit," *New York Times Magazine*, March 11, 2001, 40–45.

19. Following are the zone divisions:

Zone 1: Región Tuxtepec (Región de Tuxtepec, Ojitlán, Ayotzintepec, Alberto Cinta, José López Delgado, Soyaltepec, Coscomatepec, Ignacio Escobar Contreras, Alfredo V. Bonfil Acatlán).

Zone 2: Acayucan (Benigno Mendoza, Arroyo Negro and surrounding areas, Adolfo López Mateos, Alfredo V. Bonfil, Primitivo R. Valencia, Helio García Alfaro, Hilario C. Salas, 23 de Junio, Toma de Zacatecas).

Zone 3: Amatepec, Estado de México (Lázaro Cárdenas del Río).

Zone 4: Papantla (Fernando Gutiérrez Aburto, Galvarino Barria, Ursulo Galván, José Cardel, Manuel Almanza).

Zone 5: Chiapas (Salvador Allende, Santos Degollado, Roberto T. Gutiérrez, Ignacio López Rayón, Francisco Trujillo Gurría, Adolfo Ruiz Cortínez) "Dirección de comercialización de Proquivemex, Perfil Económico."

By 1976 Zone 1, Tuxtepec, would report a 17 million peso profit, selling barbasco at.50 pesos per kilo. Quoted in Isabel Cruz, *La organización campesina y la integración vertical de la agricultura.*

20. Alejandro Villar Borja, personal interview, Tlaxcala, Tlaxcala, February 12, 1999.

21. Ibid.

22. "El corrido de Proquivemex" (Proquivemex's Ballad)," November 1976. AVBP, folio "Para entregar," Mexico City.

23. Emma López, personal interview, Mexico City, April 1999.

24. H. Chávez, biologist, personal interview, Instituto Nacional de Investigaciones Forestales y Agropecuarias (INIFAP), Mexico City, November 1988; Xavier Lozoya, personal interview, IMSS, Mexico City, July 1999.

25. "Lo que queremos es competir en iguales condiciones con esas grandes empresas, dentro del régimen de economía mixta. Nosotros somos dueños del barbasco: ellos, de la tecnología, y cada quien debe defenderse como pueda." AVBP, newspaper clipping, n.d. (ca. March 1976).

26. Eduardo Domínguez, personal interview, Toluca, Estado de México, February 1999.

27. After barbasco has been placed on the cement slabs, it needs to be continuously raked so that the granules can dry evenly. Locals called them *arrigros.*

28. "Cartera vencida," *La Opinión*, Poza Rica, Veracruz, September 1975.

29. Gabriel Cué, personal interview, Tuxtepec, Oaxaca, November 1998.

30. Emilio Fortín, personal interview, Catemaco, Veracruz. 1998.

31. Lorenzo León Felipe, personal interview, Valle Nacional, Oaxaca, 1998.

32. Proquivemex, acta oficial, AVBP, sin número.

33. Apolinar, Isidro, personal interview, Chiltepec, Oaxaca, November 1998.

34. Ibid.

35. He still had a tattered copy of an earlier manual, which he had saved among his belongings.

36. Isidro Apolinar, personal interview, Chiltepec, Oaxaca, November 1998.

37. "Cartera vencida," *La Opinión*, Poza Rica, Veracruz, September 1975.

38. "Explotarán el barbasco 56 ejidos veracruzanos," *El Día*, March 29, 1975; "El manejo oficial del barbasco ahoga a la industria química: Doctor Giral," *Excelsior*, April 19, 1975; "Proquivemex, empresa estatal, industrializará el Barbasco," *Excelsior*, April 27, 1975, A-28; "El barbasco será industrializado por Mexicanos; pago justo a campesinos," *El Nacional*, April 27, 1975, 4.

39. "Cartera vencida," *La Opinión*, Poza Rica, Veracruz, September 1975.

40. Nineteen seventy-four was the first year that campesino root pickers partici-

pated in the DAAC (Department of Agrarian Affairs and Colonization) and demanded that they be given credits as an officially recognized (legitimate) group of peasants.

41. "Llegan a ésta funcionarios de varias secretarías con el fin de promover la solución de agudos problemas que tiene Oaxaca," *Oaxaca Gráfico*, March 29, 1976.

42. Leticia Reina Aoyoma, *Economía contra sociedad: El Istmo de Tehuantepec, 1907–1986* (Mexico City: Nueva Imagen, 1994).

43. "Informe sobre situación actual y perspectivas." (All of us who work at this company have your best interest at heart.)

44. "Tenemos todos lo que trabajamos en esta empresa el mayor interés de servirles." AVBP, "Cuaderno Proquivemex," ca. 1975, folder "Para entregar," Mexico City.

45. AVBP, "Cuaderno Proquivemex," ca. 1975, folder "Para entregar," Mexico City.

46. "Comité Coordinador de las Uniones de Ejidos: Boletín de Orientación No. 1." AVBP, folder and "Acta." AGN, Mexico City."

47. Ibid.

48. Descriptions of these meetings were provided by Pedro Ramírez.

49. Silvio Delgado, personal interview, Mexico City, Ministry of Credit and Public Assistance, Hacienda, June 1999.

50. Ibid.

51. Isidro Apolinar, personal interview, Chiltepec, Oaxaca, April 1999.

52. "Proquivemex fue creado para beneficiar al pueblo de México," *El Tuxtepecano*, February 6, 1977.

7. Proquivemex and Transnationals

1. Gereffi, *The Pharmaceutical Industry and Dependency in the Third World*, 135.

2. For a lengthier and more complete analysis of the interaction between Proquivemex and transnational companies, see ibid.

3. Ramo "Presidentes, Luis Echeverría Alvarez." AGN, vol. 625, acervo 95, folio 71, Mexico City.

4. Gereffi, *The Pharmaceutical Industry and Dependency in the Third World*.

5. "La situación es lo suficientemente importante para hacer una revisión cuidadosa de la política a seguir en México en relación al barbasco y las hormonas esteroides." (The situation is sufficiently important to merit a careful revision of the procedures be taken with regard to barbasco and steroid hormones in Mexico.) Arturo Gómez-Pompa, letter to Gerardo Bueno Zirión, December 6, 1974. AGN, ramo "Presidentes, Luis Echeverría Alvarez," caja 562, 96, AGN, Mexico City.

6. Before the creation of Proquivemex, companies had paid from 10 to 12 pesos per kilo.

7. AVBP, folder "Política de Ventas," 1976, 29. AGN, Mexico City.

8. "Alternativas para el uso del suelo en áreas forestales del trópico húmedo," *Publicación Especial* 28 (1981): 21.

9. Gereffi, *The Pharmaceutical Industry and Dependency in the Third World*, 138.

10. Alberto Perezleyva, "Proquivemex contra las transnacionales que sangran la economía del país: Villar Borja," *El Nacional*, March 13, 1976.

11. Estimates in 1975 for barbasco purchases by the six leading laboratories were 12,000 tons, yielding a total of approximately 234 million pesos. AVBP, March 3, 1976.

12. AVBP, folder "Política de Ventas," 1976, 30, Mexico City.

13. Ibid., 32.

14. Ibid.

15. Rendimientos del barbasco seco: Esteroides, ramas de producción y rendimientos. Apuntes elaborados por Ing. Gilberto Fabila Carrera el 18 de Enero 1975. AVBP, folder "Política de Ventas," 1976, Mexico City.

16. The report included a one-page disclaimer lamenting the fact that Proquivemex needed to do such roundabout calculations because the "secretive" companies had not been willing to offer any information. Ibid., 36.

17. Ibid., 45.

18. Another option was shifting agriculture to other materials. Soy, henequen, and sarsarspirilla were just some of the many possible starting materials.

19. Xavier Lozoya, personal interview, Mexico City, 1999.

20. "Es decir los estados de la República que producen la materia prima para abastecer al 50% del mercado mundial de medicamentos hormonales, no tienen acceso a ningún tipo de medicamentos." AVBP, folder "Política de Ventas," 1976, 52, Mexico City.

21. Perezleyva, "Proquivemex contra las transnacionales que sangran la economía del país: Villar Borja," *El Nacional*, March 13, 1976.

22. Diosynth ran out of barbasco and had to purchase at Proquivemex's new prices.

23. AVBP, folder "Política de Ventas," 1976, 52, Mexico City.

24. "Una patria más libre, más justa, y más humana." AVBP, folder "Política de Ventas," 1976, 52, Mexico City.

25. "Memorias del Lic. Alejandro Villar Borja sobre diferentes problemas de Proquivemex y del barbasco." AVBP, folder "Cartas de Uniones de Ejidos a Alejandro Villar Borja," Mexico City.

26. Perezleyva, "Proquivemex contra las transnacionales que sangran la economía del país: Villar Borja," *El Nacional*, March 13, 1976; "Nacionalizar la industria químico-farmacéutica, un imperativo," *Organización*, March 25, 1976, 4. Another powerful public relations coup was to appeal to the sentiments of

social justice by alluding to the fact that it was transnational companies that had, through their practices, retained caciques in positions of power. "10,000 millones de explotación, 6 transnacionales fomentan a caciques para llevarse barbasco," *Ultimas Noticias*, August 20, 1976.

27. "Denuncia el director de Proquivemex represión de transnacionales a productores de barbasco," *Excelsior*, March 13, 1976, 4–5.

28. Perezleyva, "Proquivemex contra las transnacionales que sangran la economía del país: Villar Borja," *El Nacional*, March 13, 1976.

29. Ibid.

30. "Los laboratorios transnacionales quieren monopolizar el mercado, y no encontraron mejor forma de hacerlo que instalando cadenas de farmacias, verdaderos pulpos al servicio antipopular." (Transnational companies want to monopolize the market, and they found no better way to do it than installing pharmacy chains, real octopi.) *El Día*, March 27, 1976.

31. Ibid., n.d.

32. "El precio que se le ha pagado al campesino arrancador, siempre ha sido remunerativo." Letter from Beisa, Syntex, Diosynth, Proquina, Searle, and Steromex to Hugo Cervantes del Río, December 23, 1974. AGN, Ramo "Presidentes, Luis Echeverría Alvarez," vol. 625, acervo 95, folio 71, Mexico City.

33. Ramo "Presidentes, Luis Echeverría Alvarez." Letter from Alejandro Villar Borja to Fernando Córdoba Lobo, Director General de Quejas, March 24, 1975. AGN, vol. 625, acervo 95, Mexico City.

34. Gereffi, Pharmaceutical Industry and Dependency in the Third World, 142.

35. "Sánchez Mejorada: 'Si hacemos caso de todo lo que piden los campesinos' ¿A dónde iremos?" *El Día*, March 17, 1976.

36. "Los hombres del campo están cansados de que otros exploten los recursos naturales que legalmente les corresponden, y cuyos beneficios son llevados al extranjero." Alejandro Villar Boria, personal interview, Tlaxcala, Tlaxcala, February 1999.

37. Steromex reportedly owed $52,242,715.00; Diosynth, $69,630,392.50; Proquina, $105,194,327.50; Beisa, $26,114,122.50; and Syntex, $87,050,675.00. (All amounts in pesos.) Various letters from Licenciado Avila Salado to Richard Miller, manager of Steromex, to Eduardo Mass, manager of Diosynth, Francisco Salgado Valle, Technical Manager of Proquina, to Carlos Manero Romero, general manager of Beisa, and Esteban Kausman, general manager of Syntex. AVBP, folio "Derecho de Monte."

38. "Lo único que se contrató fue la fuerza de trabajo para ir arrancar un producto de la naturaleza. Tan es así que no se pagaban derechos de monte ni ningún otro derecho de las comunidades." Alejandro Villar Borja, personal interview, Tlaxcala, Tlaxcala, February 1999.

39. Sources for this section: "Investigar fraudes de los laboratorios, cosa de Ha-

cienda, no de Proquivemex," *Diario de México*, August 17, 1976, 3; "En peligro el mercado mexicano del Barbasco," *El Sol de México*, August 21, 1977, 1; "Dice Proquivemex: Transnacionales defraudan al fisco y campesinos con la venta del barbasco," *Ovaciones*, August 17, 1976, 4–6; "Proquivemex con toda deslealtad compite contra empresas mexicanas"; "Los productores de Barbasco, firmes en que se les paguen 70 pesos por kg," *El Día*, August 16, 1976; "Los empresarios insisten: El barbasco resulta incosteable," *El Día*, August 16, 1976, A6; "Campesinos emplazan a 6 Transnacionales: Deben a los productores de barbasco 471 millones," *Diario de México*, August 17, 1976, 9; "Es de justicia que se pague un mejor precio por el barbasco a campesinos: Pérdidas económicas por exportar materia prima," *El Heraldo de México*, August 20, 1976, 3–6; "El escándalo del barbasco," *El Día*, August 21, 1976, 5; "El barbasco: Historia de una lucha campesina por su reinvidicación," *El Nacional*, September 17, 1976, 9; "El barbasco mexicano, incosteable: Afirma la CONCAMIN que Proquivemex hace campaña para nacionalizar el barbasco," *El Universal*, August 18, 1976, 13.

40. Gereffi, *Pharmaceutical Industry and Dependency in the Third World*, 145.

41. David Colmenares, "La exportación disfrazada de utilidades y la evasión fiscal," *El Día*, January 29, 1980.

42. Gereffi, *Pharmaceutical Industry and Dependency in the Third World*, 145.

43. Ibid.

44. "Nacionalizar la industria farmacéutica y asegurar el derecho del pueblo a la salud," *El Día*, March 26, 1976; Irma Alvarez, "Proquivemex debe procesar el barbasco: F. Gómez Jara," *El Sol de México*, August 24, 1976, B1, 4.

45. "Nuestro gobierno está transitando el difícil camino que conduce a la salud como parte de la justicia social, con lo cual estamos cerrando un ciclo vital de la Revolución Mexicana." "El boicot al barbasco, denunciado en el Coloquio sobre las Plantas Medicinales," *Excelsior*, March 20, 1976, A30.

46. Ibid.

47. Carlos Tello, "La economía Echeverrista balance provisional," *Nexos* 11, no. 1 (November 1978).

48. *Business Latin America*, March 24, 1976, 90.

49. "Combatiremos las leyes que el Estado aplica con discrecionalidad excesiva: La estatización lleva a la dictadura," *El Día*, March 17, 1976.

50. "Para la Confederación de Cámaras Industriales no hay más que empresas mexicanas. Toda empresa que se forma en México, dentro de las leyes mexicanas es mexicana, para efectos de la CONCAMIN." *El Día*, March 17, 1976.

51. "Sánchez Mejorada: 'Si hacemos caso de todo lo que piden los campesinos' ¿A dónde iremos?" *El Día*, March 17, 1976.

52. Ibid.

53. "Este es un problema de agitación, es un problema manejado, y lo digo así con toda claridad." *El Día*, March 17, 1976.

54. "Sabe que tiene las de perder, porque no se siguen las mismas reglas del juego." Ibid.

55. "En mayo saldrá al mercado la píldora contraceptiva mexicana." Ibid.

56. "El ingeniero Roberto Pena Razo, director de operación de Productos Quími-cos Vegetales de México informó que esta empresa estudia la posibilidad de producir comercialmente una hormona esteroidal extraída del barbasco, con la cual se puede combatir eficazmente a las ratas y a las moscas del campo, que tanto dañan a la agricultura. Dijo que esta hormona, producto de la tecnolo-gía mexicana, puede esterilizar ratas y moscas sin daño a la vida vegetal ni a otras especies animales. Explicó que el barbasco, rico en esteroides, del cual se pueden extraer 540 derivados químicos, abunda en México y es una raíz silvestre. De ahí es donde la tecnología mexicana consiguió extraer el esteroide contra ratas y moscas." "Estudia Proquivemex la producción de una hormona del barbasco." August 28, 1976, A19.

57. Xavier Lozoya, personal interview, Mexico City, July 19, 1999.

58. Theodore Moran, *Multinational Corporations and the Politics of Dependence: Copper in Chile* (Princeton: Princeton University Press, 1974). Moran illus-trated in his book how the Chilean government, faced with similar conditions of attempting to harness a lucrative natural resource, opted to create its own domestic industry, effectively removing multinational corporations from the copper industry. Many of the ensuing problems—lack of technology, lack of trained professionals, and an unclear understanding of the fluctuating world demand for copper—would be reproduced in the Mexican case of Proquivemex and the steroid hormone industry.

59. Echeverría was called "brother of campesinos" and "the Agrarista President," and the new Law of Agrarian Reform was occasionally labeled "Ley Echeverría." *Organización*, March 25, 1976.

60. "El régimen mixto establecido por la Constitución presupone que la inversión pública tiene la fuerza suficiente para dirigir el crecimiento. La libre empresa sólo puede ser fecunda si el gobierno posee los recursos suficientes para coordi-nar el cumplimiento de los grandes objetivos nacionales." Quoted in Carlos Tello, "La economía echeverrista balance provisional," *Nexos* 1, no. 11 (Novem-ber 1978).

61. "La Primera Reunión de Balance y Programación," *Organización* 25 (March 1976): 2.

62. Armando Bartra, *Notas sobre la cuestión campesina, México 1970–1976*, 46.

63. Diario Oficial de la Federación, April 16, 1971.

64. *Organización*, 1976.

65. *Política de desarrollo, política agraria*. AGN, ramo "Presidentes," vol. 629, exp./ acervo 96, 708/8, Mexico City.

66. Ibid.

67. Ibid.

68. AGN, ramo "Presidentes," LEA, vol. 619, caja 95.

69. Letter from Manuel González Cosío to Ignacio Ovalle Fernández, June 6, 1973, ibid.

70. Letter from Manuel González Cosío to Ignacio Ovalle Fernández, May 17, 1973, ibid.

71. This made reference to an earlier letter in which 100 *ixtleros* and their families would be selected to live in a community called Tipo, where they would learn to live off the desert. Letter from Manuel González Cosío to Ignacio Ovalle Fernández on May 25, 1973, ibid.

72. Ibid.

73. The reference to braceros was literal as in "men who work with their arms" or day laborers, and not a reference to the official Bracero Program, which ended in 1964.

74. Fertimex (fertilizers), Cordemex (henequen), and Tabamex (tobacco) are just some examples of how the state envisioned its role as administrator in the countryside.

8. Barbasqueros into Mexicans

1. Author interviews with Eusebio Jiménez, a pseudonym, in the Tuxtepec region, June 1998.

2. Displaced from their lands, these campesinos were forcibly assimilated into neighboring ejidos or were given rocky, nonarable plots of land. Others would become permanent migrants, finally receiving reparation for their lands in the mid-1990s. Bartolomé and Barabas 1990, *Etnicidad y pluralismo cultural*.

3. The process of how the UNPRB emerged, stayed in power, and eventually imploded is briefly addressed in the following chapter.

4. In the late 1950s Syntex started experimental camps in and around San Juan Evangelista, Veracruz, devoted to studying barbasco reproduction and maintaining a germ plasm bank of *Dioscorea* species from around the world. The camp was abandoned without any published results. Syntex later started another camp in the Costa Chica, in Chiapas. But it was not the only company conducting experiments on a wide scale on barbasco. Searle had a camp in Amatatlán de los Reyes, Veracruz, while Proquina experimented with *Dioscorea composita* and *D. floribunda* in Acayucan and Playa Vicente; Beisa had one near Tuxtepec, Oaxaca. "Investigación sobre domesticación y cultivo de barbasco realizada por las empresas farmacéuticas," Reunión para el análisis y reorientación de investigación sobre el barbasco, Córdoba, Friday November 7–10, 1979, Publicidad Especial no. 21, August 1980. INIF: Mexico, 125–26. Found in AGN, galería 2, Caja 18, Proquivemex Archives.

5. A similar process of identity formation has been analyzed using the henequen workers of Yucatán after the creation in 1964 of Cordemex and the introduction of the *desfibradores*' (shredders') first labor union, "José María Morelos y Pavón," started in 1974. For more on the *henequeneros*, see Luis A. Várguez Pasos, *Identidad, henequén y trabajo.*

6. For example, the files of the Unión Región Tuxtepec of the National Peasant Confederation, CNC, which spanned 1975 to 1989, were burned in March of 1999 to make room for office space.

7. *El Sol de México*, March 13, 1976.

8. As mentioned in chapter 7, after Proquivemex opened its doors and became the intermediary between transnational corporations and peasants, the companies decided not to purchase any barbasco from Proquivemex and instead decided to wait out the end of Echeverría's presidential term. They were able to successfully do this, because five of the six pharmaceuticals had hoarded barbasco since 1974.

9. Ejidos de la Unión Arroyo Negro, letter to Luis Echeverría Alvarez, August 15, 1976, Minatitlán, Veracruz. AVBP, folder "Cartas a LEA," n.d.

10. Gereffi, *The Pharmaceutical Industry and Dependency in the Third World.*

11. When speaking of a limited natural resource sought by all, Garrett Hardin's *Tragedy of the Commons* (*Science* 162 [1968]: 1243–48) article immediately springs to mind: "Freedom in the commons brings ruin to all," or "All must agree to preserve the commons but any one can force the destruction of the commons." Nevertheless this "free for all" attitude in ejidos was addressed in the 1970 Law of Agrarian Reform, which, for the purposes of this argument, I include in its entirety. Article 138, II, c stated, "La explotación comercial de los montes o bosques propiedad de ejidos o comunidades agrícolas o forestales, así como la transformación industrial de sus productos, deberá hacerse directamente por el ejido o comunidad, previo acuerdo de la Asamblea General. Cuando las inversiones que se requieren rebasan la participación estatal, en primer lugar, o alguna empresa privada, ofreciere condiciones ventajosas para el ejido o comunidad, podrá la asamblea acordar la explotación, conforme a *contratos debidamente autorizados por el Departamento de Asuntos Agrarios y Colonización, siempre que garanticen plenamente los intereses de ejidatarios y comuneros*" (emphasis mine). B. B. Martínez Garza, *Evolución legislativa de la Ley Federal de Reforma Agraria* (Mexico City: Textos Universitarios, 1975), 682. Although initially unregulated, the harvest of barbasco by landless camepesinos changed after barbasqueros formed a union. After that point, landless pickers had to pay a "fee" to the owners of the ejidos if they collected barbasco in ejido lands. The fact that transnational corporations *never* paid this fee was the source of the nationalization arguments. Campesinos answers derived

from conversations with the residents of Cinco de Oro and Cerro Cangrejo in Oaxaca. April and July 1999.

12. "Exigen [campesinos] que se nacionalice la industria," *Diario de Xalapa*, March 13, 1976.
13. "Que la industria pase a manos mexicanas piden los campesinos," *Cine Mundial: Un Diario Diferente*, March 13, 1976.
14. "25 mil campesinos pidieron que se expropien 6 plantas de esteroides," *Diario de Xalapa*, March 13, 1976.
15. Acuerdo de la Secretaría de Agricultura y Ganadería. AGN, ramo "Presidentes," vol. 625, exp. 95, ca. 1974–75 (emphasis mine).
16. Juan Ballesteros Porta, "Estudio sobre formas actuales de cooperación agropecuaria," in *Los problemas de la organización campesina* (Mexico City: Editorial Campesina, 1975), 121; Ballesteros Porta, *Los campesinos: ¿Para qué organizarlos?* (Mexico City: Centro de Ecodesarrollo, 1976), 81.
17. Echeverría's tactic, blaming a presidential predecessor, would become a trademark of Mexican politics. Echeverría used it most convincingly in disassociating himself from the student revolts of 1968.
18. Hellman, *Mexico in Crisis*.
19. Ibid., 84.
20. Tulio Halperín Donghi, *The Contemporary History of Latin America* (Durham, N.C.: Duke University Press, 1993), 236.
21. Stephen Niblo, *War, Development, and Diplomacy*, 75.
22. Halperín Donghi, *The Contemporary History of Latin America*, 237.
23. Hellman, *Mexico in Crisis*, 105.
24. Ibid.
25. Ibid., 108.
26. Halperín Donghi, *The Contemporary History of Latin America*, 277.
27. Hellman, *Mexico in Crisis*, 105.
28. Cynthia Hewitt de Alcántara, *Modernizing Mexican Agriculture: Socioeconomic Implications of Technological Change, 1940–1970* (Geneva: United Nations Research Institute for Social Development, 1976), 9–16.
29. The Coalition of Workers, Peasants and Students of the Isthmus (COCEI), created in 1973, is such an example. The coalition, which gained the right to rule Juchitán (approximate population 100,000) in 1989, after fifteen years of regime-sanctioned killings, is often mentioned as a "success" story for peasant movements. The creation of COCEI in Juchitán was in direct response to violent repression against Zapotec peasant and worker leaders. The coalition formed in response to the construction of the nearby Benito Juárez Dam and the adjacent irrigation district. Peasants claimed that the dam would force them to lose their land, their livelihood, and their way of life, so they rebelled. Jeffrey

Rubin, a researcher of the movement, contends that the organization's success in challenging local and national authorities stems from the Juchitecos' ability to transform their daily activities, neighborhoods, and workplaces into sites of political discussion. For more information on COCEI, including the internal contradictions within the movement (such as oppression of women), see Jeffrey Rubin, "Ambiguity and Contradiction in a Radical Movement," in *Cultures of Politics, Politics of Culture: Re-visioning Latin American Social Movements*, eds. Sonia Alvarez et al. (Boulder: Westview Press, 1998), 141–64.

30. Juan Fernando Pelaez, presentation, Center for U.S.-Mexican Studies, University of California, San Diego, November 2000.

31. The former hacienda of Santa Catarina was taken over in April of 1972, and shortly thereafter students from the Normal in Tuxtepec joined the peasants. The crisis over land was divided in armed struggle and legal battles. However, by 1974, with the help of the UGOCP, more than 5,000 peasants from Valle Nacional and Loma Bonita, began an organized invasion of nearby ejidos. The uprising was violently suppressed with disappearances and incarcerations. Gloria Zafra and E. Salomón González, "La reforma del ejido en Tuxtepec: Campo y campesino en San José Chiltepec, San Bartolo y Santa Catarina," in *Propiedad y organización rural en el México moderno: Reforma agraria y el procede en Veracruz, Chiapas, Oaxaca y Sonora*, eds. Julio Moguel and José Antonio Romero (Mexico City: Juan Pablos, 1998), 151.

32. Simonian, *Defending the Land of the Jaguar*, 178.

33. Quoted ibid., 179.

34. Ibid.

35. These ideas would later be discussed at a symposium in Rio de Janeiro on the role of transnational corporations in Latin America. The idea of "socializing" these companies or, rather, making them conform to the specific culture of each host nation, were directly derived from Echeverría's speech at the UNCTAD. See *Excelsior*, July 27, 1975.

36. Víctor L. Urquidi, "La carta de derechos y deberes económicos de los estados: La cuestión de su aplicación," *Foro Internacional* 78, no. 20 (October–December 1979): 2.

37. Letter signed by fourteen barbasco unions, without date. AVBP, file "Ponencia," 21.

38. Moreover, in Oaxaca there was a surge of autonomous peasant organizations which functioned outside of the party's state-created and regulated CNC. Each of these organizations had specific claims and demands, but they fall within a general category that has been termed "movimiento popular en Oaxaca" by some authors. For example, see Carlos Durand Alcántara, *La lucha campesina en Oaxaca and Guerrero, 1978–1987*. The strength and diversity of these move-

ments, some of which survive today, reflect the entrenched socioeconomic, political, and racial contradictions that characterize Oaxaca, and which permit anachronistic regional cacicazgos to thrive.

39. Armando Bartra, Los herederos de Zapata, 113.
40. Ibid., 113.
41. Letter to governors. AGN, Ramo "Presidentes Luis Echeverría Alvarez," acervo 96, caja 637,717/11–1, cocosa July 8, 1975.
42. Guillermo Corea, personal interview, fideicomiso del Fondo Nacional para el Fomento Ejidal (FONAFE) central offices, Mexico City, July 1999.
43. Secretaría de Reforma Agraria, Organización, May 1978, 13.
44. Letter signed by fourteen barbasco unions, without date. AVBP, file "Ponencia," 21.
45. Melquíades Santiago, Isidro Apolinar, Pedro Ramírez, Eduardo Domínguez, and Alejandro Villar Borja all repeated this curious fact, though there were loose organizations of cane workers already in the area.
46. "Las Uniones de Ejidos, Opción Organizativa de Desarrollo y Programa Regional." AVBP, file "Ponencias—June 1976." In addition, in the region of Tuxtepec, unions based on rubber, sugar cane, bananas, and pineapple all emerged from the initial barbasco organization.
47. Horacio Mackinlay, "Las organizaciones de productores rurales y el Estado de México," paper presented at the conference "Dilemmas of Change in Mexican Politics," Center for U.S.-Mexican Studies, La Jolla, Calif., October 8–9, 1999.
48. "Se recuperó para México el Barbasco importante producto para la química," ca. 1976. AVBP, folder "Artículos Sueltos."
49. Alberto Perezleyva, "El barbasco: Historia de una lucha campesina por su reivindicación," El Nacional, ca. March 1976.
50. Letter to Luis Echeverría from Unión de Producción y Comercialización Agropecuaria "C. Hilario C. Salas," Huazuntlán Municipio de Mecayapan, Estado de Veracruz, August 14, 1976. AVBP, folder "Cartas a LEA," n.p.
51. Ibid.
52. "Muchas cosas que a México le pasan, en gran parte, se ha debido a la deficiencia que tenemos del conocimiento de las cosas en general." Eduardo Domínguez, personal interview, Toluca, Estado de México, February 3, 1999.
53. Alejandro Villar Borja, personal interview, Mexico City, 1999.
54. Guillermo Wilkins, personal interview, Tuxtepec, Oaxaca, 1999.
55. Letter to Alejandro Villar Borja from Unión Regional de Colonias Agropecuarias de la Región de Los Tuxtlas, Veracruz. August 16, 1976. AVBP, folder "Cartas a AVB," n.p.
56. "Dentro de esta Asociación, el Estado aporta la tecnología, capacidad empre-

sarial y financiamiento, siendo recomendable, que se retire una vez que las Uniones hayan desarrollado su capacidad de autogestión (se estima que el lapso puede variar de 3 a 10 años, dependiendo de la complejidad de sus operaciones). "Las Uniones de Ejidos, Opción Organizativa de Desarrollo y Programa Regional," unpublished paper, June 1976. AVBP, file "Ponencias."

57. Speech made by Alejandro Villar Borja, March 16, 1976, Veracruz. AVBP, file "Sueltos."

58. Juan Manuel Barrera, personal interview, Jacatepec, Oaxaca, April 1999.

59. Eduardo Domínguez, personal interview, Toluca, Estado de México, February 3, 1999.

60. Ibid.

61. Letter to Alejandro Villar Borja from Unión de Ejidos Licenciado Francisco Trujillo Gurría de Tacotalpa, Tabasco, August 14, 1976. AVBP, folder "Cartas a AVB," n.p.

62. Nuria Costa, *UNORCA: Documentos para la historia* (Mexico City: Costa-Amic, 1989), 165.

63. Ibid., 165.

64. Crispo Pérez, letter to Alejandro Villar Borja, ca. 1977. AVBP, folder "Ponencias," n.p. "Estoy formulando una Historia del beneficio en el cual trabajo y está vajo [sic] mi responsabilidad asi como fotografías del mismo se las embiaré [sic] por correo."

65. On June 23, 1914, the revolutionary Division of the North, led by Pancho Villa, gained control of Zacatecas.

66. It most likely belonged to Syntex because this company had control of nearly all of Veracruz.

67. AVBP, folder "Ponencias," n.p.

68. Letter to Alejandro Villar Borja from Crispo Pérez, ca, 1977. AVBP, folder, "Ponencias," n.p.

69. After Proquivemex took over barbasco production, by assembly with ejidatarios it was agreed that from each sale of barbasco, a percentage of the sale would go back to the ejido which had sold the barbasco in the form of a common account. Funds from this account could only be allocated for community projects, e.g., building a school, bringing electricity to the community, or paving streets.

70. Letter to "Sr. presidente de la República from Mario Sentís López." AVBP, file, "Ponencia," 19.

71. Letter to Lic. Alejandro Villar Borja from Federación Nacional de Colonias Agropecuarias—Confederación Nacional Campesina, August 14, 1976. AVBP, file "Ponencia," 20.

72. Interestingly *Barbasco*, a Salvadoran novel, narrates the tale of a community

of *peones*, who after decades of abuse from their *patrón*, are forced to take up arms against him when a plague of locusts destroys their maize. Barbasco, the protagonist, leads a ragtag group of peasants to demand clemency from their debts, and for this affront he is killed. It is in the name of Barbasco that the peasants ultimately revolt and burn the hacienda.

73. Speech given by Alejandro Villar Borja, representing the interests of the barbasqueros, March 12, 1976, Papantla, Veracruz. AVBP, folder "Creación."

74. Ibid.

75. "Nacionalizar los esteroides," *El Sol de México*, March 15, 1976.

76. "Si ellos tienen el derecho que les da la fuerza, nosotros tenemos la fuerza que nos da el derecho." Letter to Alejandro Villar Borja from Unión Regional de Colonias Agropecuarias de la Región de Los Tuxtlas, Veracruz, August 16, 1976. AVBP, folder "Cartas a AVB," n.p.

77. Letter to Luis Echeverría Alvarez from Unión de Ejidos de Producción y Comercialización Agropecuaria licenciado Adolfo López Mateos del Municipio de Hidalgotitlán, Veracruz, August 14, 1976. AVBP.

78. AVBP, Jaime Solis, "De como los barbasqueros ganaron su derecho," publication unknown, January 5, 1986.

79. Perezleyva, "El barbasco: Historia de una lucha campesina por su reivindicación," *El Nacional*, ca. March 1976.

80. Letter to President Luis Echeverría Alvarez from Nicolás Martínez Aguilar, president of the Unión de Ejidos 23 de Junio la Toma de Zacatecas, ca. 1976. AVBP, folder "Cartas a LEA," n.d.

81. "Con el barbasco, México recupera enorme recurso de progreso rural," *El Día*, June 2, 1976.

82. Interview with Delfino Hernández Salazar, Tuxtepec, Oaxaca, February 23, 1999.

83. Letter to Alejandro Villar Borja from Unión Regional de Colonias Agropecuarias de la Región de Los Tuxtlas, Veracruz. August 16, 1976. AVBP, folder, "Cartas a AVB," n.p.

84. Ibid.

85. Vianey Malpica was killed in November 1975, many believe because of his activities with barbasco production.

86. Letter to Luis Echeverría Alvarez from the Uniones de Ejidos Ursulo Galván, Manuel Almanza, and Fernando Gutiérrez Aburto, July 3, 1975. AVBP, folder "Cartas a LEA," n.p.

87. "Los montes que nos pertenecen." Letter to Alejandro Villar Borja from Federación Nacional de Colonias Agropecuarias—Confederación Nacional Campesina, August 14, 1976. AVBP, file "Ponencia," 20.

88. Ibid. for letter contesting newspaper article. This is partially true given the fact

that many Mexican chemists specializing in steroid hormones had been trained by Syntex or another transnational company. However, once a chemist or any other worker left a pharmaceutical company to work for Proquivemex, the person was considered a pariah. The case of Dr. Carlos Huerta who left Diosynth to work for Proquivemex in 1976 is an illustrative case. After eighteen months at Proquivemex, Huerta was offered a job with Johnson & Johnson de México. At the end of his first day of work, he was called in to Human Resources and told that he had to resign. Upon pressing the employee as to why, he was told that he had been blacklisted by foreign companies. Unable to find work in industry, he has, since then, taught at the University of Chapingo. Interview with Dr. Carlos Huerta, Mexico City, June 1999.

89. Perezleyva, "El barbasco: Historia de una lucha campesina por su reivindicación," *El Nacional*, ca. March 1976.

90. Letter to Luis Echeverría from Unión de Ejidos de producción y Comercialización Agropecuaria, Adolfo López Mateos del municipio de Hidalgotitlán, Veracruz, August 14, 1976. AVBP, folder "Cartas a LEA," n.p.

91. Letter to Luis Echeverría Alvarez from Ejidos de la Unión Arroyo Negro, Minatitlán, Veracruz, August 15, 1976. AVBP, folder "Cartas a LEA," n.p.

92. Open letter signed by a representative of the Unión Ejidal de Producción Agropecuaria Ursulo Galván of Papantla, Veracruz, ca. March 1976. AVBP, file "Ponencias," n.p.

93. Ponencia from Ejidal de Producción Agropecuaria Ursulo Galván, Papantla, Veracruz. AVBP, ca. March 1976, file "Ponencias: Sueltos" (emphasis [underlining] in original).

94. Ponencia de Gustavo Fernández Arroyo president of Unión de Ejidos Emiliano Zapata from Misantla, Veracruz. AVBP, folder "Cartas a AVB," n.p.

95. "Exigimos que nos paguen un precio justo que sea redituable a nuestra economía y al nivel de vida nuestra." (We demand to be paid a fair price that profits our economy and benefits us.) Letter from Unión Ejidal Agropecuaria Alfredo B. Bonfil to President Luis Echeverría Alvarez, ca. 1976. AVBP, folder "Ponencias," 1.

96. Letter from Unión Ejidal Agropecuaria Alfredo B. Bonfil to President Luis Echeverría Alvarez, ca. 1976. AVBP, folder "Ponencias," 1.

97. Ibid.

98. AGN, galería 1, Barbasco—exp. directo 73–61.

99. Ibid.

100. Ibid.

101. AGN, galería 1, DFS November 7, 1978.

102. De la Grange and Rico, *Marcos*, 133.

103. Fernando Rello, *El Campo en la encrucijada nacional* (Mexico City: Secretaría

de Educacíon Pública, Foro 2000; orig. pub. 1986), 31, cited in Héctor Aguilar Camín, *Después del milagro*, 93.

9. Root of Discord

1. Letter from Manuel Puebla to Ing. Jorge Gutiérrez Samperio, director general de Sanidad Vegetal. AGN, Vol. 17, PQV-D-084/80.
2. Letter from Manuel Puebla to Cuauhtémoc Cárdenas, undersecretary of Forestry and Fauna, January 14, 1980. Ibid. The following quantities were requested: Veracruz—1,000 tons, Tabasco—*en veda* (ban), Chiapas—600 tons, Oaxaca—700 tons, Puebla—300 tons, and Estado de México—100 tons.
3. AGN, Proquivemex, folio 17, May 13, 1980.
4. Steroid hormone exports had decreased 38 percent, from 750 million pesos in 1975, to 460 million pesos in 1977. "Descendió la exportación de hormonas esteroides," *El Día*, February 7, 1977.
5. Cruz, "La organización campesina y la integración vertical de la agricultura."
6. "Pérdidas en Proquivemex al desplomarse los precios del barbasco," *Excelsior*, February 28, 1980. A 1986 table used by the UNPRB to illustrate the quality of barbasco from one region to the next made it apparent that, with few exceptions, the quality of barbasco flour had gone down. For example in 1984 from one of the unions producing the most barbasco flour in Veracruz, Unión Galvarino Barría, the quality deteriorated from an initial 4.54 diosgenin content in 1982 to a mere 3.70 percentage two years later, which meant that it no longer reached the minimum percentage requirements. Even the Unión Región Tuxtepec, which prided itself on its high yield of diosgenin-rich flour, suffered a slight loss when its yield declined from 4.85 to less than 4.15 in the same two-year time span. There were some unions that reported a slight increase (e.g., Roberto T. Gutiérrez in Chiapas, from 3.88 to 4.19; Hilario C. Salas in Veracruz, from 3.50 to 3.55), but there was speculation that these unions were mixing "good" barbasco from other regions with their lower-yielding barbasco. There were also previously unknown areas that were emerging as barbasco producers, most notably Michoacán, with a poor quality yield, and Amatepec, in the state of Mexico. This expansion in turn signified a more geographically disperse population that the national union needed to control. Cruz, *La organización campesina y la integración vertical de la agricultura*.

The highly fluctuating barbasco production is shown in the following data: In 1980 total reported production was 623 tons of barbasco flour. In 1981 that total was 2,440. In 1982 a significant increase, of 3,658, was reported. In 1983 the total was 5,803, and in 1984 that total reached 5,040. In 1986, after a crisis year of next to no production, the total finally came down, to 2,900 tons. The 1985 production was negligible because that was the year when diosgenin from

China was imported (see pages 198–200 for more about Chinese diosgenin). Unión de Crédito Agropecuaria, Forestal e Industrial de los Productores de Barbasco, S.A. de C.V., "Plan de operaciones de crédito 1989," Mexico City, November 1988.

7. In 1977 Proquivemex made an agreement with Cordemex to conduct further research into the juices extracted from henequen, which are high in hecogenin, similar to diosgenin. Moreover, Proquivemex itself was researching into alternative sources such as the yucca planta or, *palma china*, and date extracts. "Descendió la exportación de hormonas esteroides," *El Día*, February 7, 1977.

8. "Privatizar paraestatales, piden empresarios a JLP," *Unomásuno*, March 16, 1980, 6–8. In spite of this, the CNC continued to implore that López Portillo nationalize the pharmaceutical industry. "Los actos delictuosos cometidos por mal llamadas empresas mexicanas y por transnacionales, en contra del patrimonio de los trabajadores de la ciudad y del campo, nos obligan a solicitar al gobierno de la República que concluya los estudios y se haga realidad la nacionalización de la industria química-farmacéutica. Consideramos que ha llegado el momento de crear una industria nacional farmacéutica, acorde con los planes y programas de desarrollo del país, y que responda a los intereses legítimos de la nación." (We believe the time has come to provide a domestic pharmaceutical company that complies with the goals of this country.) "Confederación Nacional Campesina a C. Lic. José López Portillo," *Excelsior*, February 10, 1977, A22.

9. "Debe seguir el agro en manos del productor," *Excelsior*, May 11, 1980.

10. In the early 1990s, this would once again be a problem for INBASA, the campesino-controlled company that replaced Proquivemex. "Daños a productores de barbasco por la importación de diosgenina venida de China," January 18, 1993; "En bancarrota, los productores de barbasco: Excesivas importaciones," *El Universal*, February 15, 1993; "Adquieren empresas farmacéuticas barbasco importado: Afectados, 100,000 productores," *El Universal*, March 17, 1993; "Acusa la CNC a SECOFI de permitir la compra de barbasco a precios dumping," April 28, 1993. Newspaper articles found in Archivo y Biblioteca Lerdo de Tejada, Barbasco R01314, Archivos Económicos, Mexico City; some clippings did not have the title of the newspaper.

11. AGN, Galería 2, vol. 17, PQV-D-084/80.

12. Letter to Manuel Puebla from Okamoto managing director, November 11, 1980. Ibid.

13. Letter from Manuel Puebla to Ramón González Jameson on November 24, 1980. AGN, Galería 2, vol. 17, PQV-D-084/80.

14. Letter from Manuel Puebla. February 1, 1980. Ibid. A few years later Puebla

was asked to provide receipts of his itinerary as proof that he had really been working and not touring Europe. AGN, Proquivemex, vol. 21.

15. Letter from Francisco Fernández Arteada to Manuel Puebla, August 22, 1980. AGN, Galería 2, vol. 17, PQV-D-084/80.

16. Ibid.

17. S. Janka and S. Diechtl, *Relacionario de barbasco* (INIF: Mexico City, 1982).

18. Ibid., 2.

19. Archival material found in gallery (galería) 2 of the AGN substantiates Diechtl's report.

20. Fortín Emilio, personal interview, Catemaco, Veracruz.

21. Proquivemex División Agroindustrial, S.A. de C.V. Notas a los Estados Financieros Años que Terminaron el 31 de Diciembre de 1983 y 1982, p. 11. Documents found in CNC, Tuxtepec, Oaxaca.

22. Letter from the director general of the Secretaría de Programación y Presupuesto Isaac Osorio Corpi to the Director of the Secretaría de Patrimonio y Fomento Industrial Lic. Alfredo Acle Tomasini, July 8, 1980 AGN, Galería 2, Proquivemex Collection, vol. 17, PQV-D-084/80.

23. Proquivemex División Agroindustrial, S.A. de C.V., "Notas a los Estados Financieros años que terminaron el 31 de Diciembre de 1983 y 1982," 11. Documents found in CNC, Tuxtepec, Oaxaca, 14.

24. *Informe Anual a la H. Asamblea General de Accionistas de Proquivemex División Agroindustrial, S.A. de C.V. Sobre el ejercicio fiscal 1983*, CNC, Tuxtepec, Oaxaca.

25. Fidel Santiago Hernández, personal interview, Valle Nacional, Oaxaca, July 2004.

26. Ibid.

27. Cruz, *La organización campesina y la integración vertical de la agricultura*.

28. AGN, Galería 2, Archivo Proquivemex, vol. 17.

29. "No hay hostilidad a la inversión extranjera," *El Universal*, February 11, 1977.

30. Alejandro Villar Borja, personal interview, central offices of SEDESOL, Tlaxcala, Tlaxcala, February 1999.

31. Villar Borja's "self-imposed" title was heavily criticized in the press, where it was implied that check number 8560061, cashed for 1 million pesos in the name of "expenses for the cause," was fraudulently used by him. Moreover, Villar Borja was accused of not wanting to relinquish his hold over the company and the ejidos. "El barbasco: Anticonceptivos políticos," *El Sol de Mexico*, April 24, 1977. Villar Borja retaliated in a series of letters to various Mexico City newspapers (*El Día, Excelsior,* and *El Sol de México*). AVBP, folio "Cartas a la Prensa," Mexico City.

32. "Advierten los campesinos: No se permitirán cambios en la comercialización del Barbasco," *El Día*, February 11, 1977.

33. "Campesinos 'barbasqueros' lanzan cargos al director de Proquivemex," *El Día*, April 14, 1977.

34. Ibid.

35. *"Por defender los derechos del hermano campesino, Malpica fue eliminado por un cobarde asesino."*

36. "Matan por el barbasco: Proquivemex acusa a las transnacionales," *Diario de México*, August 20, 1976.

37. *El Universal*, March 16, 1976.

38. Letter from the Uniones de Ejidos Ursulo Galván and Manuel Almanza to Luis Echeverría Alvarez, July 3, 1975. AVBP, file "Cartas a LEA."

39. Unión de ejido delegates, letter to barbasco pickers, April 27, 1977. AVBP, folio "Uniones de Ejidos."

40. "Campesinos 'barbasqueros' lanzan cargos al director de Proquivemex," *El Día*, April 14, 1977.

41. Letter from Pedro Ramírez to the secretary of the CNC, May 22, 1985. AGN, Proquivemex, vol. 70, exp. 697, 3.

42. The exchange rate, according to Proquivemex documents, was 247.44 pesos per dollar. Ibid.

43. This was not necessarily a triumph. By the mid-1980s many of the beneficios were not in use, the machinery was in disrepair, or the individual unions that controlled them had organized into other associations and had abandoned the beneficios.

44. Eduardo Domínguez, personal interview, Toluca, Estado de México, February 1999.

45. Unión de Crédito Agropecuaria, Forestal e Industrial de los Productores de Barbasco, S.A. de C.V., "Plan de operaciones de crédito 1989," Mexico City, November 1988.

46. Ibid.

47. By 1986 the UNPRB was the only campesino organization in Mexico working with credits from Citibank. Andrés Correa, personal interview, Mexico City, November 1999.

48. Barbara Caughlin, personal interview, Mexico City, June 1999.

49. Guillermo Wilkins, personal interview, Mexico City, June 22, 1999.

50. Ibid.

51. AGN, Galería 2, Proquivemex, vol. 67, exp. 660, folio 17.

52. A typical confusing comment was the following made during that meeting of July 1, 1985, "Este, estoy de acuerdo, pero yo, no basta, es como si yo aquí o en este caso, digo, sigue el problema de la importación de la diosgenina, a pero, mira yo el año pasado mandé un escrito diciéndole que no, pero el problema es que sigue, entonces vamos aliando las partes aquí, digo en un momento determinado." (This nonsensical answer explains: "Uhm, I agree, but I, it is not

enough, if I, or in this instance, I mean, the import problem with diosgenin . . .")
AGN, Galería 2, Proquivemex, vol. 67, exp. 660, folio 17, 10.

53. In 1984 he allegedly sold a kilo of processed flour for significantly lower (2,600 pesos) than the UNPRB established rate of 3,170 pesos.

54. Guillermo Wilkins, personal interview, Mexico City, June 22, 1999.

55. *Informe general de actividades 1980–1985*, UNPRB Third General Congress, Mexico, UNION report, November 1985.

56. AGN, Galería 2, Proquivemex, vol. 55, Exp. Amatepec.

57. Isidro Apolinar, personal interview, Chiltepec, 2004.

58. *Informe geneal de actividades 1980–1985*, UNPRB Third General Congress, UNION Report, November 1985.

59. Guillermo Wilkins, personal interview, Mexico City, June 22, 1999.

60. Unión Helio García Alfaro. AGN, Galería 2, Proquivemex Collection, vol. 73, PQV.

61. Letter from Eva Domínguez Choapas to Guillermo Wilkins, November 26, 1984. AGN, Proquivemex, vol. 30.

62. Letter from Movimiento Nacional Campesino "Alfredo V. Bonfil" to Guillermo Wilkins, October 25, 1983. AGN, Galería 2, Proquivemex, vol. 73, legajo Helio García Hernández.

63. Guillermo Wilkins, personal interview, Mexico City, June 22, 1999.

64. *Informe general de actividades 1980–1985*, UNPRB Third General Congress, UNION report, Mexico City, November 1985.

65. José Gasca Zamora, "Fuentes para el estudio de las empresas paraestatales de México y su privatización 1983–1988," *Comercio Exterior* 39, no. 2 (February 1989): 151–75.

66. AGN, Galería 2, Proquivemex, vol. 73, February 19, 1986.

67. Ibid. Workers of pharmaceutical companies had been rallying against Proquivemex.

68. Cordemex and Farmex made offers after it was determined that the value of the company was around 430 million pesos. Cruz, *La organización campesina y la integración vertical de la agricultura*.

69. Letter dated November 17, 1989, from Secretaría de la Contraloría General de la Federación to Asamblea General Ordinaria de Accionistas de Productos Químicos Vegetales Mexicanos, S.A. de C.V. AGN, Galería 2, Proquivemex, vol. 96., exp. 5, folio 67.

70. "A la Asamblea General Ordinaria de Accionistas de Productos Químicos Vegetales de México, 17 de Noviembre de 1989." AGN, Galería 2, Proquivemex, vol. 96, exp. 5, folio 67.

71. "Proyecto de Transferencia y Liquidación de la Empresa Productos Químicos Vegetales Mexicanos, S.A. de C.V." AGN, Galería 2, Proquivemex, vol. 96, exp. 5, folio 67.

72. "Orden del Día." AGN, Galería 2, Proquivemex, vol. 96, exp. 13, folio 16, 6.
73. Ana Paula De Teresa, Crisis agrícola y economía campesina, 93.

Epilogue

1. During three conversations with Santiago, he never mentioned his various trips to Mexico City or his meeting with President Echeverría until I explicitly questioned him about it. He was surprisingly reluctant to speak of his trip to Los Pinos, but his experience was corroborated by other campesinos.

2. Ruy Pérez Tamayo describes the role of science in twentieth-century Mexico this way. *Historia general de la ciencia en el siglo XX*. Mexico City: Fondo de la Cultura Económica, 2005.

3. "Se concede un subsidio en favor de todos los explotadores de la planta conocida con el nombre de barbasco . . . cuyo subsidio estará en vigor durante el presente año y será por el 75% de la percepción federal sobre la cuota de [Mex]$200.00 por tonelada, señalada por la ley del Impuesto sobre la explotación Forestal. . . ." Acuerdo a la Secretaría de Hacienda y C.P., February 25, 1955. And "Acuerdo por el que se concede subsidio en la explotación del vegetal conocido por Barbasco registrado con el número 281." March 30, 1955. Dirección General de Gobierno. Vol. 133, Exp.: 35 2300(2a)4033, Fs.; 4. AGN, Mexico City ". . . he dispuesto se conceda un subsidio en favor de todos los explotadores de la planta conocida con el nombre de barbasco (*Dioscoreaceas composita*), el cual estará en vigor durante todo el año de 1960 y será por el 50% (CINCUENTA) de la percepción federal neta sobre la cuota de $200.00 por tonelada. . . ." January 21, 1960. Departamento de Gobierno. 2/300(2a)/4358. Caja 6. Exp.:4, Fs.:5, AGN, Mexico City.

4. "Dominamos el mercado de hormonas: Más de la mitad del consumo universal la exporta México," April 16, 1955. "La Industria hormonal mexicana batió marcas de venta al exterior," January 25, 1958. Archivo Lerdo Tejada / Archivos Económicos. M05072/150204Biología, Genética, Hormonas, Internacional 1931–87. 12 DT.

5. "Un grupo de técnicos del I.N.I.P., fue comisionado para estudiar un plan de protección y propagación del barbasco. . . ." ("We dominate the hormone trade: Mexico exports to more than half the world" and "The Mexican hormone industry had record export sales.") *Protección Oficial a una planta que produce Hormonas*, November 27, 1961. Archivo Lerdo Tejada/Archivos Económicos. M05072/150204 Biología, Genética, Hormonas, Internacional 1931–87. 12 DT.

6. *Life*, June 6, 1951.

7. In the nearly thirty newspaper articles from this period, peasants are only mentioned as harvesters of the root. Newspaper articles of the time focus on the chemists (Marker, Rosenkranz, and Djerassi), the companies (Organon in

Holland, Scherring in Germany, and Syntex in Mexico), and how the wild yam alleviated the cortisone shortage.

8. Alejandro Villar Borja, Guillermo Wilkins, and José Luis Martinez expressed this opinion.

9. Ingeniero Cuautémoc Tejada of SEMARNAP kindly provided a copy of this letter.

10. Ibid.

Major Primary Sources

Archives

MEXICO CITY

Alejandro Villar Borja Personal Papers (AVBP)
Archivo Condumex
Archivo General de la Nación (AGN)
Archivo General de la Secretaría de Reforma Agraria
Archivo y Biblioteca Lerdo de Tejada
Hemeroteca Nacional
Registro Agrario Nacional

OAXACA

Archivo General del Estado de Oaxaca

UNITED STATES

Chemical Heritage Foundation (CHF) Archives, Philadelphia
Russell Earl Marker Papers, Paterno Library, Pennsylvania State University

Libraries

Biblioteca CIESAS-DF (Estudios Superiores Antropológicos y Sociales,
   Distrito Federal)
Biblioteca de la Reforma Agraria
Biblioteca de la Secretaría de Agricultura, Ganadería
Biblioteca de la Secretaría de Medio Ambiente, Recursos Naturales

Interviews

GENERAL

Selerino Acevedo, CNC Valle Nacional.
Ignacio Bernal, INI, Oaxaca City.

Cuauhtémoc Cárdenas Solórzano, Tucson, Ariz., and Santa Barbara, Calif.

Barbara Caughlin, Formerly of Proquivemex. Mexico City.

Rafael Ceballos, CNC, Mexico City. One of the original "Pañales."

Roberto Cervantes Alarcón, Regional Director of INI, Tuxtepec.

Guillermo Correa, FONAFE.

Andrés Correa, AMUCS.

Silvio Delgado, Hacienda. Formerly of Reforma Agraria.

Alfredo Hernandez, CNC, Valle Nacional.

Xavier Lozoya, Siglo XXI Hospital. Formerly of IMEPLAM.

José Luis Martínez, Hacienda. Formerly of Proquivemex.

Bernardo Mortera, INI, Oaxaca.

Miguel Pena, CNC, Tuxtepec.

Cuauhtémoc Tejada, INIFAP, Mexico City.

Lic. Alejandro Villar Borja, SEDESOL, Tlaxcala. Former director of
    Proquivemex.

Lic. Guillermo Wilkins, Mexico City. Former director of Proquivemex.

SCIENTISTS (BIOLOGISTS, CHEMISTS, AGRARIAN ENGINEERS)

Mstra. (Maestra) Abigaíl Aguilar, IMSS Herbarium, Mexico City.

Dr. Miguel Angel Alfaro, Jardín Botánico, Mexico City.

Ing. (Ingeniero) Salvador Anta Fonseca, SEMARNAP, Oaxaca City.

Ing. Juan Manuel Barrera, SEMARNAP, Oaxaca.

Dr. Hans Beets, San Diego, California.

Ing. Armando Cruz, independent chemist, Mexico City.

Sigrid Diechtl, former researcher for the Mexico-Germany Agreement,
    Catemaco.

Dr. Gómez-Pompa, Riverside, California.

Ing. Miguel González Corona, INIFAP, Loma Bonita.

Dr. Carlos Huerta, Universidad Autónoma de Chapingo.

Ing. Francisco Maldonado, Tuxtepec.

Ing. Luis Ernesto Miramontes, Mexico City.

Ing. Miguel Angel Plancarte, SEMARNAP, Oaxaca.

Dr. Alfredo Pérez Jiménez, Instituto de Biología, UNAM.

Ing. Galeote Reyes, SEMARNAP, Oaxaca.

Dr. Ricardo Reyes Chilpa, Instituto de Química, UNAM.

Dr. George Rosencranz, Palo Alto, California.

Ing. Cuauhtemoc Tejada, INIFAP, Mexico City.

Ing. Carlos Tello, SEMARNAP, Mexico City, November 1998.

Dr. Alejandro Zaffaroni, Palo Alto, California.

Dr. Gloria Zafra, sociologist, Universidad Autónoma Benito Juárez.

BARBASCO PICKERS: INTERVIEWS IN OAXACA;
NOVEMBER 1998, FEBRUARY, APRIL, JUNE, AND JULY 1999
*(unless otherwise specified, not listed are eighteen who asked that
their names not be used)*

Florentino Vicente Albines, Cerro de Concha.

Daniel Antonio Alejandro, Chiltepec, Oaxaca.

Fortino Alvarez, Valle Nacional.

Isidro Apolinar, Chiltepec, Oaxaca. November 1998, April 1999, November
  2001, and July 2004.

Rosa Cruz Pérez, Cerro de Concha (translated with aid of native Chinantec
  speaker).

Eduardo Domínguez, Toluca.

Lencho Domínguez, Jacatepec.

Delfino Hernández Salazar, Tuxtepec.

Eufemia Hernández, Cerro de Concha.

Fidel Santiago Hernández, Valle Nacional, 2004.

Bernardo Galindo, Cerro de Concha.

David Gamboa, Cerro de Concha.

Gregoria Gamboa, Cerro de Concha.

Tomás Felipe Gamboa, Cerro de Concha.

Pascual Gamboa Cruz, Cerro de Concha.

Aristro Lara, Valle Nacional.

Lorenzo León Felipe, Valle Nacional, Oaxaca. 1999, 2001.

Cristina López, Jacatepec.

Faustino López, Jacatepec.

Porfirio Martínez, Jacatepec.

Juan Martínez Ferrer, Cerro de Concha.

Próspero Mendoza, La Gran Lucha.

Panuncio Ortega, Tuxtepec.

Abel Perez Vicente, Cerro de Concha.

Pedro Ramírez Rodríguez, Mexico City.

Francisco Rosas, Jacatepec.

Melquíades Santiago, Valle Nacional, Oaxaca. 1999, 2001.

M. Santos, Tuxtepec, Oaxaca. July 1999.

Alejandro "El Turco" Weber, Jacatepec. 1999, 2001, 2004.

FORMER AND CURRENT BENEFICIO OWNERS

Gabriel Cué, Tuxtepec, Oaxaca.

Emilio Fortín, Catemaco, Veracruz.

Newspapers

Acción de Tuxtepec	*El Heraldo de México*
Diario de México	*New York Times*
El Día	*La Prensa*
El Nacional	*Unomásuno*
El Sol de México	*Vientos del Sur*
Excelsior	

Secondary Sources

Abel, Christopher, and Colin M. Lewis. *Latin America: Economic Imperialism and the State.* London: University of London Press, 1985.

Acevedo Cárdenas, Conrado. *Echeverría y su pensamiento educativo.* Mexico City: Editorial Libros de México, 1974.

Aceves Lozano, Jorge E. *Historia oral e historias de vida: Teoría, métodos y técnicas.* Mexico City: CIESAS, 1996.

Adelson G., Lief. "Coyuntura y conciencia: Factores convergentes en la fundación de los sindicatos petroleros de Tampico durante la década de 1920." In *El trabajo y los trabajadores en la historia de México,* edited by Elsa Cecilia Frost. Mexico City: University of Arizona Press, 1979.

Adler Hellman, Judith. *Mexico in Crisis.* New York: Holmes and Meier Publications, 1978.

Aguilar Camín, Héctor. *Después del milagro.* Mexico City: Cal Editores, 1989.

———. "El deceno del milagro: El sistema político mexicano 1940–1984." In *Primer simposio sobre historia contemporánea de México 1940–1984: Inventario sobre el pasado reciente.* Mexico City: Instituto Nacional de Antropológica e Historia, 1986.

Aguirre, Norberto. *Cuestiones agrarias: Cuadernos de Joaquín Mortiz.* Mexico City: Editorial Joaquín Mortiz, 1977.

Aguirre Beltrán, Gonzalo. *Pobladores del Papaloapan: Biografía de una hoya.* Mexico City: Casa Chata, 1992.

Alonso, Ana Maria. "The Effects of Truth: Re-presentations of the Past and the Imagining of Community." *Journal of Historical Sociology* 1 (March 1, 1988): 33–57.

"Alternativas para el uso del suelo en áreas forestales del trópico húmedo." *Publicación Especial* 29, no. 4 (1981).

Amin, Samir, Giovanni Arrighi, Andre Gunder Frank, and Immanuel Wallerstein. *Transforming the Revolution: Social Movements and the World-System.* New York: Monthly Review Press, 1990.

Andersen, John, and Birte Siim, eds. *The Politics of Inclusion and Empowerment: Gender, Class and Citizenship.* New York: Palgrave Macmillan, 2004.

Anderson, Benedict. *Imagined Communities*. London: Verso, 1995.

Anderson, Warwick. *Colonial Pathologies: American Tropical Medicine, Race, and Hygiene in the Philippines*. Durham: Duke University Press, 2006.

Anta Fonseca, Salvador. *Ecología y manejo integral de recursos naturales: En la región de la Chinantla*. Mexico City: PAIR-UNAM, 1992.

Anzures y Bolaños, María del Carmen. *La medicina tradicional en México*, Mexico City: UNAM, 1989.

Appadurai, Arjun. "Disjuncture and Difference in the Global Cultural Economy." *Theory, Culture and Society* 7, nos. 2–3 (1990): 295–311.

———. "Introduction: Commodities and the Politics of Value." *The Social Life of Things: Commodities in Cultural Perspective*, edited by Arjun Appadurai. New York: Cambridge University Press, 1986.

Applezweig, Norman. "The Big Steroid Treasure Hunt." *Chemical Week* (January 31, 1959): 38–52.

———. *Steroid Drugs*. New York: McGraw-Hill, 1962.

———. "Steroids." *Chemical Week* (May 17, 1969): 58–68.

Arellanes, Anselmo, ed. *Historia de la cuestión agraria mexicana: El Estado de Oaxaca*. Vols. 1, 2. Mexico City: Juan Pablo Editores, 1988.

———. *Oaxaca: Reparto de tierra: Alcances, limitaciones y respuestas*. 2nd ed. Mexico City: UNAM, 1999.

Arellanes, Anselmo, Víctor Raúl Martínez Vásquez, and Francisco José Ruiz Cervantes. *Oaxaca en el Siglo XX: Testimonios de historia oral*. Mexico City: Ediciones Meridiano 100, 1988.

Armus, Diego. *Disease in the History of Modern Latin America: From Malaria to AIDS*. Durham: Duke University Press, 2003.

Arnove, Robert F., and Carlos Alberto Torres. "Adult Education and State Policy in Latin America: The Contrasting Cases of Mexico and Nicaragua." *Comparative Education* 31, no. 3 (November 1995): 311–25.

Asbell, Bernard. *The Pill: A Biography of the Drug That Changed the World*. New York: Random House, 1995.

Asociación rural de interés colectivo, internal document. Mexico City, 1986.

Avila Camacho, Manuel. "Address to the Mexican Agronomists," National and International Problems Series, no. 8. Mexico City: Talleres Gráficos de la Nación, 1941.

———. *Segundo plan sexenal*. Partido Revolucionario Institucional, Comité Ejecutivo Nacional, Comisión Nacional Editorial, 1976.

Ayensu, Edward S. "Comments on Old and New World Dioscoreas of Commercial Importance." In *Primer Simposio Internacional sobre Dioscoreas, Publicación Especial*, no. 3 (August). Mexico City: SAG, 1972.

Azpeitia Gómez, Hugo. *Compañía Exportadora e Importadora Mexicana, S.A. (1949–1958)*. Mexico City: CIESAS, 1994.

Azpeitia Gómez, Hugo, et al., eds. *Historia de la cuestión agraria mexicana: Los tiempos de la crisis (primera parte), 1970–1982*. Mexico City: Siglo Veintiuno Editores, 1990.

Bade, Bonnie. "Contemporary Mixtec Medicine: Emotional and Spiritual Approaches to Healing." In *Cloth and Curing: Continuity and Change in Oaxaca*, edited by G. Johnson and D. Sharon. San Diego Museum of Man *Papers*, no. 32. San Diego: San Diego Museum of Man.

Bakhtin, M. M. *The Dialogic Imagination*. Austin: University of Texas Press, 1981.

Ballesteros, Juan, Matthew Edel, and Michael Nelson. *La colonización del Papaloapan: Una evaluación socioeconómica*. Mexico City: Centro de Investigaciones Agrarias, 1970.

Ballesteros Porta, Juan. "Estudio sobre formas actuales de cooperación agropecuaria," in *Los problemas de la organización campesina*. Mexico City: Editorial Campesina, 1975.

——. *Los campesinos: ¿Para qué organizarlos?* Mexico City: Centro de Ecodesarrollo, 1976.

Banco Nacional de Comercio Exterior, S.A. Translated by Susana Gamboa. *Mexico City 1976: Facts, Figures, Trends*. Mexico City: Banco Nacional de Comercio Exterior, S.A., 1977.

Barabas, Alicia, and Miguel Bartolomé, coordinadores. *Etnicidad y pluralismo cultural: La dinámica étnica en Oaxaca*. Mexico City: Dirección General de Publicaciones, 1990.

Barahona, Marvin. *El silencio quedó atrás: Testimonios de la Huelga Bananera de 1954*. Tegucigalpa: Editorial Guaymuras, 1994.

Barham, Bradford L., and Oliver T. Coomes. *Prosperity's Promise: The Amazon Rubber Boom and Distorted Economic Development*. Boulder: Westview Press, 1996.

Barnet, Richard J., and John Cavanagh. *Global Dreams: Imperial Corporations and the New World Order*. New York: Touchstone, 1994.

Barrios de Chungara, Domitila. *Let Me Speak! Testimony of Domitila: A Woman of the Bolivian Mines*. New York: Monthly Review Press, 1978.

Barthel, Diane. *Historic Preservation: Collective Memory and Historical Identity*. New Brunswick, N.J.: Rutgers University Press, 1996.

Bartolomé, Miguel Alberto, and Alicia Mabel Barabas. *La Presa Cerro de Oro y el Ingeniero El Gran Dios: Relocalización y etnicidad chinanteco en México*. Vol. 2. Mexico City: Instituto Nacional Indigenista. 1990.

Bartra, Armando. *Notas sobre la cuestión campesina, México 1970–1976*. Mexico City: Editorial Macehual, 1979.

——. *Los herederos de Zapata: Movimientos campesinos posrevolucionarios en México*. 2nd ed. Mexico City: Editorial Era, 1992.

Bartra, Roger. *La jaula de la melancolía: Identidad y metamórfosis del mexicano.* Mexico City: Grijalbo, 1987.

———. "Peasants and Political Power in Mexico: A Theoretical Approach." *Latin American Perspectives* 5 (1975): 125–45.

Becker, David G. *The New Bourgeoisie and the Limits of Dependency: Mining, Class and Power in "Revolutionary" Peru.* Princeton: Princeton University Press, 1983.

Behrman, Jack. *Review of Multinational Corporations in Brazil and Mexico: Structural Sources of Economic and Noneconomic Power.* New York: Council of the Americas, 1975.

Beltrán, Enrique. *Los recursos forestales y su utilización.* Mexico City: Subsecretario de Recursos Forestales y de Caza, 1963.

———. *Los recursos naturales de México y el crecimiento demográfico.* Mexico City: Fundación para Estudios de la Población, 1973.

Beltrán, Gonzalo Aguirre. *Cuatro nobles titulados en contienda por la tierra.* Mexico City: Centro de Investigaciones y Estudios, 1995.

Bennett, Douglas C., and Kenneth E. Sharpe. *Transnational Corporations versus the State: The Political Economy of the Mexican Auto Industry.* Princeton: Princeton University Press, 1985.

Bermúdez, Antonio J., and Octavio Vejar Vázquez. *No dejes crecer la hierba . . . (El Gobierno avilacamachista).* Mexico City: Talleres de B. Costa-Amic, 1969.

Bernstein, Seymour. "Historic Reflections on Steroids: Lederle and Personal Aspects." *Steroids* 57 (1992): 392–402.

Berry, Charles R. *The Reform in Oaxaca, 1956–76: A Microhistory of the Liberal Revolution.* Lincoln: University of Nebraska Press, 1981.

Bethell, Leslie, and Ian Roxborough. "Latin America between the Second World War and the Cold War: Some Reflections on the 1945–48 Conjuncture." *Journal of Latin American Studies* 20 (1988): 167–87.

Birch, Arthur J. "Steroid Hormones and the Luftwaffe: A Venture into Fundamental Strategic Research and Some of Its Consequences. The Birch Reduction Becomes a Birth Reduction." *Steroids* 57 (1992): 363–77.

Birn, Anne-Emanuelle. *Marriage of Convenience: Rockefeller International Health and Revolutionary Mexico.* Rochester, N.Y.: University of Rochester Press, 2006.

Bissett, Jim. *Agrarian Socialism in America.* Norman: University of Oklahoma Press, 1999.

Blancarte, Roberto, ed. *Cultura e identidad nacional.* Mexico City: Consejo Nacional para la Cultura y las Artes, 1994.

Bliss, Katherine Elaine. *Compromised Positions: Prostitution, Public Health, and Gender Politics in Revolutionary Mexico City.* University Park: Pennsylvania State University Press, 2001.

Bloch, Konrad. "Sterol Molecule: Structure, Biosynthesis, and Function." *Steroids* 57 (1992): 378–83.

Bonfil Batalla, Guillermo. *México Profundo: Reclaiming a Civilization*. Austin: University of Texas Press, 1996.

Boomgaard, Peter. "In the Shadow of Rice: Roots and Tubers in Indonesian History, 1500–1950." *Agricultural History* 77, no. 4 (Autumn 2003): 582–610.

Borges, Dain. "'Puffy, Ugly, Slothful and Inert': Degeneration in Brazilian Social Thought, 1880–1940," *Journal of Latin American Studies* 25, no. 2 (May 1993): 235–56.

Borneman, John. *Belonging in the Two Berlins: Kin, State, Nation*. Cambridge: Cambridge University Press, 1992.

Boyer, Christopher. *Becoming Campesinos: Politics, Identity, and Agrarian Struggle in Postrevolutionary Michoacán, 1920–1935*. Stanford, Calif.: Stanford University Press, 2003.

———. "Modernizing the Monte: Of Tree Tappers and Scientific Development in Postrevolutionary Michoacán." Paper presented at the LASA conference, Las Vegas, 2003.

———. "Old Loves, New Loyalties: Agrarismo in Michoacán, 1920–1928." *Hispanic American Historical Review*, 78, no. 3 (August 1999): 419–55.

Briggs, Charles. *Learning How to Ask: A Sociolinguistic Appraisal of the Role of the Interview in Social Science Research*. Cambridge: Cambridge, University Press 1996.

———. "The Meaning of Nonsense, the Poetics of Embodiment, and the Production of Power in Waroa Healing." In *The Performance of Healing*, edited by Carol Laderman. Routledge: Scholarly Resources, 1993.

Briggs, Laura. *Reproducing Empire: Race, Sex, Science, and U.S. Imperialism in Puerto Rico*. Berkeley: University of California Press, 2002.

Britton, John A. "Urban Education and Social Change in the Mexican Revolution, 1931–40." *Journal of Latin American Studies* 5, no. 2 (November 1973): 233–45.

———. "Indian Education, Nationalism, and Federalism in Mexico, 1910–1921." *Americas* 32, no. 3 (January 1976): 445–58.

Brockway, Lucile H. "Plant Science and Colonial Expansion: The Botanical Chess Game." In *Seeds and Sovereignty: The Use and Control of Plant Genetic Resources*, edited by Jack Kloppenburg Jr. Durham: Duke University Press, 1988.

Brown, Richard Harvey. "Modern Science: Institutionalization of Knowledge and Rationalization of Power." *Sociological Quarterly* 34, no. 1 (1993): 153–68.

Burke, Michael E. "The University of Mexico and the Revolution, 1910–1940." *Americas* 34, no. 2 (October 1977): 252–73.

Byrne, David. *Social Exclusion*. Buckingham: Open University Press, 1999.

Cabarrús, Carlos Rafael. *Génesis de una revolución: Análisis del surgimiento y desarrollo de la organización campesina en el Salvador*. Mexico City: Casa Chata, 1983.

Calhoun, Craig. *Social Theory and the Politics of Identity*. Oxford: Blackwell, 1994.

Calingaert, Edgar, and R. E. Marker. *Journal of the American Chemical Society* 51 (1929): 1483.

Callan, Eamonn. *Creating Citizens: Political Education and Liberal Democracy.* Oxford: Clarendon Press, 1997.

Campbell, Elmer Grant. "What Is a Weed?" *Science* 58, no. 1490 (July 20, 1923): 50.

Campos, Navarro. *Nosotros los curanderos.* Mexico City: Nueva Imagen, 1997.

Cantú Peña, Fausto. *Café para todos.* Mexico City: Grijalbo, 1989.

Carabias, Julia, Enrique Provencio, and Carlos Toledo. *Manejo de recursos naturales y pobreza rural.* Mexico City: Fondo de Cultura Económica, 1994.

Cárdenas, Lázaro. "Message to the People of Mexico on the Occasion of the 28th Anniversary Celebration of the Mexican Revolution." Delivered November 20, 1938.

———. "New Year's Message." Delivered January 1, 1938.

Cardoso, F. H., and E. Faletto. *Dependency and Development in Latin America.* Berkeley: University of California Press, 1979.

Carter, Erica James Donald, and Judith Squires. *Space and Place: Theories of Identity and Location.* London: Lawrence and Wishart, 1994.

"Cartera vencida." *La Opinión.* September 1975. Poza Rica, Veracruz.

Casas-Andreu, Gustavo, et al. "Anfibios y reptiles de Oaxaca: Lista, distribución y conservación." *Acta Zoológica Mexicana*, no. 69 (1996): 1–35.

Castañeda, Jorge. *Perpetuating Power: How Mexican Presidents Were Chosen.* New York: W. W. Norton, 2000.

———. *Utopia Unarmed: The Latin American Left after the Cold War.* New York: Knopf, 1993.

Castellanos, Rosario. *Balún-canán.* Mexico City: Fondo de Cultura Económica, 1957.

Castillo, Heberto. *Desde la trinchera que fue excelsior.* Mexico City: Editorial Posada, 1976.

Celis Ochoa, Humberto. *Papaloapan: Cuentos del llano el río.* Jalapa, Veracruz: Editiv, 1950.

Chacón, J. C., and S. R. Gliessman. "Use of the 'Non-Weed' Concept in Traditional Tropical Agroecosystems of South-Eastern Mexico." *Agro-Ecosystems* 8, no. 1 (1982): 1–11.

Chambers, David Wade, and Richard Gillespie. "Locality in the History of Science: Colonial Science, Technoscience, and Indigenous Knowledge." In *Osiris* (series edited by Kathryn M. Olesko). Vol. 15: *Nature and Empire: Science and the Colonial Enterprise*, edited by Roy MacLeod. Chicago: University of Chicago Press, 2000.

Chassen-López, Francie. *From Liberal to Revolutionary Oaxaca: The View from the South, Mexico 1867–1911.* University Park: Pennsylvania State University Press, 2004.

Chenaut, Victoria. *Procesos rurales e historia regional (sierra y costa totonacas de Veracruz)*. Mexico City: CIESAS, 1996.

Ciba Foundation. *Ethnobotany and the Search for New Drugs*. Chichester, N.Y.: John Wiley and Sons, 1994.

Ciencia Forestal: Revista de la Dirección General de Investigación y Capacitación Forestales 3, no. 13 (May–June 1978).

Clarke, Adele E. "Controversy and Development of Reproductive Sciences." *Social Problems* 37 (1990): 18–37.

―――. "Research Materials and Reproductive Science in the United States, 1910–1940." In *Physiology in the American Context*, edited by Gerald L. Geison. Bethesda, Md.: American Physiological Society, 1987.

Clayton, Lawrence, and Michael Coniff. *History of Modern Latin America*. Fort Worth: Harcourt Brace College Publishers, 1999.

Cole, Blaiser. *The Hovering Giant: U.S. Responses to Revolutionary Change in Latin America*. Pittsburgh: University of Pittsburgh Press, 1976.

Collier, George A. *Basta! Land and the Zapatista Rebellion in Chiapas*. Oakland, Calif.: Institute for Food and Development Policy, 1994.

Colmenares, Ismael. *Cien años de lucha de clases*. Mexico City: Ediciones Quinto Sol, 1994.

Comaroff, John L., and Jean Comaroff. *Civil Society and the Political Imagination in Africa: Critical Perspectives*. Chicago: University of Chicago Press, 1999.

Comisión de Estudios sobre la Ecología de Dioscoreas. *V Informe, 1967–1968*. Vol. 2. Mexico City: Instituto Nacional de Investigaciones Forestales.

"Comments on Old and New World Dioscoreas of Commercial Importance." *Publicación Especial*, no. 3 (August). Mexico City: SAG, 1972.

"Con capital del Estado, el Barbasco dejará de ser fuente de explotación del campesino." *El Día*. March 1976.

Conniff, Michael. *Latin American Populism in Comparative Perspective*. Albuquerque: University of New Mexico Press, 1982.

"Contribuciones al estudio ecológico de las zonas cálido-húmedas de México." *Publicación Especial*, nos. 3, 6, 7. Mexico City: SAG, 1964.

Cook, Noble David. *Born to Die: Disease and the New World Conquest, 1492–1650*. New York: Cambridge University Press, 1998.

Cooper, Frederick. *Confronting Historical Paradigms: Peasants, Labor, and the Capitalist World System in Africa and Latin America*. Madison: University of Wisconsin Press, 1993.

Coronel, Gustavo. *The Nationalization of the Venezuelan Oil Industry*. Lexington, Mass.: Lexington Books, 1983.

"Cortisone from Giant Yam." *Life* (July 23, 1951): 75–77.

Cosío Villegas, Daniel. *El estilo personal de gobernar*. Mexico City: Editorial Joaquín Mortiz, 1974.

Costa, Nuria. *UNORCA: Documentos para la historia*. Mexico City: Costa-Amic, 1989.

Cotter, Joseph. "The Rockefeller Foundation's Mexican Agricultural Project: A Cross-Cultural Encounter, 1943–1949." In *Missionaries of Science: The Rockefeller Foundation in Latin America*, edited by Marcos Cueto. Bloomington: Indiana University Press, 1994.

———. *Troubled Harvest: Agronomy and Revolution in Mexico, 1880–2002*. Westport, Conn.: Praeger, 2003.

Coursey, D. G. *Yams: An Account of the Nature, Origins, Cultivation, and Utilisation of the Useful Members of the Dioscoreaceae*. London: Longmans, Green and Co., 1967.

Crapo, Lawrence. *Hormones: The Messengers of Life*. New York: W. H. Freeman and Company, 1985.

Cresswell, Tim. "Weeds, Plagues, and Bodily Secretions: A Geographical Interpretation of Metaphors of Displacement." *Annals of the Association of American Geographers* 87, no. 2 (June 1997): 330–45.

Criollo, Armando Alonso, Arturo Ruiz López, and Ana M. Alvarado Juárez. *Salud y tradiciones reproductivas en la Sierra Norte de Oaxaca: Un estudio de caso*. Donato Ramos Pioquinto, coordinador. Oaxaca City: Universidad Autónoma "Benito Juárez" de Oaxaca, 1998.

Crosby, Alfred W. *The Colombian Exchange: Biological and Cultural Consequences of 1492*. Westport, Conn.: Greenwood Press, 1972.

———. *Ecological Imperialism: The Biological Expansion of Europe, 900–1900*. Cambridge: Cambridge University Press, 1986.

Cruz, Isabel. *La organización campesina y la integración vertical de la agricultura*. Mexico City: AMUCS, 1986.

Cuadernos del Sur 13 (1998). Mexico City.

Cutler, Stephen J., and Horace G. Cutler. *Biologically Active Natural Products: Pharmaceuticals*. Boca Raton, Fla.: CRC Press, 2000.

Cvetkovich, Ann, and Douglas Kellner. *Articulating the Global and the Local: Globalization and Cultural Studies*. Boulder: Westview Press, 1997.

Dallek, Robert. "The Medical Ordeal of JFK." *Atlantic Monthly* 290, no. 5 (December 2002): 49–61.

———. *An Unfinished Life: John F. Kennedy, 1917–1963*. Boston: Little, Brown, and Company, 2003.

Dalton, Margarita. *Oaxaca: Una historia compartida*. Mexico City: Instituto de Investigaciones Dr. José María Luis Mora, Gobierno del Estado de Oaxaca, 1990.

Dean, Warren. *Brazil and the Struggle for Rubber: A Study in Environmental History*. New York: Cambridge University Press, 1987.

Deans-Smith, Susan. *Bureaucrats, Planters, and Workers: The Making of the Tobacco Monopoly in Bourbon Mexico.* Austin: University of Texas Press, 1992.

De Cárdenas, Juan. *Primera parte de los problemas y secretos maravillosos de las Indias.* Mexico City: Academia Nacional de Medicina, 1978.

De la Concha Ahuja, Silvia Elena, and Ana Luisa Gisholt Orozco. *El curandismo en el Distrito Federal.* Mexico City: UNAM.

De la Cruz, Martín. *Libellus de Medicinalibus Indorum Herbis.* Mexico City: Fondo de Cultura Económica and Instituto Mexicano del Seguro Social, 1964; orig. pub. 1552.

De la Garza Toledo, Enrique, coordinator. *Crisis y sujetos sociales en México.* Mexico City: Centro de Investigaciones Interdisciplinarias en Humanidades UNAM, 1992.

De la Grange, Bertrand, and Maite Rico. *Marcos: La genial impostura.* Mexico City: Ediciones Santillana, 1997.

De la Peña, Guillermo. *Herederos de promesas: Agricultura, política y ritual en los altos de Morelos.* Mexico City: Casa Chata, 1980.

Del Castillo, Gustavo. *Crisis y transformación de una sociedad tradicional.* Mexico City: Casa Chata, 1979.

De Teresa, Ana Paula. *Crisis agrícola y economía campesina: El caso de los productores de henequén en Yucatán.* Mexico City: Grupo Editorial Miguel Angel Porrúa, 1992.

———. *Población y territorio en la región chinanteca de Oaxaca.* UAM-1: Departamento de Antropología, Reporte de Investigación, no. 11, November 1997.

De Vos, Jan. *Oro Verde: La Conquista de la selva lacandona por los madereros tabasqueños, 1822–1949.* Mexico City: Fondo de Cultura Económica, 1996.

Deininger, Klaus W., and Bart Minten. "Poverty, Policies, and Deforestation: The Case of Mexico." *Economic Development and Cultural Change* (1999): 313–44.

Diechtel, Sigrid. "El barbasco mexicano: Condiciones y perspectivas de su aprovechamiento." *Ciencia Forestal: Revista de la Dirección General de Investigación y Capacitación Forestales* 5, no. 28 (November–December 1980): 1–43.

Djerassi, Carl. "The Making of the Pill: Russell Marker's Extraction of Sex Hormones from Mexican Yams Was Only the Beginning." *Science* (November 1994): 127–29.

———. *The Pill, Pygmy Chimps, and Degas' Horse.* New York: BasicBooks, 1992.

———. *Progestins in Therapy—Historical Developments.* New York: Raven Press, 1983.

———. *Steroids Made It Possible.* Washington, D.C.: American Chemical Society, 1990.

————. *This Man's Pill: Reflections on the 50th Birthday of the Pill*. Oxford: Oxford University Press, 2001.

Domínguez Vidal, Mario J. *Las selvas de Tabasco: Orígenes de la revolución de 1910 y 1913*. Mexico City: Editorial Polis, 1942.

Dorfman, Ariel, and Armand Mattelart. *How to Read Donald Duck: Imperialist Ideology in the Disney Comic*. New York: International General, 1971.

Dulles, John W. F. *Yesterday in Mexico: A Chronicle of the Revolution, 1919–1936*. Austin: University of Texas Press, 1961.

Durand, Jorge. *La ciudad invade al ejido*. Mexico City: Casa Chata, 1983.

Durand Alcántara, Carlos. *La lucha campesina en Oaxaca y Guerrero, 1978–1987*. Mexico City: Universidad Autónoma Chapingo, 1989.

Ege, Seyhan N. *Organic Chemistry: Structure and Reactivity*. Boston: Houghton Mifflin, 1992.

"El barbasco será industrializado por Mexicanos; Pago justo a campesinos," *El Nacional*, April 27, 1975:4.

Engel, Leonard. "ACTH, Cortisone, & Co." *Harper's Magazine* 201, no. 1203 (August 1951): 25–33.

————. "Cortisone and Plenty of It." *Harper's Magazine* 201 (September 1951): 56–62.

Espinosa, Mariano. *Apuntes históricos de las tribus chinantecas, mazatecas y popolucas*. Mexico City: Museo Nacional de Antropología, 1961.

Etnografía contemporánea de los pueblos indígenas de México—Valles Centrales. Mexico City: INI, 1995.

Evans, Peter. *Dependent Development: The Alliance of Multinational, State and Local Capital in Brazil*. Princeton: Princeton University Press, 1979.

"Explotaciones forestales en la cuenca del Papaloapan." In *Recursos naturales de la cuenca del Papaloapan*. Mexico City: SARH Comisión del Papaloapan Instituto Mexicano de Recursos Naturales Renovables, 1977.

Featherstone, Mike. *Undoing Culture: Globalization, Postmodernism and Identity*. London: Sage Publications, 1995.

Feierman, Steven. *Peasant Intellectuals: Anthropology and History in Tanzania*. Madison: University of Wisconsin Press, 1990.

Ferguson, James. "Cultural Exchange: New Developments in the Anthropology of Commodities." *Cultural Anthropology* 3, no. 1 (February 1988): 488–513.

Fieser, Louis F., and Mary Fieser. *Steroids*. New York: Reinhold Publishing, 1959.

Fitzgerald, Deborah. "Exporting American Agriculture: The Rockefeller Foundation in Mexico, 1943–1953." *Social Studies of Science* 16, no. 3 (August 1986):457–83.

Florentine Codex: General History of the Things of New Spain. School of American Research and the University of Utah, no. 14, pt. 12 (1963).

Foley, Michael W. "Agenda for Mobilization: The Agrarian Question and Popular Mobilization in Contemporary Mexico." *Latin American Research Review* 26, no. 2 (1991): 39–74.

Fondo Mixto Revolvente para Estudios de Preinversión. Secretaría de Recursos Hidráulicos Comisión del Papaloapan y Nacional Financiera. February 1972.

Fortes, Jacqueline, and Larissa Adler Lomnitz. *Becoming a Scientist in Mexico: The Challenge of Creating a Scientific Community in an Underdeveloped Country.* University Park: Pennsylvania State University Press, 1994.

Fortin, Carlos, and Christian Anglade, eds. *The State and Capital Accumulation in Latin America.* 2 vols. Pittsburgh: University of Pittsburgh Press, 1985–90.

Fowler-Salamini, Heather. *Agrarian Radicalism in Veracruz, 1920–38.* Lincoln: University of Nebraska Press, 1971.

Frayre-Torres, M., et al. "Mortalidad por contacto traumático con serpiente y lagarto venenoso, México 1979–2003." *Gaceta Médica de México* 142, no. 3 (2006): 209–13.

Freebairn, Donald K. "The Dichotomy of Prosperity and Poverty in Mexican Agriculture." *Land Economics* 45, no. 1 (February 1969): 31–42.

Freyermuth Enciso, Graciela. *Médicos tradicionales y médicos alópatas: Un encuentro difícil en los altos de Chiapas.* Mexico City: CIESAS, 1993.

Fried, Josef. "Hunt for an Economical Synthesis of Cortisol: Discovery of the Fluorosteroids at Squibb (A Personal Account)." *Steroids* 57 (1992): 384–91.

García, J. *Problemas campesinos México, 1977.* Mexico City: Estudios Sociales, 1977.

García Canclini, Nestor. *Hybrid Cultures.* Minneapolis: University of Minnesota Press, 1995.

García Hernández, Tomás. *Tuxtepec ante la historia.* Mexico City: Culturas Populares de México, 1997.

Garner, Paul. *Regional Development in Oaxaca during the Porfiriato (1876–1911).* University of Liverpool, Research Paper, no. 17, 1995, 8.

Gasca Zamora, José. "Fuentes para el estudio de las empresas paraestatales de México y su privatización 1983–1988." *Comercio Exterior* 39, no. 2 (February 1989): 151–75.

Gates, Marilyn. *In Default: Peasants, the Debt Crisis, and the Agricultural Challenge in Mexico.* Boulder: Westview Press, 1993.

Gaudilliere, Jean-Paul. "Better Prepared than Synthesized: Adolf Butenandt, Schering Ag, and the Transformation of Sex Steroids into Drugs (1930–1946)." *Studies in History and Philosophy of Science Part C: Studies in History and Philosophy of Biological and Biomedical Sciences* 36, no. 4 (December 2005): 612–44.

Gay, José Antonio. *Historia de Oaxaca.* Mexico City: Editorial Porrúa, 1982.

Gereffi, Gary. *The Pharmaceutical Industry and Dependency in the Third World.* Princeton: Princeton University Press, 1983.

Gereffi, Gary, and Peter Evans. "Transnational Corporations, Dependent Development, and State Policy in the Semiperiphery: A Comparison of Brazil and Mexico." *LRR* 16, no. 3 (1983): 31–64.

Gereffi, Gary, and Miguel Korzeniewicz, eds. *Commodity Chains and Global Capitalism.* Westport, Conn.: Praeger, 1994.

Gerhard, Peter. *A Guide to the Historical Geography of New Spain.* Cambridge: Cambridge University Press, 1972.

Goldman, Michael. *Privatizing Nature: Political Struggles for the Global Commons.* London: Pluto Press, with Transnational Institute, 1998.

Gomezperalta, Mauro. *Cuatro años y un embajador, 1967–1971.* Mexico City, 1973.

Gómez Pompa, Arturo. "El Instituto de Investigaciones sobre Recursos Bióticos, A.C. (INIREB)." In *Estado actual del conocimiento en plantas medicinales mexicanas.* Mexico City: Instituto Mexicano para el Estudio de las Plantas Medicinales, 1976.

———. "La investigación botánica en México en los últimos diez años." *Biología* (1978): 25–29.

———. "Las raíces de la etnobotánica Mexicana." In *logros y perspectivas del conocimiento de los recursos vegetales de México en vísperas del Siglo XXI,* edited by S. Guevara, P. Moreno-Casasola, and J. Rzedowski. Xalapa, Veracruz: Instituto de Ecología and Sociedad Botánica de México, 1993.

González, A. "Biopiratería o apoyo al desarrollo comunitario? La Guerra por los microorganismos." *La Jornada* (January 10, 2000).

González, Alvaro, and Marco Antonio Vásquez, eds. *Etnias, desarrollo, recursos y tecnologías en Oaxaca.* Oaxaca City: CIESAS, 1992.

González Leija, Luis. "Algunas investigaciones sobre la domesticación del barbasco." *Ciencia Forestal: Revista de la Dirección General de Investigación y Capacitación Forestales* 3, no. 13 (May–June 1978): 1–15.

González Leija, Luis, and Ramiro Reyes Carmona. "Ensayos sobre técnicas de propagación vegetativa del barbasco." *Boletín Técnico* 62 (October 1980): 1–34.

González Leija, Luis, and Ana Cecilia Mañón. "Estudios ecológicos sobre el barbasco." 9 Mexico City: INIF.

González Montalvo, Ramón. *Barbasco.* Mexico City: Departamento Editorial del Ministerio de Cultura, 1960.

González y González, Luis. *Todo es historia.* Mexico City: Cal y Arena, 1989.

Goodman, Jordan, and Vivien Walsh. *The Story of Taxol: Nature and Politics in the Pursuit of an Anti-cancer Drug.* Cambridge: Cambridge University Press, 2001.

Goonatilake, Susantha. *Aborted Discovery: Science and Creativity in the Third World.* London: Zed Books, 1984.

Gootenberg, Paul E. *Between Silver and Guano: Commercial Policy and the State in Post-Independence Peru*. Princeton: Princeton University Press, 1989.

———. *Cocaine: Global Histories*. New York: Routledge, 1999.

Grant, Ellen. *The Bitter Pill*. London: Elm Tree Books, 1985.

Grindle, Merilee S. "Policy Change in an Authoritarian Regime: Mexico under Echeverría." *Journal of Interamerican Studies and World Affairs* 19, no. 4 (November 1977): 523–55.

Gruening, Ernest. *Mexico and Its Heritage*. New York: Century Company, 1928.

Gupta, Akhil, and James Ferguson. *Culture, Power, Place: Exploration in Critical Anthropology*. Durham: Duke University Press, 1997.

Haber, Stephen. *Industry and Underdevelopment: The Industrialization of Mexico, 1890–1940*. Stanford, Calif.: Stanford University Press, 1989.

Halperin Donghi, Tulio. *The Contemporary History of Latin America*. Durham: Duke University Press, 1993.

Hamilton, Nora. *The Limits of State Autonomy*. Princeton: Princeton University Press, 1982.

Handler, Richard. *Nationalism and the Politics of Culture in Quebec*. Madison: University of Wisconsin Press, 1988.

Hann, C. M. *Property Relations: Renewing the Anthropological Tradition*. Cambridge: Cambridge University Press, 1998.

Hardin, Garrett. "Tragedy of the Commons." *Science* 162 (December 13, 1968): 1243–48.

Hart, John Mason. *Empire and Revolution: The Americans in Mexico since the Civil War*. Berkeley: University of California Press, 2002.

Haskell, Thomas L., ed. *The Authority of Experts: Studies in History and Theory*. Bloomington: University of Indiana Press, 1984.

Hayden, Cori. *When Nature Goes Public: The Making and Unmaking of Bioprospecting in Mexico*. Princeton: Princeton University Press, 2003.

Hernández Cárdenas, Gilberto, and Martha Pérez García. "Diagnóstico ambiental y del deterioro de la Chinantla." In *Reporte de Investigación No. 1*. Mexico City: UAM-I, 1998.

Hernández Díaz, Jorge. *El café amargo: Diferenciación y cambio social entre los chatinos*. Mexico City: U.A.B.J.O., 1987.

Hernández Díaz, Jorge, Parra Mora León Javier, and Manuel Matus Manzo. *Etnicidad, nacionalismo y poder: Tres ensayos*. Mexico City: Universidad Autónoma "Benito Juárez" de Oaxaca, 1993.

Hernández Pallares, Luis. "Manual para la producción de barbasco." *Folleto Técnico*, no. 5. Mexico City: SARH, 1992.

Hernández Pallares, Luis, and Ramiro Reyes Carmona. "Ensayos sobre técnicas de propagación vegetativa del barbasco." *Boletín Técnico*, no. 62 Mexico City: SARH, 1980.

Hernández Rodríguez, Rogelio. *Empresarios, banca y estado: El conflicto durante gobierno de José López Portillo, 1976–1982*. Mexico City: Facultad Latinoamericana de Ciencias Sociales, Grupo Editorial Miguel Angel Porrúa, 1988.

Hernández Xolocotzi, Efraím, Arturo Gómez-Pompa, and Javier Chavelas Polito. "Contribuciones de la Comisión de Estudios sobre la Ecología de Dioscoreas, en México 1959–1970." *Publicación Especial*, 8, no. 11. Mexico City: INIF, n.d.

Hewitt de Alcántara, Cynthia. *Anthropological Perspectives on Rural Mexico*. London: Routledge, 1984.

———. *Modernizing Mexican Agriculture: Socioeconomic Implications of Technological Change, 1940–1970*. Geneva: United Nations Research Institute for Social Development, 1976.

Hewitt de Alcántara, Cynthia, ed. *Economic Restructuring and Rural Subsistence in Mexico: Corn and the Crisis of the 1980s*. La Jolla, Calif.: Center for U.S.-Mexican Studies, 1994.

Hill, Jonathan D. *Rethinking History and Myth: Indigenous South American Perspectives on the Past*. Urbana: University of Illinois Press, 1988.

Holloway, John, and Eloina Pelaez. *Zapatista: Reinventing Revolution in Mexico*. London: Pluto Press, 1998.

Holzner, W., and M. Numata, eds. *Biology and Ecology of Weeds*. The Hague: Dr. W. Junk Publishers, 1982.

Humboldt, Alexander von. *Political Essays on the Kingdom of New Spain*. Norman: University of Oklahoma Press, 1988.

Ideario Luis Echeverría March 11, 1970–April 4, 1970, Vol. 4. Mexico City: PRI, 1970.

"Informe general de actividades 1980–1985." UNPRB Third General Congress, Mexico, UNION report, November 1985.

"Informe sobre situación actual y perspectivas." Proquivemex, S.A. de C.V. AGN, Galería 2, vol. 22, Fs, estado actual.

Instituto de Estudios Políticos, Económicos y Sociales. *Reunión Nacional sobre Sector Agropecuario*. Mexico City: Partido Revolucionario Institucional, 1976.

Intervención del Dr. Rodolfo Tuirán. Mexico City: CONAPO, October 31, 2001.

Jackson, Myles W. *Spectrum of Belief: Joseph von Fraunhofer and the Craft of Precision Optics*. Cambridge, Mass.: MIT Press, 2000.

Janka, Helmut, and S. Diechtl. *Relacionario de barbasco*. Mexico City: INIF, 1982.

Jiménez, Michael. "Class, Gender and Peasant Resistance in Central Colombia, 1900–1930." In *Everyday Forms of Peasant Resistance*, edited by Forest D. Colburn. Armonk, N.Y.: M. E. Sharp, 1989.

Jones, Ewart R. H. "Early English Steroid History." *Steroids* 57 (1992): 357–62.

Joseph, Gilbert M., and Daniel Nugent, eds. *Everyday Forms of State Formation:*

Revolution and the Negotiation of Rule in Modern Mexico. Durham: Duke University Press, 1994.

Kearney, Michael. *Reconceptualizing the Peasantry: Anthropology in a Global Perspective*. Boulder: Westview Press, 1996.

Keen, Benjamin. *Latin American Civilization: History and Society, 1492 to the Present*. Boulder: Westview Press, 1986.

Kefauver, Estes. *In a Few Hands: Monopoly Power in America*. New York: Pantheon Books, 1965.

Kepner, Charles David, Jr., and Jay Henry Soothill. *The Banana Empire: A Case Study of Economic Imperialism*. New York: Vanguard Press, 1935.

Keyman, E. Fuat. *Globalization, State, Identity/Difference: Toward a Critical Social Theory of International Relations*. Atlantic Highlands, N.J.: Humanities Press, 1997.

Kicza, John, ed. *The Indian in Latin American History: Resistance, Resilience and Acculturation*. Wilmington, Del.: Scholarly Resources, 1993.

King, Lawrence J. *Weeds of the World: Biology and Control*. New York: Interscience Publishers, 1966.

Klooster, Dan. "Campesinos and Mexican Forest Policy during the Twentieth Century." *Latin American Research Review* 38, no. 2 (2003): 94–126.

Kluckhohn, Frank L. *The Mexican Challenge*. Garden City, N.Y.: Doubleday, 1939.

Knight, Alan. "Peasants into Patriots: Thoughts in the Making of the Mexican Nation." *Mexican Studies/Estudios Mexicanos* 10, no. 1 (Winter 1994): 135–61.

Knochenhauer, Guillermo. *Organizaciones campesinas: Hablan diez dirigentes* Mexico City: El Día, 1990.

Kohler, Robert E. *Landscapes and Labscapes: Exploring the Lab-Field Border in Biology*. Chicago: University of Chicago Press, 2002.

Korten, David C. *When Corporations Rule the World*. Bloomfield, Conn.: Kumarian and Berrett-Koehler, 1995.

Krauze, Enrique. *Biography of Power*. New York: Harper Perennial, 1998.

Kreig, Margaret B. *Green Medicine: The Search for Plants that Heal*. Chicago: Rand McNally, 1964.

Lafuente, A., A. Elena, and M. L. Ortega, Eds. "Ciencia, descubrimiento y mundo colonial." *Mundialización de la ciencia y cultural nacional*. Madrid: Ediciones Doce Calles, 1991.

La Goff, Jacques, and Pierre Nora, eds. *Faire de l'histoire: Nouveaux problèmes*. Paris: Gallinard, 1974.

Lange-Churión, Pedro, and Eduardo Mendieta, eds. *Latin America and Postmodernity: A Contemporary Reader*. New York: Humanity Books, 2001.

Lartigue, François. *Indios y bosques: Políticas forestales y comunales en la sierra tarahumara*. Mexico City: Centro de Investigaciones y Estudios Superiores en Antropología Social, 1983.

Latour, Bruno. "Give Me a Laboratory and I Will Raise the World." In *Science Observed: Perspectives on the Social Study of Science*, edited by Karin Knorr-Cetina and Michael Mulkay. London: Sage Publications, 1983.

Latour, Bruno, Alan Sheridan, and John Law. *The Pasteurization of France*. Cambridge, Mass.: Harvard University Press, 1988.

Lehmann, Pedro A. "Early History of Steroid Chemistry in Mexico: The Story of Three Remarkable Men (Marker, Somlo, and Lehmann)." *Steroids* 57 (1992): 403–8.

———. "Russell E. Marker: Pioneer of the Mexican Steroid Industry." *Chemical Education* 50 (March 1973): 195–96.

Levi-Strauss, Claude. *Structural Anthropology*. New York: Basic Books, 1963.

Locke, John. *Two Treaties of Government*. New York: Cambridge University Press, 1960.

López Díaz, Pedro. *Capitalismo y crisis en México*. Mexico City: Ediciones de Cultura Popular, 1979.

"Los laboratorios venderán medicina barata vía Conasupo." *Novedades*, June 18, 1975.

Love, Joseph L. "Economic Ideas and Ideologies in Latin America since 1930." In *Cambridge History of Latin America*, edited by Leslie Bethell. Vol. 6. New York: Cambridge University Press, 1994.

Lowe, Henry. *Jamaica's Ethnomedicine: Its Potential in the Healthcare System*. Kingston: University of the West Indies, 2000.

Loyola Díaz, Rafael. *Una mirada a México: El Nacional, 1940–1952*. Mexico City: Instituto de Investigaciones Sociales, UNAM, 1996.

Lozoya Legorreta, Xavier. *Estado actual del conocimiento en plantas medicinales*. Mexico City: Instituto Mexicano para el Estudio de las Plantas Medicinales, 1976.

———. *La herbolaria en México*. Mexico City: Consejo Nacional para la Cultura y las Artes, 1998.

———. *La medicina tradicional en México: Experiencia del IMSS-COPLAMAR*. Mexico City: IMSS, 1988.

———. "La medicina tradicional y la atención a la salud en la América Latina." In *Rituales y Fiestas de las Américas*. Bogotá: Ediciones Uniandes, 1988.

———. "An Overview of the System of Traditional Medicine Currently Practised in Mexico." In *Economic and Medicinal Plant Research*, edited by H. Wagner. London: Academic Press, 1990.

———. "Two Decades of Mexican Ethnobotany and Research in Plant Drugs." In *Ethnobotany and the Search for New Drugs*, ed. by G. T. Prance, Derek J. Chadwick, and Joan Marsh. Ciba Foundation Symposium Series 185. Chichester, N.Y.: J. Wiley, 1994.

Lozoya Legorreta, Xavier, Georgina Velázquez Díaz, and Angel Flores Alvarado. *La medicina tradicional en México: Experiencia del programa* IMSS-COPLAMAR *1982–1987.* Mexico City: IMSS, 1988.

Macías, Jesús Manuel, Blanca Díaz Torres, and Lourdes Alvarez Fragoso. *Espacios campesinos y expansión del capital.* Mexico City: Centro de Investigaciones y Estudios Superiores en Antropología Social, 1987.

Mackinlay, Horacio. "Las organizaciones de productores rurales y el Estado de México." Paper presented at the conference "Dilemmas of Change in Mexican Politics," Center for U.S.-Mexican Studies, University of California, San Diego, October 8–9, 1999.

MacLeod, Roy. *Nature and Empire: Science and the Colonial Enterprise.* Chicago: University of Chicago Press, 2000.

Magdaleno, Angeles. "Papelito habla: El Fondo de Gobernación. Sección DFS." Paper presented at the "Cárdenas, Echeverría, and Revolutionary Populism" conference, University of Arizona, Tucson, April 7–8, 2006.

Maisel, Albert Q. *The Hormone Quest.* New York: Random House, 1965.

Maldonado Alvarado, Banjamín, Mauricio Maldonado Alvarado, and León Javier Parra Mora. *Entre la abundancia y la desnutrición: Invitación a pensar la alimentación, la salud y la historia política de los pueblos indios de Oaxaca.* Oaxaca City: Anadeges del Sur Pacifico, 1995.

Mallon, Florencia. *Peasant and Nation: The Making of Postcolonial Mexico and Peru.* Berkeley: University of California Press, 1995.

Mariátegui, José Carlos. *Seven Interpretative Essays on Peruvian Reality.* Austin: University of Texas Press, 1971.

Marichal, Carlos. *A Century of Debt Crises in Latin America: From Independence to the Great Depression, 1820–1930.* Princeton: Princeton University Press, 1991.

Marker, R. E. *Journal of American Chemical Society* 71 (1949): 2656, 4149.

Marker, R. E., and E. J. Rohrman. *Journal of American Chemical Society* 61 (1939): 846.

Marker, R. E., E. L. Wittle, and E. J. Lawson, "Sterols. XLIX. Isolation of Pregnanediols from Bull's Urine." *Journal of the American Chemical Society* 60 (1938): 2931–33.

Marker, R. E., and J. López. *Journal of American Chemical Society* 69 (1947): 2373–83.

Marker, R. E., and N. E. Gordon. "Effect of Hydrogen-Ion Concentration on Compound Formation and Absorption of Dyes by Mordants." *Industrial and Engineering Chemistry* 16 (1924): 1186–88.

Marker, R. E., and R. B. Wagner. *Journal of American Chemical Society* 69 (1947): 2167.

Marks, Lara V. *Sexual Chemistry: A History of the Contraceptive Pill.* New Haven, Conn.: Yale University Press, 2001.

Marshall, T. H. *Class, Citizenship, and Social Development: Essays by T. H. Marshall.* Garden City, N.Y.: Doubleday, 1964.

Martin, Franklin W., and Murria H. Gaskins. "Cultivation of the Sapogenin-Bearing *Dioscorea* Species." *Agricultural Research Service, Production Research Report* no. 103. Washington, D.C.: U.S. Department of Agriculture, 1974.

Martínez Borrego, Estela. *Organización de productores y movimiento campesino.* Mexico City: Siglo Veintiuno, 1991.

Martínez Garza, B. B. *Evolución legislativa de la Ley Federal de Reforma Agraria.* Mexico City: Textos Universitarios, 1975.

Martínez Vásquez, Víctor Raúl. *Movimiento popular y política en Oaxaca (1968–1986).* Mexico City: Dirección General de Publicaciones del Consejo Nacional para la Cultura y las Artes, 1990.

———. *Orale, Santo, no seas puñal.* Mexico City: Ediciones Meridiano Cien, 1986.

Mathews, Andrew Salvador. "Mexican Forest History: Ideologies of State Building and Resource Use." *Journal of Sustainable Forestry* 15, no. 1 (2002): 17–28.

———. "Suppressing Fire and Memory: Environmental Degradation and Political Restoration in the Sierra Juárez of Oaxaca, 1887–2001." *Environmental History* 8, no. 1 (January 2003): 77–108.

McBeth, B. S. *Juan Vicente Gómez and the Oil Companies in Venezuela, 1908–1935.* Cambridge Latin American Studies Series. Cambridge: Cambruidge University Press, 1983.

McCook, Stuart. "Giving Plants a Civil Status: Scientific Representations of Nation and Nature in Costa Rica and Venezuela." *Americas* 58, no. 4 (April 2002): 513–36.

McCreery, David J. "Coffee and Class: Structure and Development in Liberal Guatemala." *Hispanic American Historical Review* 56, no. 3 (1976): 438–60.

"Medicinas baratas." *Novedades,* June 18, 1975.

Medina, Luis. *Historia de la Revolución Mexicana, periodo 1940–1952: Del cardenismo al avilacamachismo.* Mexico City: El Colegio de México, 1978.

Meixueiro, Anselmo Arellanes. *Asuntos agrarios del Estado de Oaxaca: Conflictos por límites, bosques y las tierras comunales.* Oaxaca City: SEP, CONACYT, SIBEJ, and Instituto Tecnológico de Oaxaca 2002.

Menchú, Rigoberta. *Me llamo Rigoberta Menchú y así me nació la conciencia.* Mexico City: Siglo Veintiuno, 1985.

"Mexican Hormones." *Fortune* (May 1951): 86–90, 162–62, 166, 168.

México, Comisión del Papaloapan. *El Papaloapan, obra del Presidente Alemán: Reseña sumaria del magno proyecto de planificación integral que ahora se realiza en la cuenca del Papaloapan.* Mexico City: Secretaría de Recursos Hidráulicos, Comisión del Papaloapan, 1949.

Mexico 1976: Facts, Figures, Trends. Mexico City: Banco Nacional de Comercio Exterior, 1976.

Meyer, Michael C., William L. Sherman, and Susan M. Deeds. *The Course of Mexican History*. New York: Oxford University Press, 2007.

Migdal, Joel. *Strong Societies and Weak States: State-Society Relations and State Capabilities in the Third World*. Princeton: Princeton University Press, 1988.

Miller, Francesca. *Latin American Women and the Search for Social Justice*. Hanover, N.H.: University of New England Press, 1991.

Mintz, Sidney. *Sweetness and Power: The Place of Sugar in Modern History*. New York: Viking, 1985.

Mintz, Sidney, and Eric Wolf. "Reply to Michael Taussig." *Critique of Anthropology* 9 (1989): 25–31.

Miranda, Faustino, Efraím Hernández Xolocotzi, and Arturo Gómez-Pompa. "Un método para la investigación ecológica de las regiones tropicales." *Anvarios del Instituto Biológico UNAM, Servicios Botánicos* 38, no. 1 (1967): 101–10.

Mitman, Gregg. *The State of Nature: Ecology, Community and American Social Thought, 1900–1950*. Chicago: University of Chicago Press, 1992.

Modena, María Eugenia. *Madres, médicos y curanderos: Diferencia cultural e identidad ideológica*. Mexico City: Casa Chata, 1990.

Moguel, Julio. "La cuestión agraria en el periodo 1950–1970." In *Historia de la cuestión agraria mexicana: Política estatal y conflictos agrarios, 1950–1970*. Mexico City: Siglo Veintiuno, 1989.

Moguel, Julio, and José Antonio Romero. *Reforma agraria y el procede en: Veracruz, Chiapas, Oaxaca y Sonora*. Mexico City: Juan Pablos, 1998.

Moran, Theodore. *Multinational Corporations and the Politics of Dependence: Copper in Chile*. Princeton: Princeton University Press, 1974.

Monardes, Nicolás. *Herbolaria de Indias*. Mexico City: Instituto Mexicano Del Seguro Social, 1990.

Monteón, Michael. *Chile in the Nitrate Era: The Evolution of Economic Dependence, 1880–1930*. Madison: University of Wisconsin Press, 1982.

Mumme, Stephen P., C. Richard Bath, and Valerie J. Assetto. "Political Development and Environmental Policy in Mexico." *Latin American Research Review* 23, no. 1 (1988): 7–34.

Murphy, Arthur D., and Alex Stepick. *Social Inequality in Oaxaca: A History of Resistance and Change*. Philadelphia: Temple University Press, 1991.

"Nacionalizaremos los esteroides, si presionan las transnacionales." *El Universal*, March 11, 1976.

Nash, June. *We Eat the Mines and the Mines Eat Us: Dependency and Exploitation in the Bolivian Tin Mines*. New York: Columbia University Press, 1993; orig. pub. 1979.

Newfarmer, Richard S., and Willard F. Mueller. *Multinational Corporations in Brazil and Mexico: Structural Sources of Economic and Non-economic Power*. Washington, D.C.: U.S. Government Printing Office, 1975.

Niblo, Stephen R. *War, Development, and Diplomacy: The United States and Mexico, 1938–1954*. Wilmington, Del.: Scholarly Resources, 1995.

"No hay hostilidad a la inversión extranjera." *El Universal*, February 11, 1977.

Novo, Salvador. *La vida en México en el periodo presidencial de Manuel Avila Camacho*. Mexico City: Consejo Nacional para la Cultura y las Artes, 1994.

Olivares, Felipe León. "Syntex, origen, apogeo y pérdida de una industria estratégica para México." M.A. thesis, UNAM, 1999.

Onwueme, I. C. *The Tropical Tuber Crops: Yams, Cassava, Sweet Potato, and Cocoyams*. Chichester, N.Y.: John Wiley and Sons, 1978.

"Opening Remarks: 4th International Congress on Hormonal Steroids, September 2–7, 1974, Mexico City." *Journal of Steroid Biochemistry* 6 (1975): 1.

Ortiz, Fernando. *Cuban Counterpoint: Tobacco and Sugar*. Durham: Duke University Press, 1995; orig. pub. 1940.

Osuji, Godson, ed. *Advances in Yam Research: The Biochemistry and Technology of the Yam Tuber*. Enugu, Nigeria: Biochemical Society of Nigeria in collaboration with Anambra State University of Technology, 1985.

Oudshoorn, Nelly. *Beyond the Natural Body: An Archeology of Sex Hormones*. London: Routledge, 1994.

Painter, Michael, and William H. Durham, eds. *The Social Causes of Environmental Destruction in Latin America*. Ann Arbor: University of Michigan Press, 1995.

Palacios, Guillermo. "Post-revolutionary Intellectuals, Rural Readings, and Shaping of the 'Peasant Problem' in Mexico: El Maestro Rural, 1932–34." *Journal of Latin American Studies* 30, no. 2 (May 1998): 309–39.

Palacios, Marcos. *El café en Colombia: Una historia económica, social y política*. Mexico City: Colegio de México, 1983.

Parker, M. G. *Steroid Hormone Action*. New York: Oxford University Press, 1993.

Partido Revolucionario Institucional. *The Second Six-Year Plan, 1941–1946: Mexico Builds*. Mexico City, 1939.

Paz, Octavio. *Labyrinth of Solitude: Life and Thought in Mexico*. New York: Grove Press, 1962.

Peard, Julyan G. *Race, Place, and Medicine: The Idea of the Tropics in Nineteenth Century Brazilian Medicine*. Durham: Duke University Press, 1999.

Pelaez, Juan Fernando. Weekly presentations, Center for U.S.-Mexican Studies, University of California, San Diego, November 2000.

Pérez Jiménez, Luis A. "Trabajos desarrollados sobre vegetación y etnobotánica: La vegetación de Pichucalco, Chiapas." M.A. thesis, UNAM, 1967.

"Pidieron a Echeverría la nacionalización de laboratorios químicos de esteroides." *Ovaciones: El Diario de México*, March, 13, 1976.

Piñón Jiménez, Gonzalo, and Jorge Hernández. *El café: Crisis y organización*. Mexico City: UABJO, 1998.

Pisan, Donald J. "Forests and Conservation, 1865–1890." *Journal of American History* 72, no. 2 (September 1985): 340–59.

Planeación Integral Empresarial de México, S.A. de C.V. *Mecanismos para el desarrollo de las regiones del sureste*. Mexico City: Instituto de Proposiciones Estratégicas, 1992.

Plotkin, Mark J. *Medicine Quest: In Search of Nature's Healing Secrets*. New York: Viking, 2000.

Poleman, Thomas T. *The Papaloapan Project: Agricultural Development in the Mexican Tropics*. Stanford, Calif.: Stanford University Press, 1964.

Poniatowska, Elena. *Fuerte es el silencio*. Mexico City: Ediciones Era, 1988.

Popkin, Samuel. *The Rational Peasant: The Political Economy of Rural South Vietnam*. Berkeley: University of California Press, 1979.

Popol Vuh: A Sacred Book of the Maya. Translated by V. Montejo. Toronto: Groundwork Books, 1999.

Potter, Jonathan. *Representing Reality: Discourse, Rhetoric and Social Construction*. London: Sage Publications, 1996.

Primer Simposio Internacional sobre Dioscoreas: Realizado en México, D.F., del 14 al 16 de octubre de 1970 / con el patrocinio y la organización de Subsecretaría Forestal y de la Fauna, S.A.G. y Asociación de Fabricantes de Esteroides, A.C. Mexico City: Secretaría de Agricultura y Ganadería, Subsecretaría Forestal y de la Fauna, Instituto Nacional de Investigaciones Forestales, n.d. (ca. 1973).

Proquivemex División Agroindustrial, S.A. de C.V. "Notas a los Estados Financieros Años que Terminaron el 31 de Diciembre de 1983 y 1982." CNC, Tuxtepec, Oaxaca.

Quintero, Rafael. *El mito del populismo en el Ecuador*. Quito: Universidad Central del Ecuador, 1983.

Rajchman, John. *The Identity in Question*. New York: Routledge, 1995.

Ramírez, M. "Mexico's Development Experience, 1950–1985: Lessons and Future Prospects." *Journal of Interamerican Studies and World Affairs* 28 (Summer 1986): 39–66.

Raspe, Gerhard. *Advances in the Biosciences: Schering Symposium on Biodynamics and Mechanism of Action of Steroid Hormones Berlin 1968*. Oxford: Pergamon Press, 1969.

Recursos naturales de la cuenca del Papaloapan. Vol. 2. Mexico City: Instituto Mexicano de Recursos Renovables, SARH, Comisión del Papaloapan, 1977.

Reeves, Richard. "John F. Kennedy." In *Character above All: Ten Presidents from FDR to George Bush*. New York: Simon and Schuster, 1997.

Reid, W., et al. *Biodiversity Prospecting: Using Genetic Resources for Sustainable Development*. Washington, D.C.: World Resources Institute, 1993.

Reina Aoyama, Leticia. *Economía contra sociedad: El Istmo de Tehuantepec, 1907–1986*. Oaxaca City: Nueva Imagen, 1994.

"Reunión para el análisis y reorientación de investigación sobre el barbasco, Córdoba, Friday November 7–10, 1979." *Publicidad Especial*, no. 21 (August 1980): 125–26. Mexico City, INIF. Proquivemex Archives, Galería 2, caja 18.

Reyes Carmona, Ramiro. "Ensayos sobre técnicas de propagación vegetativa del Barbasco." *Boletín Técnico* 62 (October). Mexico City: SARH, 1980.

Reyes Serrano, Angel C. *Trinchera. . . . ! Lucio Cabañas, Genaro Vázquez y su guerrilla*. Mexico City: Coasta-Amic Editores, 1985.

Riddle, John M. *Eve's Herbs*. Cambridge, Mass.: Harvard University Press, 1997.

Robertson, Roland. *Globalization: Social Theory and Global Culture*. London: Sage Publications, 1992.

Rodriguez, Julia. *Civilizing Argentina: Science, Medicine, and the Modern State*. Durham: Duke University Press, 2006.

Rogozinski, Jacques. *High Price for Change: Privatization in Mexico*. New York: Inter-American Development Bank, 1998.

———. *La privatización de empresas paraestatales*. Mexico City: Fondo de Cultura Económica, 1993.

Romero, J. "Crecimiento y comercio." In *Una historia contemporánea de México*, edited by Ilan Bizberg and Lorenzo Meyer. Mexico City: Océano, 2003.

Romero, Matías. *El Estado de Oaxaca*. Barcelona: Tipográfica de Esparza y Campo, 1886.

Ronefledt, David. *Atencingo: The Politics of Agrarian Struggle in a Mexican Ejido*. Stanford, Calif.: Stanford University Press, 1973.

Rosenkranz, George. "From Ruzicka's Terpenes in Zurich to Mexican Steroids via Cuba." *Steroids* 57 (August 1992): 409–18.

Rowe W., and V. Schelling. *Memory and Modernity: Popular Culture in Latin America*. London, New York: Verso, 1990.

Rubin, Jeffrrey. "Ambiguity and Contradiction in a Radical Movement." In *Cultures of Politics, Politics of Culture: Re-visioning Latin American Social Movements*, edited by Sonia Alvarez et al. Boulder: Westview Press, 1998.

Said, Edward W. *Culture and Imperialism*. New York: Vintage, 1994.

Saldaña, Juan José. *Science in Latin America*. Austin: University of Texas Press, 2006.

Saldaña, Juan José, ed. *Cross Cultural Diffusion of Science: Latin America*. Mexico City: Sociedad Latinoamericana de Historia de las Ciencias y la Tecnología, 1988.

Sanabria, Harry. *The Coca Boom and Rural Change in Bolivia*. Ann Arbor: University of Michigan Press, 1995.

Santiago, Myrna. *The Ecology of Oil: Environment, Labor, and the Mexican Revolution, 1900–1938*. Cambridge: Cambridge University Press, 2006.

Sarukhán Kermez, José. *Estudios sucesionales de un área talada en Tuxtepec, Oax.*

Publicación Especial Instituto Nacional Investigaciones Forestaces, no. 3 (1964): 107–72. Mexico City, INIF.

Scherr, Sara J., and Thomas T. Poleman. *Cornell/International Agricultural Economics Study: Development and Equity in Tropical Mexico. Thirty Years of the Papaloapan Project*. Ithaca, N.Y.: Cornell University, Department of Agricultural Economics, 1983.

Scherrer García, Julio, and Carlos Monsiváis. *Parte de guerra: Tlatelolco 1968. Documentos del general Marcelino García Barragán*. Mexico City: Nuevo Siglo, 1990.

Schiebinger, Londa. *Nature's Body: Gender in the Making of Modern Science*. New Brunswick, N.J.: Rutgers University Press, 2004.

Schnedel, Gordon. *Medicine in Mexico: From Aztec Herbs to Betatrons*. Austin: University of Texas Press, 1968.

Schryer, Fran. *Ethnicity and Class Conflict in Rural Mexico*. Princeton: Princeton University Press, 1990.

Scott, James. *Weapons of the Weak: Everyday Forms of Peasant Resistance*. New Haven, Conn.: Yale University Press, 1985.

Sears, Paul B. "Botanists and Conservation of Natural Resources." *American Journal of Botany* 43, no. 9 (November 1956): 731–35.

Secretaría de Recursos Hidráulicos, Comisión del Papaloapan, México. "Programa de Desarrollo del Papaloapan." Mexico City: SRH, 1964.

Segura Gómez, Abel. "Estudio de la distribución de diosgenina en rizomas de *Dioscorea composita*." *Ciencia Forestal: Revista de la Dirección General de Investigación y Capacitación Forestales* 7, no. 39 (September–October 1982): 3–13.

Senerviratne, H. L. *Identity, Consciousness and the Past: Forging of Caste and Community in India and Sri Lanka*. Oxford: Oxford University Press, 1997.

Shapin, Steve. "The House of Experiment in Seventeenth-Century England." *Isis* 79, no. 3 (1988): 373–404.

Sharon, Douglas. *Wizard of the Four Winds: A Shaman's Story*. New York: Free Press, 1978.

Sheahan, John. *Patterns of Development in Latin America: Poverty, Repression, and Economic Strategy*. Princeton: Princeton University Press, 1987.

Shiva, Vandana. "Bioprospecting as Sophisticated Biopiracy." *Signs: Journal of Women in Culture and Society* 32, no. 2 (2007): 307–13.

———. *Monocultures of the Mind: Perspectives on Biodiversity and Biotechnology*. London: Zed Books, 1993.

Simonian, Lane. *Defending the Land of the Jaguar: A History of Conservation in Mexico*. Austin: University of Texas Press, 1995.

Simposio sobre Historia Contemporánea de México, 1940–1984. *Inventario sobre el pasado reciente: Primer simposio sobre historia contemporánea de México*

1940–1984. Mexico City: Dirección de Estudios Históricos, Instituto Nacional de Antropología e Historia, 1986.

Sloan, John. *Public Policy in Latin America: A Comparative Survey*. Pittsburgh: University of Pittsburgh Press, 1984.

Smith, Carol. "Local History in Global Context: Social and Economic Transitions in Western Guatemala." *Comparative Studies in Social History* 26, no. 2 (April 1984): 193–228.

Smith, Hobart M., and Edward H. Taylor. *An Annotated Checklist and Key to the Snakes of Mexico*. Washington, D.C.: Smithsonian Institution, 1945.

Snyder, Richard, ed. *Institutional Adaptation and Innovation in Rural Mexico*. La Jolla, Calif.: Center for U.S.-Mexico Studies, 1999.

Sorkin, Michael, ed. *Variations on a Theme Park: The New American City and the End of Public Space*. New York: Noonday Press, 1992.

Sosa Velarde, Carlos Eugenio. *Determinacón del mejor mes y parte óptima del rizoma para una siembra vegetativa del "barbasco" (Dioscorea composita Hemsl)*. M.A. thesis, UNAM, 1987.

Soto, William Reuben. *Los campesinos frente a la nueva década: Ajuste estructural pequeña producción agropecuaria en Costa Rica*. San José, Costa Rica: Editorial Porvenir, 1989.

Stavenhagen, Rodolfo. *Agrarian Problems and Peasant Movements in Latin America*. Garden City, N.Y.: Doubleday, 1970.

Stepan, Nancy Leys. *The Hour of Eugenics: Race, Gender, and Nation in Latin America*. Ithaca: Cornell University Press, 1996.

Stern, Alexandra Minna. "Responsible Mothers and Normal Children: Eugenics, Nationalism, and Welfare in Post-Revolutionary Mexico, 1920–1940." *Journal of Historical Sociology* 12, no.4 (1999): 369–97.

Stern, Steve J. *The Secret History of Gender: Women, Men, and Power in Late Colonial Mexico*. Chapel Hill: University of North Carolina Press, 1995.

Steward, Julian H. *The People of Puerto Rico*. Urbana: University of Illinois Press, 1956.

Strathern, Andrew J. *Body Thoughts*. Ann Arbor: University of Michigan Press, 1996.

Sturchio Jeffrey L. Interview of Russell E. Marker, Pennsylvania State University, April 17, 1987. Oral History Transcript #0068, Chemical Heritage Foundation, Philadelphia.

Suarez, L. *Echeverría Rompe el Silencio*. Mexico City: Editorial Grijalbo, 1976.

Subsecretaría Forestal de la Fauna. *Plan Nacional Forestal 1982–1986*. Mexico City: Talleres Gráficos de la Unidad de Apoyo Técnico de la SFF, 1981.

Syntex. *Stockholder's Report*. Mexico City: Syntex, 1982.

Taussig, Michael. *The Devil and Commodity Fetishism in South America*. Chapel Hill: University of North Carolina Press, 1980.

———. "History as Commodity: In Some Recent American (Anthropological) Literature." *Crtique of Anthropology* 9 (1989): 7–23.

———. *The Magic of the State.* New York: Routledge, 1997.

Taylor, William B. *Drinking, Homicide, and Rebellion in Colonial Mexican Villages.* Stanford, Calif.: Stanford University Press, 1979.

Tello García, Carlos. "La economía echeverrista balance provisional." *Nexos* 11, no. 1 (November 1978).

Thomas, Nicholas, and Caroline Humphrey, eds. *Shamanism, History, and the State.* Ann Arbor: University of Michigan Press, 1994.

Thompson, E. P. *The Making of the English Working Class.* New York: Pantheon Books, 1963.

Todos con México, Reuniones nacionales de estudio, discursos de Luis Echeverría, 1970. Mexico City: Editorial Imprenta Casas, 1970.

Topik Steven, and Allen Wells. *Second Conquest of Latin America: Coffee, Henequen, and Oil during the Export Boom, 1850–1930.* Austin: Institute of Latin American Studies, University of Texas Press, 1998.

Topik, Steven, Carlos Marichal, and Zephyr Frank. *From Silver to Cocaine: Latin American Commodity Chains and the Building of the World Economy, 1500–2000.* Durham: Duke University Press, 2006.

Tulchin, Joseph. *The Aftermath of War: World War I and U.S. Policy toward Latin America.* New York: New York University Press, 1971.

Turner, Christena. *Japanese Workers in Protest: An Ethnography of Consciousness and Experience.* Berkeley: University of California Press, 1995.

Turner, John Kenneth. *Barbarous Mexico.* Austin: University of Texas Press, 1969; orig. pub. 1910.

Tutino, John. *From Insurrection to Revolution in Mexico: Social Bases of Agrarian Violence, 1750–1940.* Princeton: Princeton University Press, 1986.

Unión de Crédito Agropecuaria, Forestal e Industrial de los Productores de Barbasco, S.A. de C.V. "Plan de operaciones de crédito 1989," Mexico City, November 1988.

United States Senate. *Wonder Drugs: Hearings before the Subcommittee on Patents, Trademarks, and Copyrights of the Committee on the Judiciary, U.S. Senate, 84th Congress, 2nd session, Pursuant to S. Res. 167, on Licensing of United States Government Owned Patents; Removal of Obstacles to the Production of Essential Materials from the Cheapest Source for the Manufacture of Cortisone and Other Hormones. July 5 and 6, 1956.* Washington, D.C.: U.S. Government Printing Office, 1957.

Uribe Ruiz, Jesús. "El Instituto Mexicano de Investigaciones para la Industria Química Vegetal A.C. (IMIQUIVE)." In *Estado actual del conocimiento en plantas medicinales mexicanas,* edited by Xavier Lozoya. Mexico City: IMEPLAM, 1976.

Urquidi, Víctor L. "La carta de derechos y deberes económicos de los estados: La cuestión de su aplicación." *Foro Internacional* 78, no. 20 (October–December 1979).

Valenzuela Arce, José Manuel, ed. *Decadencia y auge de las identidades: Cultura nacional, identidad cultural y modernización.* Mexico City: El Colegio de la Frontera Norte, 1992.

Van Cott, Donna Lee. *Indigenous Peoples and Democracy in Latin America.* New York: St. Martin's Press, 1994.

Van Sittert, Lance. "The Seed Blows about in Every Breeze: Noxious Weed Eradication in the Cape Colony, 1860–1909." *Journal of Southern African Studies* 26, no. 4, special issue, *African Environments: Past and Present* (December 2000): 655–74.

Van Young, Eric. "To See Someone Not Seeing: Historical Studies of Peasants and Politics in Mexico." *Mexican Studies / Estudios Mexicanos* 6, no. 1 (Winter 1990): 137–59.

Várguez Pasos, Luis A. *Identidad, henequen y trabajo: Los desfibradores de Yucatán.* Mexico City: Colegio de México, 1999.

Vaughan, Mary Kay. "Cultural Approaches to Peasant Politics in the Mexican Revolution." *Hispanic American Historical Review* 79, no. 2, special issue *Mexico's New Cultural History: Una Lucha Libre* (May 1999): 269–305.

———. "Education and Class in the Mexican Revolution." *Latin American Perspectives* 2, no. 2, special issue *Mexico City: The Limits of State Capitalism* (Summer 1975): 17–33.

———. "Women, Class, and Education in Mexico, 1880–1928." *Latin American Perspectives* 4, nos. 1/2, special issue *Women, Class, and Struggle* (Winter–Spring, 1977): 135–52.

Vaughan, Paul. *The Pill on Trial.* New York: Coward-McCann, 1970.

Velez-Ibanez, Carlos G. *Visiones de frontera: Las culturas mexicanas del suroeste de Estados Unidos.* Tucson: University of Arizona Press, 1999.

Veliz, Claudio. *The Politics of Conformity in Latin America.* London: Oxford University Press for the Royal Institute of International Affairs, 1996; orig. pub. 1967.

Villanueva Mukul, Eric. *Crisis henequenera, reconversión económica y movimientos campesinos en Yucatán 1983–1992.* Mexico City: Maldonado Editores, 1993.

———. *Crisis henequenera y movimientos campesinos en Yucatán, 1966–1983.* Mexico City: Instituto Nacional de Antropología e Historia, 1985.

Villa Rojas, Alfonso. *El Papaloapan, obra del Presidente Alemán: Reseña sumaria del mango proyecto de planificación integral que ahora se realiza en la cuenca del Papaloapan.* Mexico City: Offset Internacional, 1949.

———. *Las obras del Papaloapan, 1947–1952.* Mexico City: Offset Internacional, 1952.

Viotti da Costa, Emilia. "Experience versus Structures: New Tendencies in History of Labor and the Working Class in Latin America—What Do We Gain? What Do We Lose?" *International Labor and the Working Class History* 36 (Fall 1989): 2–50.

Viqueira, Carmen. *Percepción y cultura: Un enfoque ecológico.* Mexico City: Casa Chata, 1977.

Wade, Peter. *Race and Ethnicity in Latin America.* Chicago: Pluto Press, 1997.

Walsh, Casey, Elizabeth Emma Ferry, Gabriela Soto Laveaga, and Paola Sesia. *The Social Relations of Mexican Commodities: Power, Production, and Place.* La Jolla, Calif.: Center for U.S.-Mexican Studies, University of California, San Diego, 2003.

Warman, Arturo. *Corn and Capitalism: How a Botanical Bastard Grew to Global Dominance.* Translated by Nancy L. Westrate. Chapel Hill: University of North Carolina Press, 2003.

———. *Ensayos sobre el campesinado en México.* Mexico City: Nueva Imagen, 1980.

Warman, Arturo, and Arturo Argueta. *Nuevos enfoques: Para el estudio de las etnias indígenas en México.* Mexico City: Centro de Investigaciones Interdisciplinarias en Humanidades, UNAM, 1991.

Warren, Dean. *With Broadaxe and Firebrand: The Destruction of the Brazilian Atlantic Forest.* Berkeley: University of California Press, 1995.

Wasserman, Mark. "Foreign Investment in Mexico, 1876–1910: A Case Study of the Role of Regional Elites." *Americas* (1979): 3–21.

Weber, Max. *The Protestant Ethic and the Spirit of Capitalism.* Boston: Unwin, 1976.

Weinstein, Barbara. *The Amazon Rubber Boom, 1850–1920.* Stanford, Calif.: Stanford University Press, 1983.

Weitlaner, Roberto J., comp. *Relatos, mitos, y leyendas de la Chinantla.* Mexico City: Instituto Nacional Indigenista, 1977.

Wells, Allen, and Joseph Gilbert. *Summer of Discontent, Seasons of Upheaval: Elite Politics and Rural Insurgency in Yucatan, 1876–1915.* Stanford, Calif.: Stanford University Press, 1996.

Wetten, N. "México rural." *Problemas Agrarios e Industriales de México* 5, no. 2 (April–June 1953).

White, Hayden. *Tropics of Discourse: Essays in Cultural Criticism.* Baltimore: Johns Hopkins University Press, 1978.

Wilson, Charles L., and Charles L. Graham. *Exotic Plant Pests and North American Agriculture.* New York: Academic Press, 1983.

Wilson, Rob, and Wimal Dissanayake. *Global/Local: Cultural Production and the Transnational Imaginary.* Durham: Duke University Press, 1996.

Winn, Peter. *Weavers of Revolution: The Yarur Workers and Chile's Road to Socialism*. Oxford: Oxford University Press, 1986.

Wolf, Eric R. "Agrarian Rebellion and Defense of Community: Meaning and Collective Violence in Late Colonial and Independence-Era Mexico." *Journal of Social History* (Winter 1993): 245–69.

———. *Europe and the People without History*. Berkeley: University of California Press, 1982.

Zafra, Gloria, and E. Salomón González. "La reforma del ejido en Tuxtepec: Campo y campesino en San José Chiltepec, San Bartolo y Santa Catarina." In *Propiedad y organización rural en el México moderno: Reforma agraria y el procede en Veracruz, Chiapas, Oaxaca y Sonora*, edited by Julio Moguel and José Antonio Romero. Mexico City: Juan Pablos, 1998.

Zamora, Gustavo. "Del barbasco a la progesterona." In *La investigación científica de la herbolaria medicinal mexicana*. Mexico City: SSA, 1993.

Zamora Martínez, Marisela C., and Miguel González Corona. *Catálogo de especies de plantas útiles con importancia económica el ex-distrito de Tuxtepec, Oaxaca. Catálogo*, no. 11 (November 1993). Mexico City, SARH.

Zamosc, Leon. "Peasant Struggles in Colombia." In *Power and Popular Protest: Latin American Social Movements*, edited by Susan Eckstein and Manuel Antonio Garretón Merino. Berkeley: University of California Press, 1989.

Zolov, Eric. *Refried Elvis: The Rise of the Mexican Counterculture*. Berkeley: University of California Press, 1999.

Page numbers in italics refer to illustrations.

barbasco (*continued*)

66, 135, 182–83; film on, *111*; guerillas and, 114; healers use of, 72; history
of, 6, 75; in literature, 35, 75; as metaphor, 13; myths about, 110–11; native
uses of, 72–75; Papaloapan Commission on, 36–37; peasant knowledge of,
107–9; permits for harvesting, 98–99,
123; production levels of, 4, 232; price
of, 153–55, 160–61; purity of, 100, 153–
54, 198, 210; revenues of, 36; shortage
of, 99, 100, 134–35; significance of,
59–60; socioeconomic impact of,
7, 23, *86*, 88; study of, 103–6, 272–
73 n. 4; supply of, 199–200; to test
adultery, 73; today, 235; as tool for
progress, 133; transformative aspects,
133; transporting of, 79, *80*, 85, *86*,
142–43; value of, 2–3, 172–73. *See also*
barbasco trade; diosgenin

Barbasco (González Montalvo), 75, 278
n. 72

barbasco trade: attitude toward, 71–72;
changes in, 137–38; collection sites of,
81, 83–85; credit union of, 207–8; decline of, 217, 221–22; dependence on,
86; development and, 14, 73; effect of
economy on, 200–202; income from,
35, 36–37; media coverage of, 122–23,
131, 133, 168; memories of, 223–34;
Mexican scientists in, 13–14; middlemen in, 80–83; nationalization of, 21,
130, 132; permits for, 98–99, 123; price
war in, 153–55; production in, 36–37,
197–98; under Proquivemex, 139–40;
significance of, 228; socioeconomic
impact of, 7, 23, *86*, 88–89; students
in, 120–22; as tool for progress, 134;
transformative aspects of, 15, *86*,
190–91; women in, 216–17; zones of,
14, 137. *See also* barbasco; pharma-

ceutical companies, transnational;
regulation of barbasco trade; unions

barbasqueros: alliance of, with students, 119–20; characteristics of,
224; control of, 115; definition of,
22; on ejidos, 181–82; empowerment
of, 1, 144–46, 149–50; exploitation
of, 81–82, 135, 172, 182–83; images of,
158, 159; knowledge of, 107–9, 131–32,
185–86; legitimacy of, 2, 7, 8, 207;
media coverage of, 114–15, 157, 163;
on modernization, 191; on nationalization, 171–73, 189; origin of, 36–37;
Proquivemex and, 140, 184–85, 209–
11; protection of, 133; resistance from,
85; scientists and, 102, 105–6; significance of, 7, 51, 69, 70; social mobility
of, 223–26; socioeconomic conditions
of, 76, 88–89; transformation of, 190,
191; use of science and, 6–9, 226; as
victims, *159*; working conditions of,
77–80. *See also* ejidos, ejidatarios;
identity, barbasquero; peasants

Bartra Armando, 165

Beisa, 93, 151, 272–73 n. 4

Beltrán, Enrique, 99, 103

beneficios: description of, 85, 87–88; ejidatarios and, 187; photos of, *87*, *154*;
under Proquivemex, 140; union control of, 207. *See also* barbasco trade

Benito Juárez Dam, 274–75 n. 29

Biomedical Research Center in Traditional Medicine and Natural Products, 127

bioprospecting, 9–11

Botanica-Mex S.A., 57, 94

botanists, 12, 47–49, 74, 93

Boyer, Christopher, 12, 13

Bracero Program, 177, 178

Brauer Herrera, Oscar, 119

business of science, 56–58

Butenandt, Adolf, 246–47 n. 24
buyers. *See* middlemen

Cabañas, Lucio, 178
cabeza de negro, 49, 53, *59*, 59–60, *64*.
   See also dioscorea
caciques, 182, 188–89, 206
Calderón del la Barca, Manuel, 204
campesinos. *See* barbasqueros; peasants
Cárdenas, Lázaro, 53, 174–76, 258 n. 52
carestía program, 177
cartoons, 158, *159*
Castañeda Aviles, Loreto, 210
Catemaco, Veracruz, *xiv*, 16, 17
Caughlin, Barbara, 208
Ceballos, Rafael, 120
Cerro de Oro dam, 34, 169
Cervantes del Rio, Hugo, 158
Chassen-López, Francie, 17, 28
chemistry, chemists. *See* Mexican sci-
   ence, scientists; science, scientists
Chiapas, 21, 113, 119, 121, 132, 233
Chiltepec, Oaxaca, *xiv*, 24, 242 n. 2. *See
   also* Papaloapan
Chinantecos, 25, 27, 34
Chinantla, Oaxaca, 20, 24, 27–28, 36
Chinese diosgenin, 198–200, 280–81 n. 6
cholesterol, steroids from, 44, 47, 93
Ciba-Geigy, 246 n. 20
class divisions, 81–82, 118
CNC. *See* National Peasant Confedera-
   tion
Coalition of Workers, Peasants, and
   Students of the Isthmus, 274–75 n. 29
coca, compared to barbasco, 9
COCEI (Coalition of Workers, Peasants,
   and Students of the Isthmus), 274–75
   n. 29
coffee crops, *35*
collection sites, 80, 81, 83–85. *See also*
   beneficios

commercial agriculture. *See* agriculture,
   commercial
Commission for the Study of the
   Ecology of Dioscoreas, 14, 20,
   103–6
Commission of the Papaloapan River
   Basin, 26, 32–34, 36–37
commodities, exploitation of, 9–11
commodity fetishism, 110
common fund (*fondo común*), 188
competition in steroid hormone indus-
   try, 20, 66, 153, 158, 163, 199
Compound A, 61
Compound E, 61
Conabio, 17
CONAPO (National Population Coun-
   cil), 126
CONASUPO (National Company of
   Popular Subsistence), 125, 143, 194
CONCAMIN (Confederation of Trade
   Organizations), 163
Confederación de Estudiantes Chiapanecos, 120–22
Confederación Nacional de Campesinos, 120
Confederation of Trade Organizations,
   163
Consejo Nacional de Poblacíon, 126
contraceptives, oral: diosgenin and, 3;
   FDA approval of, 71; history of, 69;
   hormones role, 126; importation of,
   125; Mestril, 164; Mexican research,
   66–67; origins of Mexican, 239–40
   n. 6; yams and, 2
Cordemex: henequen from, 272 n. 74; as
   parastatal, 181; Proquivemex and, 281
   n. 7, 284 n. 68; workers, 273 n. 5
Córdoba, Veracruz, *xiv*
corruption: government, 190; in organizations, 178; at Proquivemex, 22, 149;
   union, 207, 213

189–90, 192. *See also* derechos de
monte; unions
Ejidos Helio García, Unión de, 213
Ejidos Lázaro Cárdenas, Unión de, 186
El Hule, Oaxaca, 30
El Sol de México, 171–72
El Tajín, Beneficio, 201
El tesoro de la selva (Alfaro Siqueiros),
15
Emiliano Zapata Salazar, Unión, 188
empowerment, 1, 144–46, 149–50
endocrinology, 42–43, 246–47 n. 24
enganchar (hooking labor), 30, 82
Enovid, 69, 71
Esteroidal S.A. de CV, 57
estrogens, 43
estrone, 46
ethnic groups, 21, 23, 25
eugenics, in Latin America, 5
European steroid cartel, 44, 61, 66
Excelsior, 114–15, 122–23, 159, 191
experimental camps, 170–71
exploitation: of barbasco, 66, 135, 182–
83; of barbasqueros, 81–82, 135, 172,
182–83

Farmex, 284 n. 68
Farm Workers Obligatory Social Secu-
rity Regulation, 128
Farquinal, 66, 100
FDA (Food and Drug Administration),
66, 71
Feierman, Steven, 8
female hormones, 45–46
fermentation chemistry, 62
Fertimex, 272 n. 74
floods, 32–33
Florentine Codex, 75, 105
FONAFE (Fondo Nacional de Fomento
Ejidal), 120, 135, 180
fondo común (common fund), 188

Fondo Nacional de Fomento Ejidal, 120,
135, 180
Food and Drug Administration, 66, 71
Fortín, Emilio, 85, 87, 140
Fortune magazine, 3, 55, *64*
Fourth International Congress of
Hormonal Steroids, 126
fraud, tax, 161–62
fungicides, 164

Gabarrino Barria Union, 214
García Hernández, Tomás, 33
García Márquez, Gabriel, 75
Gedeon Richter S.A., 57
Gereffii, Gary, 60, 134, 160, 162
Germany, Germans, 61, 91, 111, 258
n. 44. *See also* Schering Corporation
Getty, J. Paul, 32
Gilardo Muñoz, Ejido, 201
Giral, Francisco, 100
glands, 42, 43. *See also* steroid hor-
mones
Gómez-Pompa, Arturo, 100–103, 105,
130
gonads, 43. *See also* steroid hormones
González, Manual, 167
González Montalvo, Ramon, 75
Gordillo, Gustavo, 196
Grant, Dr. Barrie, 45
grazing land, *35*
guerillas, 114

haciendas of Tuxtepec, 28
Harpers Bazaar, 63
Hart, John, 49
healers, barbasco used by, 72
healthcare, 123–24, 127–29
hecogenin, 248 n. 35
henequen extracts, 281 n. 7
Hernández, Delfino, 111–12, 190–91
Hernández, Paulino, 78

Hilario C. Salas, Unión, 213
hooking labor, 30, 82
hormones, steroid. *See* steroid hormone industry
Hormosynth S. A., 57
horses, steroid hormones from, 45

identity, barbasquero: assertion of, 189, 191–93; belonging and, 215; Boyer on, 13; characteristics of, 169–71; establishment of, 184, 194–95; ownership of, 230–31; self perception and, 21, 185
illiteracy, in Papaloapan, 26
IMEPLAM (Mexican Institute for the Study of Medicinal Plants), 123, 130
IMIQUIVE (Mexican Institute for the Chemical Vegetable Industry), 123–24
IMSS (Mexican Institute for Social Security), 124, 138
INBASA, 220, 281 n. 10
indigenous settlements, 24, 33, 242 n. 22
industrialization. *See* Mexican Miracle, the
Industria Nacional Quimico Farmacéutica S.A. de C.V., 66
INIF (National Institute for Forestry Research), 134
Inmecafe, 181
Institute de Química, 61
Institutional Revolutionary Party, 73, 163, 178–79
intermediary steroids, 202
International Symposium for the Ecology of Discoreas, 106
ixtle (fiber), 167

Jacatepec, Oaxaca, *xiv*, 17
Jacobs, Walter A., 247–48 n. 31
Jaramillo, Rubén, 178
Jiménez, Eusebio, 169

Joseph, Gil, 12
Juárez, Benito, 27–28. *See also* Benito Juárez Dam
Julian, Percy, 94
jungle laboratories, 12, 199, 202–3

Kennedy, John Fitzgerald, 42
Kew Gardens, 100
Knight, Alan, 12
Koch, Frank, 57–58

Laboratorios Hormona S.A., 55
land: distribution of, 175, 177, 220–21; invasions, 178, 179; ownership of, 28, 172, 173–74, 185. *See also* ejidos, ejidatarios
Latin America, 2, 5, 133, 179–80. *See also* Mexico
lechuguilla, 167
Lehman, Federico, 55, 251 n. 90
Lehmann, Pedro, 251 n. 90
León Felipe, Lorenzo, 82, 108–9, 136, 140–41
Lescohier, Dr. Alexander W., 52–53
Levene, P. A., 247–48 n. 31
Libertad, 207–8
Lic. Adolfo López Mateos, Unión, 190
Life magazine, 64, 232
loans, 143–44
López, Emma, 138–39
López, Mateos, Adolfo, 177, 232
López Portillo, José, 163–64, 198, 204
Los Pañales, 113, 120
Lozoya, Xavier, Dr., 127, 165, 263–64 n. 58

Macías Arellano, Luis, 99
Madero, Francisco I., 248 n. 33
male hormones, 246–47 n. 24
Mallon, Florencia, 12
Malpaso Dam, 119, 120

MAP (Mexican Agricultural Program), 105

Marker, Russell: achievements of, 47, 70; childhood of, 40; *Dioscorea mexicana* search by, 48–51; film about, *111*, 251–52 n. 93; hormone development and, 19, 39–40; laboratories of, 54, 56–57; peasants and, 7, 39–40, 58; professional development of, 41; research agenda of, 46, 47; retirement of, 57–58, 63; Syntex and, 20, 55–57; in Veracruz, 39, 50, 251–52 n. 93

massacre of students, 116, 261 n. 18

Master Plan for Organization and Peasant Training, 180–81

Mayer, Oscar, 251 n. 80

Mayer, Víctor, 112

Mazatecos, 27, 34

McCook, Stuart, 12

McCormick, Katharine, 66

media: advertisements in, 124; barbasco coverage in, 114–15, 122–23; cartoons, 158–59; drug costs in, 125; on nationalization, 171–72

medicinal plants: bioprospecting for, 9–11; cost of, 124; for hormone production, 46–48, 63; at Proquivemex, 199; quest for, 72, 123; study of, 105–6, 124, 127, 130, 229

Medicine Quest (Plotkin), 75

medicines, 123–25, 127–28, 136

Merck & Company, 61

mestizos, as middlemen, 81

Mestril, 164

methodology, of author, 15–20, 171

Mexican Agricultural Program, 105

Mexican Chemical Society, 57, 59

Mexican Chemical Vegetable Products. *See* Proquivemex

Mexican Institute for the Chemical Vegetable Industry, 123, 124

Mexican Institute for the Study of Medicinal Plants, 124

Mexican Institute of Medications, 125

Mexican Institute of Social Security, 124, 138

Mexican Liberal Party, 29

Mexican Miracle, the, 12, 99, 117, 174, 178

Mexican science, scientists: attitudes of, 101–2, 105; barbasco trade and, 13–14; chemists, 13–14; in Commission for the Study of Dioscoreas, 20; in Instituto de Química, 61; in Mexican Chemical Society, 57, 59; in Mexican Institute for the Chemical Vegetable Industry, 123, 124; status of, 115; subsidized, 107; transnationals and, 20. *See also* science, scientists

Mexican Workers Party, 193

Mexico: attitudes toward, 53; dependence of, on transnationals, 123–26, 151; economy of, 95–96, 174–77, 200; health issues in, 123; independence of, 27–28; modernization in, 6, 99, 114, 208, 224; oil expropriation in, 9, 53; oral contraceptives of, 164; population growth in, 117, 125, 177; under Porfirio Dìaz, 28; protectionism by, 95–96, 198; revolution of, 15, 28, 173–74, 176; social movements of, 119; status of, 112; urbanization in, 36; United States and, 89, 92, 94. *See also* countryside, the; Echeverría Álvarez, Luis; Latin America; Papaloapan; pharmaceutical industry, Mexican

Mexico City, 117, 177–78, 190, 191

Mexico-Germany Accord on Forests, 201

middlemen: displacement of, 135, 141, 181, 196; practices of, 80–83

Miguel Alemán Dam, 34

Nueva Málzaga, 212

Nugent, Daniel, 12

Oaxaca, Mexico, 27–31. *See also* Papaloapan; *and under names of specific towns*

Ogden Corporation, 92

oil companies and commodities, 9, 53, 90, 176

oral contraceptives. *See* contraceptives, oral

Organización, 165

Organon, 92, 246 n. 20

Orizaba, Oaxaca, *xiv*

OrthoNovum, 71

Oscar Mayer, 251 n. 80

Ovalle, Ignacio, 167

overpricing, 162

Palo Alto, California, *97*, 98

pamphlets, Proquivemez, *145*, *147*

Pañales, the, 112, 119, 120

Papaloapan: commercial agriculture in, 23–25, 31, *35*; Commission, 32–34, 36–37; demographics of, 25; development in, 34; flooding of, 32–33; history of, 26–35; laboratory in, 199; labor issues of, 23, 28, 30; poverty in, 25–26; topography of, 24, *35*, 38. *See also* Oaxaca, Mexico

parastatals: dissolution of, 218–20, 221; privatization of, 198; types of, 165, 167, 181. *See also* Proquivemex

Parke-Davis laboratories, 52

patents: cases for, 60, 92; manipulation of, 246 n. 20; for oral contraceptives, 17, 68; significance of, 91; Subcommittee on Patents, Trademarks and Copyrights and, 66

Paula De Teresa, Ana, 220

Peasant Intellectuals (Feierman), 8

peasants: attitude of, toward barbasco trade, 71–72; attitudes toward, 101; concept of, 13; economic conditions of, 107; health care for, 128–29; image of, 115; as landless, 173; migration of, 177–78; removal of, 169; significance of, 7, 51, 56; struggles of, 118–19; women, 17–18. *See also* barbasqueros

Pennsylvania State University, 41, 46

penogenina, 210

peptide hormones, 246 n. 14

Pérez, Crispo, 186–88, 206

permits, barbasco harvesting, 98–99, 123

pharmaceutical companies, transnational: concerns of, 53–54; cooperation of, with government, 104; dependence on, 93, 165, 167, 168; environmental abuses of, 179; European, 44, 60, 61, 256 n. 8; as exploiters, 155, 182–83; images of, 158, *159*; marketing by, 46; price gouging by, 124–25; profits of, 98; Proquivemex and, 139, 151–52; subsidiaries of, 124; supporters of, 163; tax violations of, 161–62; transfer pricing by, 162. *See also* barbasco trade; nationalization of steroid hormone industry

pharmaceutical industry, Mexican: attitudes toward, 53; on cost of medications, 124; Echeverría on, 127; laboratories, 38, 66, 100, 123; products of, 164; proposal for, 125; as subsidiaries, 124; Syntex's place in, 55. *See also* nationalization of steroid hormone industry

physician strikes, 116

Pill, the: creation of, 246–47 n. 24; FDA approval of, 71; Mexican contributions to, 2–4, 66–67, 69; patent

Pill, the (*continued*)
    holders of, 3, 17, 68, 115; price of, 153;
    use of, 73. *See also* contraceptives,
    oral
Pincus, Dr. Gregory, 3–4, 66
pineapple crops, *35*
Plan de Hidalgo, Ejido, 201
plantations, 28, 30
plants, medicinal. *See* medicinal plants
Plotkin, Mark, 75
political unrest, 178–79
Popolucas, 25, 27
population control, 4, 125
populism, 21, 115–16, 133, 151, *159*. *See
    also* Echeverría Álvarez, Luis
poverty in Papaloapan, 25–26
prednisolone, 96
prednisone, 96
PRI (Institutional Revolutionary Party),
    73, 163, 178–79
prices, triangulation of, 138
privatization of parastatals, 198
Productos Químicos Vegetales Mexica-
    nos S.A. *See* Proquivemex
profits, triangulation of, 98
progesterone, synthetic: in barbasco, *38*;
    for cortisone production, 63; efficacy
    of, 66; knowledge of, 1–2; in mares,
    247 n. 26; Russell Marker and, 46;
    yams and, 2
progestogen, function of, 43
Proquina, 151, 179, 272 n. 4
Proquivemex: administration of, 138–
    39, 204–5, 208; Agroindustrial and,
    203; ballad of, 138–39; barbasqueros
    and, 184–85; board of, 151–52; com-
    petitiveness of, 163; decline of, 202–3,
    210, 233; dissolution of, 22, 218–19;
    economy's effect on, 200; education
    programs by, 144–47, 168; establish-
    ment of, 153; financial problems of,

210–11; financing of, 151; globally, 197,
    199, 234; goals of, 135–37, 164–65, 168,
    205; images of, 158; market shares
    of, 200; operations of, 137, 140–44;
    origins of, 5, 21; as peasant run, 220,
    281 n. 10; populism of, 21, 151; pricing
    by, 152–55, 156; products of, 164, 199;
    purpose of, 133–34; reactions to, 158;
    transformative aspects of, 137; trans-
    nationals and, 161–62, 168; unions
    and, 205–6, 209–12, 217; zone chiefs
    and, 149, 207. *See also* Villar Borja,
    Alejandro
protectionism, Mexican, 95–96, 198
Puebla, Manual, 197, 204–5
Puebla, Oaxaca, *xiv*, 14
purity, of barbasco, 100, 153–54, 198, 210

Ramírez, Pedro, 76, 226, 239 n. 1, 76
rancherías, 242 n. 22
Red Mocaf, 17
regulation of barbasco trade: through
    permits, 98–99, 123; Proquivemex's
    role, 135, 152, 165; through protec-
    tionism, 94; through taxation, 95–96.
    See also Commission for the Study of
    the Ecology of Dioscoreas
Rello, Fernando, 196
reorganization, of countryside, 133–34,
    136, 166, 180–81, 195–96
reproduction research, 246–47 n. 24
research camps, 170–71
Revolution, the (1910), 15, 28, 173–74,
    176
Reyes Chilpa, Ricardo, Dr., 251 n. 31
rhetoric: of Echeverría, 148, 151, 230; of
    human rights, 222; of imperialism, 15;
    nationalist, 190, 195; peasant use of,
    170, 180, 190; against pharmaceutical
    companies, 11; in Proquivemex goals,
    133

rheumatoid arthritis, 61–62
Roche Pharmaceuticals, 15, *59*
Rock, Dr. John, 69, 71
Rockefeller Foundation, 25, 105
Rockefeller Institute, 41, 46
Rodríguez, Angel, 109
Romero, Matías, 28–29, 31
Rosenkranz, George, 56, 60, *68*
Rubin, Jeffrey, 274–75 n. 29
Ruiz Cortines, Adolfo, 95, 231
rural Mexico. *See* countryside, the

SAG (Secretaría de Agricultura y
  Ganaderia), 262 n. 36
Salinas de Gortari, Carlos, 22, 221
Sánchez Mejorada, Jorge, 163–64
San Diego, Ejido, 201
San Escobal, Beneficio, 202
Sanger, Margaret, 2–3, 66
San José Chiltepec. *See* Chiltepec,
  Oaxaca
San Luis Rey Equine Hospital, 246
  n. 20
Santa Catarina, 274–75 n. 29
Santiago, Melquíades, 1–2, 7, 225
Santiago, Myrna, 12
Santiago Hernández, Fidel, 203
saponin compounds and sapogenins,
  47, 75–76
SARH (Ministry of Water Resources),
  135, 201
sarsaparilla, 47, 135
Schally, A. V., 250–51 n. 80
Schering Corporation, 14, 21, 63, 91, 246
  n. 20
science, scientists: business of, 56–57;
  fermentation chemistry, 62; globalized, 2, 8; peasants and, 6–9, 58,
  108–9, 226–27, 229; transformative
  aspects of, 5, 7, 12, 227–28. *See also*
  Mexican science, scientists

Searle Pharmaceutical, 71, 151, 239 n. 6,
  272–73 n. 4
Secretaría de Agricultura y Ganadería,
  262 n. 36
Secretariat of Agrarian Reform: barbasqueros in, 193; creation of, 181; on
  derechos de monte, 161; education
  programs of, 148; origins of, 165;
  peasants and, 166, 171; Proquivemex
  and, 137, 141, 151–52; representatives
  of, 141; significance of, 195. *See also*
  agrarian reform
Secretariat of Agriculture and Livestock, 119, 152
Secretariat of Energy, Mines, and State
  Owned Industries, 203
Secretariat of the Environment, Natural
  Resources, and Fishing (SEMARNAP),
  17, 234, 249 n. 63
Secretariat of the Treasury and Public
  Credit, 151
Secretary of Treasury, 162
Seferino, Don, 214
SEMARNAP (Secretariat of the Environ-
  ment, Natural Resources and Fish-
  ing), 17, 234, 249 n. 63
Sentís López, Mario, 188
settlements, indigenous, 24, 242 n. 22
sex endocrinology, 43
sex hormones, 43–46
Siqueiros, David Alfaro, *59*
snakebites, 255 nn. 31, 33
Social Darwinism, in Latin America, 5
social mobility of peasants, 7, 21–22, 111,
  169, 225–26
social movements, 119
Social Security Law of 1943, 128
Sollins, Irving V., 98
Somlo, Emeric, 55
Spaniards in Gran Chinantla, 27
SRA. *See* Secretariat of Agrarian Reform

Standard Fruit Company, 31
Starling, Ernest Henry, 245 n. 1, 246
n. 13
Stern, Steve, 17–18
Steroid Drugs (Applezweig), 40
steroid hormone industry: cartel of, 44,
61, 66; competition in, 66, 153, 158,
163, 199; conferences for, 126; history
of, 41; Marker and, 39–40; Mexican
dominance of, 92–93; role of technology in, 93, 165, 167–68; transformative aspects of, 231. *See also*
nationalization of steroid hormone
industry; pharmaceutical companies;
pharmaceutical industry, Mexican;
Proquivemex; steroid hormones
steroid hormones: demand for, 198;
intermediary, 202; research and
development of, 7, 44–46; structure
of, *44*; synthesis of, 2; types, 43; from
urine, 44–45, 52, 69
sterols, vegetable, 47
Steromex, 151
St. Louis University School of Medicine, 45
Stoller, Ezra, 69
Storyteller, The (Vargas Llosa), 75
Students, 113–14, 116, 119–23
Subcommittee on Patents, Trademarks
and Copyrights, 92. *See also* patents
sugar cane crops, *35*, 116
Synalar, 4, 155, 214
Syntex: administration of, 60; barbasco
zones of, 14; competition and, 57, 66,
94, 96; congressional investigation of,
92, 96; cortisone and, *38*, 63; emergence of, 20, 55–56; experiments by,
272–73 n. 4; founders of, 257 n. 43;
growth of, 94, 97; investments in
Proquivemex by, 151; laboratory of,
64, *65*; Marker and, 20, 55–57; as a

monopoly, 92; oral contraceptive
research by, 66–67, 239 n. 6; Ortho-
Novum by, 71; patent issues of, 60, 92

Tabamex, 181, 272 n. 74
Taussig, Michael, 110
tax fraud, 161–62
technology: demand for, 93; dependence on, 165, 168; peasants and, 167;
in steroid hormone industry, 93, 165,
167–68
testosterone, 46
Texcoco laboratory, 56
tobacco crops, 23, 29, 272 n. 74
transfer pricing, 162
transnational pharmaceutical companies. *See* pharmaceutical companies,
transnational
Treasure of the Jungle (Siqueiros), *59*
triangulation: of prices, 138; of profits,
98
tropical forest. *See* Chinantla, Oaxaca
tubers. *See* barbasco
Turner, John Kenneth, 29–31
Tuxtepec, Oaxaca: barbasco industry
in, 7, 12; barbasco zone, 137; barbasqueros from, 157; commercial agriculture in, 28, 31–32; development
of, 14, 73; flooding of, 33; health unit
of, 25; location of, xiv; unions in, 212,
273 n. 5

UC MEXUS (University of California
Institute for Mexico and the United
States), xii, 264 n. 66
UNAM (Universidad Nacional
Autónoma de México), 31, 61, 255
n. 31
UNCTAD (United Nations Conference
on Trade and Development), 179, 275
n. 35

unions: complaints of, 205–6; expansion of, 208; formation of, 148; government sanctioned, 182–84; independence of, 203–4, 206–7; on nationalization, 157; problems of, 203–4; Proquivemex and, 142–43; purpose of, 181; significance of, 182, 187, 189; transnationals and, 161. *See also* ejidos and ejidatarios

United Fruit Company, 31, 32

United Nations Conference on Trade and Development, 179

United States, 92; Department of Justice, 246 n. 20; Mexico and, 89, 94; reliance of, on barbasco, 96–97

University of California, Riverside, 264 n. 66, 273 n. 5

UNPRB. *See* National Union of Producers and Gatherers of Barbasco

Upjohn Pharmaceuticals, 62–63, 66, 200

urine, for steroids, 44, 45, 52, 69

Valdés, Miguel, 118–19

Valle Nacional, Oaxaca, *xiv*, 27, 29–30, 31

Valley of Death, 29

Vargas Llosa, Mario, 75

vegetable sterols, 47

Veracruz: barbasco and, *xiv*, 4, 14, 134, 160; beneficio workers in, *143*, 202; Catemaco, 18; environment of, 32; location of, *xiv*, 24; Marker in, 39, 40, 50; oil in, 12; research camps in,

272–73 n. 4; unions in, 210, 212; zone of, 14. *See also* Moreno, Alberto

Vianey Malpica Bernabé, Mario, 56–57, 191, 205–6

Villa de Tapijulapa, 186

Villar Borja, Alejandro, 16; as consultant, 205; on derecho de monte, 161; on drug costs, 127; as national security threat, 193–94; on pricing, 153; at Proquivemex, 138–39; removal of, 204

Weber, Alejandro, 81

Wetten, Nathan, 107

Whitmore, Frank, 41, 54

WHO (World Health Organization), 4, 127–28

wild yams. *See* barbasco

Wilkins Chapoy, Guillermo, 208, 213, 215, 239 n. 1

women, 17, 45–46, 216–17

Worchester Foundation for Experimental Biology, 62

World Health Organization, 4, 127–28

yam pickers. *See* barbasqueros

yams, 60, 74. *See also* barbasco

Yaqui, 29

Zafra, Gloria, 179

Zamosc, Leon, 119

Zapotecos, 25, 227

zone chiefs, 149

Gabriela Soto Laveaga is an assistant professor of history at the University of California, Santa Barbara.

Library of Congress Cataloging-in-Publication Data
Soto Laveaga, Gabriela, 1971–
Jungle laboratories : Mexican peasants, national projects, and the
making of the Pill / Gabriela Soto Laveaga.
p. cm.
Includes bibliographical references and index.
ISBN 978-0-8223-4587-9 (cloth : alk. paper)
ISBN 978-0-8223-4605-0 (pbk. : alk. paper)
1. Pharmaceutical industry—Social aspects—Mexico. 2. Barbasco
(Dioscorea mexicana) 3. Proquivemex. I. Title.
HD9670.M62S68 2009
338.4'7615324—dc22   2009032836